Capital Markets
and Trade

THE UNITED STATES AND EUROPE IN THE 1990s

CAPITAL MARKETS AND TRADE
Claude E. Barfield and Mark Perlman, editors

INDUSTRY, SERVICES, AND AGRICULTURE
Claude E. Barfield and Mark Perlman, editors

POLITICAL POWER AND SOCIAL CHANGE
Norman J. Ornstein and Mark Perlman, editors

RESHAPING WESTERN SECURITY
Richard N. Perle, editor

Capital Markets and Trade

The United States Faces a United Europe

Edited by
Claude E. Barfield and Mark Perlman

The AEI Press

Publisher for the American Enterprise Institute
WASHINGTON, D.C.
1991

Distributed by arrangement with

University Press of America
4720 Boston Way   3 Henrietta Street
Lanham, Md. 20706   London WC2E 8LU England

Library of Congress Cataloging-in-Publication Data

Capital markets and trade : the United States faces a united Europe / edited by Claude E. Barfield and Mark Perlman.
    p. cm.—AEI studies ; 522)
Includes bibliographical references.
ISBN 0-8447-3751-8
    1. United States—Commerce—European Economic Community countries. 2. European Economic Community countries—Commerce—United States. 3. Capital market—United States. 4. Capital market—European
Economic Community countries. I. Barfield, Claude E. II. Perlman, Mark. III. Series.
HF3500.5.C37   1991
332'.0414'0973—dc20   91-26670
                                                                                                CIP

ISBN 0-8447-3751-8

1   3   5   7   9   10   8   6   4   2

AEI Studies 522

© 1991 by the American Enterprise Institute for Public Policy Research, Washington, D.C. All rights reserved. No part of this publication may be used or reproduced in any manner whatsoever without permission in writing from the American Enterprise Institute except in the case of brief quotations embodied in news articles, critical articles, or reviews. The views expressed in the publications of the American Enterprise Institute are those of the authors and do not necessarily reflect the views of the staff, advisory panels, officers, or trustees of AEI.

The AEI Press
Publisher for the American Enterprise Institute
1150 17th Street, N.W., Washington, D.C. 20036

Printed in the United States of America

Contents

ACKNOWLEDGMENT	ix
CONTRIBUTORS	xi
INTRODUCTION *Claude E. Barfield and Mark Perlman*	1

PART ONE
THE EUROPEAN COMMUNITY IN THE INTERNATIONAL TRADING SYSTEM

1	THE FUTURE OF THE INTERNATIONAL TRADING SYSTEM *Brian Hindley*	11
2	COMMENTARIES ON PART ONE *Herbert Giersch, Jules L. Katz, and Norbert Walter*	46

PART TWO
IMPLICATIONS FOR JAPAN AND THE NICs

3	EXTERNAL TRADE IMPLICATIONS OF EUROPE 1992 FOR JAPAN *Masaru Yoshitomi*	59
4	THE ROLE OF THE ASIAN NICs IN THE 1990s *Raymond J. Ahearn and Anne Dibble*	73
5	COMMENTARIES ON PART TWO *Stephen Chen, Thomas W. Robinson, G. Selvadas, John Richardson, and Vitthya Vejjajiva*	119

Part Three
Financial Integration and Fiscal Harmonization

6 European Financial Integration and Its Implications for the United States — 137
Ingo Walter

7 German Banking and Monetary Policy — 187
Anthony Saunders

8 Fiscal Harmonization in the European Community — 222
G. K. Shaw

9 Commentaries on Part Three — 284
Leon Gordon, William Haraf, Paul Mentré, Patrice Vial, and Norbert Walter

Notes — 307

List of Tables
3-1. Discriminatory Quantitative Restrictions on Japanese Products by EC Member Countries, June 1988 61
4-1. Per Capita Gross Domestic Product of the East Asian NICs, 1980–1988 77
4-2. Export Orientation of Asian NICs, 1982–1988 78
4-3. Taiwan's Export Orientation, 1982–1988 79
4-4. South Korea's Export Orientation, 1982–1988 79
4-5. Hong Kong's Export Orientation, 1982–1988 80
4-6. Singapore's Export Orientation, 1982–1988 80
4-7. U.S. Trade with Asian NICs, 1985–1989 87
4-8. U.S. Trade with Taiwan, 1985–1989 88
4-9. U.S. Trade with South Korea, 1985–1989 88
4-10. U.S. Trade with Hong Kong, 1985–1989 89
4-11. U.S. Trade with Singapore, 1985–1989 89
4-12. Asian NICs' Trade with the European Community, 1984–1988 89
4-13. Hong Kong's Trade with the European Community, 1984–1988 90
4-14. Taiwan's Trade with the European Community, 1984–1988 90
4-15. South Korea's Trade with the European Community, 1984–1988 91
4-16. Singapore's Trade with the European Community, 1984–1988 91

4-17. Trends in Japan's Manufactured Imports, 1985–1988   104
4-18. Asian NICs' Trade with Japan, 1984–1988   106
4-19. Hong Kong's Trade with Japan, 1984–1988   107
4-20. Singapore's Trade with Japan, 1984–1988   107
4-21. Taiwan's Trade with Japan, 1984–1988   107
6-1. Volume of Corporate Sector Capital Market Financing by Regional Corporations in Their Home Markets, 1988   158
6-2. Foreign Investment of Private Sector Pension Assets, 1980–1992   162
6-3. Volume of Completed International Merger and Corporate Transactions, United States, 1985–1989   165
6-4. Volume of Completed International Merger and Corporate Transactions, Europe, 1985–1989   166
7-1. Mean Values of Major Economic Indicators, 1975–1987   192
7-2. West German Money Growth, Target and Actual, 1975–1989   194
7-3. The European System of Central Banks   196
7-4. The Institutional Structure of the German Banking System   203
7-5. German Banks among European Top Fifteen, 1988   205
7-6. Predominant Form of Financial Service Integration in the G-10 Countries   206
7-7. Permissible Banking Activities under Europe 1992   207
7-8. Deutsche Bank's Expansions   208
7-9. Differences in Prices of Standard Financial Products Compared with the Average of the Four Lowest National Prices for Eight EC Countries   212
7-10. Potential Big Bank Targets   214
7-11. German Investment Funds, 1980–1988   217
7-12. West German Household Savings, 1970–1987   217
8-1. Members of the European Parliament   224
8-2. Tax Revenues of EC Member States, 1986   225
8-3. Value-added Tax Rates in EC Member States, 1987   247

8-4. Indirect Taxes in the Public Finances of Eight EC Member States, 1984   248
8-5. Excise Duty on Alcoholic Drinks in EC Member States, 1986   249
8-6. Cigarette Taxation in EC Member States, 1986   252
8-7. Excise Duty on Motor Fuel in EC Member States, 1986   253
8-8. Revenue Consequences of Fiscal Approximation Assuming Unchanged Spending Patterns   255
8-9. National Tax Rates for Various Countries, 1988   266
8-10. Withholding Tax Rates for Various Countries, 1988   267
8-11. Required Pretax Rates of Return for Various Countries   269
8-12. Summary Appendix: A Statistical Overview of Europe and Its Major Industrial Competitors, Various Years, 1985–2000   276

LIST OF FIGURES
6-1. Trading Volume of Derivative Securities for Europe, Asia, and Other Locations, 1985–1989   161
8-1. The Economics of Tax Harmonization   223
8-2. The Existing System of the Value-added Tax   239
8-3. The Proposed System of the Value-added Tax   242
8-4. Changes in Indirect Tax Burden by Income Decile, United Kingdom   259
8-5. Differential Taxation and Capital Allocation   260

Acknowledgment

The American Enterprise Institute would like to thank the following foundations and corporations for their support of the AEI project, The United States and Europe in the 1990s: The Pew Charitable Trusts, the General Electric Company, the German Marshall Fund of the United States, IBM, the American Express Company, the Samsung Group, Robert Bosch Gmbh, and the Swedish Employers' Confederation.

Contributors

CLAUDE E. BARFIELD is the coordinator of Trade Policy Studies at the American Enterprise Institute.

MARK PERLMAN is the University Professor of Economics at the University of Pittsburgh.

RAYMOND J. AHEARN is a specialist in trade relations for the Foreign Affairs and National Defense Division, Congressional Research Service.

STEPHEN CHEN is the principal deputy representative of the Coordinating Council for North American Affairs.

ANNE DIBBLE is president of Mehta Trading Company.

HERBERT GIERSCH is president of the Keil Institute for World Economics.

LEON GORDON is adviser to the director-general of Customs Union and Indirect Taxation at the Commission of the European Communities.

WILLIAM HARAF is vice-president of Citicorp.

BRIAN HINDLEY is a professor of economics at the London School of Economics.

JULES L. KATZ is deputy U.S. trade representative.

PAUL MENTRÉ is president director general of Crédit National.

JOHN RICHARDSON is director of U.S.-E.C. Affairs at the Commission of the European Communities.

THOMAS W. ROBINSON is director of the China Studies Program at the American Enterprise Institute.

ANTHONY SAUNDERS is a professor of finance at the Stern School of Business, New York University.

G. SELVADAS is first secretary, economics, at the Embassy of Singapore in Washington, D.C.

G. K. SHAW is the Rank Foundation Professor of Economics at the University of Buckingham.

VITTHYA VEJJAJIVA is former ambassador of Thailand to the United States and is currently permanent secretary.

PATRICE VIAL is under secretary for forecasting for the French Ministry of Finance.

INGO WALTER is the Abraham L. Gitlow Professor of Economics and Finance at the Stern School of Business, New York University.

NORBERT WALTER is director of Deutsche Bank AG.

MASARU YOSHITOMI is director general of the Economic Research Institute at the Economic Planning Agency of Japan.

Introduction
Claude E. Barfield and Mark Perlman

Trade and investment flows between the United States and the European Community (EC) provide the binding cement for the most important economic partnership among advanced industrial economies. The numbers tell the story clearly and succinctly. During the 1980s, the European Community took about 23 percent of U.S. exports and in turn provided 18 to 20 percent of U.S. imports. In 1989, Europeans were the single most important market for U.S. goods, buying over $86 billion in U.S. exports (Canada was the second largest U.S. export market, with $78 billion, and Japan, third, with $44 billion. Although the United States ran a substantial trade deficit with the Community from 1984 to 1988, this balance shifted to a growing surplus in 1989 and 1990.

U.S.–European Financial Ties

The economies of EC member states and the United States are closely intertwined through longstanding, large-scale, cross-border capital investments. In 1989, U.S. direct investment in the Community amounted to $150.6 billion and represented almost half of total U.S. direct foreign investment. (This figure undoubtedly understates the real value of U.S. investments in Europe because only the original value of the investments is reported, not the current value.) Conversely, total direct investment in the United States by EC countries in 1988 stood at $235.6 billion or just above 50 percent of total foreign investment in this country.

Contrary to popular—and populist—opinion, EC nations, not Japan, lead the way in direct investment in the United States (1989— U.K., $119 billion; Netherlands, $61 billion; Germany, $28 billion; and Japan, $70 billion).

The most optimistic analysts predict that European integration will result in a 7 percent increase in EC gross domestic product, a 6 percent reduction in prices, and the creation of 5 million jobs. Even discounting somewhat this robust optimism, the longstanding economic, political, and social ties between Western Europe and the United States suggest that the creation of a single European market will provide a substantial boost to U.S. investment and trade opportunities.

The chapters in this volume analyze in substantial detail the implications of European integration—both the opportunities and the challenges—for the United States and other major trading and financial powers. Together, the United States and the member states of the European Community have provided the leadership for the multilateral trade and financial system of the postwar era. The Bretton Woods agreement and the multilateral institutions for trade and for bringing the lesser-developed countries into the international economic system—the General Agreement on Tariffs and Trade (GATT) and the World Bank—were significant factors in producing postwar decades of unprecedented economic growth.

Now, as the chapters in this volume make clear, fundamental questions are being raised about the utility and viability of the postwar multilateral system and the institutions it encompasses. In this context, the moves toward greater European economic and political integration are taking place at a crucial period for the world economy—and Europe's decisions regarding its place and responsibility in that system will be an important factor in either the continuation or the modification of international economic and financial institutions and policies. Most particularly, how Europe shapes its own trade, banking, and fiscal policies will assume large-scale significance in its relations with the outside world. This reality is made abundantly clear by the first chapter of this volume, which deals with the future of the international trading system.

The Chapters

The overriding theme of Brian Hindley's chapter on the future of the international trading system is that the United States, beginning in 1945 and continuing today, is the linchpin of that system. As he states at the outset, "That law should replace power in international economic relations is—or was—a U.S. idea." Conversely, he argues, both the European Community and Japan, for very different reasons, have always felt more comfortable with the idea that "trade relations should be controlled, not by international law, but by the requirements of broader diplomacy," and in the case of Japan by the requirements of a resource-starved economy.

Hindley fears that a confluence of factors may be weakening the U.S. commitment to multilateralism and the GATT. The GATT, he states, has always served two functions: first, to provide an efficient and equitable means for resolving international trade disputes; and second, to be a vehicle for liberalizing trade and opening markets. These goals, he points out, can conflict with one another, if either is pursued at the expense of the other. For instance, attempting to achieve "liberalization" by fiat or unilateral action can very easily destroy the utility of GATT as a mediating institution. And in recent years, U.S. actions, in the name of "liberalization," have often undermined the balance of these twin GATT objectives.

The bulk of Hindley's chapter describes and analyzes three policy alternatives ("U.S. nostrums"), which the United States has flirted with during the 1980s because of its inability to deal with the seemingly intractable issue of a large external trade deficit. These three alternative paths are bilateralism, reciprocity, and regional trade blocs. Hindley examines in detail the implications of each of these policies, including the conditions under which they would further the goals of multilateralism and the GATT and the circumstances in which they could undermine and even destroy the multilateral system. He also describes what is for him the particularly pernicious consequences of the "dangerous . . . self-righteousness" embodied in the so-called Super 301 section of the 1988 U.S. trade act.

Hindley then turns to an analysis of the threats to multilateralism posed by EC trade policy. He focuses on two areas: the emergence of antidumping actions as a major tool for protection and the invocation of "strict" reciprocity provisions to produce similar protectionist results.

In his concluding section, Hindley is only cautiously optimistic about the future. He states:

> No doubt there will in the year 2000 be a GATT. . . . There may be contracting parties and more frequent meetings of trade ministers than now. But it is the state of trade relations beyond that facade that is relevant to the question posed here. There is a clear risk that trade relations will be increasingly discriminatory and chaotic—and that however splendid the GATT . . . as a venue for trade ministers or bureaucrats, it will have no impact on . . . trade relations.

Part two of the volume contains two chapters that explain the implications of European integration for Japan and for the newly industrialized economies of Asia. In his chapter, "The External Trade Implications of Europe 1992 for Japan," Masaru Yoshitomi mounts a sustained attack against what he asserts are the European Community's incorrect assumptions that Japan pursues "aggressive external expansion" through "predatory exports," while maintaining a closed market at home.

INTRODUCTION

In building his case, Yoshitomi sets out to answer three questions: (1) is there a causal link between Europe 1992 and the creation of a "fortress Europe," particularly against Japan? (2) why is Japan being singled out, and how valid are the underlying assumptions about Japanese predatory export practices and its closed domestic market? and (3) what are the global implications of Europe 1992?

In answering the first question, Yoshitomi presents the evidence for what he contends are signs of increasing harassment of foreign firms by the European Community—antidumping, local content, and rules of origin regulations, which distort trade and investment, and, he argues, are directly linked to the drive toward European integration. He also sees EC merger and competition policy as following the same path of internal protectionist goals.

To make his case regarding the second question, Yoshitomi extensively reviews recent economic literature, arguing that "Japan's distinctive trade structure essentially reflects its equally distinctive comparative advantage," composed of a relative abundance of human skills, capital, and technological sophistication and a relative scarcity of land and natural resources. The results of his study do not support the conclusion that Japan's export surpluses result from predatory competition.

Yoshitomi also defends Japan against the charge that its internal industrial organization unfairly restricts foreign firms from access to the Japanese market. On efficiency grounds he defends the *keiretsu* (corporate alliance) system and the close and longstanding connection between producers and suppliers. Hands-off relationships, or "the anonymous market," he argues, "cannot always effectively secure no-defect, high-quality products, prompt and punctual delivery or technological information flows as to specific components and capital goods."

In answering the third question, Yoshitomi reiterates his strong defense of the Japanese system and his criticism of EC moves toward protection against the consequences of that system. He concedes, however, that there is a real need for new international rules to harmonize divergent and potentially conflicting national systems of competition and industrial organization.

Raymond Ahearn and Anne Dibble, in their study of the role of the newly industrialized countries (NICs) of Asia (South Korea, Taiwan, Hong Kong, and Singapore) in the world economy, focus on four main trends: (1) the process by which the four East Asian NICs emerged as key players in the world trading system; (2) recent developments in U.S. trade policy that have had a direct impact on the NICs; (3) the current and potential impact of EC 1992 on the four countries; and (4) the recent growth of intra-East Asian export trade. A concluding section lays out a set of policy recommendations to further the evolution of a more balanced trading relationship between the Asian NICs and the rest of the world.

In the first section of the chapter, Ahearn and Dibble describe the underlying forces that shaped the extraordinary growth of the Asian NICs over the past two decades, a period in which the average rate of growth of the NICs was two to three times faster than most developed countries. They show that this phenomenal record was export led and beyond that relied heavily on the import of manufactured products into the markets of developed countries, particularly the United States. In 1988, for instance, the United States, the European Community, and Japan accounted for 58 percent of Asian NIC exports. Taiwan and South Korea were the most dependent on the United States, which took almost 40 percent of Taiwan's exports and about 35 percent of South Korea's exports.

The very success of the penetration of the U.S. market by the NICs was one cause of the great debate over U.S. trade policy that took place during the 1980s. Congress and affected industries pressed strongly for more active trade policy measures, and a number of initiatives were undertaken by the administration, including direct bilateral trade and currency negotiations, increased antidumping and countervailing duty actions, and the use of Section 301 of the basic U.S. trade act as a tool against allegedly unfair foreign trade practices. Section two of the chapter describes these U.S. actions and their impact on U.S.-Asian NIC trade patterns.

Part three provides a similar analysis of import restrictions placed on Asian NIC exports by the European Community. These include voluntary export restraints (steel, textiles, clothing, agricultural products, machine tools, automobiles, and electronic products), antidumping actions, local content and rule-of-origin requirements, and a strict definition of market access reciprocity. The goal of these policies, state the authors, is summed up in a speech by an executive from Fiat, who calls for a "common defense and retaliatory policy" to prevent the "economic colonization of [Europe]."

In the final section of the chapter, Ahearn and Dibble describe the responses of the Asian NICs to the adverse trade policies of the United States and the European Community. These include currency reform, direct investment in both the European Community and the United States to get around import restrictions, government-sponsored campaigns to increase imports, and preliminary moves toward East Asian economic integration. The authors also assess one major complicating factor: the growing role of Japanese investment and trade within the Asian region.

INTRODUCTION

Ahearn and Dibble conclude with a set of recommendations for each of the major players (the European Community, the United States, Japan, and the four NICs) to achieve more balanced trade patterns and relations.

Part three of this volume consists of three chapters: a detailed analysis of the EC moves toward financial market integration and of the implications of these changes for non-European countries; a study of the dominant role of German banking and monetary policy; and finally, a description of the difficulties surrounding moves toward fiscal harmonization among the nations in the single market.

Ingo Walter's chapter provides a comprehensive analysis of the complicated and controversial path toward financial integration in Europe. He examines the Single Market program as a force for change in conjunction with the institutional problems of converging macroeconomic policy, which can impede the process. He delves into the array of economic, political, and technological pressures transforming financial markets and makes the critical distinction between market enhancing deregulation and intra-European integration.

Major issues Walter discusses include the prospects for the European monetary system and the role of an EC central bank, liberalization of intra-EC banking activities, taxation of investment income, and the competitive dynamics of European financial markets. After examining the geographic and sectoral revolutions that are occurring simultaneously in Europe, Walter concludes that the Community banking and financial market will become the world's most competitive and innovative and that the monetary integration as envisioned in the Delors report, although desirable, is not a prerequisite. He traces the steps taken toward integration over the past two decades, providing an informed discussion of the associated opportunities, risks, and obstacles that still need to be overcome. He also offers a view of the emerging European capital market as one that encompasses both the individual markets of the member states and the London-based Euromarket.

Walter then turns to the prospective role of U.S.-based financial firms in a dynamic, integrated, and supercompetitive European financial market, highlighting the dependence of these firms on reciprocity provisions and on U.S. regulatory structures. Walter closes his analysis with the provocative conclusion that American regulatory hands—not European—will largely determine the long-run competitive impact of the 1992 financial liberalization program on the United States and that without significant U.S. reform the asymmetries between the American and the evolving European structure will hamper and potentially undermine the future competitive position of U.S. financial institutions.

Anthony Saunders's assignment was undertaken before the events that led to the swift unification of Germany. These events, however, serve only to reinforce the analysis and conclusions of his chapter. Saunders argues that the comparative strength and efficiency of the West German banking system will dominate the transitional integration of the various EC communities. He foresees an eventual all-European central bank (probably disciplined by its German section) and common monetary and even fiscal policies. Saunders also devotes considerable attention to specific regional problems. Finally, he predicts that bilateral exchange rates will be irrevocably fixed and that the various national currencies will be replaced by a single European currency.

In the final chapter of this volume, G. K. Shaw offers a detailed analysis of the intricate and fractious issue of fiscal harmonization in Europe. He presents a simple formal model to illustrate the dilemma between efficiency and sovereignty that confronts Europeans as they abolish fiscal frontiers and struggle with finding a viable balance between a "hands-off" market approach and intro-European policy coordination.

The major issues he explores include the efficiency and equity implications of capital migration and proposed measures for tax harmonization; the intransigence of the Thatcher administration; the macroeconomic and, in particular, the revenue consequences of harmonization; the need for coordination of national spending programs; and the impact of the dramatic changes in Eastern Europe on the Single Market program.

Shaw concludes that the combination of these factors will slow the pace of fundamental change and increase the losses of efficiency, at least in the short term. Special attention is given to the "long and inglorious" history of corporate tax harmonization in the Community and the current program of the Commission of European Communities. The complexity of the process and the lack of political commitment, Shaw concludes, will likely preclude the implementation of the ambitious agenda in the early 1990s. Instead, he offers the radical proposition that the corporate income tax be abolished altogether.

This book is one of four volumes published from the AEI project, The United States and Europe in the 1990s. Under the auspices of this major research effort, AEI commissioned a series of twenty-eight papers analyzing the problems and prospects for U.S.-European relations in trade, finance, agriculture, defense, social policy, political institutions, and world diplomacy.

In March 1990, AEI convened a four-day conference in Washington, D.C., to present the analysis and conclusions of the commissioned papers. Panels of experts on the subject matter of the individual chapters were asked to provide supporting or dissenting conclusions. These written statements are also included here.

The other volumes in this series are:

Industry, Services, and Agriculture: The United States Faces a United Europe, Claude E. Barfield and Mark Perlman, eds.

Political Power and Social Change: The United States Faces a United Europe, Norman J. Ornstein and Mark Perlman, eds.

Reshaping Western Security: The United States Faces a United Europe, Richard N. Perle, ed.

PART ONE
The European Community in the International Trading System

1
The Future of the International Trading System

Brian Hindley

"May you live in interesting times" runs the Chinese curse. We live in interesting times, but we do not yet know whether that will prove to be a curse or a blessing.

The extraordinary events in Eastern Europe may seem to have little to do with the structure of the international trading system, which is the subject of this chapter. The affected economies do not bulk sufficiently large to make a major impact on either international trade or the international trading system, at least in the immediate future. But international economic relations are a part of a broader system of international relations. When that broader system changes, international economic relations are unlikely to remain constant.

The world contains four nations or groups of nations with claims to superpower status. The distribution of powers between them, however, is curiously uneven. Only the United States is a superpower in both economic and military terms. The Soviet Union is a military superpower but not an economic one. The European Community (EC) and Japan are economic superpowers, but not military ones.

The inability of Europe and Japan to defend themselves in a world in which attack seemed possible—and at times even probable—has been a central element in international relations. If the need of Europe and Japan for assistance in defense is greatly diminished, as now seems possible, then radical alterations in relations between the nations of the West are also possible. Moreover, these changes are likely to display themselves most prominently, at least initially, in economic relations.

These comments are not an introduction to lengthy prognostications. They are intended to make the simple point that what appeared to be a relatively straightforward assignment in early 1989 is no longer straightforward. In early 1989, the topic of U.S.-EC trade relations in the 1990s seemed susceptible to an almost technical treatment, at least in its broad outlines. That is no longer true. Ordinary mortals cannot even make a plausible pretense of knowing how matters might stand in the year 2000.

But if it is impossible to know what the world will look like in 2000, some of the factors that will shape its appearance can be identified. In this chapter, therefore, I first seek to identify trends and tendencies in the recent trade policies of the United States and the European Community and in public discussion of them. Initially, this is without reference to events in Eastern Europe. The final section of the chapter, however, discusses the effects that the events in Eastern Europe might have when they are superimposed on the trends identified.

The United States and the European Community in the International Trading System

The most evident trend in the trade policies of the United States and the EC is toward bilateralism. Although the primary concern of both the United States and the EC is trade relations with the Far East, and especially Japan, however, and although "fair trade" marks the routes to bilateralism of both the United States and the EC, the routes themselves are different.

To cope with its "problems" with Japan and the Far East, the EC has developed antidumping action as a protectionist bilateral device (Hindley 1988, 1989). The primary bilateral weapon of the United States, in contrast, is the threat of 301 and super-301 action. In the present context, however, it is the significance of the movement to bilateralism that is important, not the nature or the operational details of the vehicles used to get there.

The international trading system is principally defined by the rules of the General Agreements on Tariffs and Trade (GATT), and, with respect to the GATT, the U.S. defection from multilateralism is more significant than that of the EC. The European commitment to multilateralism has always been more tepid than that of the United States.

That law should replace power in international economic relations is—or was—a U.S. idea, as is the corollary that remedies should be independent of the identity of the economy against which they are directed. They were not U.S. ideas in the sense that everyone, or even a majority in the United States, held them. But, in the mid-1940s, the United States was probably the only country in which these ideas were supported by a substantial body of opinion—and, moreover, opinion in the administration.

Europeans deferred to the United States in the matter, but, by and large, Europeans were—and still are—more comfortable with the traditional and opposed view that trade relations should be controlled, not by international law, but by the requirements of a broader diplomacy. The United States may now be shifting toward the position that international law should give way before exigency and power. If so, that is a major change, and portends major changes in the structure of international relations.

But the United States has a tradition of schizophrenia in these matters. U.S. trade policy mixes blatant and immediate self-interest with acts and proposals that are consistent with a much more broadly based conception of U.S. interests. Even when U.S. policy seems to be driven by immediate self-interest, moreover, it seems natural for those who make U.S. trade policy to think in terms of a global interest. Their identification of that global interest is sometimes suspect, and they do not always—and sometimes cannot—act upon their perception of it. But the idea that there *is* a global interest, which ought to be identified in the process of making trade policy, is not alien or offensive to them.

The continuing U.S. trade deficit, however, is tilting U.S. schizophrenia into paranoia. The administration apparently would like to continue the traditional U.S. role as the leading policy maker in the international trading system. That role cannot be sustained, however, if immediate U.S. interest is the sole reference point for its policy. And the Congress is unlikely to welcome actions that it perceives to be against immediate U.S. interests.

There is another reason that the U.S. drift from multilateralism is more significant than that of the EC. If any external factor could check the movement of the EC toward bilateralism, it would be a determined push by the United States for a return to multilateralism. In present circumstances, however, such a push is unlikely.

Policy makers in the EC do not naturally think in terms of a wider interest than that of the EC. The EC is the world's largest trading block, but EC officials tend to think like the representatives of some minor country without influence on the state of the world trading system. Of course, they are determined not to be pushed around as though they were the representatives of a minor country, but they cannot seem to find positive uses for the influence that falls to a major state.

The early submissions in the Uruguay Round illustrate these tendencies. The U.S. submissions are almost academic in their focus on the underlying issues and in their attempts to define the principles that should apply to the problem at hand. The EC submissions are conceptually cramped, defensive, and introverted. Even with four years of negotiation ahead, they are swamped by the burdens of practical and parochial politics.

These are the central players in the game to be discussed.[1] So far as any role in the world economy is concerned, one has little practice in raising its sights much above the interests of weekend farmers in Bavaria and may lack the capacity to lift them higher. The other has the capacity to think in broader terms, but may lack the political ability to put such thoughts into effect. If these are the primary players in the cast that will determine the future of the GATT, does the GATT have a future?

The GATT

When Professor Lester Thurow pronounced the GATT dead in February 1989, an audience of businessmen is reported to have applauded enthusiastically. Professor Rudiger Dornbusch (another member of the MIT faculty) has recently denounced "the tedium of the GATT" and has suggested instead an EC-U.S. alliance to "peel the Japanese onion" by threatening to close the markets of the EC and the United States to Japanese products unless the markets of Japan are opened to U.S. and EC products.

The GATT *is* tedious. Most legal processes are tedious to outside observers, but that is a poor reason to abandon legal process. To join the mob on its way to burn down the courthouse and string up the prisoners might give a spurious feeling of *doing* something—even of doing something constructive. But it is almost certainly more constructive in fact to explore the issues and problems that underlie dissatisfaction with the GATT. Intelligent judgments require some thought about the problems the GATT was designed to solve, about whether those problems still exist, and, if so, about how they might be solved in the absence of the GATT—and about the alternatives to the GATT.

Two Primary GATT Functions. The GATT has two primary functions. The first function derives from the interdependence of countries that trade with one another. The trade policy of the government of a country—or, indeed, its policies in areas other than trade—affect the trade and investment flows of its trading partners and the fortunes of their residents.

Members of governments cannot as a matter of course be expected to accept passively grievances of their constituents about the actions of foreign governments (and even if members of governments do passively accept them, members of oppositions certainly will not). Trade and other economic relations between sovereign states hold the potential of creating *political* tensions.

Historically, the problem has been handled in various ways. At one extreme is war or the threat of war. At another extreme are treaties, peacefully arrived at, that specify the rights and duties of the parties involved in economic relations with one another. Peaceful treaties have clear advantages. There is a further clear advantage in negotiating a single multilateral treaty rather than a very large number of bilateral ones.[2]

The GATT is that multilateral treaty. Over a certain range of international economic activity, notably that involved in international trade in goods, the GATT specifies rights and obligations of governments with respect to trade policy and, therefore, with respect to one another. Moreover, the GATT provides a "courthouse" in which disputes about the interpretation of the rights and obligations specified by the treaty can be adjudicated.

To compare the GATT to a system of criminal law in which there is a police force to arrest and charge those who break the law is an egregious, but widespread, error. The GATT is a treaty. It establishes a system of international law, analogous to *civil* law, that endows the contracting parties (CPs)—the governments of the signatory states—with rights that they can enforce through litigation.

Saying that the GATT has been unable to prevent changes or to adapt to them can be too easily misunderstood as meaning that some central organization ("the GATT") has powers of decision and execution but has failed to exercise them properly. There is no such organization. The GATT is the basis for a system of civil, not criminal, law—there is no GATT police force to apprehend wrongdoers. A statement less open to misinterpretation is that the contracting parties to the GATT could not agree on a response to the changes (whatever they may have been).

All GATT activities and actions are ultimately activities and actions of the CPs. The panels that adjudicate disputes are composed of the representatives of CPs other than those in dispute. A multilateral trade negotiation (MTN) is about obtaining agreement of CPs to reductions in tariffs, or modifying, changing, or adding to, the terms of the treaty.

This structure has a variety of consequences. For example, representatives of CPs sitting on a panel adjudicating a dispute may have neither the legal skill nor the objectivity of a judge in proceedings under domestic civil law. And the requirement that all CPs must agree to changes in the terms of the GATT leads to inertia.

Nevertheless, what is ultimately at issue in GATT reform is not a firing of some staff and a reshuffling of others—as might be the case

15

at, say, the World Bank or the International Monetary Fund (IMF). GATT reform raises far more fundamental and intractable questions about the relations between sovereign states.

The second function of the GATT is "liberalization." By the usual standards of international treaties, the preamble to the GATT is mercifully short. It says that those signatories:

> Recognizing that their relations in the field of trade and economic endeavour should be conducted with a view to raising standards of living, ensuring full employment and a large and steadily growing volume of real income and effective demand, developing the full uses of the resources of the world and expanding the production and exchange of goods,
>
> Being desirous of contributing to these objectives by entering into reciprocal and mutually advantageous arrangements *directed to the substantial reduction of tariffs and other barriers to trade and to the elimination of discriminatory treatment in international commerce,*
>
> Have through their representatives agreed as follows: [and then follows the text of the agreement] [emphasis added].

The objective of obtaining a "substantial reduction in tariffs and other barriers to trade" has now been pursued through seven MTNs or "rounds." The Uruguay Round, the eighth, latest, and most ambitious, goes far beyond reductions in tariffs.

The "success" of the GATT is almost invariably judged entirely by this second, liberalizing, function. One conventional assessment of that success is that successive MTNs have indeed reduced tariffs. But, it is said, tariffs have been replaced by nontariff barriers (NTBs), and the reduction or elimination of NTBs has proved much less amenable to the GATT process than tariffs.

The facts upon which this conventional assessment is based—the reduction of tariffs to very low levels (at least in developed countries) and the difficulties of dealing with NTBs by traditional GATT means—are certainly correct. They are open to different interpretations, however. It is sometimes suggested, for example, that the replacement of tariffs by NTBs has been complete. Were that so, the GATT would have had very little effect on total protection. In this view, the entire GATT process has been a charade and a waste of time.

That view is almost certainly wrong, however. It is difficult to argue persuasively that NTBs have *fully* replaced tariffs as protective devices. For one thing, the substitution of nontariff for tariff protection explains only some NTBs. Many NTBs have always been present. They have become a central concern *because* tariffs have fallen, making the NTBs more visible and their effects on trade flows more relevant.

Certainly, throughout the existence of the GATT, the volume of international trade has risen more rapidly than output, which has itself risen at rates that are very high by historical standards. This fact strongly suggests (though it does not prove) that there has been a substantial effective liberalization of trade.

Another interpretation of the basic facts comes closer to current policy relevance. Holders of this second interpretation grant that the GATT process was successful in reducing both tariffs *and* the total protection. But, they say, the GATT has come to the end of the line—GATT procedures eventually depend upon legal compliance, and legal compliance does not work with NTBs. Even if the rules for removal of an NTB are followed, another NTB is always available to put in its place. In this view, the GATT cannot cope with the NTBs that block trade in the modern world. Something more is needed.

The "something more" is usually an exercise of power. Released from the bonds and constraints of the GATT, the argument goes, our government could threaten to close the markets of our country to foreign products unless foreign markets were *genuinely* opened to our products.

Potential Conflict between GATT Objectives. A problem is that the role of defuser of trade tensions and that of agent of liberalization potentially conflict with each other. The conflict is well illustrated in a recent pamphlet by Rudiger Dornbusch, Paul Krugman, and Yung Chul Park. The central arguments of the pamphlet are discussed below. What is of interest in the present context is the curious direction in which they are led by their emphasis on liberalization. "The GATT," the authors complain (p. 31), "is legalistic, relying on abstract principles rather than judgment . . . *disputes are to be settled through argument in court rather than by administrative fiat*" (emphasis added).

How strange that U.S. academics should appear to prefer administrative fiat to "legalism"! GATT legal process—and the authors do not distinguish clearly between "legalistic" and legal process—is very much a reflection of U.S. tradition. That tradition, moreover (or so one might have thought), is deep and honorable.

But if fiat, whose? Dornbusch, Krugman, and Park's apparent preference for administrative fiat—for criminal law and a police force rather than civil law and litigation—does not seem to have been preceded or modified by any thought about who might exercise the police power.

Perhaps they take for granted that the United States will be able to do so—or perhaps simply think that it ought to be able to do so. Alternatively, their complaint is consistent with a belief that there is some known objective—"liberalization"—shared by all GATT CPs, and whose achievement, therefore, becomes a mere technical problem. That supposition is so far from the facts, however, that to attribute the belief to Dornbusch, Krugman, and Park is insulting. More likely, they suppose that some such belief ought to be shared by all CPs. If there actually is no such shared objective, the proposition that there ought to be is not very useful.

An international trading system in which "liberalization" is implemented by administrative fiat may just be conceivable. But the other GATT function—neutralizing the political content of disputes about trade—clearly cannot be achieved by fiat. A treaty solely concerned with such neutralization would allow on the basis of political exigency numerous actions that could not be justified on economic grounds—as, of course, the GATT does, to the often-expressed disgust of economists.

The United States, for example, probably could find GATT justification for a general tariff on balance-of-payments grounds (Article XII) were its balance-of-trade adjustment difficulties to become severe. Conventional economics cannot justify that. Politics can.

Democratic governments sometimes experience political pressures too intense to be resisted. How should an agreement such as the GATT cope with that unpleasant fact, when the pressure is for actions that are inconsistent with the core purposes of the GATT?

There is an argument for "punishing" the offender. That argument is that the prospect of punishment will stiffen the resistance to pressure of governments, and reduce the probability that the offending action will be taken.

When the circumstances in which irresistible pressure might arise can be foreseen, however, there is also an argument for setting up the agreement to allow exceptions in those circumstances. The argument is that in such circumstances, no punishment that GATT CPs can or will inflict will have any substantial effect on the probability that the offending action will be taken. In that case, a ban upon the action would risk the defection of the government under pressure. It is much more sensible, says the second argument, to ensure that the deviation is temporary, and that the affected government returns to normal disciplines when it is able to do so.

Suppose, for example, that the U.S. government finds the trade deficit creates so much pressure for increased protection that it cannot (in terms of practical politics) be resisted. From a global point of view, what is then lost by giving the U.S. government the legal right to do (on balance-of-payments grounds) what it will do anyway? If the United States has that right, such action will not, as might otherwise be the case, wreck the agreement. Authorization of the deviation in "special" circumstances increases the probability that the deviation will be temporary. Moreover, the preservation in these circumstances of the GATT structure provides a legal bulwark against retaliation by U.S. trading partners. Such retaliation would threaten to convert a temporary deviation into a much more protracted and bellicose affair.

What is true for the United States is also true for other CPs. The GATT after all is a voluntary organization. A rigid structure, such as might stem from a commitment to, say, "efficient global resource allocation" or "free trade" might be very worthy. But an organization based upon such a commitment probably would have rather few members.

To neutralize the political tensions that inevitably derive from trade issues, the GATT must be elastic. Its structure must be based on an answer to the question of what is the *political* alternative to allowing deviations from the path of "liberalization." Sensible people might answer that question in ways that permit sizable deviations.

Although the two GATT functions potentially conflict, the tension between them is productive. Pressure for liberalization and reform gives the GATT a focus and a purpose. Without it, the GATT would be at risk of aimless drifting—of having no greater objective than maintaining or increasing its membership.

To pursue "liberalization" at the expense of all else, however, is to risk both all else and liberalization. Diplomatic problems cannot be resolved by administrative fiat. Attempts to do so will lead to resistance and revolt, and to the de facto (and possibly de jure) end of the GATT.

U.S. Nostrums

If the next few years bring major changes in the legal structure of the international trading system, the changes probably will originate in the United States. The reason lies in the U.S. trade deficit and its effect on discussion of trade policy in the United States.

The trade deficit has very little to do with trade policy, despite the frequent link between them in popular discussion. The size of the trade deficit is determined primarily by macroeconomic factors. It makes little sense to focus on trade policy, whether that of the United States or of other countries, if correcting the trade deficit is the primary problem.[3]

Nevertheless, the U.S. trade deficit, together with a sense within the United States of its declining power, but, also, an enhanced sense of the possibilities that power might yield in trade policy, creates an environment in which trade-policy nostrums flourish. Most are constructed from some combination of the same basic building blocks.

Two of the building blocks are bilateralism and reciprocity. There is a third, however, which is sometimes seen as an opportunity, sometimes as a threat. It focuses on the formation of regional trading blocks. These three will be discussed in turn. The same question will be asked by each, namely, Is this a cure or a route to another set of problems?

Bilateralism. That the United States will gain from bilateralism is the central position taken by Dornbusch, Krugman, and Park. The authors are eminent international economists (and the first two are regarded by many as being among the most eminent of this generation). A pamphlet that bears their names should, therefore, be taken seriously.

The U.S. budget and trade deficits and the corresponding buildup of foreign holdings of U.S. assets, create the backdrop for the authors' argument:

> At the end of 1988, the U.S. net debt stood at about $550 billion, and was continuing to grow at an annual rate of $150 billion. Even if the current account deficit declines steadily over the next five years to zero, the debt will eventually amount to about $1 trillion, or perhaps 15 percent of gross national product. The size of this foreign debt will imply a deficit on investment income of perhaps $70 billion, or more than 1 percent of GNP.
>
> If the United States is going to balance its international accounts—which it will eventually have to do—this deficit on investment income due to our debt will have to be balanced by a surplus on merchandise trade. . . .
>
> . . . Thus, a first pass estimate would suggest an increase in the demand for U.S.-made manufactures of 3–4 percent of GNP. That is, there will be a growth in demand for manufactures arising from the need to stop borrowing abroad and pay the bill on our accumulated debt of about 3–4 percent of GNP, over and above any growth in domestic demands for manufactures.
>
> This may not sound like a large number, but given the relatively small share of manufacturing in the U.S. domestic economy, it is actually quite large. In 1987, manufacturing accounted for 22 percent of the value added in the economy. . . . If the U.S. current account deficit is to come into balance over a five-year period, manufactures output would have to rise at an annual rate of almost 6 percent, more than twice as fast as gross national product. Thus, we

are probably headed for a period of marked reindustrialization. (p. 6)

Dornbusch, Krugman, and Park do not think that trade policy has been helpful to U.S. manufactures:

> Our trade policy has steadfastly advocated open markets. Our market is, indeed, more open than virtually any other. But this trade policy has not given our firms any extra advantage. In the level playing field, the best team wins and our team is no longer the best. Therefore trade policy should have looked for special opportunities, not in the direction of market closing and protectionism, *but in opening markets for our firms, ahead of the competition.* As a result of the asymmetry between the administrative closedness of foreign markets and the wide-open nature of our own, we have been losing out in world competition. (p. 8: emphasis added)

Nevertheless, for the most part, the policies that Dornbusch, Krugman, and Park advocate to facilitate the reindustrialization that they forecast do not directly affect trade policy. Those policies include, for example, budgetary reduction and interest rate and exchange rate policy, policies toward domestic saving and investment, and toward foreign investment (where they advocate a policy of openness), and education. Indeed, they expressly play down the significance of trade policy:

> Trade policy in the manufacturing sector is sometimes assigned more significance than it deserves—for example, Japan's interventionist trade policy of the past 35 years is often given credit for the extraordinary export success of that nation; credit that really rests primarily with a high savings rate, an education system that produced a highly skilled work force, and the resulting rapid increase in productivity and quality throughout the economy. *Still an effective U.S. trade policy could reduce significantly the costs associated with the necessary reindustrialization of our economy—while a failure of trade policy could make those costs much higher.* (p. 31: emphasis added)

In the view of Dornbusch, Krugman, and Park, an effective U.S. trade policy would entail:

> An aggressive effort to secure access to world markets for U.S. manufactured goods—bearing in mind that these exports will have to expand rapidly as the U.S. moves toward external balance.
>
> But how is this to be accomplished? At the risk of being excessively blunt, we would argue that for manufactures

trade at least there is little to be accomplished through continuing multilateral negotiations under the GATT framework. Almost surely it will be necessary, if we are going to have an effective policy, to engage in bilateral and regional arrangements—preserving what we can of the GATT, but looking for new alternatives as well. (p. 34)

Despite the strong words, much of what they propose is actually quite consistent with the GATT. Two of their proposals, however, are in potential conflict with the GATT obligations of the United States.

The first such point of potential conflict, perhaps more properly described as an observation rather than a proposal, turns upon a vision of the 1990s in which the EC turns inward and "French-style administrative barriers and voluntary export restraints are used to close the European market to any increase in imports from the U.S. or from developing countries. Meanwhile, developing countries continue to pursue export-oriented policies that aim at large trade surpluses without offering an opening to goods from the U.S." (p. 34), and Japan "through its cartelized distribution system and through red-tape barriers prevents more than a marginal rise in U.S. manufactured exports" (p. 34).

Dornbusch, Krugman, and Park note that this is "probably an overdrawn scenario" (p. 33) (and might also have noted that it requires a rather substantial dash of paranoia). Nevertheless, they go on to ask, "In such a situation, why should the U.S. rely on dollar depreciation rather than protection to turn its trade balance around? After all, dollar depreciation, by leading us to sell our own goods more cheaply, tends to reduce our real income; a tariff that does not cut our prices but simply discourages imports does not" (p. 34).

This is the argument that protection will improve the U.S. terms of trade. Although it may be a policy that Dornbusch, Krugman, and Park would recommend in the circumstances they sketch, they say that they would prefer to avoid it: "The market opening strategy is by far preferred to a policy of import protection" (p. 38).

The second point of conflict between their proposals and the GATT obligations of the United States is the centerpiece of their recommendations. This is for market access agreements that set quantitative targets for U.S. exports:

Such agreements are a new and largely untried tool of policy. They have been referred to, sarcastically, as "affirmative action" for U.S. exports. The comparison has some merit. Market access agreements are intended to counter the effects of a pattern of discrimination that does not constitute an explicit violation of the legal rules—in this case the

GATT—but that is nonetheless real and needs to be corrected.

It remains to be seen what can actually be accomplished through such agreements. However, in dealing with East Asian nations, it makes sense to try novel tools. As we pointed out in Chapter III, Japan and other East Asian nations remain *de facto* closed to many U.S. exports. Despite the combination of a low dollar and a rise in Japanese manufactured imports, the increase has been concentrated in labor-intensive goods from the newly industrializing countries (NICs) rather than U.S. goods. Negotiating over the letter of the trade law does not seem to work. Thus there is a strong case for trying a more result-oriented trade policy in specific cases (p. 37).

Even this proposal does not clearly run counter to the GATT; however Dornbusch, Krugman, and Park treat the proposition that U.S. exports to East Asia are blocked by NTBs of one kind or another as demonstrated.[4] But if the United States *were* able to demonstrate persuasively that the application of NTBs by Japan or other East Asian countries was reducing U.S. exports to Japan, there is legal recourse for the United States in the GATT.

Article XXIII of the GATT is headed "Nullification or Impairment." It can be applied:

1. If any contracting party should consider any benefit accruing to it directly or indirectly under this Agreement is being nullified or impaired or that the attainment of any objective of the Agreement is being impeded as a result of

  (a) the failure of another contracting party to carry out its obligations under this Agreement, or

  (b) *the application of another contracting party of any measure, whether or not it conflicts with this Agreement,* or

  (c) *the existence of any other situation,*

  . . . the matter may be referred to the *contracting parties.* If the *contracting parties* consider that the circumstances are serious enough to justify such action, they may authorize a contracting party or parties to suspend the application of such concessions or other obligations as they determine to be appropriate in the circumstances. [emphasis added]

One issue, therefore, is that of proof. Article XXIII is very broadly drawn. It clearly covers the kind of complaint that Dornbusch, Krugman, and Park make. If the United States could *prove* that its exports to Japan are as seriously impeded by NTBs as Dornbusch, Krugman, and Park suggest, the United States could retaliate *within* the GATT framework.

But even such proof would not allow the United States to open, as Dornbusch, Krugman, and Park (p. 8) put it, "markets for our firms, ahead of the competition." Japanese market-opening measures taken through the GATT (accepting for the sake of argument that the Japanese market *is* artificially closed) could not be overtly structured in such a way as to favor the United States—unless the United States could show that Japan had discriminated against it in favor of, say, the EC—a seemingly bizarre hypothesis.

Moreover, a U.S. attempt to obtain an outcome that favored U.S. exports to Japan and the East Asian NICs (newly industrialized countries) over those of other exporters would almost certainly lead to a de facto breakup of the GATT. The EC would not passively accept such a position. If it could not obtain from Japan and the East Asian NICs the advantages given to the United States, the EC would at minimum raise barriers against exports from those countries.

The disappearance of the GATT will not help the United States to solve the problem that Dornbusch, Krugman, and Park pose. As they say, the United States must move into substantial trade surplus over the next few years. The implied increase in U.S. exports will raise protectionist sentiment elsewhere. To eliminate the GATT would be to create the conditions for their "overdrawn scenario," in which the United States withdraws into protectionism because everyone else protects against U.S. exports. Without the GATT, the rest of the world would be free to increase its protection against U.S. products, not merely by covert means (accepting for the sake of argument their view of the world), but also by overt means.

To create such freedom for other countries also casts doubt on the ability of the United States to improve its terms of trade through protection. An increase in U.S. protection that is met by an increase in foreign protection against the United States is unlikely to increase either U.S. economic welfare or that of the rest of the world.

Reciprocity. Reciprocity is sometimes treated as an end in itself, which is a mistake. Reciprocity is a mode of travel, not a destination. People go into shops with the understanding that reciprocity will be observed. They do not usually think that is enough to tell them what to buy. The idea of reciprocity seems currently to be surrounded by confusion. Much of it derives from a failure to answer the question, Reciprocity in what?

One kind of reciprocity is *first-difference* reciprocity. GATT negotiations are an example of first-difference reciprocity. An MTN is about reciprocal exchanges of concessions, where a "concession" is a relaxation in impediments to imports. Thus, *changes* in import regimes are traded. Under first-difference reciprocity, the government of a heavily protected economy can trade equal concessions with the government of a lighly protected economy. Both can *change* their import regime by the same amount, but after the change, the more heavily protected economy remains more heavily protected.

Absolute reciprocity, which has recently come into vogue on both sides of the Atlantic, is different. Senator Robert Dole gave a clear definition some years ago. "Reciprocity," he said, "means that other countries should provide us with trade and investment opportunities equal not simply to what they offer their most-favored trading partners but equal to what we afford them."

A corollary of Senator Dole's definition presumably is that we will afford them only the trade and investment opportunities that they afford us. Under absolute reciprocity, it is possible and likely that country A will have different levels of protection against similar products from different sources. Protection by A against traders from country B may be low because the B level of protection against A is low. Protection by A against similar traders from country C may be high because the C level of protection against A is high.

Under absolute reciprocity, that is, country A can only have the same trade regime toward all of its trading partners if all of them have the same trade regime as one another. Even leaving aside the central question of who is to judge the relative opportunities offered by the different protective structures of different countries, that is a most unlikely state of affairs. Absolute reciprocity and nondiscrimination— the cornerstone of the GATT system—are compatible only in extraordinary circumstances. Adoption of absolute reciprocity is tantamount to rejection of the GATT system—and, in the case of the United States, that means destruction of the GATT system.[5]

In the present context, however, it is the moral element in the argument for absolute reciprocity that is of primary importance. Bilateralism urges the use of power in trade relations. Absolute reciprocity purports to supply a moral justification for that position. The idea that foreign nations ". . . should provide us with trade and investment opportunities equal . . . to what we afford them," has, at first blush, a ring of justice and fairness to it.

One justification for absolute reciprocity is results. Suppose that the world contains two countries, one, H, with a high level of protection, and the other, L, with a low one. If L adopts absolute reciprocity and the implied threat causes H to reduce its protection to the low level of L, it is likely that the residents of *both* L and H will experience economic gains in the aggregate.

Part of the problem with this justification is that the opposite consequence is also possible. Country H may refuse to lower its level of protection. Country L's adoption of absolute reciprocity then will have the result that L adopts the high level of protection of H.

Reciprocitarians cannot claim improvements in economic welfare as a justification for their preferred policy. A proposal to match the level of protection of one's trading partners is not tantamount to a proposal to maximize economic welfare, whether that of one's countrymen or that of the world as a whole. The actions required by adherence to absolute reciprocity will sometimes be the same as those that would be required to maximize one or the other of those magnitudes, but they are not always, or even typically, the same.

Rather than pursue imponderables, a backward step may serve to clarify issues. One way to come to grips with the economic issues involved in reciprocity is to view reciprocity from the perspective of the last century.

A classic nineteenth-century free-trade position called for *unilateral* abolition of tariffs. Holders of that position rejected the need for reciprocal tariff cuts by trading partners, and in that sense were *anti*reciprocity. Many advocates of this position based their argument on the proposition that a country would secure economic gains through free trade, whatever the trade policies of other countries.

In terms of pure economics, however, the superiority from a national standpoint of free trade over protection can only be demonstrated for quite limited circumstances. The proposition ignores the possibility that a country can shift its terms of trade with the rest of the world in its own favor by imposing a tariff on imports, thereby gaining at the expense of the rest of the world. Even if a country will gain by eliminating its tariff, moreover, a country that can influence its terms of trade will gain more if it can arrange matters so that other countries remove or reduce their tariffs at the same time—that is, by reciprocity.

More sophisticated nineteenth-century advocates of unilateral free trade conceded both of these points, but were not impressed with the terms-of-trade argument, either on moral grounds or in terms of the practicality of calculating or implementing it (Irwin 1988 and Bhagwati and Irwin 1987, discuss these debates). And the antireciprocitarians observed that a government could spend decades trying to link lower tariffs at home with lower tariffs abroad—all the while maintaining its own, probably costly, tariff. Our own tariff, they said, can be eliminated now, without any negotiation with other governments. Forgoing the present gains available from unilateral action for the prospect of even greater gains that may never come, they said, is not smart. Unless there is good reason to suppose that reciprocal tariff cuts can be arranged in the very near future, they concluded, unilateral free trade is a better policy than an indefinite wait for reciprocal concessions.

That conclusion may be correct. Right or wrong, however, it does not derive from economic logic, but from judgment.

Yet, although the logic of the unilateralist position is vulnerable, it has a merit that is absent from much current debate on reciprocity. Advocates of the unilateralist position keep sight of the objective of the game. They keep the score in terms of the overall effect on the economic welfare of members of the community. A focus on opening up foreign markets, however, easily degenerates into the belief that the score should be kept in terms of the gains of domestic producers as against foreign ones.

Of course, the game can be played, and the score kept, in that way. But to keep the score *solely* in terms of the relative gains of differently located producers cannot be justified in broader terms. Buyers count, too. In economic terms, when the United States or the EC allow foreign producers easy access to their markets, they are doing a favor to buyers and users of such goods in the EC and the United States. Foreign producers may gain as well, but that, in itself, is hardly a reason to bar their access.

"Justice" and "fairness" are difficult terms. It is useful to pose the issues in terms of property rights. Thus, an argument that first-difference reciprocity is just can be founded on the premise that each government has the right to set the level of protection for its economy (except when it has voluntarily limited that right by binding within the GATT or by some other means). It follows from that premise that if the government of country A wants a lower level of protection by country B, it must "pay" for it—in GATT terms, by offering to reduce its own level of protection against B products.

Absolute reciprocity implies another allocation of "property rights" between governments. Then, in effect, the government of A claims the right to make B "pay"—by raising the level of protection of A against B—if the B level of protection is regarded as too high by the government of A.

In what terms might this allocation of "property rights" be described as just? A possible starting point is that the level of protection chosen by B affects A. That evident fact might be taken to supply a foundation for a proposition that A should have a right to intervene directly in the decisions of B. But that is not a very sound argument. The crucial difference between first-difference reciprocity and absolute reciprocity does not lie in the right of A to intervene in B's decision-making process, but in how the intervention may be made. Under first-difference reciprocity, A can only offer to "buy" reductions in protection from B. If absolute reciprocity rules, A can threaten to impose costs upon B if B does not reduce its level of protection.

Of course, as in any buyer-seller interaction, some piece or pieces of protection by B may be worth more to B than any amount that A is willing to offer to remove them. In such a case, first-difference reciprocity will not be able to dislodge those pieces of protection. Absolute reciprocity might be able to do so (though it also might not).

But does that make a case for absolute reciprocity? Suppose that A and B were individual persons. A wants something from B, but is not prepared to offer for it any amount that B is willing to accept. We do not normally suppose that B's refusal gives A a right to threaten B with violence unless B gives A what he wants.[6]

In the actual case, however, A and B are not individuals but governments. Part of the problem in thinking about reciprocity—and about many other problems of trade policy—is that no one believes that governments act to maximize the economic welfare of their populations—an objective that is taken by many to be the proper objective of governments.

Thus, country B does not contain one interest but many. Notably, there is the interest of the B government and the different interests of the members of the B economy. Part of the ethical case for absolute reciprocity seems to be that the failure of the B government to "properly" represent the economic interests of the residents of B in some sense entitles the A government to act on their behalf by seeking liberalizations that the B government will not concede.

That is a deeply suspect position. If the government of B is subject to politics, so is the government of A—and it is most unlikely to properly represent—in terms of aggregate economic welfare—the interests of A residents, never mind those of B. But even if it did, the claim that it should also be able to represent the interests of B residents, if in its view they are not properly represented by the B government, is absurdly presumptuous.

The actions of governments often win the disapproval of economists. Yet, a viable constitution for international trading relations surely can be based only on the legal fiction that governments *do* represent the interests of their populations. Governments control the policy tools that are the proper subject of such an agreement. It must in the first instance, therefore, be governments that create any international agreement concerning the use of them.

Absolute reciprocity, of course, is a prerogative of large countries. The United States and Sri Lanka can, in principle, exchange equal concessions—they can engage in first-difference reciprocity. And Sri Lanka and the United States can threaten each other with the closure of their respective markets. But only one of those threats is likely to be effective. Absolute reciprocity is not the basis for an international constitution. It is a formula for domination by the strong.

The outcomes that are now complained of in the United States were legally achieved under a system of which the United States was the primary architect. That system never promised equality of trading opportunity. That it has not delivered such equality cannot, therefore, form the basis of an ethical case that the United States should be relieved of any of the obligations that it has accepted under that system. Nor can any demands imposed upon the United States by the U.S. trade deficit make an ethical case to that effect. It is the United States that bears the responsibility for its budget deficit and, therefore, for its trade deficit.

It is a tradition of U.S. boxing (at least in fiction) that the manager of the loser shouts "We wuz robbed" and demands a rematch. And if one is big enough and makes enough noise, a rematch is probable.

Power is power. Academic analysis cannot affect it greatly. It can usefully deduce the consequences of particular exercises of power, and it can analyze claims made in their own justification by those who exercise power. Absolute reciprocity is an excuse for the exercise of power, but it is not a good excuse. Its adoption by the United States is unlikely to have good consequences either for the United States or for the world at large.

Trading blocs. Trading blocs are a focus of much current concern. One reason is the EC 1992 project, which much of the rest of the world regards as a threat. Another reason derives from the sense that the old international trading order is passing, and that its replacement is likely to be based in some way upon a division of the world into three trading blocs clustered around the United States, the EC, and Japan. But that thought also gives rise to the notion that the formation of blocs yields opportunities for gain.

Most of the legitimate concern about the formation of blocs is political. Economic and legal issues do not in themselves give grounds for concern. From a purely economic standpoint, there is nothing intrinsically wrong with blocs. Kemp and Wan (1976) demonstrate that *any* two countries forming a customs union have available to them a tariff that makes their residents better off, in aggregate, without worsening the economic welfare of the rest of the world. Of course, the countries may not adopt that tariff, but that does not affect the general point that formation of a customs union or bloc is not in itself inimical to world economic welfare.

Nor is there anything illegal about blocs. GATT Article XXIV permits the formation of customs unions or free trade areas, subject to the conditions that:

> (a) duties and other restrictive regulations of commerce . . . are eliminated with respect to substantially all the trade between the constituent territories . . . (Article XXIV[8]), and
>
> (b) . . . the duties and other regulations of commerce imposed . . . shall not on the whole be higher or more restrictive than the corresponding duties and other regulations of commerce existing in the same constituent territories prior to the formation of the union (or free trade area) . . . (Article XXIV[5]).

Potential problems arise at the political level. Concerns about the way in which the formation of a bloc might change the behavior of its constituent parts can be formulated in a variety of ways, all leading in the same direction. For example, it is plausible that:

- The larger a bloc, the higher will be its optimal tariff.
- The larger a bloc, the closer it will feel itself to be to self-sufficiency, and thus to a sense that foreign trade is a dispensable luxury.
- The creation of a bloc identity requires the reinforcement of divisions between insiders and outsiders—protection against imports being a clear example of such a division.

These three propositions or any combination of them lead to the conclusion that the formation of customs unions or free-trade areas may—GATT Article XXIV(8) notwithstanding—lead to higher protection.

These propositions will be discussed later on, when the focus turns to the EC. In the context of U.S. trade policy, the more relevant issue is the contention that the formation of free-trade areas gives the United States a solution to its trade problems. Dornbusch, Krugman, and Park illustrate the U.S. concern with trading blocs both as a threat and as an opportunity. On the potential threat, they comment (p. 23) that:

> A regional arrangement in Asia, accompanying an increased move towards increased regional emphasis in Europe, threatens to leave the U.S. isolated. This issue is all the more serious if inward-looking regional associations emerge abroad at precisely the time at which the U.S. must undergo a major economic structuring that has to be outward-looking.

The comment really does seem tinged with paranoia. What does "isolation" mean? Does their definition of that term allow the possibility of closer regional groupings in Europe and Asia that would not "isolate" the United States?

The formation of "inward-looking regional associations" would, indeed, be a serious matter—and not only for the United States. But, once again, if that is a real prospect, does it make sense for the United States to follow the advice of Dornbusch, Krugman, and Park and break up the GATT? The United States thereby forgoes real GATT constraints on the operation of regional associations. What does it get in return?

Dornbusch, Krugman, and Park also see opportunities for U.S. policy in bloc formation, however. They explain (pp. 36–37) that the United States has much to gain and little to lose from forming free-trade areas with highly protected Latin American countries—especially Mexico and Brazil. In particular, if European and Japanese firms were still subject to high tariff barriers in the Latin American countries, while U.S. firms were not, U.S. firms would have a substantial advantage in those markets.

That U.S. advantage is not costless to its free-trade-area partners, however. After the formation of such a free-trade area, U.S. and Japanese personal computers both might cost $5,000 in Mexico. If the cost of the Japanese computer is made up of $3,000 paid to the Japanese manufacturer and $2,000 duty paid to the Mexican government on entry into Mexico, however, while the cost of a similar U.S. computer is $5,000 paid to the U.S. manufacturer, Mexico loses $2,000 on every purchase switched from Japanese to U.S. sources.

Moreover, much of the high protection against imports in Latin America is directed against the United States. And, if Latin American governments want the undoubted economic benefits of trade liberalization, they obviously can obtain them more efficiently by unilateral action. Why, then, would these countries be interested in forming a free-trade area with the United States?

Dornbusch, Krugman, and Park explain that:

> The reason is that the large and now wide-open U.S. market might close. Moreover, even if the U.S. market might not close altogether, the increasing interference with trade by application of the U.S. trade laws raises the costs of and uncertainty of exporting to the U.S. market. Individual developing countries would therefore find it of interest to strike a bargain where unimpeded access to the U.S. market is the *quid pro quo* for a privileged opening to the U.S. of their own markets (p. 36).

Now there's a sound basis for friendship and cooperation! To an outsider, it seems that Mexico has a variety of sound reasons to contemplate forming a free-trade area with the United States. But the proposition that Mexico should join a free-trade agreement with the United States that is economically disadvantageous for Mexico, to avoid the even greater costs that the United States may impose upon it in the future, might not appear on more conventional lists.

Nevertheless, the proposition is illuminating. The comment ". . . that application of U.S. trade laws raises the costs of and uncertainty of exporting to the U.S. market"—presumably referring to 301, super-301, and antidumping and countervailing duties imposed by the United States—is the only point at which Dornbusch, Krugman, and Park concede that the United States has its own nontariff barriers (NTBs). The proposition that Mexico might join a free-trade arrangement with the United States solely to avoid those NTBs suggests a different view of the United States than does the rest of the Dornbusch, Krugman, and Park pamphlet. There, the United States appears as a virtuous nation badly treated by others.

The difference is important. To view the United States as one among many sinners (although its sins may be fewer than those of others) is to see a common problem that requires multilateral solutions. To present the United States as a virtuous nation badly treated by others lays the moral foundation for a self-righteous approach to unilateral or bilateral action.

U.S. Nontariff Barriers—and Section 301. What really makes the present mood in the United States look dangerous, as seen from the outside, is the sense of self-righteousness, of virtue outraged, that currently seems to affect influential sections of U.S. opinion. And, in large degree, that sense depends upon a belief that the United States has no NTBs, while the rest of the world has many.

Although the rest of the world regrettably has many NTBs, it is not true that the United States has none. Taking antidumping and countervailing duty actions together, for example, the United States takes action almost twice as often as the next most frequent user.[7] And, it is quite clear that the U.S. antidumping procedure is heavily biased against exporters and contains very large elements of administrative discretion (Palmeter 1989). U.S. antidumping law in its current form is an effective NTB—and Congress continually modifies it to make it even more effective (Finger and Murray 1989).

And then, of course, there are 301 and super-301. So far, the primary effect of these measures has been to open markets. Their retaliatory provisions, which do not have that effect, have not yet been deployed in full force.

This is not the place to discuss the technical details of 301. But Hudec 1990, makes a point that is particularly relevant to the subject of this paper. He observes that the United States does not itself meet the standards that it sets for others in Section 301: "In all, that makes seven cases in which the United States has violated the new Section 301 deadlines in the past two years. Only one case has been found during this period where the United States complied with its 301 deadlines—a case in which the panel ruled that the United States was not in violation" (p. 54):

> The 1988 version of Section 301 is a bad law. But its evil is not that it authorizes violation of GATT law in pursuit of law reform objectives. Some such authority should be part of any government's arsenal of legal policy options.
> What is wrong with the new Section 301 is that it seeks to employ such authority for law reform objectives that, in their present form, do not have the remotest claim to legitimacy. The heart of the problem is that the law is based on an outrageous premise—namely, that the commands of Section 301 do not apply to the United States. The new Section 301 is a law for the rest of the world only. Besides being wrong in itself, the one-sided premise has also corrupted the substantive content of the new Section 301, leading Congress to include many substantive standards that are wholly unreasonable on any terms (pp. 72–73).

For discussion of the future of the international trading system, however, it is what lies behind this situation that is relevant. A self-righteous U.S. Congress, acting out of a misplaced sense of injured innocence, is capable of inflicting much more harm on the international trading system than is Section 301.

Boring at the GATT. In terms of trade policy, the EC is less interesting—less *explosive*—than the United States. Large solutions are mooted in the EC to problems that usually involve Japan and East Asia. But it is difficult to portray the international trade problems of the EC as being on the same scale as those of the United States. Save for Eurozealots, therefore, it is difficult to demonstrate the need for large "solutions."

There is no pressure for the EC to withdraw from the GATT, nor to take actions that are tantamount to withdrawal. A substantial section of opinion in the EC is unenthusiastic about the idea of the GATT as a body of enforceable international law, and would prefer it to be merely a forum—a talking shop and international meeting place. And, consistent with that view, the EC is prepared to take actions that risk the de facto end of the GATT as an effective constitution for international trade—EC manipulation and antidumping policy, to be discussed later, is an example.

Each of the three issues just discussed in a U.S. context has a counterpart in the EC. The EC has discovered how to achieve bilateralism within the GATT. It has experimented with reciprocity, especially in financial services. And the 1992 project of the EC is responsible for much of the concern in the rest of the world at the possibility of the world dividing into three protectionist trading blocs—a move triggered by an EC retreat into "Fortress Europe."[8] Each is discussed in turn.

Antidumping Action and EC Bilateralism. The EC has been uncomfortable with some of its GATT obligations for quite a while. In the Tokyo Round, the EC tried very hard to obtain agreement to an amendment of Article XIX that would give importers the right to act unilaterally and selectively against "disruptive imports"—that is, imports from new and efficient suppliers, primarily located in Japan and the East Asian NICs. The EC regarded this as a matter of major importance—it claimed at one point that acceptance of its proposals on Article XIX was a *sine qua non* for EC acceptance of the outcome of the rest of the Tokyo Round.

During the event, the EC proposals were rejected and the EC did not block the Tokyo Round. But the commission has now learned to use antidumping action to create the situation that the EC tried and failed to get in the Tokyo Round. Moreover, it does not need the agreement of other GATT members to obtain that position, as it did with its suggestions for reform of Article XIX.

The essentials of the EC method have been discussed in detail elsewhere (Hindley 1988, 1989) and do not require extensive rehearsal here. The basic elements are:

- biases in the calculation of dumping margins, so that "dumping" can be found in a broad range of cases, regardless of whether products are in objective terms dumped (Hindley 1988)
- the creation of a legal position in which refunds of antidumping duties are difficult or impossible to obtain, so that to be found to dump in the EC and subjected to antidumping duties is very expensive for exporters—and they will pay a considerable amount to avoid that situation (Hindley 1989)

These combined elements provide the commission with a threat that is credible in a wide variety of circumstances. Action built upon them can potentially spread the effects of EC antidumping activity over a very much broader range of products than those directly affected by official EC antidumping procedures. Confronted with a threat of EC antidumping action, a "disruptive" exporter to the EC is likely to be responsive to suggestions that he behave more "responsibly." The mere threat should be sufficient to restrict the flow of exports to the EC—without deployment of any obvious protective device.

Thus far, virtually all of the targets for this kind of treatment by the EC have been in the Far East. But the EC policy has a final twist that brings it into potential conflict with the United States (and actual conflict in one recent case). The so-called screwdriver-plant regulation—Article 13(10) of the EC dumping regulation (Regulation 2423/88)—permits the commission to extend an antidumping duty imposed on a final product to components of the product shipped to the EC for assembly *without separate investigation of the conditions of sale of the components.*

The commission maintains that Article 13(10) is needed to prevent "circumvention" of antidumping duties imposed by the EC. If it did not have the powers conferred upon it by Article 13(10), it says, the imposition of antidumping duties could be avoided merely by exporting the components of the affected product from, say, Japan, and assembling them in the EC in plants requiring no higher level of technical sophistication than a screwdriver. Article 13(10) is, nevertheless, the subject of a complaint by Japan in the GATT.[9]

The EC also provides an escape route, however. Article 13(10) duties on components can be avoided if at least 40 percent of the parts of the product assembled in the EC come from countries other than the home country of the putative dumper.

Moreover, Article 13(10) applies only if "the assembly or production operation was started or substantially increased *after the opening of the antidumping investigation*" [emphasis added].

In effect, these provisions promise that sufficient *current* EC investment will be rewarded by exemption from most of the unpleasant effects of EC antidumping action. An exporter who thinks that he might *in the future* be hit by EC antidumping action has a substantial incentive to invest in the EC *now*—an incentive that is greater the more aggressive is EC antidumping action.

Hence, in particular cases, Article 13(10) changes the nature of the threat posed by EC antidumping action. The rule of origin contained in Article 13(10) gives an exporter threatened by antidumping action the option of shifting the manufacturing point for his EC sales. The words of Article 13(10) do not require this shift to be to the EC (and could not do so without breaching the GATT). In practice, though, exporters to the EC will often contemplate a shift of manufacturing to the EC.

Article 13(10), therefore, creates an incentive for investment in the EC. Many current concerns about rules of origin, especially in the United States, derive from the impact of the rules on the location of foreign investment.[10]

Antidumping policy as developed by the EC, however, has a wider significance than its direct impact on Japan and the United States. In particular, EC antidumping policy poses a fundamental threat to the GATT. The importance to the GATT of the rules that define dumping and that control antidumping procedure is difficult to overestimate. Were GATT members allowed unrestricted access to antidumping action under definitions and procedures decided by themselves, much or all of the rest of the agreement would be deprived of effect.

In a world in which each GATT member could devise its own definition of dumping, and take whatever action it deemed appropriate against "dumpers," a government could always discriminate between similar imports from different sources, merely by claiming that imports from one source were dumped. Without the controls incorporated in Article VI and the code, the GATT would be an effective multilateral agreement in form only—any contracting party could take bilateral action whenever it deemed such action to be in its interests.

Moreover, GATT bargaining would be fatally undermined. To negotiate reciprocal reductions in levels of protection with a government that can reimpose protective barriers at a whim, in the form of antidumping duties, cannot be a very useful activity—even for another government in the same position.

GATT authorization of antidumping action poses a threat to world trade and the world trading system. Article VI of the GATT is intended to *control* that threat by controlling antidumping action. But the EC has emasculated those controls, threatening the integrity of the GATT quite fundamentally.

The new European Commission, which took office in January 1989, may be taking a more liberal approach to many matters of trade policy than its predecessor. The antidumping policy of the European Community may have left its former aggressive course. Even if that is so, however, the regulations that enabled it to move along that route are still in place.

Whatever the current stance of the EC, its use of antidumping action in the recent past has shown that reform of Article VI and the Antidumping Code are urgently needed. What will be the EC's response to attempted reform in the Uruguay Round? That the EC has "solved" a number of its trade "problems" through the use of antidumping action provides it with interesting possible negotiating positions.

First, the EC appears to be maintaining the position on selectivity that it took in the Tokyo Round. It no longer needs that revision, however. The problem that the amendment was intended to meet has been solved by the manipulation of antidumping action. The EC can, therefore, give up its position on selectivity. And, though the withdrawal would in fact be costless, the EC might be able to represent it as a concession—and to demand reciprocal concessions from others.

Second, the EC has created through antidumping action threats that have the potential to create the same behavior on the part of exporters as voluntary export restraints (VERs), *but without the need for formal negotiation or agreement.* Hence, the EC is in a position to support, and possibly to suggest, a ban in the GATT on such formal VERs. Such a course has another virtue from the standpoint of the commission—a GATT ban on VERs would limit the ability of the member states to compete with the commission as suppliers of protection against competition from imports.

For these two moves to be viable, however, the EC must defend its "right" to take antidumping action in its current form. If it follows this route, therefore, it must reject any movement toward reform of the Antidumping Code.

Other negotiating strategies are possible, however. The EC could permit reform of the Antidumping Code. It could give up its ability to manipulate antidumping action in exchange for authorization to use selectivity in the application of Article XIX. The way in which the EC juggles these balls in the Uruguay Round has much to say about its underlying stance in trade policy matters.

EC Experiments with Reciprocity. The reciprocity condition that has alarmed bankers (both inside and outside the EC) appears as Article 7 of the Second Banking Directive. In a speech delivered in July 1988, Willy de Clercq, then commissioner for external relations, offered an interpretation of the reciprocity demanded by the EC in banking. According to de Clercq:

- subsidiaries of non-EC banks already licensed in a Community country might be prevented from obtaining the full benefits of the single market; that
- reciprocity ". . . meant equal access," defined by ". . . whether similar institutions from all member states are given the same treatment in the non-Community country concerned"; and that

- in many cases, the EC would ". . . pursue a symmetry not so much in the legal conditions of access to markets, but rather an equivalence in their economic effects."

That de Clercq would have made such a statement without discussion and support for his position in the commission seems very unlikely. Nevertheless, the outcry that followed his speech caused the commission to draw back from his more adventurous notions.

In its major statement so far on the external implications of 1992 (issued after de Clercq's speech) the commission stated that:

> Non-Community countries will benefit [from the 1992 proposals] to the extent that a mutual balance of advantages in the spirit of GATT can be secured. The Community may thus have to negotiate bilaterally with its partners in order to obtain satisfactory access to their markets. In other words, the Commission reserves the right to make access to the benefits of 1992 for non-Member countries' firms, conditional upon a guarantee of similar opportunities—or at least non-discriminatory opportunities—in those firms' own countries (European Commission 1988, p. 2).[11]

"A guarantee of similar opportunities," of course, differs greatly from "at least non-discriminatory opportunities," and much depends upon what the EC finally decides that it is seeking. The statement is amplified in the following terms:

> The Community will offer free access to 1992 benefits for firms from countries whose market is already open or which are prepared to open up their markets on their own volition or through bilateral or multilateral agreements.
>
> It [reciprocity] does not mean that all partners must make the same concessions nor even that the Community will insist upon concessions from all its partners. For example, it will not ask the developing countries to make concessions that are beyond their means. Nor does it mean that the Community will ask its partners to adopt legislation that is identical to its own. Nor does it mean that the Community is seeking sectoral reciprocity based on comparative trade levels, this being a concept whose introduction into United States legislation has been fought by the Community (European Commission 1988, p. 2).

These statements clearly represent a withdrawal from the position taken by de Clercq in his speech, but they do not represent a total withdrawal.

A central question concerns the definition of "a service provider from a non-Member country." The substance of the issue is whether the commission will attempt to apply reciprocity retroactively. If already established subsidiaries of non-EC companies (for example, American Express or Citibank) are EC residents, reciprocity cannot apply to them. Reciprocity would affect only new entrants to the EC market.

The European Economic Community Treaty contains what appears to be a substantial legal barrier to any attempt by the commission to subject already established subsidiaries of non-EC enterprises to a reciprocity test. It lies in Article 58, which (in its entirety) says that:

> Companies or firms formed in accordance with the law of a Member State and having their registered office, central administration or principal place of business within the Community shall, for the purposes of this Chapter [that is, chapter 2: *Rights of Establishment*], be treated in the same way as natural persons who are nationals of Member States.
>
> "Companies or firms" means companies or firms constituted under civil or commercial law, including cooperative societies, and other legal persons governed by public or private law, save for those which are non-profit-making.

That seems clear enough. But what legal advice did de Clercq receive before he made a speech that implied that the commission could surmount the legal barrier of Article 58 in dealing with already established subsidiaries of non-EC firms?

In any event, the commission appears to disavow the possibility of dealing with the EC subsidiaries of non-EC firms differently from EC-owned firms:

> The second banking Directive [relating to financial services] being discussed by the Council provides for the possibility of reciprocity for newcomers.
>
> However, there can be no question of depriving subsidiaries of foreign firms already established in the Community of the rights they have acquired. [European Commission 1988, p. 4].

The next issue concerns national treatment as a benchmark for reciprocity. The head of the commission's banking division is reported to have told a financial conference that the commission would seek varying forms of national treatment for EC banks. A *Financial Times* report (November 8, 1988) reads in part as follows:

> Thus, in Switzerland, EC banks should be able to compete with local banks in practising "near universal" banking, while in the US, EC banks would have to respect local rules fragmenting the geographical scope and nature of banking.

"In Japan, a market particularly hard to penetrate, *a better deal might be sought than that available to Japanese banks*," Mr. Clarotti said [emphasis added].

This claim for better-than-national treatment from Japan comes to the real heart of the issue. Some of those on the protectionist side of the reciprocity debate might have wanted to use the reciprocity provisions against the United States, but it is difficult to build in the EC a coalition for aggressive action against the United States. That is not so for aggressive action against Japan. The problem for the commission, confronted with a major outcry about its reciprocity proposals from the United States (and from within the EC itself) was how to propitiate the United States while retaining the power of hostile action against Japan.

Under revised reciprocity proposals released in March 1989, the commission will make a determination of the treatment of EC banks by third countries. Only if a third country does not provide EC banks with "national treatment and the same competitive opportunities as domestic credit institutions . . . and . . . the condition of effective market access has not been secured" will the commission be able to block or delay banks from that third country in establishing subsidiaries in the community.

It is the phrase "the condition of effective market access has not been secured" that raises problems in interpreting this statement. Going back to the reported comments of Clarotti, quoted above, how in particular will that condition affect Japan?

Article 7(4) provides that if a third country does not give EC banks "effective market access and competitive opportunities comparable to those accorded by the Community," the commission may submit proposals to the council to enter into negotiations with the third country for the object of achieving such access and opportunities.

The reciprocity provisions in the Second Banking Directive as they now stand are weaker than the original ones (and very much weaker than de Clercq's interpretation of what might be done under the original ones). The idea of applying reciprocity retroactively has been firmly dismissed. The scope for the commission to act on its own initiative has been severely curtailed. The form of words moves towards a national treatment standard, but it does not go all the way, and it is in the gap that a future EC protectionism may thrive.

The EC as a Trading Bloc. Earlier, three arguments were noted, each of which suggested that the formation of a trading bloc would increase pressure for protection within the bloc. The three were:

- The larger a bloc, the higher will be its optimal tariff.
- The larger a bloc, the closer it will feel to self-sufficiency and thus to a sense that foreign trade is a dispensable luxury.
- The creation of a bloc identity requires the reinforcement of divisions between insiders and outsiders—protection against imports being a clear example of such a division.

The first of these is not important for the EC. Governments eager to "solve trade problems" by obtaining the effects of export restraints cannot plausibly be said to have favorable manipulation of the terms of trade at the center of their attention. The second and third are potentially more important, and current developments could release that potential. European commissioners and EC heads of government have offered a flood of assurances that the 1992 project does not imply any increase in protection against external suppliers. The rest of the world remains skeptical, and the rest of the world is correct.

For one thing, a political structure that, until very recently, counted the Common Agricultural Policy (CAP) as its major achievement has major protectionist inclinations. And in recent years, when high unemployment (and the need to defend "the European model of social organisation") has intensified the pressures for protection, the commission has responded with an unseemly eagerness.

That the commission and the council contain protectionist factions, however, is not in itself a good ground for a belief that Fortress Europe will appear in 1992. Those factions have always existed and probably always will exist—with or without a 1992 project. The problem is the alliances and coalitions that the 1992 project may enable the protectionists to form.

The commission and the council also contain a large party that does not care very much one way or the other about "managed" trade—or about protection that can be defended as a response to "unfair" trade. Members of that party would prefer to pursue liberal trade policies (to do so avoids tiresome arguments with other countries)—if they could achieve their other goals in conjunction with such policies.

For most of them, however, completion of the 1992 project is an overwhelming priority. And to cement the deals that are necessary to win the consent of the member states to the details of the 1992 program, they may be willing to move in a protectionist direction. The 1992 program may provide the basis for a coalition between protectionists and the very much larger number of officials and politicians who are not, in any sensible use of the word, protectionists, but who place a higher priority on completing the 1992 program than on maintaining liberal policies toward the rest of the world.

There are, however, two limits on that willingness. The first is that while the GATT exists, protective actions that run afoul of the GATT rules in a new or major way are unlikely to win approval. That is not because of any respect for, or interest in, the GATT rules or their function; it is due to a simple desire to avoid the debating disadvantage of having broken the rules. Unfortunately, the GATT rules leave a great deal of latitude for policies that are de facto protectionist.

The second limit is on actions that are overtly hostile to the interests of the United States. That is not to say that the EC will not act in ways that the United States regards as hostile. The CAP is one instance, hormones in beef another, Airbus another, and local content rules for TV broadcasting yet another.

These policies, however, have primarily domestic purposes, in areas in which the EC believes it has a legal right to act, and where harm to the United States is, seen from an EC perspective, an incidental byproduct. It remains true that building a consensus in the EC favoring protection against the United States is far more difficult than building a consensus for protection against Japan and the Far East.

The conclusion of the debate about protectionism in the commission and the council has momentous consequences, for the world as well as for the EC. During the past year, however, it has seemed more and more apparent that the liberals are winning. They have not won all of the tricks, and in matters regarding Japan and the Far East, they may have lost more than they have won. But the broad tendency of EC policy toward the rest of the world now appears to be very much less illiberal than might have been feared even a year ago.

So what will Fortress Europe look like? Clearly, it will have some kind of protective structure facing eastward. But, as matters stand at the moment, it will have only a ditch facing the United States—minimal defenses to avoid being too easily overrun. Is such a structure properly called a fortress? A more important question is, How stable will that structure be in the new international climate?

The International Trading System in the Year 2000

It is time to return to a question posed earlier. If these are the primary actors in the cast that will determine the future of the GATT, does the GATT have a future?

No doubt there will in the year 2000 be a GATT (or perhaps even a grander institution, such as an International Trade Organization, ITO). There may be more contracting parties and more frequent meetings of trade ministers than now. It is the state of trade relations in the world beyond that facade, however, that is relevant to the question posed here. There is a clear risk that trade relations will be increasingly discriminatory and chaotic—and that, however splendid the GATT or the ITO as the venue for trade ministers or bureaucrats, it will have no impact on those trade relations.

For the GATT to come to an end would not in itself be a bad thing. The GATT, as it stands, has many defects. It is easily possible to think of very much better constitutions for international trade. The forces that threaten to cripple the GATT, however, are also incompatible with a better constitution, or, indeed, with any nondictatorial constitution. Before a new constitution can appear—never mind a better constitution—those forces may have to work themselves out in trade war, or trade chaos. The realization that everyone could be better off with an effective GATT-like institution might take a very long time to strike.

No country is likely to gain from the end of the GATT as an effective institution. The last major U.S. defection from the GATT was the 1955 agricultural waiver (Dam 1970, pp. 260–73), which essentially removed agricultural trade from the GATT. That was accomplished because Section 22 of the U.S. Agricultural Adjustment Act came into conflict with the GATT rules as they originally existed.[12] At the time, Section 22 must have seemed to promise U.S. farmers much more than adherence to the GATT. In 1955 that judgment seemed sound—not even worth much thought. In retrospect, however, the current state of world agricultural trade suggests that the GATT might have been the better bet—even from the standpoint of U.S. farmers.

A broader U.S. defection from the GATT than that of 1955 is likely to have the same effects, though on an appropriately broader scale. If the United States "waives" its GATT, so will others. That is the central problem for the United States—a giant bound by cotton threads. Giants cannot actually be bound by cotton, however. It is a charade—a charade whose playing is likely at times to create great irritation. Yet, if the United States breaks the threads that bind it, it will break those of everyone else, as well. The only condition in which the United States can make full use of its economic muscle is one in which everyone else is equally free—and in that circumstance, there is no presumption that either the United States or anyone else can "win"—the best bet is that there will not be any winners.

The EC will not break its GATT bonds without a U.S. example. It will wriggle and squirm to give itself *almost* as much freedom as though there were no bonds, but it will not finally break them.

If the United States sets an example, however, the EC will follow. And how would the EC then behave? In all foreseeable circumstances, it would increase its protection against Japan and East Asia.

But there is a broader question, and it is in answering that broader question that the Eastern European unknowns enter the picture. The answer to the broader question depends not only upon the presence or absence of GATT constraints but also on the military situation on the eastern flank of the EC. Suppose that the EC were relieved of the need for U.S. military support at the same time that it was relieved of GATT constraints on its actions.

In that event, a Fortress Europe truly worthy of the name might appear. Eurozealots do exist. And there are many more Europeans, whom it would be quite inappropriate to describe as Eurozealots, who vaguely suppose that it would be a good thing to have a European superpower that could "deal on equal terms" with the United States and Japan. Confronted with a protectionist United States, the idea of a European Community stretching from the Atlantic to—where?—could become politically feasible.

Of course, all of this may be incorrect. The GATT might survive. The U.S. negotiators in the Uruguay Round might come back from Geneva with a package that disarms even the most hostile congressman.[13]

But then, again, they might not.

References

Bhagwati, Jagdish N., and Douglas A. Irwin. 1987. "Return of the Reciprocitarians—US Trade Policy Today." *World Economy* (June).

Coase, Ronald. 1961. "The Problem of Social Cost." *Journal of Law and Economics*, vol. 3.

Dam, Kenneth W. 1970. *The GATT: Law and International Organization*. Chicago: University of Chicago Press.

Dornbusch, Rudiger, Paul Krugman, and Yung Chul Park. 1989. *Meeting World Challenges: U.S. Manufacturing in the 1990s*. Rochester, N.Y.: Eastman Kodak.

European Commission. 1988. *Europe 1992: Europe World Partner*. Brussels, October 19.

Finger, J. M., and Tracy Murray. 1989. *Policing Unfair Imports: the United States Example*. Mimeo. Washington, D.C.: The World Bank.

Finger, J. M., and Andrej Olechowski. 1987. *The Uruguay Round: A Handbook of the Multilateral Trade Negotiations*. Washington, D.C.: The World Bank.

Hindley, Brian. 1988. "Dumping and the Far East Trade of the European Community." *World Economy* (December).

———. 1989. *The European Community: Drifting (or Steering) to Bilateralism*. Mimeo.

Hudec, Robert E. 1990. *Thinking about the New Section 301: Beyond Good and Evil.* Mimeo.

Irwin, Douglas A. 1988. "Welfare Effects of British Free Trade." *Journal of Political Economy* (December).

Kemp, M. C., and H. Wan. 1976. "An Elementary Proposition about Customs Unions." *Journal of International Economics* (vol. 6), pp. 95–97.

Palmeter, N. D. 1989. "The Capture of the Anti-dumping Law." *Yale Journal of International Law* (vol. 14: no. 1), pp. 182–98.

Wolf, Martin. 1989. *Liberalism, Nationalism and Mercantilism: Global Implications of the European Community's Programme for Completing the Internal Market.* New York: Manhattan Institute. Mimeo.

———. 1990. *What We Need from the Uruguay Round.* London: Chatham House.

2
Commentaries on Part One

A Commentary by Herbert Giersch

The case for the survival of GATT can be summarized briefly. First, international organizations hardly ever die, even if they have become useless. They are kept alive as a focal point for meetings and discussions. Nobody would seriously contend that GATT has become useless. New members are waiting for admission into GATT, in the hope that they will gain by becoming part of the multilateral trading system.

Second, granting and ensuring most-favored entry will therefore remain an important activity that GATT can perform. The United States will not leave GATT at a time when GATT is expanding. Moreover, the main industrial countries will continue to support GATT to avoid disappointing new members and to benefit from the extension of the multilateral trading system.

Third, world trade will grow fast in the 1990s, faster than in the 1980s. This growth will keep the spirit of GATT alive, whatever happens to the administrative aspects and the legal framework.

Let me explain my reasons for predicting fast growth in the 1990s. With high output growth and a strong propensity to invest, the world should experience vigorous economic activity. Twenty or thirty years from now, historians may speak about a new upswing, the fifth since the Industrial Revolution and the second after the Great Depression of the 1930s.

Long upswings develop when markets move faster than governments and labor organizations in major areas or regions of the world. And this can happen for two reasons.

First, progress in science and technology becomes faster. Second, bureaucratic impediments to economic development diminish as countries move ahead toward internationalization and deregulation, as they are likely to do now, in Eastern Europe as they did in Western Europe, and as they are likely to continue in the whole Organization for Economic Cooperation and Development (OECD) area.

To explain my first reason for a long upswing, progress in science and technology, I shall state a fundamental proposition. Knowledge and technical skill increase with the absolute number of capable persons participating in the creation of knowledge, a process characteristic of Western civilization.

In addition to the division of labor among hands, we recognize the division of labor among minds. The larger the number of creative minds, the more knowledge will be created. While worldwide population growth is a source of concern, it also enhances the creativity of mankind and civilization's capacity to produce new knowledge. The population explosion is leading to a knowledge explosion—and the size of Western civilization grows more than world population, as more and more people are attracted by it.

To be sure, we cannot measure this speed of knowledge creation precisely. I believe, though, that it has accelerated during my lifetime, notably in recent years.

The second reason for my belief that markets will develop faster than governments is the decline of communication costs. The world, so to speak, is shrinking. Eastern Europe has followed earlier developments in the West, as the world moves toward greater openness, in economic affairs as in politics.

And this trend toward openness has an engine behind it: as we have competition among governments, institutions, and economic orders, we now have competition among locations. Locations compete for internationally mobile resources, such as investment capital, human capital, and applicable knowledge. These mobile resources vote with their feet, in search of higher earnings—that is, in search of less regulation, lower taxes, and a more forward-looking social atmosphere.

Capital movement across frontiers and the migration of skilled labor can force a more liberal policy stance (liberal in the European sense). Movement of capital and labor enforces such liberalization on governments and on immobile local factors of production. In a dynamic environment, growth in capitalist economy arrives in three steps: (1) more factor mobility forces on government more deregulation and privatization; (2) deregulation and privatization create more opportunities for growth and employment; and (3) greater growth and high employment make it easier to call for trade liberalization, since freer imports have beneficial effects. They ease the inflation caused by excess demand, and they bring more pressure of competition to bear on domestic sellers who can stand this competition.

This is the story of a "virtuous" circle, the opposite of the vicious circle that we experienced in the 1930s and again after the 1973 oil shortage. It is this vicious circle, after 1973, that we can now reverse in the same way as postwar liberalization and growth reversed the vicious circle of the 1930s.

Let us consider induced protection and induced liberalization. In stagnation or depression, when people feel insecure, comparative advantage lies in a hazy future; what counts is survival in the short term. Instead of moving toward risky specialization, firms broaden their range of products. Instead of product innovations, they concentrate on process innovations for short-term cost cutting. Instead of looking forward, firms look inward.

The same holds for regions and countries. With profits low and unemployment high, competition is most unwelcome. The idea that imports save resources, which can be used to increase the export potential, becomes unconvincing. When resources are underemployed, both industries and regions suffer from excess capacities.

Cartels are children of need, the saying goes, and international cartels, like voluntary export restraint agreements, increase in numbers, as do acts of collusion and merger in the domestic economy—no wonder that dumping complaints become more frequent.

The induced protectionism after 1973 was certainly much less severe than the protectionism after 1929. The mistake of Smoot-Hawley was not repeated, and the tendency toward bilateralism was weaker. GATT certainly helped in avoiding previous mistakes, as did the monetary policy designed to prevent another great contraction.

Although the GATT system had a stormy period after 1973, we should not make the mistake of extrapolating the past into the future, as the stagnationists of the 1930s did. Postwar history made the stagnationists look silly in retrospect. The shift toward faster growth in the 1990s will probably make the prophets of gloom for GATT and the international trading system look ridiculous, too.

In looking at the future of world trade, we should not focus too exclusively on the United States. While North America was the engine of growth in the early 1980s, the 1990s may well become the decade of Europe. This will sound strange to those who know why I coined the term *Euro-sclerosis* in the early 1980s. Half this sclerosis was the inward-looking tendency I just described; I call it *induced protectionist*. Perhaps it was a temporary phenomenon, since over the past several years the restructuring in Europe has taken place. The prosperity after the 1987 stock exchange crash has markedly improved business conditions and the economic outlook on both sides of the River Rhine.

Surely, this prosperity also affects the East and contributed to the east-west migration of people that brought down the Berlin Wall and the frontier between the two Germanys.

Once East Germany has become a success story and once Czechoslovakia, Poland, Hungary, and Yugoslavia have started to enjoy capitalism, Europe will become a magnet for international capital investment opportunities are likely to emerge. We now look forward to a European spring as business prepares for Project 1992.

As capital flows to Europe, Europe's and even Germany's current-account-balance will deteriorate, or improve, as I would prefer to say. Exporters and mercantilists in the rest of the world will enjoy this change.

In a period of fast history, with capitalism spreading to new lands, the real rate of interest will be as high as the growth opportunities. A higher real rate of interest tells us that the time is short—and that the resources for the future are scarce. Technical progress is one means of augmenting resources, while the other possibility is more efficient use of existing resources like a better exploitation of productivity through the international division of labor.

The high interest rate, driven up by investment opportunities, forces us to make the best use of the existing capital stock, in addition to giving more weight to capital savings innovations.

The spirit of trade liberalization will therefore be strong, by necessity, at least in capital-absorbing Europe.

A Commentary by Jules L. Katz

I think the pessimism of Brian Hindley and Martin Wolf is very much overstated; there is evidence that the multilateral system is moving in ways opposite to what they have suggested. Professor Hindley said that he wanted to narrow his focus, and I will narrow it even more to address the concerns that he raised. He based his threat of the future on a somewhat curious premise, that the future of the multilateral system depends on U.S. moral and intellectual leadership and that somehow he finds that wanting at present.

His concern is largely based on the threat represented by section 301 in the dispute with Japan. He also referred to developing countries, but he did not elaborate on that. Let me first say a word about 301. Section 301 in its various forms—regular, super, and special—clearly contains controversial provisions of U.S. law, controversial not only internationally but in the United States. But one should look at the reality of section 301 or at least its application during the current administration. I would argue that there have been no violations of anything in the General Agreement on Tariffs and Trade by section 301. I distinguish between the current administration and the past administration, because I will concede there is a question about one particular case involving 301.

What we have done under 301 is literally what the law requires, particularly in super 301, which has received the greatest attention, and that is to identify trade negotiating priorities. Those priorities have subsequently been the subject of consultation and, in some cases, negotiation. We have not come to any conclusion yet about the first year under super 301. There is a deadline that will require a decision about whether and how we proceed with those cases. But Ambassador Hills has said that we intend to proceed in accordance with the multilateral system, and the assumption that we will not do so is unwarranted.

A word about Japan. It is interesting, given the main focus of this paper on the United States, and to some extent the European Community, that there was no mention made of Japan as a threat to the system. Japan is a threat to the multilateral system at this point. That is not so much because of the U.S. trade deficit. Most people in the United States in a position of responsibility, including those in Congress who have been loudest in their complaints about Japan, have conceded that the source of the deficit is not trade policy. I do not think that anybody with any understanding of the problem would argue that the problem with Japan over the deficit is one of Japanese trade policy.

Given the magnitude of that deficit for the United States or surplus for Japan, however, Japan has obligations to carry out its responsibilities, not just with respect to the trade policy, which it has largely conformed to requirements of the GATT—Japan's tariffs are low; its quotas are few. Significant barriers to penetration of the Japanese market remain, however, and those are the subject of negotiations with the United States. But Japan has a major responsibility not only toward the United States but toward the multilateral system to accept its obligations.

Not only is pessimism about the future of the multilateral system and the GATT unwarranted, but the paper's focus on the threats is exaggerated. One must understand why people focus on threats. Indeed, it is a technique of trade policy to point out the challenges and the opportunities on the one hand and the threats on the other. It is something like calling attention to the wolf.

There are bright spots ahead, however. The Uruguay Round is the major and primary focus of U.S. policy and that of many other countries in the world. Its success is not assured, but we have never had the kinds of opportunities that we have in the Uruguay Round, not only for dealing with the problems but for strengthening the multilateral system, going beyond the rules structure to improve the institutional structure of the GATT and to make it more effective.

Many countries have, in the past five years, decided that the GATT is the wave of the future and have wanted to come in. Countries are waiting to get in that we cannot handle at the moment, because of preoccupation with the Uruguay Round.

A number of important countries, particularly in the developing world, have substantially, almost in a revolutionary way, changed their trade policies. The case of Mexico is well known. Venezuela, using Mexico as a model, has sought and is about to accede to the GATT. In Brazil the candidate who argued for participation in the multilateral system and for pursuing market mechanisms is the candidate who won the election.

The trends in Eastern Europe support the strength of the GATT; it remains to be seen what the implications of the revolutionary changes in Eastern Europe will have on Europe and on European attitudes. But it is unwarranted to assume the worst-case scenarios in every instance, as the Hindley-Wolf paper does. I will stop at this point and stand as an optimist and not a pessimist.

A Commentary by Norbert Walter

There must be some understanding by the American audience that we, the Europeans, are optimistic about economic growth in Europe, given the Europe 1992 program, the recently accelerated process of monetary integration within the European Community, the imminent unification of West and East Germany, and the liberalization in Eastern Europe. Therefore, our perspective on the trade environment is optimistic as well.

Being optimistic for Europe for the next years does not mean more prosperity for Europe forever. It is obvious that, by the end of the 1990s, the United States will have the youngest population among the industrial countries because of a somewhat higher fertility and a more experienced and liberal migration policy. The Japanese are aging very quickly now, and to a large extent Europe too will have aging populations in the future, even if we allow the Poles and the Irish to move toward the center of the continent. There is a potential escape: Europe's neighboring regions, countries like Turkey and North Africa, are facing strong population growth. These regions with their growing number of young people could become a source for the rejuvenation of Europe's labor force. To be able to benefit from this source, however, Europe would have to provide free access to its labor markets. But I believe there will be hesitation to do so. Therefore, Europe will be a positive surprise for the world only for the first half of the 1990s.

Many people in Europe have not yet recognized that they are rowing the same boat. If we really want to overcome the old structures and create a new Europe from the Atlantic to the Urals, we need a vision for this continent. Some people in Europe believe that Thatcherism hampers that vision, because of its hostility to political unity, that is, giving up sovereignty to European institutions. But Thatcherism is very constructive in a sense. If we are to create a Europe with free and open markets, we need leaders to construct the architecture of Europe from the inside. Particularly, we have to have a countervailing power for some of the forces aiming at industrial policy and protectionism that are obvious in some southern European countries.

Thus the Germans especially should be careful in criticizing the views attributed to Mrs. Thatcher, because she is a natural ally for an open-minded Europe, a concept that is even more important these days given the developments in the East. The people in Eastern Europe are looking toward the West. In their opinion the EC is an attractive model for the whole continent. When they talk about Europe, they are talking about joining Western Europe, about joining the institutional center of the EC.

Therefore, it is important to give momentum to the initiative for an economic and monetary union started by Helmut Schmidt and Valéry Giscard d'Estaing and reinvigorated by the Delors report. If the Europeans are able to ensure a new momentum in this process, this would help them to remain on schedule for Europe 1992, and it would add to the attractiveness for Eastern Europe of seeking association with the EC.

Support or attention for an idea often does not develop by describing its virtues or by straightforward arguments. Sometimes, and for some concerned with their own issues, one must label a coin to gain support and to wake people up. Surely Americans did not believe us when we told them the single market in Europe holds a great fortune for everybody. Only after the Americans feared that they would not have a chance to participate in that market did they pay attention.

It was wise to develop the label "Fortress Europe," since it was activated five years before the fortress could be built. There never was a chance that it would become effective, considering the open and liberal policies of some European nations. Thus the invention of the label Fortress Europe was an excellent device for an open-market solution for Europe. Everybody considering this market an attractive one has a reason to go there, not just an economic reason but an animal-spirit incentive. If investors around the globe believe the label will become true, they will react in much the same way—they will try to invest in Europe. Thus by 1992 a protectionist policy of the EC would fail to be meaningful.

When the Cecchini report was published in 1988, it was sharply criticized in academia as being over optimistic. Now, after just the first two and one-half years of the planning process for Europe 1992, two-thirds of the growth effects that had not been expected until five years after the completion of the single market have already been realized. The critics are obviously technocrats, national accountants rather than experts understanding growth processes. If one relies too strongly on demand-driven econometric models, one never has a chance to seize the impact of a deregulation program or of a scheme of better division of labor due to more open markets.

The revitalization of the European economies is not least a consequence of the fact that in the 1980s a very high number of young people—the generation of the postwar baby boomers—entered the labor market, especially in the United Kingdom and West Germany. Young people are usually more mobile in location and profession, they are familiar with modern technology, and they speak foreign languages, thus forming the preconditions for improving the competitiveness of Europe.

To recognize how matters are running in Europe, we should concentrate our analysis on what the EC Commission does and what the European Court of Justice decides. What has happened there is certainly proof that Europe has moved away from a position of overbureaucratization and overregulation. On the contrary, Europe 1992 is a deregulation program par excellence.

I want to add another argument for European prosperity. Established nation-states have difficulties in keeping lobbies at the national level on a low key. It is practically impossible, for example, for the German government to dismantle coal subsidization through German policies. It is obviously possible, however, to get support for undoing German coal subsidies at the European level. Thus a meaningful energy policy at the European level is possible because there are strong competing forces. The nuclear power plant lobby of France, for example, is interested in selling excess electricity to the German market. If these countervailing forces are brought to one bargaining table, they can be neutralized, the result being freer markets. The EC Commission has a leading role in organizing those forces to provide Europe with an important public good, that is, with intensified competition.

Therefore, I advise business people these days, if they want to lobby successfully, to refrain from doing so in the national capitals but rather to do so in Brussels. Whereas the Japanese still have some difficulties, it is obvious that the Americans have already begun successfully to follow such a strategy. The Second Banking Directive was a marvelous example of how Americans understood how to deal with Europe and to help to keep it an open place.

After the reforms in Eastern Europe, there is even more reason to believe that heading in a generally liberal direction is a meaningful concept for Europe at large. It is obvious that the request of Eastern Europeans to become members of the EC, that is, the society of Western values and of an open trading system, will become even stronger. The EC should be open-minded and should allow for an association, a special relationship, with countries like Hungary, Czechoslovakia, and Poland, which are very determined in their economic reforms. In fact, talks on special association agreements with these Eastern European countries will start soon.

Of course, all parties involved still have a lot of work to do. The necessary reform of the EC agricultural policy seems to be especially difficult and tricky. Western Europe pursues a protectionist Common Agricultural Policy (CAP) at the expense of those countries that have comparative advantages in the agricultural sector. Nowadays third world countries especially suffer from this policy. But the CAP will also become a handicap for the more agricultural countries in east and southeast Europe. These countries cannot successfully restructure their economies unless they are given a fair chance in EC markets.

To sum up, in Europe the 1990s will be a decade of more investment and accelerated spending on consumer durables, which is an important message to bring to the United States. For a decade the U.S. administration unsuccessfully asked us to end oversavings and to be prepared for some additional spending. Europe is now prepared to do these things as a consequence of two major programs, Europe 1992 and the reforms in Eastern Europe. Now many Americans have uneasy feelings about these developments. They are afraid of losing influence, as Europe gains more strength and self-reliance, and they do not want to become isolated. Of course, the United States must define its new position in the global network of economic, military, and political relations. Yet it should recognize that it is to its benefit if Europe becomes a mature partner on the international stage. The United States will then be able to concentrate more on its own hemisphere, that is, to pay more attention to the Latin American countries and push economic development there.

Obviously, there is concern in the United States that the reforms in Europe cannot be financed without accelerating inflation and higher interest rates. But I am sure that in countries like Czechoslovakia, Hungary, and Poland released market forces will very soon initiate a dynamic growth process, which will markedly mitigate these problems, mainly through a strong capability of self-financing the reforms, a factor typically underestimated in periods of market-oriented reforms. Furthermore, the Americans and the Europeans are now able to cut defense expenditures and thus save resources for civilian use. The current period of rapidly easing political tensions should be almost the ideal time for the world economy to allow central Europe to catch up economically.

All these will be only minor issues, however, in comparison with the problems that may arise when, at the end of the 1990s, labor will become scarce for all of us. Therefore, the north, the economic north of the globe, has every reason to be very open-minded, open for trade and open to allow for considerable migration on a global scale. If we do so, there is a good chance that economic growth in the industrialized countries will continue in the decades after the turn of the millennium. This would also be to the benefit of the developing countries because it would relieve the population pressure there and intensify the relations between the north and the south.

PART TWO

Implications for Japan and the NICs

3
External Trade Implications of Europe 1992 for Japan

Masaru Yoshitomi

From the viewpoint of Japan, Europe has already been a fortress in the sense that discriminatory trade measures exclusively against Japan (and other Far Eastern countries) have mounted during the 1980s. In European eyes, however, the new effort of 1992 is aimed "at resisting the challenge from Japan, whose aggressive external economic expansion and fierce protection of its own market the Europeans resent" (Hoffmann 1989). This presumption of Japan's aggressive external expansion, sometimes called its predatory exports, coupled with its closed domestic market has been at least implicitly used as a justification for establishing a Fortress Europe against Japan.

Defining the Issue

The key issue is, therefore, What are the external implications of Europe 1992 for Japan, given such a presumption and the discriminatory actions of the past decade? In this context three specific questions should be addressed. First, what are the causal links, if any, between Europe 1992 and external barriers, in particular against Japan? The first section of this chapter discusses this issue by looking into antidumping measures, local contents requirements, rules of origin, and the recent proposal of the Commission of the European Community on motor vehicles in a single market. Second, why is Japan sometimes singled out in justifying a Fortress Europe in particular industries? What are the real issues behind Japan's "predatory" exports and its closed domestic market? The next section discusses this problem by looking into Japan's dynamic changes in comparative advantage and its industrial organization. Third, what is the heart of the trade and industrial policy debate in the context of 1992? What

---

The opinions expressed in this chapter are my own, not those of the Economic Planning Agency, to which I belong.

are the more global implications of Europe 1992? The last section briefly discusses this issue.

Are There Any Causal Links between 1992 and a Fortress Europe?

In sharp contrast to systematic plans to eliminate internal barriers in the EC as explained and effected by official documents, there has hardly been any comparably systematic description of the external trade policy of 1992. External trade policies of the EC operate at two levels: common policies at the EC level and individual policies at the national level, mostly in the form of import quotas. The EC Commission has been unable to keep various nontariff barriers out of the control of member national governments. Trade measures at the national level, however, should become ineffective in 1993 by the abolition of Article 115 of the Treaty of Rome, unless they are replaced by similar measures at the community level. Article 115 permits member governments to request the commission to suspend the free circulation of third-country goods within the community. Thereby trade deflection, that is, the entry of a product imported by one member country into other member countries, can be prevented to preserve the effects of national nontariff barriers. Will the national barriers be replaced by barriers at the community level in 1992 and later?

Because trade policy is the exclusive responsibility of the community, the commission's strategies are even more important determinants of the external policies of Europe 1992. The commission's efforts to reconcile international trade policies at the two levels will be critical in determining the external implications of Europe 1992.

After briefly looking at nontariff barriers at the national level, let us examine the commission's external trade policies—those that have been adopted and those under serious consideration.

Quantity Restrictions at the National Levels. There are two kinds of import quantity restrictions at the national level: those authorized under Article 115 and those not authorized, that is, unilateral actions and gentlemen's agreements among business associations.

Import quantity restrictions were in force on 131 Japanese products in 1988, as shown in table 3-1. (Such restrictions existed on approximately 700 items from all third countries.) Four member countries—Spain (41 items), Italy (36), Portugal (23), and France (17)—accounted for the bulk of the EC's discriminatory measures against Japan. Electrical appliances (such as radios and television sets), ceramics, vehicles (motorcycles and passenger cars), metal products, and general machinery were the main products under the

TABLE 3-1
DISCRIMINATORY QUANTITATIVE RESTRICTIONS ON JAPANESE
PRODUCTS BY EC MEMBER COUNTRIES, JUNE 1988

Country	Number of Items	Main Products
France	17	Ceramic tiles, knives, radios, television sets, electric measuring apparatus
Benelux	7	Footwear, tableware of pottery
West Germany	2	Tableware of pottery
Italy	36	Silk yarn, tableware of pottery, knives, radios, television sets, motor bicycles, automobiles
Denmark	2	Knives, spoons
Greece	2	Cells and batteries
Ireland	1	Bags and sacks for packing
Spain	41	Glasswares, iron and steel products, processing machinery, radios, television sets, motor bicycles
Portugal	23	Yarn of man-made fibers, tableware of pottery, metal products, processing machinery, automobiles, motor bicycles
Total	131	

SOURCE: Author.

quantitative restrictions. In March 1989 it was announced that restrictions on 68 of the 131 items would be abolished. Most of those 68 items, however, were those whose exports are virtually nil today or in which Japan lost its comparative advantage a long time ago. Examples are silk products, radios, knives, cells and batteries, and toys.

Since the elimination of frontier controls by abolishing Article 115 will make these national quotas totally ineffective, a critical issue is through what mechanisms, for what products, and at what protective levels the commission will meet the demand of member countries for community-wide quotas. This issue remains extremely uncertain.

Trade Policies at the Commission Level. Common measures of external trade policies at the commission level consist of (1) antidumping measures, (2) local contents requirements and rules of origin, (3) import monitoring and safeguards, and (4) common tariffs. Other common measures are to be determined for foreign automobiles in a single market.

It is reported that the commission proposed in November 1989 to do away with national quotas on automobiles by asking Japanese firms for voluntary restraint agreements (VRAs) on the total number of their car exports to Europe and their cars produced in Europe, perhaps until the late 1990s. An important difference from traditional VRAs found in the commission's proposal is that the newly proposed VRAs would include not only cars imported from Japan but also cars produced by Japanese transplant factories located in the EC. In exchange for such restraints on market share in the EC as a whole, Japan would be given access to markets in France, Italy, and Spain, where national quotas have been imposed to limit Japanese car imports to a 2 to 3 percent market share. In other words, the commission seeks to establish VRAs on all Japanese cars sold in Europe regardless of their production base either in Japan or in the EC. Such VRAs in the form of market share would only gradually be revised upward during the 1990s from the present level of about 11 percent, so that European cars would not be crowded out.

This market share restraint arrangement would be further complicated by the provision that any cars produced by Japanese transplant factories in third countries would not be included in the calculations. There could be a sudden surge of imports from such factories, which would have to be monitored by the commission to satisfy the objective of the market share VRA. According to the commission, Japan would no longer have to meet local content requirements and could decide for itself whether to fill its allotted market share with imports or locally manufactured motor vehicles.

This example of motor vehicles vividly indicates how complex causal links can be between 1992 and a Fortress Europe. It clearly demonstrates that causal links cannot be analyzed simply by looking into the possibility of replacing national quotas by community-level conventional restrictive measures. Such links must be analyzed in a broader context, particularly since trade policies of recent years are no longer aimed simply at import protection but involve the issue of local content and the country of origin. In other words, the latter issue involves "foreign firm harassment" as a new element.

Harassment of Foreign Firms. This new element has become increasingly vital to the commission's trade policy as high-technology products have occupied a rising share of imports, particularly from Japan and other Far Eastern countries (Davenport 1989). Antidumping proceedings have increasingly been targeted at high-technology products of these countries since the middle of the 1980s. Electronic typewriters (investigation started in 1984), their components (1987), photocopiers (1985), printers (1987), semiconductors (1987), electronic scales (1987), compact disc players (1987), and audiocassettes and tapes (1989) are subjects of the main antidumping actions against Japan.

Reacting to antidumping actions against an imported product, the firm in question may start to assemble that product in the community by importing components from the original dumping country. The antidumping duty would be extended, however, to the imported components without a new investigation into those components if more than 40 percent of the value of components still came from the country concerned. A reason why the antidumping policy has been amended in this way and extended so as to harass foreign firms that set up plants in the community is partly that the concept of a "screwdriver" plant is ill defined. The ill-defined concept of screwdriver assembling expresses ignorance of the following three factors: first, how high value added is gained from the final assembling of high-techology products; second, how important for assemblers are the quality of products, punctual delivery, and postsales technological information services with respect to components and specific capital goods; and, finally, what steady steps foreign direct investment will have to take to enhance local contents so as to meet the quality and delivery requirements for specific components and capital goods. The requirement of high local contents even at the initial stage of the operation of newly set-up plants tends to harass foreign firms, whose activities would otherwise contribute to faster technological innovations, management efficiency, more sophisticated skill formation, and higher employment over the long run in host countries.

Closely associated with local contents requirements is the concept of the country of origin of a product, which was until recently defined as the country where the last substantial transformation or operation is performed in economically justifiable ways. In the past this concept was used for the purpose of assessing tariffs and duties and hence had nothing to do with dumping or local contents (Advisory Committee for Trade Policy and Negotiations 1989). In 1988, however, this concept was redefined so as to extend antidumping duties to Japanese photocopiers. Even if photocopiers are produced in the community, their country of origin can be defined as Japan if the most sophisticated components are still produced there. The commission has recently argued that certain photocopiers assembled in the United States should be classified as Japanese on the grounds of their high proportion of sophisticated Japanese components. The country of origin of videocassette recorders and computer printers can be judged on the basis of the technological significance of various components.

The case of integrated circuits is yet another example of new rules of origin. The country where the etching of circuits onto blank silicon wafers takes place would be defined as the country of origin. It seems extremely arbitrary and uncertain for the commission to decide what particular components or what particular production processes will be construed as technologically sophisticated or significant.

The application of antidumping regulations not only to imports of high-technology products but also to components of screwdriver plants and the redefining of the concept of the country of origin both indicate the commission's efforts to establish Europe's high-technology industries in the hands of European companies. It is now argued that it is essential for Europe to have a strong electronics base to revitalize its manufacturing sectors, since electronics has significant spinoff or spillover effects on manufacturing industry as a whole. Instruments for achieving this purpose are voluntary export restraints, local content measures, broadened VRAs, and redefined rules of origin, leading to trade protection and harassment of foreign firms. What is at issue is no longer simply whether value added can be preserved and increased in host countries by trade protection or the inflow of foreign direct investment but firms of what nationalities should reap the benefit of the preserved and increased value added.

Therefore, as long as these instruments are continually adopted by the commission, reflecting compromises among member countries, the possibility that Europe 1992 will intensify techno-Europeanism must be high in the 1990s. This is ironic simply because the national origin of multinationals is becoming increasingly blurred through global scope of the location of research and development, components production, assembling, marketing, and headquarters.

Relation between External Trade and Competition Policy. It is still too early to tell how the community policy on mergers and acquisitions can be compatible with the fundamental objective of 1992, that is, greater exposure of European firms to competition through deregulation and the resultant greater efficiency of European industries. Mergers that could impede effective competition would be incompatible with this objective.

At the same time, a merger that was found incompatible could nevertheless be authorized by the commission on the grounds that its contribution to improving the competitive structure within the single market through economies of scale and the learning curve outweighs the damage to effective competition. In other words, the need for European industries to be internationally competitive can be a strong justification for the approval of mergers even when they may reduce effective competition in the single market. If such a commission policy on mergers were integrated with the aforementioned antidumping regulations, local contents and rules-of-origin measures, and VRAs on products including those made by multinational firms in host countries, Europe 1992 would end up with an intensified fortress Europe in specific industries. The commission may have a greater temptation and greater incentives to protect European industries that may reap large economies of scale in high-technology industries such as consumer microelectronics, supercomputers, aircraft, and universal satellites.

The greatest contradiction can be found between the 1992 integration as an instrument for achieving greater efficiency through tougher competition by way of deregulation, on the one hand, and Europe 1992 as the integrated mechanism for insulating the single market from international competition in high-technology industries, on the other. The commission's external trade policy can be liberal and can invite greater international competition, or it can restrict such competition. Correspondingly its policy on mergers can be strongly antimonopoly or can aim at strengthening the international competitiveness of European industries at the expense of effective competition in the single market. The relation between the commission's trade policy and its merger policy should be explicitly spelled out. The issue of whether the commission's policy on mergers is likely to result in an interventionist European industrial policy or in a more genuine competition policy must be profoundly associated with its external policy of 1992, as suggested by new strategic trade theory. The commission's external trade policy may contradict its merger policy if the former is liberal and the latter allows monopoly formation or if the former is protective in specific industries and the latter encourages more competition.

The case of Daimler-Benz's takeover of MBB and the joint bid by GEC and Siemens for Plessey may suggest that the commission's national policy on mergers now caters to industrial policy aimed at strengthening high-technology European industries such as aircraft and consumer electronics, rather than enhancing competition and efficiency. What can really vitalize European industries, however, is intensified pressure on European business to innovate and improve management. This should entail not only the existence of at least several firms in an industry but also the absence of barriers for foreign products and for new firms, including foreign enterprises. If the commission's merger policy reduced the number of European firms in an industry and its external trade and direct investment policy raised barriers for both foreign high-technology products and foreign direct investment through antidumping regulation and harassment of foreign firms, Europe 1992 would revitalize European industries in vain.

Do Japan's Trade Practices Justify a Fortress Europe?

European protectionist policy against Japan has often been claimed to be justified at least implicitly as a reaction to Japan's predatory exports and closed domestic market. The extensive application of antidumping measures has directly or indirectly demonstrated this. Two specific questions should be addressed to this presumption about Japan's trade behavior and structure. One is, What are the real issues behind the extremely aggressive external expansion? What accounts for the Japanese business behavior that leads to Japan's being blamed for predation? The other question is, How closed are Japanese domestic markets and how can their closedness or openness be measured? The ultimate policy question is whether Japanese domestic markets are so distinctively closed that a Fortress Europe against Japan can be justified.

Economic Fundamentals behind the Allegedly Closed Market and Aggressive Exports of Japan. The allegation that the Japanese market is closed is almost always based on the extremely small proportion of Japan's manufactured imports relative to total imports or to gross national product.

The issue is whether this distinctively low import penetration is a reflection either of trade barriers (official or nonofficial) or of the equally distinctive features of the endowment of production resources in Japan. This issue has been intensively studied (see, in particular, Saxonhouse 1983; Leamer 1988; and OECD 1989). The results are that Japan's distinctive trade structure reflects its equally distinctive comparative advantage, determined by interindustry differences in the intensities of its production factors. The comparative advantage theorem puts a stress on the relative abundance of particular production factors compared with other factors. Even if absolute levels of accumulated human skills and physical capital are the same in Japan as in other countries, the relative abundance of such skills and capital is much greater for Japan since its lands and natural resources are extremely scarce, as reflected, for example, in the extraordinarily high GNP per acre in Japan (more than thirty times and five times as high as the United States and West Germany, respectively). The dynamic changes in comparative advantage of Japan from unskilled-labor-intensive to capital-intensive and to research and development–intensive manufactured products over nearly the past two decades have also been econometrically demonstrated (Balassa and Noland 1989; Grossman 1989). Thus Japan's trade structure and its evolution can be explained largely by the variables drawn from the Heckscher-Ohlin factor proportions theory of trade.

While such production factor proportions can account for the distinctive features of Japan's interindustry trade structure, another distinctive feature of Japan's external trade has been pointed out: that is, its extremely low participation in intraindustry trade. An empirical examination of Japan's participation in intraindustry international trade for 1985 indicates that actual imports of manufactured goods were about 40 percent less than the theoretically expected levels that would have been witnessed if there had been no barriers (Lawrence 1987). The substantial appreciation of the yen after 1985, however, appears to have overcome "invisible private barriers," which are not like import quotas but like tariffs (Lawrence 1987). The volume of Japan's imports of manufactured goods jumped by 110 percent from 1985 to 1989, which would have not happened under barriers like import quotas. Furthermore, serious misspecifications have been pointed out with regard to Lawrence's econometric estimation of intraindustry trade (Srinivasan and Hamada 1989).

A small but growing number of recent empirical studies attempt to analyze the interrelations between international trade and industrial organization or market structure. These studies depart from the traditional premise by treating firms as oligopolists rather than anonymous pure competitors. Both domestic and foreign firms may thus engage in an oligopoly game, and therefore the market share in world trade can be an outcome of international oligopolistic interactions. Such an outcome can be determined by certain strategic variables such as product differentiation, research and development, and tangible investment committed by oligopolistic firms (Yamawaki and Audretsch 1988). While these studies are conducted cross-sectionally for one specific year, more dynamic, time-series approaches have been adopted to highlight dynamic changes in technology-trade relations across sectors over time (Owen 1988; Owen and van der Loeff 1989).

Both cross-sectional and time-series approaches have demonstrated that research and development expenditures and other strategic variables in trading countries (the United States and Japan in Yamawaki and Audretsch and the United States, Japan, and France in Owen and van der Loeff) are determinants of trade shares in industries (at the three-digit level). More important, the research and development intensities of individual sectors relative to those of other industries not only diverge within a country but also vary among countries for a specific year and evolve differently over time. In particular, Owen and van der Loeff have found that Japanese research and development play a more critical role than American technological investment, accounting for Japan's relatively better trade performance, especially in its market share in world trade rather than in bilateral trade between the United States and Japan. This finding is consistent with findings of other empirical studies that Japanese research and development expenditures have concentrated on process innovations of improvement in product quality and cost reduction.

All these studies tend to suggest that the alleged closed market (that is, the low imports of manufactured goods) and extremely rapid expansion of exports of Japan are a reflection of two economic fundamentals. One is Japan's distinctive endowment of production factors in Heckscher-Ohlin terms. The other is the dynamic and rapid advancement in Japan's trade structure due to increasingly intensified research and development expenditure in manufacturing, particularly in high-technology industries. An important policy implication can be drawn from this: the Japanese market is not so distinctively closed as to justify a Fortress Europe against Japan.

Market Access and Industrial Organization in Japan. Market access to the Japanese economy is an important economic issue, but unfortunately often debated only emotionally. Since tariffs or quotas are insignificant for Japan's imports of manufactured goods, the lack of market access often refers to a set of official guidelines and private business practices that effectively deny entry of foreign manufactured goods into the Japanese market. Particularly when business practices lead to anticompetitive or entry-deterring results, market access is often said to be restricted. If foreign firms encounter predatory or entry-deterring practices by incumbent Japanese large-scale oligopolies, foreign firms will complain about market access (Harris 1989).

In this specific context it is worth understanding the basic functions of the *keiretsu* (postwar corporate alliances) in Japan. This example may highlight how important industrial organization is for developing high-technology products.

Two kinds of business groups exist in Japan: (1) the *zaibatsu* (prewar corporate alliances) successors and non-*zaibatsu* principal bank groups and (2) groups composed of large firms and their subsidiaries. The two groups are not mutually exclusive. An important difference between the two kinds of groups is that the first have neither a centralized decision-making unit nor a well-established way of regulating their members, whereas the second groups centralize decision making in the parent company, followed by a large number of subsidiaries. Stockholdings, strong transaction relationships, interlocking directorates, and financial dependence are more or less common to both kinds of groups (Goto 1982).

Most important economic functions performed by these second business groups are associated with the transactions of intermediate and capital goods within a group. In the intermediate and capital goods markets, buyers' demand is often characterized by extremely detailed specifications for various dimensions of the product and hence can be satisfied by a very small number of suppliers of such a specific product. Three consequences arise from this character: first, transaction costs would be high if the negotiations and maneuvering involved were to be repeated for each transaction; second, how to secure a stable supply of such specific products becomes even more important for keeping operations going smoothly in large assemblers; third, obtaining precise technological information on specific products both before and after transactions is indispensable for securing the quality of both components and final products as well as for uninterrupted production processes in parent firms. Under these circumstances firms seek to lower transaction costs, secure procurements, and obtain technological information.

Can firms satisfy these three requirements by relying on the general anonymous market or by integrating transactions vertically in an enterprise through in-house production of necessary components and capital goods? The problem with the anonymous market is that such a market cannot always effectively secure no-defect, high-quality products, prompt and punctual delivery, or technological information flows about specific components and capital goods. There is also a serious problem with in-house production, because in-house production of a large number of necessary components and capital goods may entail diseconomies of scale for such captive products. Transactions in a business group can be interpreted to be designed to overcome the problems associated with either the anonymous market or the in-house production system, so as more effectively to guarantee the quality of specific products, punctual delivery, and the provisions of before and after sales information services (for a concrete example, see Asanuma 1985). Such transactions are, therefore, conducted neither through the anonymous market nor through in-house production but through the customized intermediate market of a business group. If so, the existence of business groups cannot be identified as a structural impediment to new entry. But the long-term, repetitive relationship between large parent companies and subcontractors can be seen as a barrier to new entry, both domestic and foreign, in procurements of intermediate and capital goods.

What is profoundly associated with such business practices is the extremely low penetration of foreign direct investment in Japan. This problem reflects not government restrictions, the low profitability of such investment, or appreciation of the yen but difficulties in reaching customers who prefer long-term relationships, in hiring good personnel (partly because of the lifetime employment custom), or in obtaining effective sales channels in Japan's complex distribution system (Booz, Allen & Hamilton 1987).

All these evidences tend to suggest that the limit to market access in Japan should be associated not with artificial barriers but with the Japanese production and management system as a whole.

Conclusions—More Global Implications of Europe 1992

In the 1980s the EC Commission has made increasingly active and even innovative use of antidumping regulations, particularly against Japanese high-technology products such as office machines and consumer microelectronics. The concept of the country of origin has been redefined so as to protect European firms from Japanese competition regardless of the location of Japanese firms. The commission's proposal on VRAs on Japanese cars, including not only those imported but also those produced by European-based Japanese firms, suggests that Europe 1992 could produce a Fortress Europe for particular industries of particular countries. A new element in recent trade protection measures is harassment of foreign firms in the face of increasing globalization of the activities of multinational companies.

Europe 1992 is in part a reaction to the declining competitiveness of European firms vis-à-vis the American and especially the Japanese in high-technology industries. The commission attempts to coordinate trade, competition, and technology policies so as to reduce Japanese dominance in so-called strategic industries.

Furthermore, the allegedly predatory exports and closed domestic market of Japan have often been used to justify European protectionist policies. The real issue behind such an allegation, however, is the combined effects of Japan's distinctive endowment of production factors in Heckscher-Ohlin terms and its extremely rapid and dynamic advancement of trade structure due to the intensification of research and development expenditure by Japanese firms in high-technology industries. Closely associated with this allegation is the often emotionally debated issue of access to the Japanese market. This issue is largely a reflection of Japan's industrial organization, featured by *keiretsu* transactions. *Keiretsu* transactions are essentially those in customized intermediate markets that guarantee the quality of the product, prompt and timely delivery, and the postsales flow of technical information about specific components and capital goods in a more cost-effective fashion than the general anonymous market or in-house production systems. The long-term repetitive transactions in *keiretsu* or a business group, however, can work as barriers to market access for new entrants because of their nature, even when competition among different *keiretsu* or business groups is fierce and *keiretsu* transactions are not engaged in predatory or entry-deterring practices.

The external implications of Europe 1992 for Japan are essentially twofold. One is that Europe 1992 may intensify discriminatory actions against not only imports of Japanese high-technology products but also Japanese multinationals. The other is that Europe 1992 highlights fierce competition not only among different nationalities of multinational companies but also among different production and management systems and industrial organizations unique to each nation. Industrial organization affects both firms' performance and the market access of new entrants.

In a world increasingly interdependent because of the increasingly globalized activities of multinational companies, there is a growing pressure for international harmonization of the rules of the game to avoid an industrial policy war in strategic industries (Krugman 1987, but only for an intra-Europe war).

References

Advisory Committee for Trade Policy and Negotiations. 1989. *Europe 1992*.

Asanuma, Banri. 1985. "The Organization of Parts Purchases in the Japanese Automotive Industry." *Japanese Economic Studies* 13, no. 4 (Summer) 32–53.

Balassa, Bela, and Marcus Noland. 1989. "The Changing Comparative Advantage of Japan and the U.S." *Journal of Japanese and International Economies* 3: 174–88.

Booz, Allen & Hamilton. 1987. *Direct Foreign Investment in Japan: The Challenge for Foreign Firms*. A study for the American Chamber of Commerce in Japan and the Council of the European Business Community. September.

Davenport, Michael. 1989. "The Charybdis of Anti-dumping: A New Form of EC Industrial Policy?" Royal Institute of International

Affairs, RIIA Discussion Paper no. 22.

EC Commission. 1988. "The Economics of 1992." *European Economy*.

Goto, Akira. 1982. "Business Groups in a Market Economy." *European Economic Review* 19: 53–70.

Grossman, Gene M. 1989. "Explaining Japan's Innovation and Trade: A Model of Quality Competition and Dynamic Comparative Advantage." Working Paper no. 3194 (December), National Bureau of Economic Research.

Harris, Richard. 1989. " 'Market Access' in International Trade." In *Trade and Investment Relations among the United States, Canada, and Japan*, ed. Robert M. Stern. Chicago: University of Chicago Press.

Hoffmann, Stanley. 1989. "The European Community and 1992." *Foreign Affairs* (Fall).

Krugman, Paul. 1987. "Economic Integration in Europe: Some Conceptual Issues." In *Efficiency, Stability, and Equity: A Strategy for the Evolution of the Economic System of the European Community*, ed. Tomaso Padoa-Schioppa. New York: Oxford University Press, pp. 117–40.

Lawrence, R. Z. 1987. "Imports in Japan: Closed Markets or Minds?" Brookings Papers in Economic Activity, no. 2.

Leamer, Edward. 1988. "Measures of Openness." In *Trade Policy Issue and Empirical Analysis*, ed. R. E. Baldwin. Chicago: University of Chicago Press.

OECD. 1989. *Economic Surveys: Japan, Paris, 1989*. Annex III, "Overview of the Empirical Research on Imports in Japan," pp. 119–21.

Owen, Robert F. 1988. "The Evolution in Japan's Relative Technological Competitiveness since the 1960s: A Cross-sectional, Time-Series Analysis." *Bank of Japan Monetary and Economic Studies* (November).

Owen, Robert F., and Sybrand Schis van der Loeff. 1989. "A Dynamic Prospective on R&D as a Determinant of Japanese and American Trade Flows: A Disaggregate Analysis." (Mimeo.).

Saxonhouse, Gary. 1983. "The Micro- and Macro-economics of Foreign Sales to Japan." In *Trade Policies in the 1980s*, ed. W. Cline. Washington, D.C.: Institute for International Economics.

Srinivasan, T. N., and K. Hamada. 1989. "The U.S.-Japan Trade Problem." Paper presented at Columbia University Conference on Trade.

Yamawaki, Hideki, and David B. Audretsch. 1988. "Import Share under International Oligopoly with Differentiated Products: Japanese Imports in U.S. Manufacturing." *Review of Economics and Statistics* (November) 569–79.

4
The Role of the Asian NICs in the 1990s

Raymond J. Ahearn and Anne Dibble

The Asian newly industrialized countries (NICs)—South Korea, Taiwan, Hong Kong, and Singapore—play a role in the world economy that is far out of proportion to their size, locations, and disparate political situations. As a group they constitute only 1 percent of the world population, and all are highly dependent on the outside world for critical supplies of natural resources. Given unique geopolitical positions, they all have very different and limited capacities to influence the outside world.

South Korea, the largest of the four with a population of 40 million, is a divided country and a longstanding center of big power rivalries. Taiwan, the second largest with a population of 20 million, survives with an ambiguous diplomatic status as an offshore province of China. Hong Kong, the third largest with a population of 6 million, is a British colony but will revert back to China in 1997. Singapore, the smallest of the four with a population of less than 3 million, is a high-technology city-state the size of Chicago.

Even though the Asian NICs are more different than they are alike and two of the four (Hong Kong and Taiwan) lack the full trappings of modern states, they have been lumped together as a group primarily because of their individual economic accomplishments and the collective challenge they and other countries in Asia pose to the West. Following in Japan's path, the NICs have come to symbolize a massive shift in location of wealth and power to the Pacific region.

As a part of the most economically dynamic region in the world, the Asian NICs have accomplished in twenty-five years what most developing countries have not been able to accomplish in a century. Their long-term economic growth has been about three times as fast as world trade. Since the 1960s the NICs have been growing at rates significantly higher than industrialized countries. Their average annual growth rate was 9 percent in the 1960s and 1970s and 8 percent in the 1980s. Already some analysts predict that 70 percent of global manufacturing production will take place in East Asia in the twenty-first century.

The emerging economic power of the Asian NICs has generated a mixture of admiration and anxiety among the U.S. policy-making, business, and academic communities. The admiration stems from the fact that between 1980 and 1988 the Asian NICs managed to double their share of world merchandise exports to $220 billion—an amount surpassed only by Japan, West Germany, and the United States.

Conversely, American anxiety arose from the NICs' rapid penetration of an excessive dependence on the U.S. import market during a period of massive U.S. trade deficits. In 1988 alone the United States purchased nearly one-third of all Asian NIC exports; these purchases accounted for one-fourth of the $119.1 billion merchandise trade deficit in the United States accumulated (USITC 1989, 13). Collectively the NICs were able to run a $32 billion current account surplus in 1988, a $41 billion turnaround from their $9 billion current account deficit position in 1980.

The trading success of the NICs in the 1980s focused international attention on their economic and industrial promotion policies. Owing substantially to their rising balance-of-payments surpluses and heavy dependence on the U.S. market, they came to be recognized as major players in the world trading system and as part of the problem in reestablishing more balanced global trading relations.

It is widely appreciated that the United States bears the greatest responsibility for correcting the politically destabilizing global payments imbalances. But as the United States continues to move to correct its twin deficits—its external current account and its related domestic budget deficit—the Asian NICs along with the European Community (EC) and Japan will have to facilitate the adjustment.

The NICs face two fundamental policy questions in seeking to facilitate the development of more balanced global trade relations. First, what kinds of economic policies should they adopt to facilitate the adjustment without endangering their own growth prospects and political stability? Second, how should they engage in a more constructive dialogue with other members of the industrialized world to ensure that the transition does not undermine the multilateral world trading system (East-West Center 1989, 26)?

The response of the NICs to these questions is being influenced by a changing world trade environment in North America, Europe, and Asia. First, in North America pressures that developed in the 1980s for a more aggressive and unilateral U.S. trade policy have forced the NICs, particularly South Korea and Taiwan, to appreciate their currencies and to liberalize their trade and investment controls. To lessen the NICs' heavy dependence on exports as a source of growth, additional changes in their economic structures may be necessary.

Second, to diversify exports and become less dependent on the U.S. market, the NICs have expanded their trade relations with the EC in recent years. But a number of developments in the EC, particularly growing antidumping actions against Asian manufactured exports, together with increasingly stringent local content and product standards requirements, have ignited fears among East Asian manufacturers that a united Europe in 1992 may serve to reduce their access to that important consumer market.

Third, NIC efforts to adjust and accommodate to the necessary changes in trade imbalances will be affected by the trend toward a more economically integrated East Asian trading community. Spurred by a more open Japanese market, economic reform in China, and *perestroika* in the Soviet Union, a more economically integrated East Asia may play a larger role in absorbing a greater share of Asian NIC exports in the 1990s.

Accordingly, this paper seeks to analyze how a changing world trade environment is affecting the Asian NICs and their role in the world trading system. The paper will focus on four main trends: (1) the emergence of the East Asian NICs as key players in the world trading system; (2) recent developments in U.S. trade policy affecting the NICs; (3) the potential impact of EC 1992 on the NICs; and (4) East Asia as a growing market for NIC exports.

A concluding section assesses how the changing world trade environment is affecting both the shape of the world trading system and the role of the NICs in the system. In addition, a set of policy recommendations is provided to enhance the evolution of more balanced trading relations between the NICs and the rest of the world.

The Rise of the Asian NICs

The rapid rise of the Asian NICs in the world economy during the 1980s is well known. Their growing prosperity has been export driven, with a heavy reliance on the production of manufactured goods for sale in markets of developed countries. South Korea and Taiwan have been transformed from agrarian economies to industrial powerhouses. And Hong Kong and Singapore have been transformed from colonial trading posts to economies based on a sophisticated combination of industry, financial services, and port facilities.

Prosperity through Exporting. The rapid growth of the Asian NICs has depended on a high level of exports. The NICs are among the world's most export-dependent economies, with exports ranging from 45 percent of gross national product in South Korea to 130 percent in Singapore (Hanazaki, 1989, 15).

Dramatic increases in shares of world exports illustrate their exporting prowess. In 1960 the Asian NICs had less than a 2 percent share of world exports, but by 1988 their share had quadrupled to 8 percent. This share was based on a combined trade volume of about $220 billion—a volume that far surpassed those of France and the United Kingdom and that was only 15 percent less than the $260 billion exported by Japan during the same year (World Financial Markets 1989, 1).

This exporting prowess has allowed the Asian NICs to run up large current account surpluses. In 1988 the group together ran a current account surplus of $32 billion, a $41 billion turnaround since 1980, when they collectively experienced a $9 billion current account deficit. This strong external financial position has been reinforced by high foreign reserves. By year-end 1988 Singapore was reported to have the highest reserve position per capita in the world at $6,459 and Taiwan the third highest at $4,012 (FEER 1989b). With reserves valued at over $16 billion and $75 billion respectively, Singapore and Taiwan are capable of using their excess domestic savings for "global" investments. South Korea and Hong Kong have also been in a position to export capital in recent years.

In addition to stimulating industrial efficiency and expanding economies of scale, rapid export growth has enabled the NICs to boost per capita incomes by approximately 38 percent between 1980 and 1986. Per capita incomes of roughly $8,000 in Singapore and Hong Kong now surpass those of some poorer European nations (table 4-1). Taiwan and South Korea, with per capita incomes in excess of $6,000 and $4,000 respectively, still have far to go in catching up to many industrialized countries.

The still relatively low per capita incomes in Taiwan and South Korea are indicative of the scope in each country for faster growth in domestic consumption and higher living standards. These would require a major shift in resources from export to domestic uses.

Reliance on Manufactured Exports. Manufactured goods have constituted the lion's share of the total Asian NIC exports. During the period 1980–1982, 72 percent of all NIC exports to the world were manufactured goods. By 1987 approximately 95 percent of total exports from the NICs to the United States and the EC were manufac-

TABLE 4-1
PER CAPITA GROSS DOMESTIC PRODUCT OF THE EAST ASIAN NICs,
1980–1988
(thousands of dollars)

Country	1980	1985	1988
Hong Kong	5,456	6,683	8,195
Singapore	4,871	6,149	7,673
South Korea	1,646	2,203	4,040
Taiwan	2,315	2,869	6,045

SOURCES: Japan Development Bank, *Research Report No. 15*, August 1989, p. 21; Morgan Guaranty Trust Company, "World Financial Markets," April 17, 1989; Trade Development Board of Singapore; Korean Economic Institute; and Economics Division, Coordination Council for North American Affairs, Republic of China.

tures, and such goods made up 60 percent of total exports to Japan.[1]

The NICs' export thrust has traditionally been strongest in miscellaneous manufactured goods; in 1986, for example, countries of the Organization for Economic Cooperation and Development (OECD) imported more than $17 billion in apparel and clothing articles from the four NICs. OECD trade data show, however, that traditional exports of leather, footwear, textiles, and apparel are declining as a percentage of aggregate NIC exports to the advanced industrialized states, although they still retained the predominant positions in the composition of sales by Hong Kong and Taiwan to developed countries.

The NICs have been able to diversify their exports, moving into increasingly sophisticated, higher-value-added, and technology-intensive products. Between 1964 and 1985 the ratio of high-technology exports to total exports from all four countries to OECD markets rose from 2 to 25 percent, and the medium-technology export ratio expanded from 14 to 22 percent; conversely, the ratio of low-technology exports to total exports declined from 80 to 53 percent over the period surveyed (OECD 1988, 24).

The export composition of the Asian NICs has matched changing trends in demand, shifting into increasingly sophisticated consumer electronics, data- and word-processing equipment, telecommunications equipment, and automobiles. Machinery exports have constituted a growing proportion of total exports. Constituting just 12 percent of total NIC exports in 1970, machinery exports made up 33 percent by 1987. Electrical machinery, consumer electronics equipment, and telecommunications equipment have shown exceptionally

TABLE 4-2
EXPORT ORIENTATION OF ASIAN NICs, 1982–1988
(percent of total exports)

	United States	Japan	European Community	Total
1982	28	7	13	48
1985	40	10	11	61
1986	33	9	11	53
1987	35	12	14	61
1988	31	12	15	58

SOURCE: IMF, *Directions of Trade*; and Trade Statistics, Republic of China.

strong export growth rates. By 1986 the Asian NICs had secured over 10 percent of the OECD market in both the office and the electrical machinery categories, with OECD imports of semiconductors from South Korea and Singapore showing exceptionally strong growth (OECD 1988, 20–24).

Differences among the countries however, are pronounced. South Korean exports tend to be finished products and the most capital and technology intensive. Taiwan has specialized in the production of components for computers and consumer electronics. Singapore has specialized in consumer electronics products produced by foreign multinationals. Hong Kong has upgraded the sophistication of its manufacturing base, but close to 50 percent of Hong Kong's total exports remain in such light industries as textiles and garments.

Reliance on Developed Country Markets. Developed countries have been the primary purchasers of Asian NIC exports. In 1982 the United States, the EC, and Japan accounted for 48 percent of Asian NIC exports. By 1987 and 1988 these percentages had grown to 61 and 58 respectively (table 4-2).

Among the developed countries, the United States has been the dominant market for the Asian NICs, accounting for as high as 40 percent of total NIC exports in 1985. But by 1988 the export dependence of the NICs on the U.S. market had dropped to 31 percent.

As the Asian NIC dependence on the U.S. market dropped by nine percentage points between 1985 and 1988, Japan and the EC increased their shares of Asian NIC exports by seven percentage points from 1982 to 1988. Japan's share rose from 7 percent in 1982 to 12 percent in 1988 while the EC share rose from 13 percent to 15 percent.

Of the four NICs, Taiwan and South Korea are most dependent

TABLE 4-3
TAIWAN'S EXPORT ORIENTATION, 1982–1988
(percent of total exports)

	United States	Japan	European Community
1982	39	11	12
1985	48	11	10
1986	48	12	12
1987	44	13	14.5
1988	39	14.5	16.3

SOURCE: Trade statistics, Republic of China.

TABLE 4-4
SOUTH KOREA'S EXPORT ORIENTATION, 1982–1988
(percent of total exports)

	United States	Japan	European Community
1982	29	16	13
1985	36	15	11
1986	40	16	12
1987	39	18	14
1988	35	20	13

SOURCE: IMF, *Directions of Trade*.

on the United States. Taiwan's dependence reached almost 50 percent in the mid-1980s but declined to 39 percent by 1988 (table 4-3). South Korea's dependence on the U.S. market peaked at 40 percent in 1986 and declined to 35 percent by 1988 (table 4-4). Hong Kong (table 4-5) and Singapore (table 4-5 and 4-6) are also heavily dependent on the U.S. market, with one-fourth of their exports sent to that market.

Japan in 1988 purchased 20 percent of South Korea's and 14.5 percent of Taiwan's exports but only 9 percent of Singapore's and 6 percent of Hong Kong's exports. The EC purchased approximately 16 percent of Hong Kong's and Taiwan's exports and 13 percent of South Korea's and Singapore's exports in 1988.

U.S. Trade Policy

Pressures for Reform of U.S. Trade Policy. The growing success of the Asian NICs in the U.S. market became part of the U.S. trade debate in the 1980s. Between 1980 and 1985 U.S. purchases of foreign

TABLE 4-5
HONG KONG'S EXPORT ORIENTATION, 1982–1988
(percent of total exports)

	United States	Japan	European Community
1982	29	4	18
1985	31	4	12
1986	31	5	14
1987	28	5	16
1988	25	6	16

SOURCE: IMF, *Directions of Trade*.

TABLE 4-6
SINGAPORE'S EXPORT ORIENTATION, 1982–1988
(percent of total exports)

	United States	Japan	European Community
1982	13	11	10
1985	21	9	11
1986	24	8	11
1987	24	9	12
1988	24	9	13

SOURCE: IMF, *Directions of Trade*.

manufactured imports rose from $125 billion to $247 billion, an increase largely fueled by the appreciation of the dollar by some 58 percent against other major currencies on a real, trade-weighted exchange basis during that period. In addition to pricing U.S. exports out of the market, the strong dollar acted like a magnet for low-cost East Asian exports.

At the dollar's peak in 1985, the United States absorbed $39.1 billion in goods from the Asian NICs—almost double the value of Asian NIC exports to the United States in 1981 (Burton 1988, 244–45). In contrast, the United States exported only $16.5 billion to the Asian NICs in 1985, resulting in a $22.6 billion deficit with those countries—approximately 15 percent of the $152 billion U.S. trade deficit that year. Combined with Japan's bilateral trade surplus of $47 billion, these five East Asian countries accounted for over 55 percent of America's record trade deficit in 1985.

Concern over the ballooning trade deficit and growing frustration with the Reagan administration's refusal to fight foreign unfair trade practices or to provide adjustment assistance to firms hurt by import competition led to rising pressures on Congress to take action. Congress responded with an outpouring of legislative proposals designed to force the administration to take a tougher position on foreign trade barriers and to provide greater protection to domestic industries hard hit by import competition.

By the summer of 1985 the enactment of some restrictive trade bills had emerged as a top congressional issue. The Reagan administration was most concerned about the Jenkins textile bill, which called for a 40 percent reduction in textile imports from twelve countries, and the Bentsen-Gephardt-Rostenkowski bill, which would have imposed a 25 percent surcharge on imports from countries that did not take immediate remedial action to reduce their excessive trade surpluses with the United States.

Although much of the legislation was aimed at opening up the Japanese market to American goods and services, U.S. legislators were not unmindful of the weight of the Asian NICs in the U.S. global trade deficit. Indeed, many in Congress had come to view the Asian NICs—South Korea and Taiwan in particular—as "mini-Japans" that sought to emulate the Japanese government's role in creating competitive advantage through protectionist practices together with financial, administrative, and informal domestic arrangements. Their success at combining a rolling infant industry strategy and sophisticated trade protection was perceived by Congress not only as unfair but also as a threat to America's comparative advantage (Ahearn 1987, 27).

Seeking to deflect growing protectionist sentiment in Congress, the Reagan administration unveiled a major trade initiative in September 1985 centered on a tougher stand on unfair foreign trading practices. President Ronald Reagan's "free but fair" trade policy sought to broaden the scope of U.S. action against such practices by rigorous enforcement of U.S. antidumping and countervailing duty laws and the self-initiation of section 301 investigations against Brazil, Japan, and South Korea. This last action set an important precedent, given that all previous section 301 cases had been initiated in response to petitions from private industry.

An integral part of the administration's new trade policy also focused on the need for surplus nations to shoulder more responsibility for the stability and continued growth of the global economy. Japan, West Germany, and the Asian NICs were perceived by the Reagan administration as countries that could absorb more of the world's imports through a revaluation of their currencies and the removal of macroeconomic distortions to international trade flows. U.S. pressure on the two leading surplus nations, Japan and West Germany, was especially intense in this regard, given that the United States was absorbing roughly 66 percent of manufactured goods from the rest of the world, compared with 7 percent for Japan and 25 percent for the EC. Taiwan and South Korea were also targeted for negotiations to liberalize their markets and revalue their currencies.

South Korea and Taiwan also figured prominently in the congressional debate accompanying enactment of the Omnibus Trade and Competitiveness Act of 1988. A number of the provisions were drafted in ways that were likely to target these countries for action. Provisions of the act dealing with currency manipulation and unfair trade practices under "super 301" and "special 301," in particular, were written with these two Asian NICs in mind.

While not abandoning in principle the longstanding U.S. commitment to the General Agreement on Tariffs and Trade (GATT) and multilateralism, administrative and congressional actions in the latter half of the 1980s had the combined effect of nudging U.S. trade policy in a more activist direction. Greater emphasis on bilateral negotiations backed by threats of retaliation, tightened sectoral agreements, and administrative procedures for gaining import relief from unfair competition, along with the negotiation of free trade areas with Israel and Canada, prompted concern, particularly among foreigners, that U.S. trade policy was moving in a less nondiscriminatory and less open direction. Most important, U.S. actions sent a clear message to the NICs that access to the U.S. market was not without limitations and conditions.

U.S. Actions Directed at the NICs. The U.S. government took a number of actions to stem the rapid surge in NIC exports to the United States during the 1980s. These included more vigorous enforcement of U.S. countervailing duty and antidumping statutes, negotiation of bilateral restraint agreements affecting textiles and steel, and the elimination of tariff preferences under the U.S. Generalized System of Preferences (GSP). To boost U.S. exports to the NICs, the United States engaged in a series of bilateral negotiations designed to appreciate the value of the South Korean won and the new Taiwan dollar and to reduce barriers to U.S. exports. In addition, considerable U.S. pressures were directed at South Korea and Taiwan to undertake basic structural changes in their economies that would provide greater emphasis on domestic consumption as a source of economic growth. The purpose of these pressures was to make these two economies less dependent on an export-led growth strategy resulting in excessive trade surpluses.

Import-related actions. Between 1980 and 1987 the United States initiated 411 antidumping investigations and 283 countervailing duty investigations. Approximately 41 percent of the antidumping investigations and 51 percent of the countervailing duty investigations targeted NIC products (Kelly 1988).

Since 1981 thirty-eight antidumping and countervailing duty investigations have been initiated against South Korean manufactured exports, seventeen of these resulting in positive determinations of injury to U.S. domestic producers (*Business Korea* 1988b). On December 31, 1988, antidumping and countervailing duty orders were in effect against twelve Taiwanese products, three products from Singapore, and one product from Hong Kong (USITC 1989).

A variety of bilateral restraint agreements covering textiles and apparel and steel have affected NIC exports to the United States. Agreements concerning textiles and steel have been perhaps the most onerous. By year-end 1988 the United States had negotiated bilateral textile agreements with forty-five countries, including the four Asian NICs. Taiwan, South Korea, and Hong Kong, together with China, clearly dominate the flow of textile imports from developing countries into the United States, accounting for 41 percent of such imports in 1988 (USITC 1989, 150).

U.S. pressures to place tighter quotas on Hong Kong's exports have been a constant source of tension. Textiles account for about 42 percent of Hong Kong's domestic exports, and more than 40 percent of that total goes to the United States. Hong Kong exporters like to point out that much of the textile product that Hong Kong exports is manufactured with fabrics that have to be imported into Hong Kong from other countries, including the United States. They further point out that the Hong Kong market is an open one and that U.S. textile producers wishing to export to Hong Kong can do so without encountering any tariffs or other, nontariff barriers (Dumbaugh 1989, 5).

Another import-related action eliminated the eligibility of the NICs under the U.S. duty-free GSP. In January 1988 President Reagan decided to graduate Hong Kong, Singapore, South Korea, and Taiwan from the program, ostensibly because of "their remarkable economic advancements and improved trade competitiveness" (USTR 1988). One year before their graduation Taiwan, South Korea, and Hong Kong were the top three GSP beneficiaries, accounting for 51.4 percent of total GSP imports in 1987.

Singapore, in particular, was upset by the decision. Although Singapore had long been prepared for the loss of GSP preferences because of its attainment of middle-income status, Singaporean officials had been led to believe that the preferences would be extended for an indefinite period if Singapore adopted a copyright law covering intellectual property rights.

It was widely believed that the decision to include Singapore in the action in spite of an apparent earlier U.S. commitment stemmed from the desire of senior U.S. officials to find a more "objective" rationale than simple retaliation to deal with South Korea's resistance to U.S. market-opening measures. As a result, this viewpoint holds, the administration decided to revoke GSP privileges for the NICs as a group, casting the action as a positive step to graduate the NICs from "unneeded preferential treatment." From the perspective of the NICs, however, the U.S. action was another indicator of a shift toward a tighter and more restrictive trade policy (Cronin 1989).

Despite an increase in the number and scope of U.S. import-related actions, the U.S. restrictions have been "leaky." This statement is supported by a number of indicators showing that the Asian NICs have been able to increase their market shares of manufactured goods in the United States. For example, the four NICs captured 18.6 percent of the developing countries' 21.2 percent share of total U.S. manufactured imports in 1987—up considerably from their 14.7 percent share in 1981. The Asian NICs also increased their U.S. market share in all major categories of manufactured goods (less nonferrous metals) between 1981 and 1987. Asian NIC manufactured exports to the U.S. rose in value from $21 billion in 1981 to $59 billion in 1987—an estimated 88 percent of the total value of developing countries' manufactured exports to the United States in 1987.

Currency negotiations. Since the unveiling of President Reagan's "free but fair" trade policy initiative in September 1985, the U.S. government has followed a two-track approach in negotiations on East Asian trade and monetary policies. While discussions on trade issues have, for the most part, been undertaken by the U.S. trade representative on a formal basis under section 301 of the 1974 Trade Act, discussions on exchange rates and macroeconomic policies with the NICs have been conducted more informally by the U.S. Treasury Department, with a view forcing them to pursue policies that would allow their currencies to reflect their economies' strong underlying fundamentals (G-6 Communiqué 1987).

Before 1985 the Asian NICs avoided any major misalignments in their exchange rates. After the Plaza agreement in September 1985 the exchange rates of Singapore and Hong Kong, on the one hand, and Taiwan and South Korea, on the other hand, followed opposite patterns. The Singapore and Hong Kong dollars tended to fluctuate in parallel with the U.S. dollar. But the Taiwan dollar and the South

Korean won did not begin to rise against the U.S. dollar for several years. Between 1985 and 1988 the dollar had fallen 83 percent against the yen but only 49 percent against the new Taiwan dollar and 34 percent against the South Korean won. As a result, Taiwanese and South Korean exporters gained a competitive edge in shipping to the United States, particularly from 1986 through 1987 (Cooper 1989).

In mid-1986 the Treasury Department began holding discussions with South Korea and Taiwan to influence authorities in those countries to allow the value of their currencies to reflect the underlying strength of their economies. The 1988 Trade Act provided an impetus to this process by requiring that the secretary of the Treasury issue periodic reports on exchange rate policy and determine which countries were manipulating their exchange rates to gain an unfair competitive advantage in international trade.

In addition to focusing on currency manipulation, the Treasury Department suggested that South Korea and Taiwan undertake other structural reforms to give greater emphasis to domestic consumption as a source of economic growth and to liberalize financial markets. The Treasury maintained that a combination of currency appreciation, trade liberalization, and increased government spending on infrastructure projects would help achieve the dual objectives of reducing excessive trade surpluses and increasing living standards at home (U.S. Senate 1989).

Both South Korea and Taiwan have been responsive to U.S. pressures. The currencies of both countries have appreciated further, contributing to a reduction in their trade surpluses. The appreciation of the new Taiwan dollar has been facilitated by the adoption of a more market-sensitive exchange rate system in April 1989. In the first month following the changes, the new Taiwan dollar appreciated 8 percent in nominal terms against the U.S. dollar in one month (U.S. Senate 1989).

Appreciation of the won accelerated in late 1988 after release of the first mandated Treasury Department report on exchange rate manipulation. Under pressures from exporters South Korean authorities resisted further significant won appreciation in 1989, reflecting concern over a slowdown in exports and failures of firms that came as a result of won appreciation and steep wage increases. In its October 1989 report the Treasury Department determined that Taiwan's currency was no longer undervalued but that the South Korean won still was. South Korean authorities rejected this conclusion by arguing that the current exchange rate was already bringing South Korea's trade surplus down to a low level.

South Korea and Taiwan have also made some adjustments in

their growth orientation. Vigorous increases in domestic demand powered economic growth in both countries during 1988. Spending on consumption, infrastructure projects, and productivity-enhancing investments in sophisticated technology have lessened their dependence on exports as the overwhelming source of economic growth. Hong Kong and Singapore to a lesser extent are also increasing their reliance on domestic demand for output growth. As described by a *World Financial Markets* report, "Taiwan is in the vanguard of this adjustment, Korea is in train, and Singapore and Hong Kong are just getting started" (World Financial Markets 1989).

Market-opening pressures. U.S. market-opening pressures have been directed mostly at South Korea and Taiwan. Both Hong Kong and Singapore maintain open policies applied to trade in goods, services, and investments. South Korea and Taiwan, however, have pursued more interventionist policies in promoting industrialization.

In response to U.S. pressures both South Korea and Taiwan have implemented an extensive series of reductions in both tariff and nontariff barriers. The liberalization measures adopted reflect a transition from the traditional perception of being poor and developing economies to that of being middle-ranking industrialized economies. Despite objective improvements, there appears to be much scope for both countries to do more to support the open trading system from which they have so greatly benefited. Government pronouncements and reports in both countries have reflected an awareness that more liberalization and opening of their economies to outside participation will be supportive of their own prosperity and security.

Nevertheless, South Korea's average tariff of 12 percent remains high. Agricultural commodities, in particular, are still shielded by high tariffs. South Korea also uses import bans to shield its agricultural sector, particularly on beef imports. U.S. efforts to open up South Korea's cigarette market in the mid-1980s proved extremely contentious. In addition, the United States has pressed South Korea to open up its banking and insurance sectors to foreign competition. Currently, South Korea has been designated by the United States for priority attention in regard to its restrictions on telecommunications equipment trade and for its inadequate protection of intellectual property rights. Barring some unilateral concessions, the United States may respond with retaliatory actions against South Korea.

Reducing Taiwan's high tariffs has been a principal U.S. market-opening objective. Taiwan's nominal average tariff rate was about 28 percent until 1986, but after several tariff cuts it is now about 16 percent. The U.S. government contends that more tariff cuts are necessary, particularly on meat products, fish, fresh fruits and vege-

TABLE 4-7
U.S. Trade with Asian NICs, 1985–1989
(billions of U.S. dollars)

	Exports	Imports	Balance	Balance as % of World Deficit
1985	16.5	39.1	−22.6	17.9
1986	17.5	46.1	−28.7	20.2
1987	22.9	57.7	−34.8	22.7
1988	34.2	63.2	−29.0	24.2
1989	38.2	62.9	−24.7	23.0

Source: U.S. Trade Representative, *Trade Net*. 1989 data are projections based on January–September data.

tables, textiles, and footwear. Through import quotas Taiwan also heavily restricts a variety of agricultural products.

As a result of bilateral negotiations Taiwan has reduced its nontariff barriers in the banking, insurance, wine, and tobacco markets. Although the Taiwanese have enacted laws to protect patents and copyrights, negotiations to improve protection of intellectual property have continued.

Trade Impact. The U.S. merchandise trade deficit with the Asian NICs increased from $23 billion in 1985 to $35 billion in 1987 (table 4-7). At its peak in 1987 the trade deficit with the Asian NICs accounted for nearly one-fourth of the total U.S. trade deficit. But by year-end 1989 the NIC surplus was reduced by $10 billion from 1987, to $25 billion. Despite this drop, it continued to constitute approximately 23 percent of the more than $100 billion U.S. trade deficit.

Taiwan accounted for nearly $4 billion, South Korea $3 billion, and Hong Kong $2.7 billion of the $10 billion improvement in the trade deficit from 1987 to 1989 (tables 4-8, 4-9, and 4-10). Taiwan still accounts for over half of the total NIC trade surplus and South Korea for one-fourth.

Most of the reduction in the U.S.–Asian NIC trade deficit has been due to an increase in U.S. exports. U.S. exports to the Asian NICs more than doubled from $16.5 billion in 1985 to over $38 billion in 1989. At the same time U.S. imports from the Asian NICs increased 62 percent, rising from $39 billion in 1985 to $63 billion in 1989.

The improvement in U.S. exports primarily reflects the effects of the decline in the value of the dollar against the South Korean won and the Taiwan dollar. Rapid economic growth and to a lesser extent more open markets also contributed to the pickup in U.S. exports.

TABLE 4-8
U.S. Trade with Taiwan, 1985–1989
(billions of U.S. dollars)

	Exports	Imports	Balance	Balance as % of World Deficit
1985	4.5	16.4	−11.9	9.5
1986	5.2	19.8	−14.6	10.3
1987	7.2	24.6	−17.4	11.4
1988	11.9	24.8	−12.9	10.6
1989	10.4	24.2	−13.7	12.7

Source: U.S. Trade Representative, *Trade Net*. All 1989 data are projections based on January–September data.

TABLE 4-9
U.S. Trade with South Korea, 1985–1989
(billions of U.S. dollars)

	Exports	Imports	Balance	Balance as % of World Deficit
1985	5.7	10.0	−4.3	3.4
1986	5.9	12.7	−6.8	4.8
1987	8.8	18.0	−9.3	6.1
1988	10.6	20.2	−9.6	7.9
1989	13.8	20.1	−6.3	5.9

Source: U.S. Trade Representative, *Trade Net*. All 1989 data are projections based on January–September data.

The decline in U.S.-NIC trade deficits in 1988 and 1989 appears to have ended a pattern of growing NIC surpluses with the United States. The Asian NICs have been able to lessen their dependence on the U.S. market. Increased reliance on the EC market has been one important factor in allowing them to begin to make this transition without undercutting economic growth.

The European Community as a Growing Market for NIC Exports

Current Trade Trends. For more balanced and harmonious trade relations to develop in the 1990s, the EC will have to become a more important market for the East Asian NICs. This is already occurring to a certain extent. Since 1985, the Asian NICs have increased their aggregate trade surplus with the EC from $300 million to almost $9 billion in 1988 (table 4-12). This success is largely a consequence of

TABLE 4-10
U.S. Trade with Hong Kong, 1985–1989
(billions of U.S. dollars)

	Exports	Imports	Balance	Balance as % of World Deficit
1985	2.8	8.4	−5.6	4.4
1986	3.0	8.9	−5.9	4.1
1987	4.0	9.9	−5.9	3.8
1988	6.0	10.2	−4.6	3.8
1989	6.6	9.7	−3.2	3.0

SOURCE: U.S. Trade Representative, *Trade Net*. All 1989 data are projections based on January–September data.

TABLE 4-11
U.S. Trade with Singapore, 1985–1989
(billions of U.S. dollars)

	Exports	Imports	Balance	Balance as % of World Deficit
1985	3.5	4.3	−0.8	0.6
1986	3.4	4.7	−1.4	1.0
1987	4.0	6.2	−2.2	1.4
1988	5.7	8.0	−2.3	1.9
1989	7.4	8.9	−1.5	1.4

SOURCE: U.S. Trade Representative, *Trade Net*. All 1989 data are projections based on January–September data.

TABLE 4-12
Asian NICs' Trade with the European Community, 1984–1988
(billions of U.S. dollars)

	Exports	Imports	Balance
1984	12.2	10.6	1.6
1985	11.6	11.3	0.3
1986	15.9	12.7	3.1
1987	24.3	17.9	6.5
1988	29.7	20.9	8.8

SOURCE: International Monetary Fund, *Directions of Trade*.

TABLE 4-13
HONG KONG'S TRADE WITH THE EUROPEAN COMMUNITY, 1984–1988
(billions of U.S. dollars)

	Exports	Imports	Balance
1984	4.1	3.2	0.9
1985	3.7	3.4	0.3
1986	5.1	4.1	1.0
1987	7.7	5.4	2.3
1988	9.4	6.3	3.1

SOURCE: International Monetary Fund, *Directions of Trade*.

TABLE 4-14
TAIWAN'S TRADE WITH THE EUROPEAN COMMUNITY, 1984–1988
(billions of U.S. dollars)

	Exports	Imports	Balance
1984	2.7	1.9	0.8
1985	2.6	2.0	0.6
1986	4.3	2.7	1.5
1987	6.9	4.3	2.7
1988	7.9	4.2	3.7

SOURCE: Trade Statistics, Republic of China.

two factors: European currency appreciation vis-à-vis the dollar, in which Asian NIC exports are denominated; and more aggressive marketing campaigns aimed at capturing greater shares of the European market for consumer goods.

Taiwan and Hong Kong have been the most successful exporters to the EC. Rapid export growth has accounted for a large increase in each country's trade surplus with the EC. Hong Kong's exports rose by about 150 percent while imports did not quite double from 1985 to 1988, thus contributing to an improvement of $2.8 billion in Hong Kong's trade position with the EC (table 4-13). Similarly, Taiwan's exports rose faster than imports from 1985 to 1988, thus contributing to a $3.1 billion improvement in Taiwan's trade balance with the EC (table 4-14). Together Taiwan and Hong Kong accounted for nearly 70 percent of the improvement in the Asian NICs' trade balance with the EC over this period.

South Korea also has an important and growing trading relationship with the EC. By 1987 the EC had become South Korea's third largest trading partner, accounting for 13.9 percent of its total exports

TABLE 4-15
SOUTH KOREA'S TRADE WITH THE EUROPEAN COMMUNITY, 1984–1988
(billions of U.S. dollars)

	Exports	Imports	Balance
1984	3.3	2.8	0.5
1985	3.3	3.0	0.3
1986	4.3	3.2	1.1
1987	6.6	4.6	2.0
1988	7.6	5.5	2.1

SOURCE: International Monetary Fund, *Directions of Trade*.

TABLE 4-16
SINGAPORE'S TRADE WITH THE EUROPEAN COMMUNITY, 1984–1988
(billions of U.S. dollars)

	Exports	Imports	Balance
1984	2.1	2.7	−0.6
1985	2.0	2.9	−0.9
1986	2.2	2.7	−0.5
1987	6.1	6.9	−0.8
1988	6.8	6.9	−0.1

SOURCE: International Monetary Fund, *Directions of Trade*.

and 11 percent of its total imports. South Korea nearly doubled its trade surplus with the EC from 1986 to 1987 and 1988 (table 4-15).[2] Singapore is the only NIC still running a trade deficit with the EC (see table 4-16).

Current EC Restrictions. In mid-1989 the Roundtable of European Industrialists expressed fear that the trade trends discussed above are indicative of a domino process, whereby one European industry after another will fall to East Asian domination unless countermeasures are adopted. Speaking on behalf of many European industrialists, the managing director of Fiat called for a "common defense and retaliatory policy" to fight the "economic colonization of [Europe]" (FEER 1989a).

In response to industry pressure, the EC Commission announced its determination to "apply vigilantly the instruments of commercial policy it has at its disposal" to safeguard European interests and prevent nonmember countries from obtaining any cost-free benefits from the economic integration of its twelve member states (FEER 1988b).

The trade policy instruments available to the EC Commission to protect the interests of domestic firms are quite similar to those employed by the United States. They include escape clause legislation and a New Commercial Policy Instrument considered to be a version of section 301 of the U.S. Trade Act of 1974. Unlike section 301, which has been increasingly used by the U.S. executive branch to fight unfair trade practices, the EC's New Commercial Policy Instrument has rarely been applied; rather, the EC Commission has increasingly opted to use its antidumping and antisubsidy legislation in tandem with voluntary export restraints to stem the flow of imports from Japan, the Asian NICs, and state trading companies.

Voluntary export restraints. Asian NIC exports to the EC are currently constrained by a variety of restrictions. In 1988 the EC accounted for 138 of the 261 known voluntary export restraints applied by industrial countries (excluding quotas concluded under the Multifiber Agreement—MFA). The number of such restraints applied on either an EC-wide or a national basis doubled between September 1987 and April 1988, compared with a 74 percent increase for the rest of the world (Kelly et al. 1988, 14, 92).

European voluntary export restraints are generally negotiated on a government-to-government basis and are currently maintained on imports of steel, textiles, clothing, agricultural and food products, machine tools, automobiles, and electronic products. Japan and the East Asian NICs are among those countries most affected by the EC's quantitative restrictions, with such restraints currently imposed on eighty-nine Japanese and thirty South Korean products. European trade barriers now affect over 40 percent of all South Korean exports to the EC (Harrison et al. 1989; Business Korea 1988b).

Significant restrictions on the export of textiles from the Asian NICs to the EC were put into place during the negotiation of the third MFA in 1981–1982. At that time the EC secured cutbacks in the quotas of its dominant suppliers (Hong Kong, South Korea, Taiwan, and Macao) ranging from 4 to 8 percent in the "very sensitive" group I (textiles and clothing) product categories, coupled with extremely low growth rates for future years (Howell and Noellert 1986). The EC continues to restrict textile exports from the Asian NICs under the fourth MFA, which covers the five-year period 1987–1991.

Although Sir Leon Brittan, EC commissioner for competition policy, has strongly rejected EC-wide quotas to restrict imports after 1992, there are strong pressures for continuing some form of quotas during a "transition period." How long the transition period will last and which industries will be covered remains uncertain. In addition to textiles and apparel, EC producers of cars, footwear, and consumer electronics are lobbying Brussels for protection.

Antidumping procedures. In June 1987 the EC Commission introduced new antidumping rules to restrict cut-price dumping of Asian parts and components used in "screwdriver" assembly plants. The new regulations enable the EC to take action if the commission finds that more than a specified portion of components used in a particular assembly plant are imported from the investor's country of origin; in the case of Asian screwdriver plants, at least 40 percent of parts and components must ostensibly be sourced from European firms to avoid antidumping penalties. The EC argues that the new regulations are necessary to counter East Asian attempts to circumvent European antidumping duties through increased use of screwdriver plants. For their part, Asian exporters charge that European manufacturers are attempting to shore up their post-1992 defenses by expanding the number and scope of antidumping investigations against Asian manufactured products as a means of increasing the local content of products assembled in Europe and forcing Asian companies to transfer new technologies.

After the 1987 modifications in the EC's antidumping law, eight antidumping actions were brought against South Korean firms in 1988, and another nine investigations were pending in 1989. The bulk of EC antidumping actions against South Korea involve consumer electronics goods and office equipment, although investigations are also being conducted against South Korean pianos and photo albums. Hong Kong has also been the focus of eight EC antidumping investigations since 1987 on its exports of audiocassettes and videocassettes, televisions, cellular telephones, tungsten, silicon, photograph albums, and cotton denim cloth.

Some Asian exporters allege that the EC's method of calculating dumping duties is arcane and unfair, aimed at inflating the manufacturer's domestic price by deducting certain charges from EC prices that are not deducted from Asian prices. Furthermore, it is argued that the EC Commission penalizes any new exporter from a dumping country even if it is not named in a given ruling.

Asian companies have no real legal recourse against EC anti-Asian dumping decisions, given that the European Court of Justice, which arbitrates such disputes, has rubber-stamped most EC antidumping findings over the past five years. The commission rebuts such criticism by claiming that its methods conform to the GATT's antidumping code. Some observers note that the arbitrariness of the EC's antidumping legislation allows the commission to pursue industrial policy goals beyond those relating to short-term trade problems (Economist 1989).

Generalized System of Preferences. In 1986 the EC revised its GSP scheme for developing countries to graduate products from countries with a per capita income exceeding $2,000 whose share of EC industrial imports of the product concerned exceeded 20 percent of the total import market. The exports of South Korea, Hong Kong, and Singapore were among those affected. In late 1987 GSP benefits on all products were withdrawn from South Korea on the grounds that it provides discriminatory protection for intellectual property rights. The removal of GSP benefits was damaging to South Korea, given that over one-fifth of its total exports to the EC had been entering duty free. Finally, the EC decided to withdraw GSP benefits beginning in 1988 for countries with per capita income exceeding $2,000 whose share of EC textile imports exceeds 10 percent of the total market (Kelly et al. 1988, 101).

Singapore, with a per capita income of $7,673, could be affected by this new requirement when its GSP benefits come up for review in 1990. Currently, eight of Singapore's exports that receive preferential treatment under the EC's GSP program are subject to quota restrictions, including color television sets, telecommunications equipment, semiconductor devices, and certain machine tools.

Potential Impact of EC 1992. The reduction of internal market barriers will provide a significant boost to the European economy, resulting in faster growth, more jobs, and lower consumer prices. A booming Europe, in turn, should stimulate the world economy and lead to increased demand for foreign products. Foreign exporters, particularly the Asian NICs, will also benefit from the convenience and transaction-cost reduction in trading with a single market. Instead of having to meet twelve different sets of health, safety, and technical standards, foreign exporters will be faced with a broadly uniform set of standards.

Nevertheless, demands by prominent EC officials for reciprocity in trade and banking services, increased use of EC antidumping actions, and stricter language on European rules of origin gave rise in early 1988 to fears that the EC was constructing a "Fortress Europe"— fears exacerbated by the lack of any official statement by the EC on the kind of external trade regime envisioned for the single market. In reaction to East Asian and U.S. concerns, the EC Commission issued a detailed statement in October 1988 on the EC's intentions toward its trading partners. The document, entitled "Europe World Partner," sought to dispel the notion of a Fortress Europe by highlighting the

EC's dependence on external markets as a percentage of GNP and emphasizing its commitment to the GATT and previously negotiated bilateral agreements. While it did admit that national protection might be replaced with EC-wide protection in certain cases, the commission sought to reassure its trading partners that overall levels of European protection would not increase because of the deregulatory nature of the 1992 plan. Foreign concerns, nevertheless, have centered on three elements of the EC 1992 plan: reciprocity, rules of origin, and product standards.

Reciprocity. One of the key elements of the EC's external trade policy for 1992 is "reciprocity," a term used by the EC Commission to denote the conditions under which access to the single market is to be provided to Europe's trading partners. In its general policy statement on reciprocity, issued in October 1988, the EC Commission noted that "the EC reserves the right to make access to the benefits of 1992 for non-EC firms conditional upon a guarantee of similar opportunities—or at least non-discriminatory opportunities—in those firms' own countries (EC News 1988). With the exception of the financial services sector, the commission has purposely left vague both the definition and the future application of reciprocity within its external trade policy. That vagueness has fomented fears among Europe's trading partners that in sensitive sectors the EC may abandon its commitment to such long-established principles of free trade as unconditional most-favored-nation treatment and national treatment.

The issue of reciprocity is potentially the most dangerous aspect of EC 1992 for East Asian countries. This is especially true for Japan and South Korea, which have large trade surpluses with the EC and myriad barriers to foreign goods and services. A series of speeches by European political and business leaders in the spring of 1988 clearly established that East Asia was the main target of European demands for reciprocity. In April 1988 Umberto Agnelli, deptuy chairman of Fiat, called on the EC Commission to use the single market for the benefit of Europeans first and "negotiate very specific quid pro quos" with Japan and the Asian NICs. In a subsequent speech the EC's former trade commissioner, Willy de Clercq, sent an even more emphatic message to the Asians when he stated that the EC would "use entry to the newly integrated market as a bargaining chip to demand reciprocal trade concessions from Japan and the newly industrialized Asian countries that currently restrict European products" (*LA Times* 1988).

The specter of new entry barriers to the European market led the Japanese to lobby Brussels vigorously in the ensuing months of 1988 on behalf of its trade interests and those of its East Asian neighbors. Japan was joined in such efforts by the United States, which was concerned about the impact that reciprocity would have on the access of U.S. financial institutions to the European market after 1992. In order to allay fears that reciprocity demands would be the cornerstone of a new Fortress Europe, the EC Commission issued a policy statement in October 1988 that incorporated the following negative definition of reciprocity:

> [Reciprocity] does not mean that all partners must make the same concessions nor even that the Community will insist on concessions from all its partners. For example, it will not ask the developing countries to make concessions that are beyond their means. Nor does reciprocity mean that the Community will ask its partners to adopt legislation identical to its own. Nor does it mean that the Community is seeking sectoral reciprocity based on comparative trade levels, this being a concept whose introduction into the United States legislation has been fought by the Community (EC News 1988, 4).

The EC will demand an equivalency of market opportunities in those areas not covered by multinational rules, such as the insurance, broadcasting, air and road transport, and financial services sectors. With regard to financial services, the Council of Ministers adopted a less stringent application of reciprocity than that sought by France and Italy, based on "national treatment" criteria outlined in the Second Banking Directive and subsequent modifications thereof. National treatment in this instance means that any country that treats EC financial institutions in the same manner as that accorded to local institutions would be given full rights, including a single EC banking license. The EC's banking proposal is essentially aimed at the Japanese, who control 10 percent of the deposit base in Europe, while European banks control only 0.35 percent of the deposit base in Japan (Europe 1988). EC demands for national treatment with effective market access in financial services could also affect South Korea and Taiwan, as these countries will ultimately need to establish financial concerns in Europe to service their growing manufacturing investments in the region.

In sum, the extent to which the benefits of the integrated EC market will be extended to third countries will depend on reciprocal market-opening measures by the EC's major trading partners. The EC is pursuing such measures both bilaterally and within the context of the Uruguay Round. In this regard reciprocity should be less of an issue for Singapore and Hong Kong, which are open to foreign investment and trade, and more preoccupying to South Korea and Taiwan, which impose greater restrictions on the flow of foreign goods and services. European demands for reciprocity in the area of services have generated concerns among countries like South Korea that their highly protected shipping, insurance, and financial services sectors would be forced to deal with European competition to gain access to the single market.

Local-content and rules-of-origin requirements. Local-content and rules-of-origin restrictions in the EC 1992 plan have the potential to distort international trade and investment flows, given that such requirements are designed to force foreign companies to use domestic suppliers as a major source of parts and components or, alternatively, to transfer important manufacturing and technological processes to European firms. The EC is adopting unofficial local-content requirements on a sectoral basis to protect the European market from cheap Asian automobile and consumer electronics imports, as well as to encourage local sourcing and technology transfer. Through the use of local-content and rules-of-origin requirements, the EC has made it clear that it intends to promote its electronics industry in particular by forcing East Asian companies with plants in Europe to use European electronics components.

EC trade officials deny the existence of local-content requirements in Europe in light of their nonconformity with GATT rules. Thus the EC's legislation refers not to the percentage of components and parts that must be produced locally but to the percentage that must not be imported from the investor's own country to determine a product's origin. The EC definition of rules of origin is derived from the Kyoto Customs Convention of 1965. It states that origin is to be based on "the country in which the last substantial process or operation that is economically justified was performed . . . resulting in the manufacture of a new product or representing an important stage of manufacture" (Harrison et al. 1989, 43). To guarantee European origin in sophisticated or import-sensitive product categories, the commission has found it necessary to adopt origin regulations on a product-by-product basis. Because EC rules permit negotiated local content, this process has been executed through individual negotiations with companies on the amount of European sourcing required, many times as a quid pro quo for investment subsidies and incentives.

In February 1989 the EC Commission adopted new rules of origin for semiconductors that redefine the "last substantial process" as the diffusion stage rather than the previously accepted assembly stage. The community's intent apparently was to accelerate the transfer of

U.S., Japanese, and South Korean semiconductor diffusion technology—the etching of the microcircuit onto the semiconductor wafer—to those European firms that do not possess this vital technology. Although East Asian industrialists are anxious not to offend European sensitivities in light of potential sales to the single market, they are angered by the seemingly arbitrary method with which the EC Commission is imposing local-content and origin regulations through antidumping actions. Asian manufacturers cite poor quality, high prices, and uncertain delivery schedules as the main reasons why they have been slow to comply with the community's rigorous local-content requirements.

Local-content regulations are also being applied to East Asian manufacturers of machinery, electronics, and electrical goods, in response to the proliferation of screwdriver plants set up by those countries to avoid EC antidumping penalties. Changes made in the EC's antidumping legislation in 1987 now require that a minimum of 40 percent of the parts and components used by Asian plants assembling consumer electronics products be of European or third-country origin, or the manufacturers will be slapped with antidumping duties. Similarly, radios, televisions, and ball bearings will be deemed European only when 35 to 45 percent of their value is added in the EC, and for videocassette recorders the local content required is 45 percent. Products and services destined for public procurement projects must also contain at least 50 percent local content, with companies meeting this requirement favored over suppliers of "non-EC" products and services.

Product standards. One of the most important tasks in moving the twelve member states of the EC toward a single market has been the harmonization of national standards, testing, and certification procedures. If EC product standards are not established in a transparent and fair manner but rather are designed to impede foreign access to the internal market, exporters lacking a substantial manufacturing presence in the EC could find themselves discriminated against after 1992. Because the majority of Asian exporters are too small or too provincial to invest in a manufacturing plant in Europe, they could find themselves shut out of both the EC standards-setting process and the single market after 1992.

Over 200 EC directives have already been issued that seek to integrate the approximately 100,000 industrial standards and technical regulations currently in force in the EC. The EC's new approach to standards will allow products that have been granted market access in one European member state to circulate freely in all other EC countries provided that they do not impair the health and safety of consumers (USDC).

EC-wide standards have now been established for pressure vessels, construction materials, electrical interference, machine safety, and toys. New toy standards, for example, were introduced in January 1990, but foreign firms had no advance notice. Asian companies, which produce most of the world's toys, are worried that they will not have enough time to adjust to the new standards and thus lost market share to better informed local suppliers. Unlike the situation in the United States, non-European nations are not allowed to vote on standards or participate in working group meetings and are made aware of the draft standard only when it is released to the public. That lack of access to the European standards-setting process has generated concern that new EC standards designed without foreign input will impede effective access to the integrated market.

The EC justifies its nontransparent standards-setting process by arguing that international standards, where they exist, will be adopted as the standard of first choice. International standards, however, do not exist for many products because the certification process can take up to fifteen years to complete; furthermore, the EC has reserved the right to change international standards when necessary to conform with broad 1992 requirements, thus weakening the EC's commitment to adopt international standards. Japan and the East Asian NICs are not the only countries denied access to the EC standards-setting process; U.S. standards organizations and companies have requested observer status at CEN (European Committee for Standardization) and CENELEC (European Committee for Electrotechnical Standardization) meetings, but these requests have been denied. Thus it is in the interests of the United States, Japan, the Asian NICs, and other major European trading partners that the EC adopt as many international standards as possible.

NIC Strategies to Deal with EC 1992. While U.S. corporations have generally welcomed the free market pronouncements of EC officials in recent months, East Asian industrialists remain highly skeptical that they will be able to profit from an open, integrated European market to the same extent as their American counterparts. East Asian attitudes toward EC 1992 were best described by an official of the Federation of Korean Industries: "Whatever liberalist banner the EC may hang, the nature of the beast is that an economic bloc will become more protectionist" (Business Korean 1988a). This statement reflects the fact that the East Asian NICs are now the target of the same restrictive trade policies and antidumping actions once reserved for Japan. Like Japan, the NICs now recognize that to shift their exports successfully away from the American market toward Europe, they need to become "good corporate insiders" by 1992. This means that they must increase their investment in Europe and integrate their manufacturing operations as far as possible into local European economies and societies before the 1992 deadline, in order to continue their rapid penetration of the European market and with the least amount of trade friction.

South Korea and Taiwan. Following in the footsteps of Japan, which has $25 billion invested in Europe, South Korea is seeking to develop a sizable manufacturing presence in the EC as a first step in its strategy to circumvent protectionist trade barriers and antidumping suits. In the beginning of 1989 South Korea's manufacturing investment in Europe amounted to approximately $40 million spread over 65 projects, the bulk of which were concentrated in the consumer electronics sector. With the exception of Hyundai, all of South Korea's major business groups are now present in Europe, producing goods ranging from videocassette recorders and microwave ovens to color television sets. According to the South Korean Ministry of Trade and Investment, South Korean companies plan to increase their presence in Europe to 100 manufacturing and trading concerns by 1992. Encouraged by Japan's rapid conquest of 10 percent of the European car market, two South Korean firms, Hyundai and Sunkyong, are also contemplating plans to invest in the European vehicle industry before 1992.

Similar strategies are being pursued by Taiwan, which unveiled an "EC-directed trade plan" in 1988 to increase exports to Europe from their current $10 billion to $18 billion in 1992 (Korean Business Review 1988). To attain this goal over 100 Taiwanese companies have opened product distribution or purchasing centers in Europe in recent years, as the first step toward locating manufacturing plants in the EC. To consolidate its "Look Europe" strategy, Taiwan's Ministry of Economic Affairs hopes to persuade 300 to 600 companies to invest in Europe before 1992. Large Taiwanese electronics firms like Tatung and Acer, flush with cash and facing a tight domestic labor market, are already investing heavily in Europe with the hope of capturing up to 10 percent of the regional market for color televisions and personal computers.

Both South Korea and Taiwan realize that the key to a successful manufacturing presence in Europe is the fostering of local subcontractor relationships to increase European content and avoid antidumping actions. To this end South Korea's electronics giant Lucky Goldstar recently opted to use European-made integrated circuits in its consumer electronics products. Similarly, Goldstar's largest rival, Samsung, will no longer import semiconductors from South Korea but will begin to manufacture them locally using European components. To facilitate subcontractor relationships, Taiwanese and South Korean subsidiaries are hiring local managers, increasing managerial and language training to prepare South Korean executives better for the differences among local European markets, and expanding corporate marketing and cultural exchange activities.

Another tactic used by Taiwan and South Korea to facilitate the entry of their products into the EC and improve their image with EC trade officials has been to increase imports of goods and services from European firms. Taiwan, which imported $6.2 billion from the EC in 1987, hopes to boost this figure to $17 billion by 1992 by extending to Europe trade terms similar to those granted to the United States. Taiwan has already liberalized its tobacco market, lowered its tariffs for European textile machinery, farm goods, and light industrial products, and granted European firms an edge in bidding for major construction projects traditionally won by U.S. firms (FEER 1988a).

South Korea has tried to expand European imports by drawing up a list of 215 imports currently sourced from Japan in which European manufacturers are likely to be competitive, with emphasis on the production equipment and high-technology sectors. To expedite the importation of advanced technologies from Europe, South Korea has sought to promote cooperation in the fields of semiconductors, computers, machinery, and energy with Great Britain, automation and material industry technologies with West Germany, precision chemical industry technologies and genetic engineering and ocean technologies with France, and engineering, metallic, and electronic industry technologies with Belgium. South Korea is also making efforts to increase imports of traditional European products, such as cigarettes, farm produce, dairy products, chocolates, alcoholic beverages, and textiles.

Hong Kong. Unlike South Korea's and Taiwan's, Hong Kong's manufacturing presence in Europe is largely limited to textile plants in Great Britain. Rather than invest in the European market, Hong Kong entrepreneurs have sought access to the EC by setting up assembly plants for export in neighboring mainland China, which enjoys a special relationship with the EC because of the size of its potential consumer market. Because Hong Kong exporters are largely small to medium-sized firms, they lack the necessary capital and managerial expertise to undertake significant investments in the EC, evidenced by the fact that some 93 percent of all Hong Kong firms employ nineteen or fewer employees. Consequently, Hong Kong government officials have sought to counter European protectionism and antidumping suits against their products in two ways: by stepping up trade fairs in Europe through the Hong Kong Trade Development Council to assist local exporters and by lobbying Geneva for changes in the GATT's outdated antidumping code. This campaign parallels similar efforts by Japanese trade officials, who requested the formation of a special GATT panel in 1988 to review the legality of EC antidumping regulations. This is the first time that Japan has invoked paragraph two of the GATT's Article 23 disputes settlement mechanism, an act that is significant in that it reflects a greater recognition of and reliance on GATT rules by East Asian countries.

Singapore. Despite Singapore's trade deficit with the EC in 1988, Singaporean companies are also concerned about the possibility of increased EC protectionism, particularly in the trade, direct investment, and banking areas. Consequently, the government of Singapore is urging local companies to invest in Europe before 1992 as a means of establishing local footholds in the integrated market, allowing tax write-offs on losses incurred in approved investments. The Singapore Trade Development Board has been active in the organization of trade fairs in Europe to promote local products and recently formed an International Direct Investments Board to provide logistical support to companies seeking to establish manufacturing concerns in the EC.

Because local firms tend to lack the financial strength and marketing expertise to undertake direct investments in the EC, the Singaporean government is encouraging companies to enter into joint ventures with European firms in the electronics, industrial machinery, telecommunications, aerospace, pharmaceutical, and chemical sectors as a means of gaining managerial expertise and exposure in the European market. The government is also encouraging local firms to invest in countries that are considering membership in the EC, such as Turkey, Austria, and Norway, as an indirect means of penetrating the regional market.

East Asian Economic Integration

Japan's growing role in Asia and various geopolitical developments are knitting the NICs closer into the fabric of an Asian trading community. In 1988, according to GATT data, intraregional merchandise trade grew 33 percent to $259 billion, making the Asian-Pacific region the fastest-growing trading area and the third in its share of global trade. At current growth rates intra-Asian trade will surpass the value of Asia's trade with the United States and Canada by the turn of the century (Jones 1989).

Closer economic link among the countries of East Asia hold out the promise that they will be able to sustain economic growth without overdependence on the U.S. market, reduce their vulnerability to a downturn in the U.S. economy, and eventually help alleviate the problem of global trade imbalances. At the same time the expansion of intraregional trade might develop in a manner that simply shifts the Japanese and NIC trade surpluses to the rest of Asia. Whether the United States and Europe would be prepared to accept Japanese and NIC trade surpluses generated from lower-cost bases of production in China and countries of the Association of Southeast Asian Nations remains to be seen. How the United States and Europe react to this evolution of intraregional trade and investment flows will have a bearing on whether the region moves to establish more formal consultative mechanisms.

Japan's Growing Role. *A strong yen.* The rapid appreciation of the Japanese yen since 1985 has been a major force for increasing intraregional trade and investment ties. From 1985 to 1987 the yen nearly doubled in value, strengthening from about 240 yen to the dollar to about 135 to the dollar. The appreciated yen has influenced a large number of Japanese corporations to relocate mostly labor-intensive and standard production technologies throughout the rest of Asia.

The high yen propelled a boom in Japan's imports in 1987 and 1988, particularly from the Asian NICs. Between 1985 and 1988 NIC exports to Japan rose $15 billion, from $9.8 billion in 1985 to $25 billion in 1988. In the process Japanese imports from the Asian NICs as a share of total Japanese imports increased from 7.5 percent in 1985 to over 13 percent in 1988.

The Asian NICs have accounted for the major portion of the growth in Japan's imports of manufactured goods, which accounted for 50 percent of total Japanese imports in 1989 (table 4-17). In 1985 the NICs accounted for $5.7 billion, or about 14 percent of Japan's total imports of manufactured goods. Based on phenomenal growth rates of 37 percent in 1986, 59 percent in 1987, and 46 percent in 1988, the NICs in 1988 were accounting for about 20 percent of Japan's growing manufactured imports. In contrast, the U.S. share fell from 33 percent in 1986 to 25 percent in 1988.

Most of the increase in NIC manufactured exports has been concentrated in fairly simple and standardized, low-value-added, consumer goods. Items such as apparel, calculators, black and white and color television sets, radio cassette recorders, fans, and cameras

TABLE 4-17
TRENDS IN JAPAN'S MANUFACTURED IMPORTS, 1985–1988
(hundreds of millions of U.S. dollars)

	From the World		From the United States		From the EC		From the NICs		Manufactured Imports Ratio (%)
	Amount	Growth rate (%)	Amount	Growth rate (%)	Amount	Growth rate (%)	Amount	Growth rate (%)	
1985	402	−1	142	2	77	−5	57	−1	31
1986	528	31	176	24	120	55	78	37	42
1987	660	25	177	1	151	27	125	59	44
1988	918	39	235	33	208	37	182	46	49

SOURCE: Ministry of Finance, Japan.

have made major increases in market share. The bulk of these items are produced in the Asian NICs, and a significant portion of them are produced by Japanese affiliates located in South Korea, Taiwan, Singapore, or Hong Kong.

At the same time an increasing amount of high-value-added NIC products are now reaching the Japanese market. The growing technical sophistication of the NICs and the expansion of their after-sales servicing capabilities are forcing Japanese corporations to introduce higher technological and value-added products.

The increase in imports of standardized, ready-to-consume durables reflects some change in Japanese attitudes generally and toward the Asian NICs specifically. In the past, Asian NIC products suffered from a reputation of being cheap but of poor quality. But in recent years the Japanese press and ministries have been taking a much more positive attitude toward the Asian NICs.

Increased financial links. The more favorable attitude toward the products of the Asian NICs is substantially related to the rise in Japanese investment in these countries since 1985. In March 1989 Japanese investment in Asia totaled over $32 billion, or about 17 percent of Japan's $186 billion in direct investments. This total included $10 billion invested in Indonesia, $6 billion in Hong Kong, $4 billion in Singapore, $3 billion in South Korea, $2 billion in China, and almost $2 billion in Taiwan (Keizai Koho Center 1990).

Many of the new Japanese investments are geared to developing production networks with components of final products sourced throughout Asia. Nissan Motors, for example, has planned a production network across Southeast Asian nations. Thailand will produce the diesel engines and molds for stamped parts. Indonesia will provide mechanical parts, the Philippines wire harnesses, and Malaysia clutches and electrical parts. By 1995 Nissan hopes to produce 120,000 vehicles in the region (Nanto 1989).

Japan's direct investment flows are reinforced by its large and growing foreign aid program. About 70 percent of Japan's rapidly growing $10 billion annual economic aid program is concentrated in Asia. The funding goes primarily for technology-intensive infrastructure projects. While an increasingly large portion of the procurement associated with Japanese aid is not formally tied to purchases of Japanese equipment, Japan tends to tie the engineering and consultancy portion of Japanese loans to Japanese business. Once the detailed specifications are drawn up by Japanese firms, procurement of major capital equipment is awarded de facto to Japanese companies (Preeg 1989).

As a result of these trends, some Japanese economists have

TABLE 4-18
ASIAN NICs' TRADE WITH JAPAN, 1984–1988
(billions of U.S. dollars)

	Exports	Imports	Balance
1984	11.1	26.0	−14.9
1985	11.4	24.5	−13.0
1986	13.5	31.4	−17.9
1987	20.5	41.3	−20.8
1988	26.0	51.5	−25.5

SOURCE: International Monetary Fund, *Directions of Trade*.

argued that the division of labor between Japan and Asia is changing from a vertical mode (featuring Japanese manufactured exports to the rest of Asia in return for basic materials) to a horizontal mode (featuring a growing intra-Asian trade in manufactured goods).[3] This kind of restructuring of the trade relationships could lessen long-standing Asian concerns that trade with Japan means importing high-value-added manufactured goods in return for low-value-added natural resource–based products. A lessening of this sensitivity, combined with the expanding trade and investment links, could also help create an atmosphere conducive to greater policy coordination among the countries in the region.

NIC trade deficits with Japan. A more open Japanese market and a restructuring of Japan's trade with the NICs and other countries in Asia offer opportunities not only for lessening the dependence of the NICs on the U.S. market but also for the development of a different triangular trading relationship among the United States, the NICs, and Japan. A more open Japanese market provides opportunities for the NICs further to reduce their reliance on the U.S. market, and the fast-growing NIC economies provide growing export opportunities for the United States in intermediate and capital goods as well as in finished products.

It is not at all clear, however, that this pattern is taking hold. The Asian NICs continue in a pattern of increasing trade deficits with Japan (table 4-18). In 1985 the deficit was $13 billion, but by 1988 it had steadily climbed to $25 billion. Hong Kong runs the largest individual deficits, followed by Taiwan, Singapore, and South Korea (see tables 4-19, 4-20, and 4-21). A reduction of U.S. trade deficits through a restructuring of the triangular trading relationship thus still appears to be mostly a theoretical possibility.

The NICs' ballooning trade deficits are due to a number of

TABLE 4-19
HONG KONG'S TRADE WITH JAPAN, 1984–1988
(billions of U.S. dollars)

	Exports	Imports	Balance
1984	1.3	6.7	−5.4
1985	1.3	6.8	−5.5
1986	1.7	7.2	−5.5
1987	2.5	9.2	−6.7
1988	2.1	11.7	−9.6

SOURCE: International Monetary Fund, *Directions of Trade*.

TABLE 4-20
SINGAPORE'S TRADE WITH JAPAN, 1984–1988
(billions of U.S. dollars)

	Exports	Imports	Balance
1984	2.0	5.3	−3.3
1985	2.1	4.5	−2.4
1986	1.9	5.0	−3.1
1987	2.6	6.6	−4.0
1988	3.4	9.6	−6.2

SOURCE: International Monetary Fund, *Directions of Trade*.

TABLE 4-21
TAIWAN'S TRADE WITH JAPAN, 1984–1988
(billions of U.S. dollars)

	Exports	Imports	Balance
1984	3.2	6.4	−3.2
1985	3.5	5.6	−2.1
1986	4.5	8.3	−3.8
1987	7.0	11.8	−4.8
1988	8.7	14.8	−6.1

SOURCE: Trade Statistics, Republic of China.

factors, including Japan's high export competitiveness, the procurement decisions of Japanese affiliates operating in Asia, and continued Japanese reluctance to cede domestic production capability to foreign sources. Japan's exports to the NICs made up 19 percent of its total exports in 1988, up from 13 percent in 1985. A large portion of

Japanese exports consists of parts and intermediate goods. South Korea, for example, is highly dependent on parts and intermediate goods from Japan. In 1982 almost half of South Korea's imports of components came from Japan, and South Korea's trade deficit with Japan in components amounted to 60 percent of its overall trade deficit with Japan (Hanazaki 1989, 103).

The procurement decisions of Japanese affiliates operating in Asia could also account for the worsening of the NIC trade balances with Japan. Japanese affiliates typically procure much less in parts and basic material from local sources than comparable foreign companies. In addition, they tend to produce much more for domestic consumption or third-country export than to export back to Japan. In the long run more outward procurement practices and a commitment to export more back to Japan may be necessary to reverse the trade deficits.

Various Japanese ministries have maintained that exporting back to Japan is becoming more prevalent among Japanese affiliates. According to one survey of the Ministry of International Trade and Industry, 15 percent of the output of Japanese companies operating in Asia was exported back to Japan in 1986–1987, and much higher percentages are predicted in the future.

While some evidence suggests that Japanese procurement practices are changing (for example, electrical machinery parts and precision machinery parts produced by Japanese affiliates now constitute a significant portion of total NIC exports to Japan), it may take many years for the imbalance in intracorporate trade to materialize. In 1987, for example, Japanese subsidiaries shipped $47 billion to their parent companies in Japan but imported $97 billion worldwide, a $50 billion surplus.

Japan still registers trade surpluses with the NICs in a wide range of standardized manufactured goods, such as textile fibers and chemicals. The NICs hold a competitive edge in producing many of these products. Japan's import penetration percentages remain low in a number of industries, providing wide scope for further penetration, especially by Asian NICs (Hanazaki 1989, 105).

Considerable scope for increased imports is also indicated by Japan's per capita consumption of imported finished goods (excluding processed foods). According to Japan's Economic Planning Agency, Japan's per capita consumption of these goods is only one-third that of the United States and one-fifth that of West Germany.

Geopolitical Changes. A variety of geopolitical conditions helped spur the NICs into becoming super exporters to the United States and other distant developed countries. Today major changes in those same geopolitical conditions are increasing the possibilities for the NICs to trade with less-developed countries closer to home.

Political conflicts in the 1950s and 1960s severed the ties of all four NICs from their traditional markets. The Chinese Communist victory of 1949 and the Korean War of 1950 severed the ties of Taiwan, Hong Kong, and South Korea to their hinterlands. Singapore was expelled from the Malaysian Federation in 1965 with a somewhat similar psychological effect. These disruptions no doubt had a profound psychological impact on the NIC populations, contributing to a certain mind-set that survival was intimately bound up with succeeding on the international trade battlefield (Whitehead 1989).

Growing recognition in both China and the Soviet Union that Marxism-Leninism and the socialist strategy of development had severe deficiencies has led to bold economic reform programs in both countries. The reform process in both countries, accompanied by the decline in postwar ideological tensions, has created new opportunities for the Asian NICs to trade closer to home.

Economic liberalization in China. China's "open door" policy, begun in 1978, has been accompanied by a large increase in external trade and inflow of foreign direct investment. Between 1979 and 1987 Chinese exports expanded 17 percent and imports 18 percent. Most analysts believe that the trend toward integration into the world economy is not likely to be substantially reversed by the military crackdown in June 1989.

While Japan has been the largest foreign investor in China, the NICs have all been active. It is estimated that over 2 million workers in Guangdong province are employed by Hong Kong firms (SRI International 1989). Taiwan and South Korea, despite lacking diplomatic relations with Beijing, have increased their trade and investment relations with China through Hong Kong. Singapore has also been very active in joint ventures in the Mandarin-speaking areas of China, particularly in turnkey projects such as hotels.

Most of China's increased trade has been transacted with neighboring Asian states. This heavy concentration is evidenced by changes in both the export and the import orientation of the NICs. In 1980, for example, China took just 2 percent of the NICs' exports, but by 1988 this percentage had increased to 8.5 percent. China's share of NIC imports went from 6 percent to 10 percent during this period (Morgan Guaranty).

Japan and the NICs export mostly capital goods and technology-intensive intermediate goods in return for agricultural commodities and raw materials. Given that nearly three-fourths of China's exports will probably consist of manufactured goods by the end of the century, the question arises of which countries will absorb those exports. If China develops a trade pattern in which exports of labor-intensive products are directed mostly to the United States and Europe and imports of capital and intermediate goods come mostly from Japan and the NICs, China might begin running large surpluses with the United States and Europe. This development could be as disturbing to industrialized countries as the trade surplus of the NICs.

Change in the Soviet Union. The dramatic political and economic changes that are occurring in the Soviet Union and Eastern Europe also have long-term implications for the economic and political orientations of the Asian NICs. Ideological barriers that have divided socialist and market economies are coming down and changing the landscape of the political economy of Asia.

On one level political and economic liberalization in the Soviet Union has the potential of affecting NIC trade opportunities in Eastern Europe and the Soviet Union. South Korea, for example, has already taken advantage of détente to improve relations with Hungary, Poland, and the Soviet Union. As a result, new markets may open up and help South Korea to diversify its exports.

On another level the dramatic changes in the Soviet Union have broader implications for changing the domestic policies of the socialist states of Indo China—Vietnam, Cambodia, and Laos. Since the end of the Vietnam War, these countries have all developed economies that are highly dependent on the Soviet Union. Abandonment of the centralized command economy mode by the Soviets and to a lesser extent by China could strengthen the positions of less ideological leaders supporting economic decentralization and restructuring in accordance with market forces. To the extent that these countries turn in the direction of going after a share of the world economic pie, it should only be natural that they will attempt to integrate their economies further with those of the Asian NICs and Japan (Burton 1989).

Prospects

A more activist and arguably less open U.S. trade policy, the drive for a single European market by 1992, Japan's growing economic and political role in Asia, and economic and political reform in the Communist world are the key elements of today's international trade environment. All these trends reflect intensified competition for an increased share of the global economic pie. On the one hand, these trends could support the development of more balanced trade relations between the NICs and the United States and bolster the postwar open and nondiscriminatory world trading system. On the other hand, the trends could undermine the development of more balanced trading relations and nudge the world trading system toward a regime of managed trade and regional trading blocs.

Trends Supportive of More Balanced Trade Relations. A more activist U.S. trade policy and the movements toward greater economic integration in Europe and East Asia are having a number of positive effects on the role of the NICs in the world economy. These include the declining dependence of the Asian NICs on the U.S. market, increasing NIC reliance on the EC, Japanese, and Chinese markets, declining NIC trade surpluses with the United States, and increasing investments of NIC companies in Europe.

U.S. trade policy pressures, combined with a weaker dollar and a stronger yen, have been important in moving the NICs to diversify their export markets. In the process, the export dependence of the Asian NICs on the U.S. market dropped from 40 percent of total exports in 1985 to 31 percent in 1988. During this same period Japan's share of NIC exports increased from 10 percent to 12 percent, and the EC's share increased from 11 percent to 15 percent. Thus growing imports to Japan and the EC picked up two-thirds of the drop in U.S. purchases from the NICs.

While the ultimate impact of EC 1992 on third countries remains to be seen, it is forcing the NICs to increase their business presence in Europe as well as to step up the pace of their own import liberalization programs. South Korean and Taiwanese firms are in a position to consider direct investments, and Singaporean local companies are considering a variety of joint ventures. These corporate tie-ups are creating the conditions for expanding trade relations. Provided capital and technology remain free to move into the EC, a more integrated and efficient world economy should result.

The growth of trade and investment flows within East Asia are also having positive effects. The trend toward East Asian economic integration, most important, is providing the NICs with the opportunity to adjust to further reductions in the U.S. market by trading closer to home. The role of Japan in this regard is critical.

As a result of Japan's dramatic increase in manufactured imports from the Asian NICs and increasing supply of capital and technology to these countries, the division of labor between the NICs and Japan may be changing to support a more self-sustaining growth path in the region. A more open Japanese market is providing opportunities for bringing greater balance into the United States–Japan–Asian NICs triangular trade relationship.

Finally, a variety of geopolitical conditions that helped spur the NICs to become super exporters to the United States are also changing. China's opening to the outside world since 1978 and the lessening of bipolar ideological competition between the superpowers are increasing the possibilities for the NICs to trade closer to home. In particular, China now accounts for 10 percent of NIC exports, up from 2 percent in 1980, and trading opportunities may open up for the NICs in Indochina and Eastern Europe.

Trends Undermining More Balanced Trade Relations. A more activist U.S. trade policy and the movements toward greater economic integration in Europe and East Asia could also have very negative effects on the NICs and the world trading system. Although it is difficult to make the case that U.S. trade policy is today overtly protectionist, it is being formulated with more incentives to retaliate against foreign unfair trade practices and with less presidential discretion not to take retaliatory action.

In view of predicted continuing large external imbalances, a more activist U.S. trade policy could be severely tested in the years ahead. Despite the fact that the current account surplus of the Asian NICs declined about $5 billion in 1989 to $25 billion, the OECD predicts little further improvement in the next two years. Moreover, the OECD predicts that the U.S. current account deficit will increase, creating the possibility that the U.S. trade deficit with the Asian NICs (which constituted nearly 25 percent of the U.S. global trade deficit in 1989) will begin to grow again (OECD 1989). Combined with Japan's 50 percent share of the U.S. global trade deficit, the Japan–Asian NIC component could easily exceed 75 percent over the next few years. This heavy Asian component of the U.S. trade deficit could be a highly visible target for U.S. trade policy activism.

In light of the deregulatory objective of EC 1992, it is uncertain whether fear of a Fortress Europe will prove well founded. The EC commissioners from the United Kingdom, Holland, and West Germany share the belief that the 1992 plan will succeed only if Europe remains open to foreign competition. In opposition to this position are the representatives from France, Spain, and other countries, who advocate protectionist directives to safeguard the interests of local firms.

The growth of large payments imbalances among EC member states and the preoccupation of West Germany with the developments in East Germany could make it more difficult for the EC simultaneously to liberalize internally and to the outside world. To provide a cushion for European firms, particularly those from countries such as France, the United Kingdom, and Italy that have weak external payments positions, pressures for the adoption of "transitional arrangements" and "reciprocity" are likely to grow. Unfortunately, such terms are often code words for indefinite protection from outside competition. Enjoying a $9 billion trade surplus with the EC, the Asian NICs would probably be a target of such transitional arrangements.

While East Asian economic integration holds out the encouraging possibility of a restructuring of the triangular trade relationship between the United States, Japan, and the Asian NICs, the necessary changes in trade flows between Japan and the Asian NICs have not yet begun to materialize. Despite some indication that Japan is opening its market to NIC imports, a pattern of growing Japanese trade surpluses with the NICs continues. Japan's trade surpluses with the NICs from 1984 to 1988 rose from $14 billion to $24 billion. In addition, Japan's imports from the NICs turned down sharply in 1989, growing at a very modest 10 percent annual rate.

Even if Japan's trade surpluses with the NICs begin to decline, there is a fear that the Japan-NIC trade surpluses could be transferred to the rest of Asia. Under such a scenario the focus of U.S.-Asian trade tensions could shift from the NICs to China, Malaysia, and Thailand.

Recommendations for More Balanced Trading Relations. The policy recommendations to achieve greater balance in trade relations are for the most part quite familiar. The problem, as with most policy recommendations, is finding the political will for implementation.

United States. To reduce or eliminate its current account deficit of more than $100 billion, the United States needs to shift resources into exporting and investment and away from consumption. Appropriate spending and tax policies, including the standard call for reduction of the federal government budget deficit, are required to slow domestic consumption and free up resources for exporting and investment in new capacity (Bergsten 1988, 7–9).

As the appropriate macroeconomic adjustments are made, the private sector needs to step up its efforts to sell to Europe, Japan, and the NICs—the regions with the largest external surpluses, which will have to import more from the United States. In particular, U.S. companies continue to underestimate the attractiveness of South Korea and Taiwan as markets and as offshore investment sites. Taiwan is the primary growth market for U.S. agricultural exports, and South Korea and Hong Kong are the second and fourth largest potential markets respectively (Journal of Commerce 1990). Anecdotal evidence continues to suggest, however, that American companies (notably manufacturers) are not nearly as aggressive and dependable as many of their Asian competitors.

European Community. As the world's largest developed market, the EC must adjust to the inevitable reversal of the U.S. external deficit. Within the EC Germany is the key to this adjustment. Germany's external surplus in 1989 was $69 billion—equivalent to Japan's surplus in absolute terms but much larger in relation to the size of its economy. To reduce its surplus Germany must ensure rapid growth of domestic demand, reorient its economy to produce more for the domestic market, and increase imports.

The EC adjustment process is complicated by the development of major external imbalances within Europe. While Germany, Belgium, and the Netherlands are experiencing growing external surpluses, the external accounts of Italy, Spain, and the United Kingdom are going in the opposite direction. Persisting high unemployment could further complicate the adjustment process.

As the EC moves toward completing the internal market, pressures for the creation of barriers against countries outside the community may well escalate. While the fears are greatest in the areas not covered by the GATT, forthcoming directives affecting government procurement and state subsidies could distort trade in goods. The EC needs to make every effort to adhere strictly to international obligations, such as the GATT, when formulating internal directives. The United States, Japan, and the Asian NICs need to pressure the EC jointly to complete the restructuring of its internal market without discriminating against the outside world.

Japan. Despite the considerable progress Japan has made in reorienting its economy toward domestic-led growth, it faces additional challenges if it is to reduce its current account surplus of $60 billion in 1989. To reduce the surplus, current domestic-demand-led expansion and a rising level of imports must be sustained and expanded. To this end many economists argue that Japan needs to consider a variety of fundamental economic and social reforms to open up its economy further to imports.

Without continued efforts to curtail formal and informal barriers to imports, Japan's external surplus may be reduced too slowly. This could lead to continued trade conflict and erosion of the multilateral trading system that the NICs depend on so heavily.

South Korea and Taiwan. Both South Korea and Taiwan need to give priority attention to the reduction of their current account surpluses. In relation to the size of their economies, the external surpluses of these two NICs remain the highest in the world. In light of their relatively low per capita incomes and correspondingly large potential for expanding living standards, these surpluses are inappropriate from both domestic and international perspectives (Bergsten 1988, 103).

Three policy measures—currency appreciation, import liberalization, and fiscal expansion—might reduce both the level of their current account surpluses and the level of trade tensions. Each measure has advantages and disadvantages.

Further currency appreciation might reduce exports and increase imports, thereby decreasing their trade surpluses. This would encourage some exporters to shift capital and workers out of the tradable goods sector to the home goods sector. A potential disadvantage of overreliance on this approach is that before resources are transferred to the home goods sector, real appreciation could lead to a rapid increase in imports, job losses in the export sector, and an economy-wide decline in production (Park 1989).

South Korea and Taiwan must also continue to press ahead on opening their economies to outside competition for trade in both goods and services. Markets in the United States and Europe are unlikely to remain open so long as NIC markets are perceived as closed. Trade liberalization, however, has political limitations in both countries, particularly as democratization proceeds and the influence of farmers remains strong. In addition, trade liberalization may simply increase imports without changing the savings and investment relations that determine a country's overall trade balance.

Because trade imbalances are essentially driven by macroeconomic factors, efforts to expand government spending could be a more effective way to reduce trade imbalances than trade liberalization and currency appreciation. Unfortunately, both governments have been slow to undertake major public investment projects. Shifting resources to nontradable sectors such as education, health and medical care, transportation, water supply, communications, and environmental protection would not only help reduce external surpluses but also contribute to higher living standards in these countries (Park 1989, 140–42).

The lack of an international forum to discuss issues of these kinds directly with South Korea and Taiwan remains a serious limitation. Neither country is a member of the OECD—the industrialized countries' forum for discussion and coordination of macroeconomic issues.

As South Korea and Taiwan graduate from developing country status and become more important players in the world trading system, it is important that they be granted membership in the OECD and assume the responsibilities of developed countries. Both countries would have much to gain by participating in the discussion of policies that will affect their positions in the world economy. The major constraints on membership—reluctance on the part of South Korea to undertake the OECD trade and financial liberalization obligations and the political problem of offending China in the case of Taiwan—need to be overcome.

In summary, it is clear that the Asian NICs and the world trading system are at a crossroads. The export-led growth strategies that served the Asian NICs well in the 1970s and 1980s have contributed to international trade tensions and to less open trade policies in the United States and Europe. Because markets today are global, there is less and less room for countries to pursue purely domestic policies without reference to their impact on other countries. Unless there is greater recognition of this interdependence through the adoption of appropriate policies, the open and multilateral postwar trading system will continue to erode. As the world shrinks to the size of everyone's hometown, institutions and forums for discussion that are inclusive and nondiscriminatory will continue to provide the best hope for constructing more balanced trade relations and an open world trading system.

References

Ahearn, Raymond J. 1987. *Trade Conflict in the 99th Congress.* CRS Report for Congress. Washington, D.C.: Congressional Research Service, August 25.

Bergsten, C. Fred. 1988. *America in the World Economy: A Strategy for the 1990s.* Washington, D.C.: Institute for International Economics.

Burton, Charles. 1989. "The Role of the Asian NICs in Southeast Asia's Political and Economic Development." *International Journal* 44 (Summer).

Burton, Daniel F., Jr. 1988. "International Pressures and Policy Choices." In *America's New Competitors: The Challenge of the Newly Industrializing Countries.* Cambridge, Mass.: Ballinger Publishing Company.

Business Korea. 1988a (October).

———. 1988b (September).

Cooper, William. 1989. *South Korea and Taiwan: Expanding Trade Ties with the United States.* Washington, D.C.: Congressional Research Service, Issue Brief 86151.

Cronin, Richard P. 1989. *Singapore-U.S. Economic Relations: Some Views from Singapore's Economic Elite*. Report 89-49F (January).

Dumbaugh, Kerry. 1989. *Hong Kong-U.S. Economic Relations: Some Views from Hong Kong's Economic Elite*. Washington, D.C.: Congressional Research Service (January).

Economist. 1989. September 9.

Europe. 1988 (December).

European Community News. 1988. "1992: Europe—World Trade Partner." October 20.

Far Eastern Economic Review (FEER). 1988a. September 15.

———. 1988b. November 3, 1988.

———. 1989a. May 18, 1989.

———. 1989b. "Singapore's Sleeping Booty." May 25.

G-6 Communiqué. February 22, 1987. In Yoichi Funabashi, *Managing the Dollar: From the Plaza to the Louvre*. Washington, D.C.: Institute for International Economics, 1988.

Hanazaki, Masaharu. 1989. *Industrial and Trade Structures and the International Competitiveness of Asia's Newly Industrializing Economies—A Search for Development in Harmony with the Industrialized Countries*. Japan Development Bank (August).

Harrison, Glennon J., et al. 1989. *European Community: Issues Raised by 1992 Integration*. CRS Report for Congress no. 89-323. Washington, D.C.: Congressional Research Service.

Howell, Thomas R. and William A. Noellert. 1986. *The EEC and the Third Multifiber Arrangement*. Washington, D.C.: Dewey, Ballantine, Bushby, Palmer, and Wood.

Jones, Steve. 1989. "Imports to Asian-Pacific Nations Increase." *Wall Street Journal*. November 9.

Journal of Commerce. 1990. "Taiwan Seen as No. 1 Mart for U.S. Farm Products." *Journal of Commerce*, January 22.

Keizai Koho Center. 1990. *Japan: An International Comparison*.

Kelly, Margaret, et al. 1988. *Issues and Developments in International Trade Policy*. IMF Occasional Paper no. 63. Washington, D.C.: International Monetary Fund.

Korean Business Review. 1988 (November).

Los Angeles Times. 1988. September 20.

Morgan Guaranty. *Wrestling with Success*. p. 4.

Morrison, Charles E., and Robert F. Denberger. 1989. *Asia-Pacific Report*. East-West Center.

Nanto, Dick K. 1989. *Pacific Rim Economic Cooperation*. Congressional Research Service. Report no. 89-472E, August 3.

Office of the U.S. Trade Representative. 1988. *Annual Report of the President on the Trade Agreements Program*, 29th issue. Washington, D.C.: USTR.

Organization for Economic Cooperation and Development. 1988. *The Newly Industrializing Countries: Challenges and Opportunity for OECD Countries*. Paris: OECD.

———. 1989. *Economic Outlook* (December).

Park, Yung Chul. 1989. "The Little Dragons and Structural Change in Pacific Asia." *World Economy* (June).

Preeg, Ernest H. 1989. *Tied-Aid Credits*. Washington, D.C.: Center for Strategic and International Studies.

SRI International. 1989. *Building Prosperity: A Five-Part Economic Strategy for Hong Kong's Future* (September).

USDC. U.S. Department of Commerce, internal memo, N.D.

U.S. International Trade Commission. 1989. *Operation of the Trade Agreements Program*, 40th report. USITC Publication 2208. Washington, D.C.: USITC.

U.S. Senate, Committee on Finance. 1989. *Hearing, Currency Manipulation*, May 12.

Whitehead, Laurence. 1989. "Tigers in Latin America?" *Annals*. AAPSS, no. 505 (September).

World Financial Markets. 1989. "The Asian NICs: Wrestling with Success." April 17.

5
Commentaries on Part Two

A Commentary by Stephen Chen

I will limit my remarks to supplying additional information about my country's position. The Republic of China does not maintain diplomatic relations with the European Community; therefore, it is not a beneficiary of the generalized system of preferences (GSP) of the EC. And it is not yet a contracting party to the General Agreement on Tariffs and Trade; so it suffers a disadvantage. But as the EC is gradually phasing out the GSP now granted to all newly industrialized countries, the Republic of China will in time compete with other NICs in the EC market on an equal footing as far as tariffs are concerned.

In view of the rapid economic development of the Republic of China, the EC took the initiative in requesting the first trade negotiations with the Republic of China in London in December 1981, and those were followed by subsequent talks. Issues of major concern to the EC include the Republic of China's procurement for major engineering projects, services such as banking and insurance, and importation of beef and liqueurs.

After bilateral trade negotiations between the Republic of China and the United States in October 1984, the Republic of China made bold tariff reductions from 65 percent to 50 percent and tariff concessions on tobaccos, wine, motion pictures, leasing, banking, and insurance to the United States. These concessions have since been applied to EC countries as well.

To cope with the dramatic change in the EC, the Republic of China government approved a four-year plan under the Outline Program for Strengthening Economic and Trade Ties with Europe in April 1989. An ad hoc committee on EC was established jointly by various ministries. We are thus accelerating our relations with the EC, and, of course, we are hoping to join the GATT. We submitted our application on January 1, 1990, as a developed country. We are also willing to join the Organization for Economic Cooperation and Development if at all possible.

We did not have any relations with Eastern Europe as a Communist bloc of nations. But, led by Poland and Hungary, these European countries have successfully undertaken dramatic reforms toward political democratization and economic liberalization since 1989, attracting worldwide attention. Now aggressive steps have been taken by the Republic of China to develop and strengthen its relations with these countries. East Germany, Poland, Hungary, Yugoslavia, Czechoslovakia, Bulgaria, and Romania have been declared countries with which the Republic of China may have direct trade. In addition, the International Economic Cooperation and Development Fund of the Republic of China, which has an initial funding of $1.2 billion and will grow to $12 billion in ten years, is now open to East European countries.

In the chapters one important point was not addressed: why the Republic of China became one of the Little Dragons. It was not at all accidental. A number of key factors played a very important role in Taiwan's economic success: the correct development strategies; detailed economic planning; an abundance of diligent and high-quality labor; and a free and prosperous international trading environment. Important to the industrial development and economic reconstruction of Taiwan during the early years was also the relocation of many skilled technocrats and technicians from the Chinese mainland to Taiwan in the late 1940s and the timely provision of U.S. aid in the early stage of economic development.

Economic development is a continuous process. The people of Taiwan enjoy a per capita income of more than $7,500, almost as much as the per capita income in some developed countries. They are now entering a critical transition period that, barring mishap, will lead to an even more advanced stage of development. A long-term perspective of Taiwan's economic development, a study commissioned by my government in 1986, foresees the emergence of a fully developed modern society in Taiwan after the completion of our economic liberalization and internationalization program before the close of this century. By that time, which is less than ten years away, my country will have assumed a voice in international affairs that befits its economic achievement and, together with other developed countries, will be working to bring the benefits of economic growth and prosperity to other peoples of the world.

A Commentary by Thomas W. Robinson

First of all, I am very grateful to the organizers of this conference for including me as a discussant on this panel. I understand I am the only nondiplomat, and I therefore intend to speak in a nondiplomatic manner about the subject.

I am very interested and also very grateful that there is a session on the Asian dimension of the question of the United States and Europe in the 1990s. I presume it is inevitable and desirable that we talk about the topic of the conference since we are fast upon 1992, but it is important that Asia be remembered in that regard.

The first thing that I wish to address is that we should not talk about Asia, as the conference seems to assume, as an external disturbing variable in American-European economic relations in the 1990s. Instead, we should discuss what Asia is already and will become: an internal determinant of what is happening within the European Community, within the United States and across the Atlantic, not only with regard to trade and investment and competition for markets in the two large entities but also in third areas. I predict that Japan will be more and more an element in the security relations across the Atlantic and on the Continent, as well. That is my first message.

The second thing I wish to note is that I experienced some difficulty with what the word "Asia" refers to here. Two of the chapters talked about Japan and the newly industrialized countries (NICs). That is not all there is to Asia, as some of the other discussants have also noted. To be sure, Asia is Japan and the NICs. In addition, Asia will not include Hong Kong in the latter 1990s because it will no longer be an independent entity. The NICs, in that sense, will be reduced to three. But Asia should also include China, India, and all the other Asian countries. That is what I mean by Asia: the entire area, not just some currently important Asian economies.

It follows, directly and immediately, that the 1990s will be a time when, first of all, Japan asserts itself as an economic superpower throughout the globe, not just in Asia, Europe, or North America. The implication is that anything the Americans and the Europeans do, together or separately, will have to be done with an eye toward Japanese cooperation or at least with the knowledge of what Japan's reaction will be in any department, not just economic.

The second thing already happening is that China is driving fast toward that same superpower status economically, aiming at becoming one of the globe's top trading nations and looking toward becoming a superpower in every sense of the term by the early part of the twenty-first century. That is one of the major trends in the area and will continue throughout the decade.

Third, this is a decade in which the Asian NICs will become even more active and consequential with regard to trade and investment throughout the globe, not just in Asia, Europe, or North America, and they will have at least one new member. My candidate is Thailand, and Malaysia is also well along the way to joining that particular club.

Fourth, the 1990s will be a decade in which India will become at least as important to trade and investment around the globe as China, to say nothing of Asia as a whole, perhaps even more so. India is, in that regard, the sleeper: we know it is there but we do not pay enough attention to it. In fact, India will come to influence us all in many regards.

The results of these four trends, which I think are inexorable, are, first, that Americans will have to be concerned about Asia as much as about Europe. With the Soviet Union going in the direction we see it, American resources will have to be drawn more and more out of Asia and into these other regions, as much as being put into Europe, as has been the case in the 1980s. In other words, more will have to be accomplished with fewer resources.

The second implication is that Pacific basin economic cooperation could go as far in the 1990s and the early 2000s as transatlantic economic cooperation went in the 1970s and 1980s. This will come about not only as a national response to the dynamism of the region but with regard to a number of other matters. One will be as a device to control Japan and to prevent American-Japanese economic relations from deteriorating further. A second will be as a means of drawing the Soviet Union into Asia on terms offered by the market economies of the region. A third will be as a response to Europe 1992 and beyond. Finally, Pacific basin economic cooperation will be a means to discipline or entice China to modify its foreign and economic policies in manners that we would all like to see.

The third thing that is happening is that we are all headed for some combination of a three-bloc world: European, North American, and Asian. That has been noted before with all that it implies for shifting alliances, alignments, and so forth.

That is not an enormously happy thing for me. I am a student of strategic triangular relationships, and I believe that a three-sided economic system, like triangles in the diplomatic, security, or other reaches of life, is about the most wicked arrangement one can imagine. So I do not necessarily think that is going to be a happy time for all of us.

In fact, I think it is heading that way now. But it could also head toward a much more complex global market economy if Asia is to be thought of not as a single economic entity but as composed of at least five major elements: America, Japan, China, the NICs (I would amalgamate the NICs in this regard), and, finally, India—and perhaps the Soviet Union. So it is going to be a very complex situation in Asia, and that complexity will influence Europe and America.

It follows that the division of labor within Europe and between the United States and Europe, which is the subject of this conference, will have to be modified in a thoroughgoing manner. Wherever we look, we are going to find Asian money, Asian technology, Asian competitiveness, Asian markets, Asian ideas, and Asian presence. Both Americans and Europeans must get used to that fact.

The final point I want to address is rather discordant. That is that any economic forecast is only as good as the political-security framework behind it allows. And in Asia the prospects for military conflict exist and in many cases are rather fearsome.

I should only note the rather tenuous and increasingly difficult situation on the Korean peninsula, the somewhat unhappy prospects that might well occur between China and Taiwan, the Chinese propensity to take military action against Vietnam in the South China Sea, what we can all read about in the paper with regard to India and Pakistan, the coming probable political and social disintegration of the Philippines, and the Cambodian situation, which is hardly fixed. This is to say nothing of the regional and perhaps global effects of Japanese disarmament, the Chinese procurement of a regionally threatening projection force, and the realization that India, in all three services, is becoming one of the world's principal military powers.

My own feeling is that the extraordinary luck of the 1980s in Asia in suffering no major international conflict will not persist into the 1990s and that war, the threat of war, and arms races could upset otherwise favorable economic conditions with regard to Asia, America, and Europe. In fact, one cannot really separate trade and economic matters, on the one hand, from these military security and general diplomatic matters, on the other hand.

As a new political and economic order is being constructed across the Atlantic and within Europe, it should also be understood that a new economic order is being built in Asia as in Europe, not only on the basis of well-known economic factors set forth in the two presentations that we have heard but also on the basis of the transformation of the Asian security system to a degree that is at least as radical as we now see occurring in Europe.

A Commentary by G. Selvadas

When I was asked to comment on these chapters, I was a little hesitant for three reasons. First, the authors showed a command of their subjects that was impressive. Second, I am neither an economist nor a political scientist. Third, the Asian dimension of U.S.-European relations is mind boggling. Sadly, however, the Asian dimension has not received as much attention as it deserves.

Before I continue, perhaps I should briefly present my country's credentials. Singapore is largely a free port. Some 96 percent of U.S. exports enter Singapore duty free. Singapore also runs an overall trade deficit. In 1989 this deficit amounted to approximately US$5.2 billion. On a per capita basis, this was more than twice the corresponding figure for the United States. And Singapore's external trade is some 300 percent of our gross national product, making us the country most affected by the vagaries of international trade. As a relatively small economy, however, Singapore cannot demand or enforce market-opening and other trade liberalization measures in other countries. Singapore does not have serious trade problems with either the United States or the European Community. The health and strength of the international trade system, however, are of vital importance to Singapore. The changes currently taking place in transpacific and transatlantic relations are thus of vital concern to Singapore.

The changes that are currently under way in the Soviet Union and Europe and in the world economy, caused by communications, computerization, sophisticated production, and management techniques, are massive upheavals in the geopolitical and economic tectonic plates. Where these plates will collide and where they will come to rest and fuse together for a new (temporary) order are impossible to predict. While I am in general agreement with the paper on the role of the Asian newly industrialized countries, I would like to make some observations of my own on the Asian dimension of changing U.S.-European relations. In my comments I will look at the recent role of the United States in Asia, the changes taking place in the EC, the Soviet Union, and Eastern Europe, how these changes affect Asia, and what could be done to take advantage of these changes.

The Recent Role of the United States. The presentation recognizes that the effects of changes in Europe on Asia cannot be assessed without factoring in the role of the United States. The current international economic and political order is the result of a world order that America largely created after World War II, and with brilliant success. After World War II the United States undertook to resurrect prosperity and create conditions for peace in Europe and Japan, contain Soviet power and expansionism, and help the poorer countries develop economically to achieve stability. The International Monetary Fund, the World Bank, the General Agreement on Tariffs and Trade, the United Nations, the North Atlantic Treaty Organization, the United States–Japan Mutual Defense Treaty, U.S. foreign military bases, foreign aid, containment, export of technology, and the role of importer of last resort were largely part of a grand design of vision by the United States. In Asia and to a lesser extent in Europe the United States provided strategic stability and order with its military presence. The United States acted as a benign superpower that did not seek to impose a hegemony over other countries. The East Asian economic miracle is partly a result of this grand design. It allowed countries in the region to develop under the American defense umbrella. It allowed Japan an avenue of constructive expression for its dynamism through economic expansion. More important, it was this strategic vision that resulted in the collapse of communism and victory in the cold war.

The EC and Its Role. Western Europe traditionally has a head start over the United States in Asia. Historically, culturally, and politically, many countries in Asia have strong links with Europe. The French were in Indochina and the Pacific, the British in Burma, Malaysia, India, Ceylon, and Singapore, the Spanish in the Philippines, the Portuguese in Malacca, and the Dutch in Indonesia. Many of the former colonies continue to enjoy a special relationship with their former metropolitan powers.

With the cold war, however, reconstruction in Europe, the formation and expansion of the EC, and the years of Eurosclerosis, Europe gradually became inward looking. Growth in economic ties between Europe and Asia did not match that with the United States. The United States as the engine of world growth and with its use of English as the language of commerce became the most important economy to much of Asia.

The resurgence of the EC economy in the 1980s was a blessing to Asian countries. It accorded them the opportunity to broaden the diversification of their trading patterns. Singapore had long recognized that the dominant American share in its global trade, though mutually beneficial, was not healthy in the long run. Continued economic growth necessitates a diversification of economic partners. Singapore therefore supports the establishment of the single European market (SEM) because of its intention to liberalize trade. We are concerned, however, about the possibility of a Fortress Europe.

The Ahearn-Dibble chapter covers the changes in EC trade policy well and outlines the many pitfalls awaiting a unified EC attempting to forge a new trade policy based on the SEM. Singapore and many of its neighbors of the Association of Southeast Asian Nations have received political assurances that there will be no Fortress Europe. We have heard that Fortress Europe was a propaganda exercise by Japan and the United States. We have accepted these assurances in the spirit in which they were made. But the external implications of EC 1992 have not been as well researched and as well explained as the 279 directives and their accompanying legislation. We remain watchful of the impact of EC 1992 on EC trade with Asia. Singapore wants the SEM to result in an economically vibrant, confident, externally oriented entity. If the EC is able to establish a greater economic presence in Asia as a result of the SEM, Singapore will welcome it.

I cannot see how such a massive shakeup in a competitive environment as that which is taking place in the EC now will not be accompanied by demands for transitional arrangements. Smaller companies in the lesser developed EC countries are almost certain to demand some safeguard to survive. In such a context the political will that must back up the assurances that there will be no Fortress Europe will be tempered with the desire for political survival. The degree and nature of these transitional arrangements, which I think are inevitable, will be the most important external phenomenon of EC 1992. Unfortunately, like most phenomena, it must have occurred and been observed before corrective action can be taken.

Already there appears to be a refocusing of the EC away from Asia toward its internal processes and the changes taking place in Eastern Europe. At the ASEAN-EC ministerial meeting in Kuching, Malaysia, in mid-February 1990, the foreign ministers of three major EC countries—France, Britain, and West Germany—were unable to attend. At the ASEAN-EC meeting there was reportedly little meeting of minds on key economic issues, such as market access, which was given only cursory attention. Perhaps this apparent waning of EC interest in Asia is only temporary. The EC cannot afford to put its relations with Asia on the back burner for long as the Pacific basin is predicted to become the world's largest and most technically sophisticated market within two generations.

Another concern about EC 1992 is its potentially distorting impact on global investment flows. Already we can observe an inflow of Japanese, American, Taiwanese, and Korean investments into the EC. If these investments are made on sound economic fundamentals, they are to be welcomed as a sign of a vibrant market at work. If, however, they are based, *inter alia*, on the desire to gain a foothold in a lucrative market before a Fortress Europe is built, that is a shame, and they could diminish the pool of available investment funds and technology for developing countries. They could thus slow the growth of less developed Asian countries that may possess comparative advantages over Europe.

The Soviet Union and Eastern Europe. In the Soviet Union President Mikhail Gorbachev has embarked on unprecedented changes. We wish him success. But the euphoria over the victory of the free world must be tempered with the recognition that Russia's historical track record has been expansionist. Although there have been Soviet troop reductions in Asia, the largest concentration of Soviet naval power remains in its Pacific fleet. The Soviet Union still maintains a powerful military concentration of submarines, SLBMs, and bombers in the Kamchatka peninsula. It continues to support troublesome regimes in North Korea and Vietnam and an illegitimate regime in Afghanistan.

The Soviet Union has recently launched a diplomatic initiative in the Asia-Pacific region. Singapore was host for the first time to a visiting Soviet prime minister. Mr. Ryzhkov also visited Thailand and Australia. Soviet diplomacy has thus now begun to focus on another frontier: the Asia-Pacific region. President Gorbachev has stated that the Soviet Union wants to be a formidable Pacific power. If this power is an economic one, built on trade, prosperity, and mutual economic gain, it will not be perceived as threatening. But if this power is accompanied by a strong security presence and a challenge to the order and stability the United States created, we would indeed be cautious. There is nothing to be gained by substituting for a friendly superpower with a benign and constructive track record one that has a less commendable record.

The changes sweeping through Eastern Europe have had two effects that are of concern to Asian countries. The first is the shifting of the EC's attention away from the Asia-Pacific and toward the economic needs and opportunities of the liberalization of Eastern Europe. The second is the rekindling of hopes for an all-European security order. The role and functions of NATO will need to be reexamined in this new European order. The results of such reexamination are likely to bring about major changes. Coupled with this is the impact of political integration, aided by the SEM, of Europe. In the past forty years Europe's identity was forged and influenced largely by the security challenge from its eastern borders. With the perception that this threat is receding, Europe will look toward the United States in forging its political identity. This would eventually pose a challenge to the United States over who possesses primacy over Atlantic relations and European security. The U.S. response to this challenge will affect its own global role and the entire global political, economic, and security orders.

The Future. What do these changes mean for Asia? First, it should be recognized that the U.S. role in Asia should continue. In some important aspects this is still a bipolar world, and only a superpower can act as a counterbalance to another superpower. Second, talk of a United States in decline is unsubstantiated. The United States may be experiencing a relative decline in economic predominance, but it will continue to be *primus inter pares*. The challenges that the United States faces in its domestic restructuring are molehills compared with Gorbachev's Everest. The United States needs to make only comparatively minor, albeit painful, adjustments to a basically sound and thriving system. Given its economic clout, U.S. management of bilateral and multilateral economic issues will continue to affect the development of Asia. The U.S. response to EC trade policy and United States–Japan economic problems could result in a resurgence of protectionism, often in disguise under the rubric of managed trade. It will be ironic that America has fought and won the cold war only to lose forty years of effort to protectionism. Fred Bergsten put it aptly by saying, "The ultimate paradox of the twentieth century would be a realization of the Marxist prophecy of inevitable conflict among the capitalist nations just as the political conflict spurred by Marxist ideology was waning." The United States should retain its commitment to multilateralism and trade liberalization, using all means at its disposal to open up the markets of mercantilist economies that are taking a free ride on the world trading system and to prevent a global slide into protectionism.

Third, the United States and other Western countries encouraged the development of Asian countries through aid, loans, market access, and technology. One of the major aims of such a policy was containment of communism through economic development. In the post-cold-war era of economic conflict, will there be a consensus of political will to help the poorer countries? Those Asian countries that have benefited from the economic environment following World War II must recognize their new responsibilities and work with the West to continue the process of international development.

Fourth, the countries that have benefited from the postwar order in Asia should recognize the role that the United States played. They should help the United States reduce its trade deficit by opening their markets, becoming exporters of capital and, if possible, of technology, and taking up an increased share of the burden of maintaining a stable Asian security order. In fact, this is already happening, and the more successful Asian states are helping development in the rest of the third world. The United States, with its massive economic power, can then continue to act as lender and buyer of last resort.

Fifth, the perceived reduction in a Soviet threat, particularly in north Asia, could lead to a desire in the United States to pursue a policy of massive military retrenchment in the Asia-Pacific. This would leave a power vacuum that the Soviets or various regional powers would try to fill. If this occurs or if the economic conflicts with Japan vitiate Japan's security alliance with the United States, Japan may feel compelled to rearm, ostensibly to defend itself. The last time Japan built an extensive military machine there were disastrous consequences for Asia. This should not be allowed to happen again. Sixth, it would be a positive and helpful factor if the United States, acting in partnership with Japan and Europe if necessary, could develop a new grand strategy aimed at maintaining and extending the hard-fought and hard-won stability in the new world that is taking shape.

A Commentary by John Richardson

In light of my own experience, the idea of Fortress Europe is a myth, a very persistent myth, particularly in Washington.

The idea that the European Community has become more protectionist recently does not seem to jibe with what has been happening to the EC-U.S. trade balance nor with the continued impressive growth of Japanese exports to the European Community.

I find it difficult to see why we should bash Japan so hard, unsuccessfully, if Japanese exports to the European Community continue to grow as they do. If we examine the trade figures in a cold, analytical light, preferably outside Washington, perhaps we will consider whether this view should be as persistent as it seems to be.

I should state clearly the European Community's position on this issue. The Commission of the European Communities has a clear policy of maintaining its liberal external trade stance and making it more liberal in the future, to the extent possible within the Uruguay Round. Our policy is not a response to the requests of our partners but a position in the community's own interests.

The European Community exports more manufactures to the rest of the world than to the United States and Japan put together. We have a stronger interest than either the United States or Japan in maintaining a liberal system of world trade.

The 1992 program is primarily about making community industry more competitive. If we want it to draw the maximum from that competitiveness, then we need liberal world markets. It would not be in our interest to go in a protectionist direction.

People often talk about a multipolar world and the trade imbalances within that world. Sometimes they describe it as a triangular world: the United States, Japan, and Europe. The persistent trade imbalances among them should be seen in perspective, though. In 1986, the European Community had a trade surplus representing about 0.4 percent of the total GDP of the OECD economies. Japan had a current account surplus representing 0.8 percent of the OECD's gross national product, and the United States, 1.3 percent. Those imbalances were a real problem in 1986, and they were dealt with.

In 1989, however, the European Community's 0.4 percent, in comparison with OECD surplus, had been turned into a zero surplus: it disappeared. The Japanese surplus had been reduced to 0.5 percent, and the U.S. deficit of 1.3 had been reduced to 0.7 percent. In those three years, the problem was halved. If it could be dealt with when it was that size, why are some hysterical about dealing with it now, when it is half the size?

Maybe the overestimation of this problem derives from the new status of the United States as a net debtor. For many decades, the United States has had an inflow of net factor income on its balance of payments, which is one of the reasons why it did not have balance-of-payments problems. In 1989 for the first time in postwar history, the United States did not have net factor income, because its net assets had declined at about the same time that the U.S. public's worries about the trade position reached their peak, particularly in Congress.

As we look at the world economy, we must take the difficult perspective of global interdependence.

Financial services is an example. Thanks to modern telecommunications, our world now has global markets in financial services. In an interdependent world, if the stock market in the United States sneezes, the European market catches a cold, to misquote an old expression.

In addition, trade flows have increased, as we know, faster than GNP almost every year since the war and every year since the creation of the GATT. Last year in our bilateral relations with the United States, for example, we had a trade flow of around $170 billion if we add the flows in each direction. What does this mean? It means simply that our economies are becoming more and more interdependent. Investment flows have been increasing as well, very often faster than trade flows. Investment flows are twice the $170 billion trade flow, in fact. Our economies, through investment, are becoming more and more heavily integrated, too.

That is part of my answer to those in the European Community and the United States who worry about the direct investment from Japan. The old story of the poor man who borrowed a thousand dollars from his bank comes to mind: because he was poor, *he* had a problem. His neighbor was rather better off; he borrowed a million dollars from the bank, and the *bank* had the problem. Perhaps the increase of investment flows should be considered in that light.

Every increase in foreign direct investment in another country— every increase of Japanese investment in the European Community or the United States—gives Japan a bigger stake in the health of the U.S. economy and that of the European Community. We are all related; we all have the same interest in maintaining the health of the system. We therefore all have the same interest in developing coherent and sensible rules for that system and in abiding by them.

European companies are, at present, revising their strategies in this interdependent world. One of the curiosities is that the events in Eastern Europe and those in the European Community's own internal market program have led many EC companies to reconsider their industrial strategies. We have been witnessing a greater realization than before of the worldwide interest of these EC companies. The regional stimulus has not led to a strategic concentration on the region but to a realization of a global interest of these companies.

All of us in the field of external economic policy have a tendency, often exacerbated by politicians and the public, to look for an outside enemy. One of the problems for the European Community and the United States is that we had an external enemy for a long time: the Communist system, personified by the USSR, and once described as an "evil empire." While that picture may not be quite as credible as it was five or ten years ago, the danger is that we will replace it with another external enemy: Japan.

We would be far better off by pursuing the more rational policy of looking for the potential global enemies that we all face—for example, the environmental crisis—to replace in the public mind the individual regional enemies we have had in the past. That might be progress for human society and for the world economic system.

The best weapon against the illegitimate exaggeration of individual enemies around the world is the GATT and the rest of the multilateral system. The best way we can deal with our collective problems is to make a success of the Uruguay Round.

That point is emphasized over and over again by Carla Hills, who is responsible for the external trade policy of the United States. I see no reason to question that commitment: we have the same one. I would emphasize that it is in the European Community's own interest to support a strong, liberal multilateral system. It should be in the interest of all.

If Japan and the United States are serious about wanting the European Community to move in a liberal direction, then all of us, with all our trading partners, can work together to deliver on that desire, and then the myth of Fortress Europe will disappear forever.

A Commentary by Vitthya Vejjajiva

I have been wondering what my contribution should be since the subject of these chapters is the European Community, the United States, Japan, and the newly industrialized countries. Thailand is not even a NIC. Nevertheless, Thailand shares many of the problems that the Asian NICs face. So our perspective is not dissimilar to that of many of our Asian neighbors.

We have heard interesting presentations in the two chapters. I listened with great interest to the arguments of Masaru Yoshitomi explaining—some people might say explaining away—the closedness of the Japanese market and also the explanation about the so-called natural barriers, as evidenced by the Japanese production and management style and so on. I cannot help wondering whether these will hold water or will be able to convince many of Japan's competitors around the world who are eyeing Japanese domestic markets and are making more and more demands on Japan.

As far as we in Thailand are concerned, we think that in spite of all these exhortations and demands on Japan, Japan can play a very positive role in two directions. One, of course, is to continue to show a willingness to share its wealth and prosperity with others, as it has been doing to some degree in the Asian NIC countries, including Thailand.

As the author brought out, Japan has a scarcity of land. Therefore, I would venture to suggest that Japan could try its best to open its agricultural sector.

My second point would be about the playing of a positive role in the world arena. I have in mind the Uruguay Round going on right now. Japan can play a very positive role, mindful of its position in the economic realm. Japan and the other key players can come together and bring about a better world system. I think we all agree that that is where our future lies.

Turning to the other chapter, by Raymond Ahearn and Anne Dibble, I find the authors' arguments very well developed. I agree with most of the points made, including both the more optimistic and the less optimistic scenarios.

My observations are more on related points, observations of one from Thailand, which looks to this changing world pattern with a bit of apprehension but not altogether without hope. I have six or seven points to make.

First, international efforts since the end of World War II to open markets have played a major role in bringing unprecedented prosperity to the nations on this earth. The successes of the NICs and Japan are only a more recent and dramatic example of that. This is a very fundamental point that we have to establish.

Second, addressing the so-called structural problems being faced by the United States, Japan, and the NICs, I want to point out that these problems are of a different nature, that they must not be allowed to detract in any way from the virtue of an open market and free trade. The easy way out through managed trade or creating some kind of mechanism to obviate or circumvent an open and free market will not be acceptable. It is not a desirable solution or approach.

Third, the NIC export successes that enriched them did of course occur at the same time that the United States faced structural imbalances. But it does not follow that restoration of American balance requires NICs or other emerging economies like Thailand to abandon economic specialization that makes full use of their comparative advantage. Competition, in other words, in the world market has often been portrayed as a zero-sum game. I contend that the reverse is true, because everyone stands to gain or to be enriched.

Fourth, it is also true that with their new wealth the NICs are in a very good position to open up their markets and eliminate market distortions. They can also play an important role in sustaining the world's economic momentum when the United States embarks on major adjustments needed to restore economic balance. Japan, the NICs, and the emerging Asian economies, India and Thailand, have reached a critical mass that can assist in counterbalancing economic slowdown in other parts of the world.

Fifth, at the same time I wholeheartedly support the notion that the rules governing the multilateral trading system must be strengthened. By this I mean the Uruguay Round.

Sixth, I would like to touch on events in my part of the world, which the author briefly mentioned. Although much remains to be done, the prospect for peace and stability in Indo China looks more promising. Much attention has been focused, and rightly so, on the momentous changes in Eastern Europe. But in Southeast Asia, too, the Communists who won their war in the 1970s have now lost their peace.

Increasing growth and prosperity of the Asian free market economies have made our Communist neighbors admit reluctantly that free and open markets work while their socialist system does not. This happened or signs of it were apparent even before the momentous events of 1989 in Eastern Europe.

Finally, I would like to express my hope that with the universal vindication and triumph of the free market economy and democracy, as championed by the two key players in the world, the United States and Europe, these two key players will not yield to narrow and domestic interests. The United States should make the hard decision to restore economic balance; the EC should continue toward its 1992 goal of integration. But both must also continue to lead the way to what is an even more open and freer world market. Thailand, and I am sure also the NICs, will gladly walk and work with you.

PART THREE
Financial Integration and Fiscal Harmonization

6
European Financial Integration and Its Implications for the United States

Ingo Walter

There is a good chance that the banking and financial markets of the European Community in the 1990s will become among the most efficient and innovative in the world, possibly surpassing those of the United States in some respects. The integration of European financial markets stands to play a role in the 1990s that is comparable to the role of the integration of product markets some thirty years earlier. Besides creating internal static and dynamic benefits for the EC regional economy, it will do much to enhance the standing of the EC in global finance and create a viable staging area for financing the economic restructuring of Eastern Europe. Monetary integration is desirable but not necessary—given the prospective breadth and depth of the evolving European hedging markets and instruments—for financial integration to generate many of the expected static and dynamic gains.

True financial market integration involves freedom for savers to place their funds, for borrowers to finance themselves, and for banks and other financial firms to pursue profit opportunities anywhere within the EC, all within a reasonably consistent and coherent regulatory framework. This issue has been formally taken up relatively late in the evolution of the community. But it has developed a powerful momentum, driven by political and economic events that began to come at a rapid pace during the 1980s and that promise to continue and perhaps strengthen further in the 1990s. The European financial industry is thus caught in a dual revolution—geographic and sectoral restructuring, which are occurring simultaneously.

In the process the EC will become among the most competitive of the world's financial markets, with large numbers of indigenous and foreign-based players clustered in distinct strategic groups. Japanese and American institutions will play significant, but different, roles in this process. Vigorous competition will also capture the financial centers of Europe, both among each other and with financial centers outside the EC.

The first section of this paper briefly traces the process of European monetary integration through the 1970s and 1980s, from the end of Bretton Woods to the 1989 agreement in principle to proceed to a European Monetary Union (EMU). The next section considers the state of the debate on problems of macroeconomic policy convergence to the extent that these are relevant to the creation of a unified EC financial market. The following section discusses the evolution of that market, with specific reference to cross-border bank lending, new issues of securities, secondary market brokerage and trading, investment management, financing of foreign direct investment activity, and mergers and acquisitions. The succeeding section focuses on the financial markets playing field that is being shaped by the EC banking and securities directives, as well as tax and investment policies. The implications of the evolving playing field are developed for financial centers in the EC as well as for banks and securities firms home based in the EC and elsewhere.

All of this carries with it significant implications for the United States. On the one hand, the allocative and growth effects of financial market integration in Europe will have positive spillover effects for the United States. On the other hand, U.S. financial markets and institutions will face new challenges and opportunities, with respect to both their links to Europe and their global competitive positioning and performance.

The Path toward Financial Integration

The concept of financial integration in Europe had its origins in the Treaty of Rome of 1957, negotiated in an environment that at the time remained dominated by a thicket of exchange controls, the Bretton Woods system of pegged exchange rates, and inefficient, fragmented, and wholly inward-oriented domestic financial markets. Consideration of EC monetary integration first took place alongside the 1955–1958 negotiation of the European Monetary Agreement (EMA), intended to liberalize exchange controls. It preceded the full restoration of external convertibility at the end of 1958, as well as adherence in 1961 by the EC member countries to International Monetary Fund Article VIII on liberalization of exchange controls.

Financial and monetary integration was seen in the 1950s by many of the EC's founders, including Robert Schumann, as a necessary component of the economic integration process. The 1957 Rome Treaty, however, stipulated only that each member state act in the "common interest" when formulating and executing its exchange rate policies (Article 107) and work toward liberalization of exchange controls (Article 67) as quickly as practicable. Violation of the general rule on exchange rate policies by a member state could be offset by the EC Commission's suspending—on recommendation of the EC Monetary Committee—internal trade liberalization measures and authorizing injured member countries to undertake specific temporary countermeasures, possibly including imposition of import quotas. Intra-EC freedom of trade in financial services was likewise implicit in the Rome Treaty, but it remained dormant for some thirty years and was brought to the surface in part by the fundamental changes that occurred in financial intermediation over the intervening decades.

Gradual liberalization of current payments and financial market transactions in the EC continued throughout the 1960s and 1970s, although there were significant leads and lags—for example, in Belgium, Greece, and Italy—and as the community grew from the original six members to the present twelve. Some capital restrictions were liberalized in 1961, and further liberalization occurred during the ensuing years.

On June 13, 1988, the Council of Ministers authorized full liberalization of capital movement (including movements affecting short-term funds flows) by the end of July 1990, with an extended adjustment period to the end of 1992 granted to Greece, Ireland, Portugal, and Spain. There are provisions for reimposition of temporary restrictions on short-term capital movements under a safeguard clause in case these seriously disturb a member country's exchange rate or monetary policies.

Meantime, the Second Banking Directive, intended to provide a consistent and level playing field for credit institutions within the EC, was proposed by the commission in early 1988 and finally acted on by the council in late 1989, to take effect at the beginning of 1993 (EC Commission 1988b). A parallel draft directive covering the securities industry—the Investment Services Directive—was circulated throughout 1988 and 1989, and rules governing the creation and EC-wide distribution of mutual funds were adopted in 1989 as well (EC Commission 1988a). By the beginning of 1990 the broad outlines of the EC financial markets for the remainder of the century had largely been set in place.

As early as 1962 the EC Commission proposed increased coordination of macroeconomic and exchange rate policies among EC finance ministers and central bank governors, with full monetary union to be achieved by 1971. Premature as it turned out to be, the proposals presaged establishment of the Committee of Central Bank

Governors in 1964 to confer periodically on members' monetary policies, as well as the release of the Barre report in 1969, promoting greater central bank coordination and leading in February 1970 to a system of short-term monetary support among EC central banks.

The Werner report in 1970 proposed creation of a single European currency, total liberalization of capital movements, freedom of establishment for financial institutions, a common central banking system essentially modeled on the U.S. Federal Reserve System, and a centralized EC economic policy-making body politically responsible to the European Parliament. Many of the Werner report's recommendations found resonance in an EC council resolution of March 1971 calling for gradual narrowing of intervention margins among the EC currencies, which were subsequently instituted in the form of the "snake" in March 1972. This involved limiting intra-EC exchange rate margins to 2¼ percent on either side of fixed reference rates, while the EC countries as a group maintained a margin of 4½ percent against the dollar under the Smithsonian Agreement of December 1981.

Running through much of the early discussions leading up to and following the signing of the Treaty of Rome had been a strong bias in favor of exchange rate stability. Perhaps more than in some other countries, therefore, the end of the Bretton Woods system in 1971 and the subsequent collapse of the short-lived Smithsonian Agreement in 1973 created a sense of unease among EC policy makers, reflected in a continuous stream of initiatives throughout the 1970s for global and regional alternatives based on exchange rate stability.

The EC currency arrangements during the 1970s, however, largely failed to live up to these expectations for stability, and by 1978 the snake consisted of a deutsche mark bloc of relatively strong currencies—those of West Germany, the Netherlands, Belgium, Luxembourg, and Denmark. Lack of internal currency stability during the decade can be traced to the failure to achieve substantial macropolicy convergence, which was rooted in the strains of turbulent times, with oil price shocks as well as monetary shocks emanating in particular from the United States.

Nevertheless, the 1970s saw renewed pressure for an intra-EC zone of monetary stability. This pressure led to the formulation of annual policy guidelines for members by the Council of Ministers (1974), creation of the European unit of account (EUA) for intra-EC central bank settlements (1975)—superseded in 1978 by the European Currency Unit (ECU)—and finally the Bremen summit creating the European Monetary System (EMS). This four-point program involved

(1) the establishment of the ECU as a weighted basket of member-country currencies; (2) implementation of an exchange rate mechanism (ERM) limiting fluctuations to 2¼ percent in relation to a bilateral parity grid based on the ECU, with no established reference rates between the ECU and non-ERM currencies; (3) creation of a European Monetary Cooperation Fund (FECOM) to which participating governments contributed 20 percent of their gold and U.S. dollar holdings in exchange for ECU balances, intended to be used in very short-term financings of intervention to maintain EMS parities; and (4) design of a fiscal transfer mechanism to ameliorate intra-EMS payments disequilibriums and facilitate adjustment. Special arrangements for Italy within the ERM grew into a 6 percent band that also applied to Spain. Greece and the United Kingdom remain outside the ERM, as does Portugal, which is due to join in 1992.

The track record of the EMS has been mixed, even though the 1980s constituted a relatively benign monetary environment within which to begin to move seriously toward monetary integration. Inflation differentials among the two principal ERM countries, France and West Germany, declined significantly over the decade, but this was also true of the principal non-ERM member countries, Italy and the United Kingdom, as well as between the EC countries as a group and the United States. Still, divergence of ERM exchange rates continued during the decade after 1978, involving eleven currency realignments, ample testimony to a continued lack of substantive macropolicy coordination among the ERM countries during the 1980s, especially in the monetary sphere.

The correlation of exchange rates among ERM participants, however, has been much higher than between members and nonmembers, indicating low intra-ERM volatility in nominal exchange rates and in nominal interest rate differentials. Moreover, the periodic currency realignments within the ERM have certainly prevented the sort of overshooting against relative purchasing power in the ERM cross-rates that has been so troublesome in the case of the United States, Japan, and the United Kingdom.

Exchange rate overshooting creates significant risk for those engaged in international trade and investment activities who are exposed to medium-term exchange rate movements. This occurs in a manner and over periods of time that make it difficult or costly to hedge against by using available financial instruments and markets. At the national level as well, resources are pulled into the tradable goods and services sectors of the economy when a currency is undervalued and expelled from those sectors when the currency is overvalued. This can create serious structural adjustment costs.

By substantially driving out medium-term exchange rate overshooting, the EMS-based combination of policy coordination and timely exchange rate realignments has effectively reduced intra-EC transactions costs and probably made a significant contribution to economic integration—despite the failure to achieve full policy coordination or substantially fixed exchange rates. The absence of the United Kingdom from this story would have been reflected in significantly higher risk exposures and adjustment costs for United Kingdom firms and investors and for the United Kingdom economy as a whole, with respect to intra-EC transactions throughout the 1980s.

The 1985 EC White Paper on Completing the Internal Market gave rise to renewed pressure for monetary integration, and events began to accelerate. In September 1987 the Basel-Nybord Agreements followed, under which EC central banks committed themselves (in the face of West German objections) to lend to each other in order to defend currency values before reaching the 2¼ percent mandatory intervention limit under the ERM. In early 1988 French Finance Minister Edouard Balladur called for establishment of a European central bank and a substantial strengthening of the EMS, and the June 1988 EC summit saw the creation of an expert group chaired by Jacques Delors to examine possible steps toward achieving a common monetary policy—avoiding all references to a common central bank at the insistence of Prime Minister Margaret Thatcher.

The Delors report, duly submitted at the June 1989 EC summit meeting in Madrid, called for a three-stage transition to full monetary union—with a gradual shift of policy-making powers from the national governments to Brussels. The first stage, intended to begin by July 1990, involved greater coordination of monetary policies and inclusion of all EC currencies in the ERM. The second stage envisages creation of a European central banking structure and narrower exchange rate intervention margins. The final stage includes fixed exchange rate parities, adoption of a single currency and central banking institution, and transfer of macropolicy to the community. The first stage of the Delors report was adopted at the June 1989 Madrid summit, as was the commitment to begin preliminary work on the two subsequent stages. The community had thus come full circle to many of the basic principles included in the Werner report almost twenty years earlier. (For a survey, see Schinasi 1989.)

Clearly, the EC initiatives on creating an integrated financial market are closely linked to the process of monetary integration. On the one hand, completely free internal financial flows in the absence of economic policy coordination could be destabilizing. On the other hand, progress toward a common currency and a unified set of economic policies would serve as a catalyst in creating a single financial market and at the same time influence a wide range of activities in financial markets, such as the ability to profit from intra-ERM exchange rate realignments and the need on the part of traders, borrowers, and investors to hedge against them.

Some Problems of Macropolicy Convergence

The issues captured in the Delors report have, of course, been widely debated by policy makers, financial market practitioners, and academics in Europe and elsewhere (see Wyplosz 1990 for a survey). They can perhaps be summarized as follows:

Burden Sharing. The argument is that under any fixed-rate regime the burden of international financial adjustment falls disproportionately on deficit countries—which are by definition under pressure from erosion of external reserve holdings and therefore to pursue deflationary monetary or fiscal policies. Surplus countries can afford to run up extensive reserves, assuming they are able to sterilize their effects on the domestic money supply. They bear a potentially significant opportunity cost by holding excess reserves but are under no immediate pressure to adjust through monetary or fiscal expansion. In the case of the ERM, increased policy coordination is required to increase the symmetry in sharing adjustment burdens (see Begg and Wyplosz 1987).

Further Erosion of Fiscal Policies. Most countries have seen government tax and expenditure policies fall into relative disuse as techniques of active macroeconomic policy, because of integrated markets and significant political and economic rigidities. In the EC context, for example, given substantially free internal trade, expansionary fiscal policies tend to spill over onto partner countries, and this reduces their domestic macropolicy usefulness (IMF 1989). Moreover, with integrated financial markets domestic interest rates may become less responsive to fiscal deficits as capital inflows prevent crowding out of private sector borrowers in national financial markets. Together with the effects of differential fiscal burdens on the location of EC economic activity, this could make it necessary to achieve a certain harmonization of fiscal charges as well.

To a significant extent such problems can be eased, as they are in federally organized countries such as the United States, through a system of fiscal transfers among the member countries. In the EC, however, where such an extensive system of transfers is unlikely to be implemented in the immediate future and where labor migration from depressed areas is culturally constrained, the problem of differential fiscal burdens may remain important.

Erosion of Monetary Independence. The argument here is that financial integration will increase inflationary pressure in low-inflation countries through the impact of capital flows on the domestic monetary base that could be difficult to sterilize (Mastropasqua et al. 1988). Countries wishing to use expansionary monetary policies to stimulate their economies may find it difficult to do so in the face of the resulting capital outflows and pressure on the ERM-linked exchange rate.

Currency-Substitution Effects. An integrated financial market will make possible substantially greater portfolio diversification among financial instruments and currencies for small investors as well as financial institutions and nonfinancial corporations. If investors actively manage these portfolios in ways that include acting on anticipated currency realignments within the integrated area, that could lead to greater monetary instability. Intensified economic policy coordination and narrower inflation differentials should limit the extent of currency-substitution effects (Dornbusch 1988).

Viability of a Deutsche Mark Anchor. Conventional wisdom has been that the natural anchor for the evolving European monetary arrangement is the mark and that members' economic policies will to a significant extent have to be aligned with those of Germany to maintain exchange rate stability—as has been the case to some extent under the ERM (Russo and Tullio 1988). Alternatives to German leadership with respect to monetary policies in the EC include some form of index of traded goods as a currency anchor or greater economic policy harmonization in which Germany gives up a significant degree of monetary policy autonomy to a central decision-making body. Failing these two options, there seems little doubt that Bundesbank leadership will have to be accepted on the matter of monetary policy formulation and that this will set both monetary and fiscal constraints for the other EC countries. At the same time the political pressures on the Bundesbank emanating from German unification have called into question the viability of a mark anchor and prompted the search for alternatives. The undersirable options, most likely to emerge in difficult economic times, include the possibility of reimposing exchange controls or continuing the 1980s pattern of periodic realignments that would negate some of the principal benefits of monetary integration (see Giavazzi and Giovannini 1989).

One can challenge conventional wisdom, however, with the notion that concerted monetary and fiscal policies of the EC members would provide stability sufficient to let the ECU be its own anchor. Such an outcome would spread fairly any gains from seigniorage and any burdens from over expansionary or over contractionary monetary policies—all dependent on the political will of the EC members to pursue common policies (Schinasi 1989).

Policy Credibility. As the foregoing discussion suggests, achieving further monetary convergence in the EC pivots on the credibility of the EC members' pursuit of common policies. If all market participants were convinced that the ERM parity grid exchange rates would be defended, no incentive would exist for destabilizing speculation. Since the 1960s, however, market participants have been skeptical about the integrity of fixed-rate regimes that lack strong demonstrations of monetary and fiscal discipline. The need for an anchor such as the mark is precisely the need to demonstrate discipline.

With full capital mobility and complete currency substitutability approaching reality in the EC, however, there is arguably a need for a stronger ERM. Assume, for example, that the EC's defense of an exchange rate is initially accepted as credible by the market but that substantial commonality of policies has not in fact been achieved. A member government could take advantage of such a situation to fund itself at the expense of other members. If the policy divergence continued, political fallout from other EC countries that bear the inflationary burden would soon contaminate the credibility of the fixed-rate policy once market sentiment changed. In a perfect capital market, pressure for realignment would take the form of complete and rapid desertion of the currency by asset holders.

An EC Central Bank. The Delors report foresees the eventual creation of a single monetary unit and central bank for the EC. This would of course eliminate national monetary autonomy altogether and create a single monetary policy, with the national central banks reduced to the role of the regional Federal Reserve banks in the United States. In this case, many of the aforementioned problems would fall away. One possibility is that such a central bank would be based in Frankfurt under the watchful eye of the Germans, although with full British participation its execution arm could be located in London as the principal EC financial center, more or less on the pattern of Washington and New York in the operations of the U.S. Federal Reserve System.

By May 1990 a prospective structure for an EC monetary organization unofficially called Eurofed began to emerge. In a commission draft paper, Eurofed would be charged with "formulating and implementing monetary policy and issuance of the ECU" (Buchan 1990). The governing body would be a sixteen-member board, of whom twelve would be governors of the national central banks and four would constitute a directorate chosen by the European Council (heads of state). One member of the directorate would be named Eurofed president in consultation with the European Parliament. Each board member would serve a five-year term and could be reappointed once. In board voting the directorate would have 30 of 120 votes, and a qualified majority of 74 votes would be needed in board decisions (meaning that eleven of twelve national central bank governors could overrule the directorate). The extent to which such a structure would guarantee a viable degree of independence from political pressures remained to be seen (Buchan 1990).

Integration of EC Banking and Securities Industries

EC financial integration can occur with or without monetary integration along the lines just described. Even if the institutional and political obstacles prove insurmountable in the near term, integration of EC debt and equity markets will proceed anyway in view of the increasingly broad and deep markets for cash, forward, futures, and options transactions that have developed throughout the EC and globally—with correspondingly broad scope for financial innovation and the creation of derivative financial instruments.

Integration of the banking and securities industries will create higher risk-adjusted asset returns to savers and lower financing costs to borrowers and issuers by reducing the cost and improving the quality of the financial intermediation process. Like integration of nonfinancial markets, this will produce static gains in the efficiency of capital allocation and higher real output in the EC and its trading partners. It may also have dynamic benefits if it leads to higher rates of saving and capital formation in the community. These economic gains will, through international trade and capital-market links, be of substantial benefit to countries such as the United States and Japan as well.

The playing field for banking and securities firms has in any case become increasingly level in recent years. In the United States, for example, the post-1933 division between commercial and investment banks (also applied in Japan after 1947) has been significantly eroded, partly through regulatory change and court decisions but perhaps more effectively by the globalization of financial firms. Japanese and U.S. subsidiaries of commercial banks engage in securities underwriting abroad despite continued home-country separation of the two spheres of activity. Japanese city banks engage in branch banking abroad even as they continue to be limited at home, while U.S. banks undertake global branching despite being prevented, until recently, from interstate branching domestically.

The regulatory environments of national bond and stock markets have changed even more dramatically. Starting with the 1975 U.S. introduction of negotiated securities commission rates on "Mayday" and working through assorted deregulation in the 1986 "big bang" reforms in London, as well as significant reforms in Tokyo, Toronto, and Paris, restrictive pricing conventions and business practices have been liberalized. While restrictions on foreign ownership of equities still remain arguably the largest regulatory obstacle to free international capital movement among the countries of the Organization for Economic Cooperation and Development, they too have declined.

EC debt and equity markets, however, have remained fragmented. Each member nation maintains its own securities exchanges. Each exchange operates according to its own regulations, which have been subject in recent years to widespread reforms. To accommodate large block trades and limited hours of exchange operations, participants have implemented over-the-counter markets in a number of EC countries. These national over-the-counter markets form a second-level structure that can be institutionalized and integrated once restrictions on ownership and capital flows have been eliminated and once the settlement procedures (for payment and delivery of financial instruments) are agreed. Internationally the Euromarkets already form an integrated, self-regulated, over-the-counter market, trading in deposits and debt securities—listed, unlisted, and derivative.

The specific form of community regulatory structures within this broader, international context will have a determining effect on how well the EC banking and securities industry does its job in the 1990s and how it links into the evolution of global financial markets. Certain areas of regulation (such as rules on capital adequacy, conditions for doing business, and transactions standards) will apply directly and specifically to the industry itself. Others (such as taxation, competition policies, and regulation of mergers and acquisitions) will have an important indirect effect.

A Level Playing Field. In the absence of a globally integrated, evenly regulated, fully competitive financial marketplace, what is required in the EC is to attain "equality of competitive opportunity"—a level playing field with maximum market access. This is an extraordinarily difficult condition to define, much less to achieve, in an industry as complex as financial services. It should, however, include at least the following five aspects (Walter 1988):

1. Freedom to establish branches, agencies, subsidiaries, representative offices, or other affiliates within a national market on a basis identical to that applying to locally owned financial institutions. National antitrust and other policies relating to establishment should bear on foreign-based players and domestic players identically.

2. Regulatory symmetry, insofar as possible, with respect to domestic and foreign competitors. This includes the incidence of prudential controls such as capital requirements, asset ratios, lending limits, and reserve requirements. It also implies equal access to domestic securities markets, including, for example, lead-managing local currency issues of securities in the local and offshore markets, as well as equal access to the national payments clearing system, money markets, central bank discount facilities, trust and investment businesses, deposit insurance, and a variety of other dimensions that can affect an institution's competitive positioning.

3. Freedom to import critical resources, including travel and resettlement of professional staff, subscriptions of capital in the case of nonbranch affiliates, data processing, and telecommunications equipment on the same basis as local firms. Equally critical is equality of access to communication and data transmission services and the freedom to establish proprietary data networks.

4. Symmetry with respect to the application of taxation and exchange restrictions, if any, between foreign and local players. This bears on capital outflows such as foreign borrowing in the local markets and local investments abroad, as well as remittances of capital earnings.

5. Equality of access to domestic client groups, financial institutions, and product markets, including branching privileges equal to those of local firms and the right to purchase shares in local financial institutions in accordance with domestic laws regarding competition.

It is against these benchmarks that the EC's commitment to an integrated financial market must be tested, including the impact of EC regulatory structures on non-EC financial institutions.

Equality of Market Access. Liberalization of intra-EC banking activities can be traced to the First Banking Directive of 1977, which allowed banks based anywhere in the EC to establish branches or subsidiaries in any other member country on the condition that banking regulations in the host country were fully observed. It also required member states to establish a licensing system for credit institutions, including minimum "fit and proper" criteria for authorization to do business.

Under the Second Banking Directive of 1988 a single EC banking license allows credit institutions authorized to do business in any single member state to have full access to other national markets for all credit services without separate authorization (see Dermine 1990). This includes deposit taking, wholesale and retail lending, leasing, portfolio advice and management, and trading in securities. In line with the broader dictates of the Basel Concordat of 1986, prudential control is exercised by home countries over all banks authorized to do business in the EC, including subsidiaries (which come under a separate 1983 EC directive on consolidated supervision).

Nonbanking securities firms are covered by the commission's 1988 draft Investment Services Directive, modeled on Britain's Financial Services Act of 1986 and scheduled to go into effect in January 1993 (see Walter and Smith 1990). Again, home-country agencies (public authorities or professional associations appointed by public authorities) will retain the power of licensing, supervising, and regulating investment firms. Institutions duly registered and supervised by EC home countries will essentially be free to establish a commercial presence and to supply securities services in any member country without separate authorization. Investment firms holding membership in stock exchanges in their home countries will likewise be free to apply for full trading privileges on all EC stock, options, and futures exchanges. Close collaboration is envisaged between the EC Commission, the authorities responsible for securities markets and institutions, and banking and insurance authorities.

The responsibility for much of the direct regulation lies with the commission's Directorate General 15 (DG-15). It has the right to countermand host-country restrictions on credit institutions and investment firms from other member countries and to make certain amendments to the banking and securities directives.

Capital Adequacy. The capital-to-assets ratio required of banks and securities firms directly affects their funding costs, as well as their ability to execute transactions, and hence their ability to offer competitive financing to clients. Japanese commercial banks, for example, have long been alleged to have an artificial competitive advantage in international markets as a result of home-country regulations permitting very low capitalization—permitting them to be exceedingly aggressive in competing for various kinds of lending business around the world. Equity-to-asset ratios have indeed differed dramatically among countries in which some of the major international financial institutions are home based. At the same time, hidden reserves are acceptable in some countries—such as Germany, Japan, and Switzerland—seriously distorting equity-to-asset ratios as a measure of capital adequacy (see Bryant 1987).

In 1986 representatives of the Federal Deposit Insurance Corporation and the Federal Reserve System renewed pressure for greater coordination of prudential controls, including capital adequacy requirements, within the broad context of the Bank for International Settlements. The move toward international agreement on this issue, however, achieved real momentum only with an Anglo-American initiative announced in January 1987 to strengthen the international banking community and create a level playing field among globally competing banks.

As agreed in the Basel Accord a year and a half later, banks will have to meet a minimum ratio of 8 percent capital (including not less than 4 percent "core" capital) to "risk assets" (defined to include off-balance-sheet exposures). Criticism of the accord is easy. The definitions of risk assets are unavoidably rough. While the definition of the required 4 percent core capital is fairly stringent, inclusion of hidden and unallocated loan-loss reserves in the definition of secondary capital makes it controversial. And the implementation period (to the end of 1992) is long. The accord's importance, however, is as a beginning. The need for international prudential capital standards was recognized and acted on and contributes significantly to a level playing field for credit institutions. In the EC context the Basel Accord has made further harmonization of capital standards for credit institutions largely superfluous.

Comparable initiatives have yet to be taken, within the EC or on a broader basis, with respect to the securities industry. Yet to create equality of competitive opportunity for all institutions supplying financial services in the community, the EC will eventually have to come to grips with the question of capital adequacy for nonbanks as well. The alternatives range from matching capital against position (market) risks to minimum levels of firm capital covering all eventualities and EC-wide enforcement of maximum exposure limits. Whatever emerges will also have to be aligned with capitalization requirements for banks to achieve regulatory parity, not least because the banking and securities business is heavily integrated in most EC countries and likely to become even more so. Indeed, implementation of the draft Investment Services Directive in the absence of an EC capital adequacy directive bearing on nonbank securities firms could lead to significant competitive dislocations among such firms and between independent securities firms and banks.

Conduct-of-Business Rules. Whereas the EC "single passport" for banks and securities firms will be under the control of home-country authorities, conduct-of-business rules regarding EC financial markets themselves will be the exclusive responsibility of host-country authorities. This split regulatory responsibility was partially designed to be responsive to fears of British regulators that complete reliance on home-country regulation might place London at a serious competitive disadvantage in light of the relatively stringent British Financial Services Act. At worst home-country regulation could lead to "regulatory arbitrage" among firms seeking the most permissive home-country environment, as well as competitive laxity in oversight and control of financial firms on the part of countries seeking to attract them.

As it stands, financial institutions will have to deal with thirteen different sets of rules (including the Eurobond market). This will increase regulatory confusion and leave open the possibility of rule-based protectionism against nondomestic firms. It seems likely, however, that EC member rules will gradually converge toward a consensus on minimum acceptable conduct-of-business standards, which will seek to optimize the balance between market efficiency and regulatory soundness.

One area of particular interest with respect to conduct-of-business rules has been insider trading. The view that insider trading is a crime, rather than a professional indiscretion, is new in most of Europe. No one in the EC has ever been jailed for insider trading, and in several member countries it is not a criminal offense. In view of major insider trading scandals in the late 1980s, the issue has become politically charged (Walter 1990).

A second example of conduct-of-business rules involves information disclosure in new issues of securities. There has been consistent opposition to efforts at standardizing the content and distribution of prospectuses covering equity, bond, and Eurobond issues for sale to individuals and institutions in the member countries. An EC disclosure directive was put forward in late 1988, for application in 1992, involving a common prospectus. All Eurosecurities, however, would be exempt from the disclosure rules if they are "not the object of a generalized advertising or canvassing campaign."

Eurobond practitioners expressed concern that any EC initiatives should be fully consistent with self-regulation in their market. Precedent has generally applied over formal rules, and the relatively loose guidelines published by the Association of International Bond Dealers (AIBD) have focused on reporting of transactions rather than market practices. Participants argue that more stringent requirements are inappropriate for a market composed entirely of some 800 professionals.

Regulation of Mergers and Acquisitions. In December 1988 the EC Commission put forward a draft directive to harmonize takeover rules. It contained three major provisions: (1) companies that offer to buy more than 33 percent of the shares in a target company must offer to buy all shares; (2) companies that launch takeover attempts must state their intentions concerning the target's future, including its activities, work force, financial structure, and debt levels, the latter criterion being aimed specifically at leveraged buyouts; and (3) certain antitakeover strategies would be prohibited, including "exceptional operations" and share sales without the agreement of existing shareholders.

Under Articles 85 and 86 of the 1957 Treaty of Rome, all distortions involving subsidies and restrictive business practices were to have been removed if they affect trade among the member countries. But serious problems in both areas remain, and can complicate merger and acquisition deals or defeat them altogether. Restrictive business practices involve market sharing, cooperative research and development, exclusive distribution, price fixing, and tied sales. Although the EC competition regulations require submission of restrictive agreements to the commission, the caseload (roughly 3,000 in 1988) ensures the persistence of competitive distortions. In addition, there are "block exemptions," specifying rules under which restrictive practices are automatically exempted from the Rome Treaty's provisions and can proceed without notifying the commission.

Power regarding EC-wide competitive structure and conduct has begun to shift to the commission's Fourth Directorate General (DG-4). It has acted against egregious use of subsidy and has attacked certain high-visibility cartel arrangements, such as in air transport and telecommunications. Future activity may target national insurance cartels, fixed commissions on securities transactions, and fixed fees on advertising. There has been increasing EC intervention in major merger and acquisition deals and a growing volume of preemptive submissions by firms seeking EC clearance of proposed transactions—nominally, EC action under Articles 85 and 86 could be taken only after takeovers were completed, but the uncertainties that would result ensure that advance clearance is the only viable option.

There have been calls from the industrial sector for the EC Commission to be given exclusive jurisdiction over all major merger and acquisition deals with respect to their competitive impact and to spell out formal merger rules that would apply on an EC-wide basis. It was originally proposed that DG-4 have exclusive power to rule on all deals valued at over 1 billion ECU, in which each company has sales of over 100 million ECU, and where at least 25 percent of the combined sales of the two companies are outside the borders of one member country and hence incorporate a "European dimension."

Amendments were subsequently put forward suggesting that the threshold for the commission's involvement should be raised to 2 billion ECU from January 1, 1993, and that there should be a transitional period during which the limit would be 5 billion ECU. The 25 percent rule was changed to 33 percent to avoid the community's becoming involved in mergers of an essentially national dimension. The commission would have six months to reach a decision, and normal antitrust considerations could be waived if the commission decided that the new entity was desirable as a "European champion." These rules were adopted at the end of 1989. They have significant extraterritoriality implications—for example, with respect to the merger of two U.S. companies whose EC operations fall under the guidelines.

The European financial market is thus in the process of achieving substantial harmonization of the statutory rules governing takeovers, which is being combined with gradual removal of the competitive distortions (such as subsidization and restrictive practices) that complicate or prevent economic restructuring.

Regulation of Mutual Funds and Unit Trusts. The EC directive governing the operation and sale of mutual funds—Undertakings for the Collective Investment of Transferable Securities (UCITS)—came into force on October 1, 1989, after fifteen years of negotiation. It specifies general rules for the kinds of investments that are appropriate for mutual funds and how they should be sold. The regulatory requirements for fund management and certification are left to the home country of the firm; specific rules for adequacy of disclosure and selling practices are left to the host countries.

Consequently, funds duly established and monitored in any EC member country, such as Luxembourg—and that are in compliance with UCITS—can be sold without restriction to investors in local markets community-wide and promoted and advertised through local selling networks and direct mail, as long as selling requirements applicable in each country are met. These include high-performance "synthetic" funds, based on futures and options, not previously permitted in some financial centers such as London. Under UCITS 90 percent of assets must be invested in publicly traded companies, no more than 5 percent of the outstanding stock of any company may be owned by a fund, and there are limits on investment funds' borrowing rights. Real estate funds, commodity funds, and money market funds are excluded.

Taxation of Investment Income. In light of free intra-EC capital mobility and the UCITS initiative, a decision on narrowing or eliminating intra-EC differentials in taxation of capital income has been of great interest (Levich and Walter 1989). In February 1989 the EC Commission formally proposed a minimum 15 percent withholding tax (administered at source) on interest income of investments (bonds and bank deposits) by residents of other EC countries. Eurosecurities and non-EC residents were exempted from the withholding tax proposal. Also exempted were savings accounts of young people and small savers that were already exempt from taxation in a number of EC countries, although member states would be free to impose withholding taxes above the 15 percent floor. Governments could exempt interest income subject to withholding at source from declaration for tax purposes. Also exempted were countries that already apply equal or higher withholding taxes on interest income. Additional aspects of the proposal concerned cooperation in enforcement and exchange of information among EC fiscal authorities. Dividends were omitted from the proposals because they are generally less heavily taxed by EC member countries and because national income tax systems were thought to capture this kind of income relatively effectively.

Supporters of abolishing investment income tax differences within the EC argued that tax harmonization was essential if financial market integration was not to lead to widespread tax evasion. The effort was led by France, together with Belgium, Italy, and Spain. All four countries also argued that absence of tax harmonization would weaken their currencies in relation to those of other EC members. All four have tax collection systems that are relatively weak in other respects.

Opponents, mainly the United Kingdom and Luxembourg as well as the Netherlands, argued that tax harmonization is both unnecessary and harmful to the functioning of efficient financial markets and that substantial investments would subsequently flow outside the EC, especially to Switzerland and Caribbean tax havens. Indeed, they argued that the proposal failed to recognize that Europe is part of a global financial market and that EC securities returns might have to be raised to levels providing equivalent after-tax returns to prevent capital outflows from becoming a serious problem. The United Kingdom was also concerned about the special role of the Isle of Man and the Channel Islands (which are "semidetached" from the EC) and their treatment in the withholding tax initiative—as well as with the tax proposal as a possible steppingstone toward harmonization of fiscal and monetary policies.

In 1988 West Germany announced consideration of a 10 percent withholding tax on interest and dividend income in what became an embarrassing demonstration that such taxes can provoke immediate and massive capital flight. Bundesbank estimates show a total long-term capital outflow of $42.8 billion during 1988 while the 10 percent withholding tax was being discussed. An estimated $10.7 billion of West German investment funds flowed into the Luxembourg bond market after the announcement that the tax was to be effective January 1, 1989. Investors' reactions to the West German tax bid up the price of Euro-deutsche mark issues and depressed yields to the point where in early 1989 it was cheaper for Pepsico to borrow marks in Luxembourg than it was for the West German federal government to do so on the domestic market. The West German authorities were subsequently induced to allow "coupon washing"—permitting investors to sell bonds immediately before the interest payment date and buy them back immediately afterward to escape the tax—by shifting the coupon payments to tax-exempt investors. Four months later, on April 27, 1989, the West German authorities announced that the withholding tax would be abolished on July 1.

After two years of intense debate on the issue, the 15 percent EC withholding tax proposal collapsed in mid-1989 as the Germans withdrew their support of the commission's initiative and joined the opposition. Nevertheless, there was little doubt that the proposal for a uniform tax on capital income and closer cooperation between EC tax authorities would eventually be revived—although harmonization of withholding tax rates and collection methods remained constrained by the possibility of capital flight to low-tax environments outside the EC.

Despite the tough sledding that various EC proposals to create a level playing field have had, there is little doubt that progress is being made. Partly this is in response to a broader search of regulatory structures that optimally combine efficiency and stability. Partly it is in response to lobbying pressure from the affected players in the banking and securities industry, inside and outside the EC, for treatment that is in their own interests. And partly it is the result of gradual movement toward economic policy harmonization among the member countries.

The Evolution of European Financial Markets

The competitive dynamics of the major world financial markets over the past quarter-century have been affected by three powerful forces—product innovation, process innovation, and technological change. Product innovation usually involves the creation of new financial instruments (for example, caps, futures, options, swaps) along with the ability to replicate certain instruments by bundling existing ones (synthetic securities) or to highlight only a single financial attribute by unbundling an existing instrument. Process innovation encompasses contract design (for example, cash settlement futures contracts), methods of settlement and trading, methods of efficient margin calculation, methods of contract pricing, and passive or index-based portfolio investment techniques, along with a range of other innovations. Technological change, primarily in telecommunications and information processing, has greatly facilitated the drive to create and broaden the market for such product and process innovations.

Both financial firms and the users of financial services have access to a broad range of location choices—including an array of foreign or offshore operations. This is certainly true at the wholesale end of the industry, and it is becoming more true at the retail end as well through the origination and distribution of asset-backed securities as well as unit trusts or mutual funds.

This is the context of financial innovation (especially in the United States and the United Kingdom) within which the European financial markets have evolved during the 1980s in linking the ultimate sources of funds with the ultimate users of funds domestically and internationally. In addition to the growth of cross-border bank lending, this has occurred in four areas: (1) new issues of securities, (2) secondary market brokerage and trading, (3) investment management, and (4) financial restructuring of corporations, including mergers and acquisitions.

All four are clearly interrelated. Performance-oriented investment management, for example, is required to create a more liquid market for mergers and acquisitions, and an active secondary market for debt and equity securities is a precondition for growth in new issues of securities. The European evolution has nevertheless been quite uneven, with the United Kingdom invariably in the lead with respect to financial innovations and deregulation and the continental European countries following with greater or lesser enthusiasm.

New Issues of Securities. European firms had long been inhibited from gaining experience with securities transactions in competitive markets for two main reasons: (1) the traditional reliance by nonfinancial corporations in Europe on bank borrowing and (2) the relatively poorly developed capital markets of a number of European countries. Since the early 1980s, however, the market for debt and equity issues in Europe has developed substantially. By the end of 1987 the total volume of new issues by European corporations in the various European capital markets was within striking distance of the world's two other principal markets, the United States and Japan, although European nonfinancial corporations still lagged their overseas counterparts by a factor of two or three to one in new issues volume relative to overall economic activity, as shown in table 6-1.

The European new issues market in effect consists of a loosely integrated three-market structure comprising (1) Eurosecurities, (2) domestic issues, and (3) foreign bonds and equities placed in domestic capital markets by issuers based in EC partner countries. The 1988 total for this three-tiered market was $244 billion, with a debt-equity split of $181 billion to $63 billion. Domestic markets remain the choice for most local firms, especially for debt securities in Germany, France, and Italy and for equity securities in Germany, France, Italy, and the United Kingdom—almost five times the volume of funds were raised domestically in 1988 as in the foreign and Euromarkets combined.

By the end of the 1980s the European new issues market had thus achieved a level of activity sufficient to supply competitively the requirements of the major European firms capable of capital markets issues. European industry has consequently reduced its reliance both on bank lending and on overseas markets—comparatively small amounts of financing were carried out by European companies in Japan and the United States in the 1985–1989 period. Nor is it any longer necessary for European companies financing outside their own markets to rely on facilities denominated in non-European currencies, as it had traditionally been for Eurodollar bond issues.

A variety of factors have contributed to the increased use of the capital markets by European companies. One of these was the sheer level of corporate funding demand in the 1980s to finance new investments, financial restructurings, and acquisitions, which encouraged companies to consider new financing options. Privatizations also had an important role on the equities side—the volume of new and secondary sales of privatization issues rose from $32.8 to $89.8 billion between 1985 and 1987, a significant part of this in the United Kingdom. The privatization process demonstrated a latent investment capacity that had been largely untapped. Though structured as domestic new equity issues, many in fact involved substantial distributions of shares in other parts of Europe, as well as the United States and Japan. This stimulated and satisfied new demand for cross-border investment within Europe and led to an invigorated marketplace for equities.

In addition, the influence of the Euromarkets can hardly be overestimated. While domestic markets for debt securities are impor-

TABLE 6-1
VOLUME OF CORPORATE SECTOR CAPITAL MARKET FINANCING BY REGIONAL CORPORATIONS IN THEIR HOME MARKETS, 1988
(billions of dollars of proceeds at average exchange rates)

	United States			Europe			Japan		
	Financial	Non-financial	Total	Financial	Non-financial	Total	Financial	Non-financial	Total
Equities	28.8	13.6	42.4	9.5	42.3	51.8	25.1	40.8	65.9
Bonds	141.1	221.9	363.0	155.2	26.3	181.5	287.7	137.9	425.6
Total	169.9	235.5	405.4	164.7	68.6	233.3	312.8	178.7	491.5
GNP (trillions)			4.88			5.27			2.9
Financing per dollar of GNP (dollars)	0.03	0.05	0.08	0.03	0.01	0.05	0.11	0.06	0.17

SOURCE: Roy C. Smith and Ingo Walter, "Reconfiguration of Global Financial Markets in the 1990s" (New York: NYU Salomon Center, 1990).

tant in total volume, each is dwarfed by the Eurobond market, which provides a continuously evolving self-regulated international structure in which domestic participants from all EC countries are actively involved and where competition based on performance and innovation are the dominant factors.

At the same time the European markets became subject to new competition beginning in 1990 as a result of the new opportunities presented by the U.S. Securities and Exchange Commission's Rule 144A, which became effective in April 1990 and offers a safe haven to any issuer (domestic or foreign) offering securities to qualified institutional investors on an unregistered basis. Rule 144A omits registration requirements altogether, thereby greatly simplifying new issue procedures for international issuers unwilling to submit to the trouble and cost of preparing a registration statement (SEC 1988).

Rule 144A contemplates a substantial increase in the number of non-U.S. debt and equity financings done in the American capital market, many of which will be offered not only to domestic investors but also, simultaneously, to investors in Europe and Japan. Issues brought to European and Japanese markets—whether by U.S. or by other corporate issuers—may also be offered to institutional investors in the United States under Rule 144A. From a regulatory viewpoint virtually all remaining obstacles to full international market integration are removed with the introduction of Rule 144A. Issuers, however, will always choose the lowest-cost market for the securities they wish to offer, which may or may not be in the United States, regardless of regulatory considerations.

One other way in which Rule 144A may affect market activities is by its use by banks to broaden and perfect their distribution of bank loans. During the 1980s many U.S. banks adopted the practice of "selling down" to other banks their participations in loans. This process could be made more efficient by securitizing the loans by using Rule 144A provisions, which would permit liquid markets to develop in the securities, and to extend the group of investors to which they are offered to encompass nonbank financial institutions. Should such practices become widespread, the U.S. bank loan market would come to be integrated with the bond market to a substantial extent, thereby facilitating the development of meaningful placing power by banks in the securities field (a strength that most banks lacked) and raising regulatory questions as to how such securities should be treated for accounting and regulatory purposes, including limitations on the extent to which government deposit insurance applies in such cases.

Secondary Market Brokerage and Trading. Intra-European secondary market trading in securities has likewise increased considerably since the mid-1980s, driven by three factors. First, the dramatic decline of the dollar against other currencies reduced the relative attractiveness of Eurodollar securities to non-dollar-based investors. Second, the upward movement of stock prices around the world created an equities euphoria such that as activity in the Eurodollar bond markets declined, trading activity in primary and secondary markets in other Eurocurrency-denominated bonds and in national stock and bond markets in the United Kingdom, Germany, and Switzerland increased. Clearly the stock market crash of October 1987 was a serious setback, with equity markets drying up throughout Europe and recovering only at the end of the decade. The third factor was deregulation. In reaction to and anticipation of this and in response to the growing interest of EC and non-European institutional investors in international diversification—a process that began in the late 1970s and has steadily expanded since—many securities firms have moved rapidly to increase their research coverage of continental European securities.

Increased volumes of new issues of securities and rising securities values necessitate increased secondary market liquidity. If this liquidity is not provided by indigenous markets—whether because of institutional inefficiency or excessive regulation—foreign markets will take up the slack. Substantial deregulation of financial markets has been seen in the United States, the United Kingdom, Australia, Canada, and France. In all cases rules restricting ownership of brokers, preserving their capital structures, and protecting their commission rates were overturned. Each of these markets has emerged stronger and larger, with increased volumes making business more viable for the survivors. But at the same time growth also placed significant strains on back-office securities clearing and delivery systems, requiring substantial upgrading of these functions to improve efficiency.

London in particular has been poised to take any dissatisfied secondary market customer from the continental European marketplace. The big bang in 1986 changed the face of the British market. It originated in a negotiated settlement, struck in 1983, of a restrictive practices suit brought in 1976 against the London Stock Exchange by the Labour government. This settlement provided for a phaseout of fixed commission rates over a three-year period and for greater participation by nonmembers in the affairs of member firms and of the stock exchange's Governing Council. After the settlement the members of the stock exchange concluded that the economics of the old system would be so severely disrupted by the move to negotiated

FIGURE 6-1
TRADING VOLUME OF DERIVATIVE SECURITIES FOR EUROPE, ASIA, AND OTHER LOCATIONS, 1985–1989
(millions)

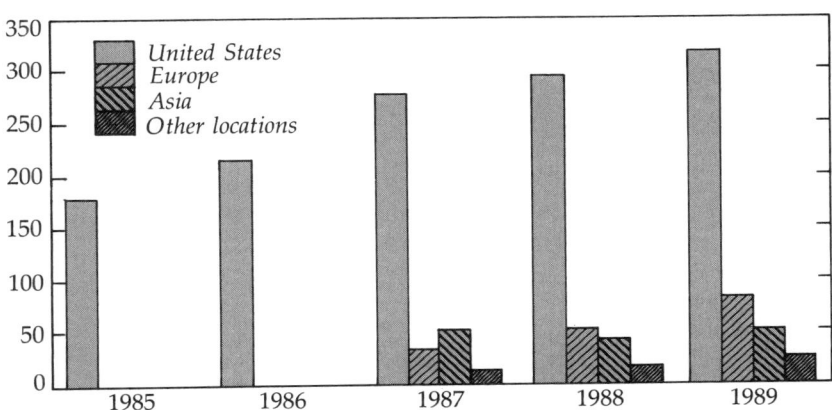

NOTE: Derivative securities include exchange-traded futures and options, stated in millions of contracts traded. Data do not include over-the-counter traded futures and options Data for Europe, Asia, and other locations not available for 1985 and 1986.
SOURCE: Futures Industry Association.

commission rates that more significant changes would have to be made. Brokers and jobbers would no longer be excluded from each other's business, and ownership restrictions on nonmembers would be lifted entirely—allowing banks, other kinds of financial institutions, and foreign firms full participation in the market. To these changes the government added reforms opening up the government securities (gilts) market. Intense competition ensued. In the gilts market alone the number of approved market makers rose from two to twenty-nine. Commissions, now fully negotiable, dropped to almost nothing on more actively traded stocks.

At the same time, trading volume in derivative securities including futures and options in Euorpe remains far behind the United States, as figure 6-1 shows—although it is growing rapidly and in the future will undoubtedly add to the financial innovation, hedging, and liquidity capabilities of the European markets.

Investment Management. Services included under investment management range from securities research and custody to the sale of

TABLE 6-2
FOREIGN INVESTMENT OF PRIVATE SECTOR PENSION ASSETS, 1980–1992
(millions of dollars and percent)

	1980		1985		1992[a]	
United States	3,300	1	27,000	3	150,000	9
Great Britain	9,700	9	40,100	18	135,000	25
Japan	400	1	7,600	8	88,000	20
Netherlands	1,500	4	5,400	9	30,000	12
Canada	2,000	7	4,100	8	20,000	10
Switzerland	1,300	4	1,700	4	12,000	8
Australia	0	0	800	8	10,000	20
Hong Kong	1,200	60	2,400	60	9,000	65
West Germany	500	2	1,000	3	9,000	6
Ireland	300	20	700	20	2,000	20
Belgium	275	25	800	30	1,800	35
France	75	1	200	2	600	3
New Zealand	0	0	0	0	400	8
Rest of world	100	2	600	3	1,200	10
Total	20,650		92,100		469,000	

a. Projected. Expressed in 1987 dollars. Assumes no change in foreign investment restrictions.
SOURCE: InterSec Research Corporation, March 1988.

options, caps, floors, futures, and swaps to private placements of securities. Central to the evolving market in Europe, however, are three functions.

First is the management of portfolios of European securities for non-European investors, predominantly for U.S. and Japanese pension funds and other institutional investors. Non-European institutional investors have traditionally retained European investment managers for portfolios of European and other international securities. The largest segment of this business has come from American pension funds, which since 1985 have been reducing domestic exposure in favor of non-U.S. equities (see table 6-2). Because of the success of this strategy, American institutions have steadily increased funds allocated to managers of international investments. On January 1, 1987, for example, the fifty largest international managers of American pension assets had approximately $50 billion under their control. Of these, some twenty-two were non-American—mostly European, mainly British merchant banks and fund managers or Swiss banks active in the private banking sector business. Of the top fifteen managers, sharing $31 billion of assets among them, five were European (Walter and Smith 1990).

Competition for international investment management business is understandably intense. European firms have the advantage of local knowledge and, for many American pension fund trustees, authenticity. They must nevertheless compete with some of the most powerful American banks and fund managers, which are perhaps more accustomed to a fiercely competitive environment and which can always hire Europeans to fill in gaps in their knowledge. American institutional investors tend to be more demanding in the standards they expect, and these higher standards are increasingly the norm for the investment management marketplace as a whole. Nevertheless, for those who do perform well, fees are attractive and usually exceed those for comparable domestic portfolio management.

The second central function in the evolving European investment industry is the management of portfolios of European and non-European securities for European institutions. European pension funds and other institutional investors have consistently invested a substantial proportion of their portfolios abroad. As much as 20-30 percent of the total assets of British and Dutch pension funds may be in non-European stocks. Competition for the management of such funds is on a global basis, with European institutions often just as willing to appoint American or Japanese advisers as domestic managers, particularly since much of the money to be invested is in any case earmarked for these two major markets. Additional competition comes from a number of continental European banks, well versed in the management of private wealth and shifting their orientation to become equally potent in the international asset management business for institutional clients.

This is the management of portfolios for European private investors. An important dimension of private wealth management has traditionally been financial secrecy, relating mainly to tax matters and transfers of funds across borders in the presence of exchange controls (Walter 1990). Confidentiality and trust have been two of the most important commodities sold by continental European banks, especially those in Switzerland, Luxembourg, and Austria, where funds have traditionally been concealed from local fiscal authorities while being prudently managed by trustworthy and reliable bankers or investment managers.

Notwithstanding these attractions, bankers in these countries are keen to be perceived as providing experienced, professional, competitive services in an environment of stability and confidentiality. Moreover, Luxembourg especially has been quick to adopt the UCITS regulations for investment funds and to position itself for pan-European fund management. These bankers are sensitive to the possibility that the EC countries will eventually come together on rules regarding personal taxation and disclosure of tax information.

With secrecy a relatively declining consideration in private banking, performance will become an increasingly important criterion for judging the competitiveness of funds managers. The traditional strength of the continental European banks' control over their clients will be severely tested. Mutual funds, investment company shares in specialized investments, and global, real-time investment services to individuals will be used to tempt clients to shift a portion of their money to new firms. The competition is bound to lower fees and commissions for investment management across the EC.

Corporate Financial Restructuring. The economic restructuring of Europe should increase the volume of corporate finance transactions such as mergers and acquisitions, leveraged buyouts, and other forms of financial restructuring (Walter and Smith 1990). First, a unified market will require longer, more competitive enterprises able to reap significant economies of scale and scope, particularly in such industries as transportation, information technology, telecommunications, financial services, food products, consumer electronics, and pharmaceuticals. Second, acquisitions of brand names and manufacturing facilities in a unified market for highly competitive products may be cheaper than *de novo* investments. Third, the growing concentration of shareholdings in institutional portfolios subject to higher performance requirements will encourage the realization of underlying equity values, and investment managers will be increasingly inclined to accept takeover bids for the short-term returns they afford. Fourth, ample financing will continue to be available from banks anxious to earn large fees and spreads on deals under Bank for International Settlements (BIS) risk-based capital standards that place all corporate lending into one category. Finally, sufficient merger and acquisition technology is in place to facilitate such transactions.

Table 6–3 indicates the global volume of merger and acquisition transactions during 1985–1989. Some 66 percent of that was domestic U.S. activity, and another 13 percent was U.S. cross-border, the bulk of the latter being acquisitions of American companies by foreign companies (Smith and Walter 1990). Thus almost 80 percent of global merger and acquisition activity during this period was United States related.

Of the $329 billion of non-U.S. merger and acquisition transactions during the 1985–1989 period, $196.4 billion, or 60 percent, were intra-European (table 6–4). An additional $156 billion (80 percent of the intra-European total) involved transactions between Europe and

TABLE 6-3

VOLUME OF COMPLETED INTERNATIONAL MERGER AND CORPORATE TRANSACTIONS, UNITED STATES, 1985–1989

(millions of U.S. dollars)

	Domestic U.S.		Cross-Border United States						Outside United States		Global Totals	
			U.S. Buyer		U.S. Seller		Total Cross-Border					
	No.	Amount	No.	Amount	No.	Amount	No.	Amount	No.	Amount	No.	Amount
1985	778 (852)	181,544.6	28 (60)	4,799.1	72 (104)	9,732.6	100 (164)	14,531.7	82 (90)	16,296.5	960 (1,106)	212,372.8
1986	1,145 (1,253)	201,745.8	35 (59)	2,905.4	147 (138)	27,280.1	182 (197)	30,185.5	132 (161)	28,728.5	1,459 (1,611)	260,659.8
1987	1,273 (1,267)	199,878.2	46 (102)	7,669.4	172 (123)	35,481.7	218 (225)	43,151.1	310 (279)	70,706.7	1,801 (1,771)	313,736.0
1988	1,510 (1,178)	286,918.8	72 (135)	5,886.6	226 (168)	60,915.9	298 (303)	66,802.5	1,115 (789)	97,798.4	2,923 (2,270)	451,519.7
1989	1,489 (1,331)	200,330.6	124 (184)	17,500.0	324 (183)	44,615.5	448 (367)	62,115.5	1,459 (1,275)	115,306.5	3,396 (2,973)	377,752.6
Total 1985–89	6,195 (5,881)	1,070,418.0	305 (540)	38,760.5	941 (716)	178,025.8	1,246 (1,256)	216,786.3	3,098 (2,594)	328,836.6	10,539 (9,731)	1,616,040.9

NOTE: Completed transactions include mergers, tender mergers, tender offers, exchange offers, purchases of stakes, divestitures, recapitalizations, exchange offers, and leveraged buyouts. The volume data are classified according to the announcement date of a transaction, not taking into consideration when a transaction is completed. Figures are in millions of dollars of purchase price—excluding fees and expenses—at current exchange rates. The dollar value includes the amount paid for all common stock, common stock equivalents, preferred stock, debt, options, assets, warrants, and stake purchases made within six months of the announcement date of the transaction. Liabilities assumed are included if they are disclosed in press releases or newspaper articles. Number of completed transactions with undisclosed dollar values in parentheses.

SOURCE: Securities Data Corporation, Mergers and Corporate Transactions database.

TABLE 6-4
VOLUME OF COMPLETED INTERNATIONAL MERGER AND CORPORATE TRANSACTIONS, EUROPE, 1985–1989
(millions of U.S. dollars)

| | Intra-European | | Europe/Non-Europe | | | | Total Cross-Border | |
| | | | Buyer from Europe | | Seller from Europe | | | |
	No.	Amount	No.	Amount	No.	Amount	No.	Amount
1985	31	8,326.0	40	6,083.2	22	2,441.0	62	8,524.2
	(32)		(44)		(40)		(84)	
1986	59	11,911.4	85	17,752.0	34	3,523.2	119	21,275.2
	(76)		(54)		(33)		(87)	
1987	189	38,335.0	111	27,825.9	45	8,307.5	156	36,133.4
	(161)		(67)		(72)		(139)	
1988	835	63,431.6	179	35,978.9	104	8,433.6	283	44,412.5
	(559)		(134)		(125)		(259)	
1989	1,090	74,432.9	255	33,367.1	180	12,671.0	435	46,038.1
	(874)		(134)		(211)		(345)	
Total 1985–89	2,204	196,436.9	670	121,007.1	385	35,376.3	1,055	156,383.4
	(1,702)		(433)		(481)		(914)	

NOTE: Completed transactions include mergers, tender mergers, tender offers, purchases of stakes, divestitures, recapitalizations, exchange offers, and leveraged buyouts. The volume data are classified according to the announcement date of a transaction, not taking into consideration when a transaction is completed. The region includes East European countries. Figures are in millions of dollars of purchase price—excluding fees and expenses—at current exchange rates. The dollar value includes the amount paid for all common stock, common stock equivalents, preferred stock, debt, options, assets, warrants, and stake purchases made within six months of the announcement date of the transaction. Liabilities assured are included if they are disclosed in press releases or newspaper articles. Number of completed transactions with undisclosed dollar values in parentheses.

SOURCE: Securities Data Corporation, Merger and Corporate Transactions database.

the rest of the world. Intra-European transactions increased by a factor of 9 during the period, while deals with the rest of the world (in which 72.6 percent of the transactions by volume involved European acquisitions of non-European corporations) grew 5.4 times. European corporations were demonstrably entering the merger and acquisition field more aggressively, with transaction volume growing far more rapidly than anywhere else in the world, during the 1985–1989 period. This expansion was occurring simultaneously on two fronts—within Europe and in other regions of global importance to European corporations, mainly the United States.

Most of the merger and acquisition activity in Europe during the period 1985–1989 (about 58 percent by volume) involved United Kingdom corporations, which have a long history and familiarity with such transactions. French and Italian corporations (together accounting for 22 percent of intra-European transaction volume) were the next most active participants, followed by German corporations, which—despite the size of the German economy—accounted for only 4.9 percent of intra-European transaction volume during 1985–1989.

A rapidly growing EC market for corporate control is both a result of and a catalyst for the economic restructuring stemming from the 1992 initiatives. There are significant constraints, however, especially on continental European merger and acquisition activity. These include limited and often fragmented public shareholdings, heavy concentrations of voting stock in the hands of management or banks, a poorly developed risk arbitrage market, corporate bylaws effectively precluding any but friendly transactions, control of share registers and nondisclosure of share ownership to outsiders, cooperative agreements between industry and banks, and government intervention in individual situations.

Whereas in the mid-1980s most of the principal of merger and acquisition bids was expressed in share exchanges of the acquiring company for the target, more recently cash bids have become more important—shareholders can more readily compare two cash bids than two bids involving paper of uncertain cash value. The rise of cash bids in the growing European merger and acquisition market has hastened the adoption of United States–style merchant banking techniques. Increased liquidity in the European merger and acquisition market is likely to lead to the development of seller-originated transactions whereby companies—mainly privately owned and smaller publicly owned businesses—"auction themselves off" to approved buyers. There will also be an increase in unfriendly takeover bids—given growing competition and the widespread presence of entrenched managements—in addition to increasing divestitures and leveraged buyouts.

The Dual Transformation of EC Financial Markets. The EC 1992 initiatives will affect financial markets in a number of ways. First, they will affect the European environment within which financial institutions and markets function, in particular the volatility of interest rates, exchange rates, and inflation rates. In particular, to the extent that there is progress toward a common currency, greater uniformity, and possibly greater stability in interest rates across the EC and greater alignment of—and possibly lower—inflation rates, transactions and risk management costs related to real sector and financial transactions will decline. This will stimulate economic activity as well as the volume of primary and secondary market financial transactions undertaken by EC and non-EC residents alike—to the point where the EC financial markets may emerge as a formidable rival to the United States and Japan.

They will also reduce or eliminate speculative opportunities and a variety of financial services driven by volatility factors, including the need for various kinds of financial markets and innovations. To the extent that such services are already provided in liquid markets with low transactions costs, monetary integration will carry lower benefits than if these markets have been fragmented, narrow, and shallow as a result of preexisting barriers to entry and innovation.

European financial markets will thus go through a dual transformation: market-enhancing deregulation and intra-European integration. Financial markets will be restructured in ways that will have profound beneficial effects on the EC regional economy and widely differing effects on EC financial centers, on banks, and on nonbank financial firms based inside and outside the community.

First, structural change in EC financial markets will continue, and there will be a rising proportion of financial flows in Europe between sources and uses of funds through the securities markets as opposed to classic banking links. This will include retail-oriented flows through mutual funds and other retail investment vehicles at one end of the financial spectrum and asset-backed securities at the other. This will develop further to circumvent in certain cases the securities industry as well—for example, through direct connections between certain issuers and investors through private placements, automated trading, and related links.

Second, interpretation of geographic and functional markets will occur in response to the EC-driven financial reforms, specifically the banking and investment services directives.

Most observers agree that the creation of a unified pan-European capital market will proceed rapidly during the 1990s, but opinions differ about the manner, timing, and likely results. Some believe that the deregulation already witnessed, which is almost certain to gather momentum with the 1992 initiatives, will render the Euromarkets redundant and that national capital market business will displace traditional Euromarket activity. Financing that was generated in the Euromarkets in the past because of exchange controls, taxation, and capital market regulation will be possible at home, and the Euromarkets will therefore fall into disuse.

Others argue that, after more than twenty-five years, the Euromarket is the single most important, technically developed vehicle for corporate new issues in Europe and is likely to remain so. Transactions costs in the national markets may well remain greater than in the Euromarket, especially if initiatives for EC withholding taxes on investment income are eventually carried through. Given a choice, most market participants will prefer an unregulated market to a regulated one, particularly if access to both can be simultaneous. Retail investors, still constituting the major part of the Euromarket, will prefer to remain beyond the view of tax collectors or other authorities that they have always sought to avoid.

Much more likely than decline and collapse of the offshore Euromarkets as a consequence of the EC 1992 initiatives is the emergence of a new intra-European integrated financial marketplace that is built on and encompasses both the various EC domestic markets and the London-based Euromarket. In such an integrated financial market, issues aimed at national investors can also be sold to Euroinvestors at the same time. Larger, regional issues normally targeted at the Euromarket should come to be marketable in national markets as well, once prospectus requirements, issuing procedures, and withholding tax matters have been harmonized. In time the distinctions between national markets and the Euromarkets will fade, and nonnational investment banks will compete, on a performance basis and in other dimensions, for the business of national companies. A substantially unified capital market that draws from all parts of Europe, from the national markets as well as from the Euromarkets, will be the most efficient way to marshal capital resources.

Implications for Financial Centers

In light of the changes affecting the European financial markets in both the macropolicy and the micropolicy spheres, there are important implications for the location of financial activities within the EC, as well as between the EC and external financial centers such as the United States, Switzerland, and Japan.

Which EC countries are likely to enjoy comparative advantages in the financial services sector in the 1990s? Clearly, those with preexisting, efficient financial service industries are key candidates. Past econometric studies suggest that the particularly successful exporters of financial services are those countries well endowed with skilled labor and having a net positive balance of trade (that is, net savers). Measures of fixed industrial plant, arable land, and unskilled labor are all shown to have negative correlations with competitiveness in financial services (Sagari 1986).

One determinant will be the constant tension (a cost trade-off) that exists between the underlying economics of decentralization and centralization of financial services. Retail financial services marketing, by definition a person-to-person activity, calls for geographical dispersion of facilities providing services. Yet the highly specialized labor needed in financial services argues for its concentration in specific locations where that expertise is available. Thus a natural spectrum exists in financial service delivery that meets these conflicting needs. The economics can change dramatically, however, for example with the ability to market investment management services by mail or retail banking by computer or telephone hookups.

At the capital-intensive end of the spectrum, where labor needs are the most specialized, international capital markets achieve their greatest degree of feasible concentration in London, New York, and Tokyo. In succession, the United Kingdom, the United States, and Japan have been the leading capital exporters of the twentieth century. They continue to be the prime sources of foreign direct investment and trade in financial services. They have achieved the critical mass that now leads them to be the major beneficiaries of foreign direct investment in the financial services sector and have developed into major exporters of financial services. The impact of an integrated financial market in the EC on all three and on the more specialized continental financial centers has been a topic of active debate.

Economic and Regulatory Competition. National regulatory authorities within the EC are increasingly competing among themselves and against non-EC financial centers to attract financial markets business. The tools of this competition include the provision of high-quality infrastructure and low net regulatory burdens (NRB) involving tax and regulatory structures (Levich 1989; Levich and Walter 1989). Financial firms clearly benefit from such competition, especially if financial innovation and technological change allow them to operate successfully at a distance from their home bases. Users of financial services also benefit to the extent that competition forces financial firms to pass through to them the lower costs that result (Kane 1987).

Compliance with regulations in onshore financial markets creates opportunities to develop a parallel, offshore market for the delivery of similar services (for example, the Euromarkets). In addition to the narrow provision of bank deposits and loans, offshore markets can be used to replicate a variety of nonbank financial instruments (such as long-term forward contracts, short-term commercial paper, long-term bonds, and Eurocurrency interest rate futures), many of which may also be regulated by onshore financial authorities. The rise of offshore markets underscores the fact that market participants face a range of alternatives for executing transactions in any of several financial centers. Consequently, if domestic regulators want to have the transactions conducted within their financial centers—driven by their desire to maintain an adequate level of prudential regulation, to sustain their revenues from the taxation of financial services, to support employment and output in the financial services industry and linked economic sectors, or simply to maximize their regulatory domain—regulatory requirements cannot be set without reference to the resulting NRB differentials between financial centers.

Within Europe, competition between London, Luxembourg, Zurich, Paris, Frankfurt, and Amsterdam in particular has intensified significantly, and there is active debate regarding future concentration or dispersion of financial transactions based on market depth, liquidity, efficiency, location of clients, and other factors. The conventional wisdom is that the size, openness of markets, trading activity, sophistication of institutional investors, quality of research, transaction services, and innovative thinking that have traditionally characterized London will be subject to challenge in specific areas by various continental financial centers, with significant implications for local employment and other real-sector considerations. The banking centers of Europe are thus caught in a vigorous struggle for market share in primary and secondary market financial transactions that are likely to grow rapidly in volume. Still, in each of the continental financial centers there are powerful entrenched interests and differences of view between the government and the financial services industry that may yet limit the competitive challenge to London, even as there are open questions about the location of the policy-making and operational arms of a future EC central bank.

Implications for Financial Institutions

Just as EC financial integration will affect the European financial centers, so too will it affect credit institutions and nonbank financial firms. Besides the sheer number of institutions intending to be significant contenders in the integrated EC financial market of the 1990s, the market is likely to be highly competitive for two additional reasons. One is the increasing financial sophistication of many banking and securities clients—"do-it-yourself banking" is creating a new generation of highly informed shoppers among major corporations and public sector institutions worldwide. The second is the long-standing nature of banking relationships in Europe, which means that taking clients away from their traditional institutions will require far more than marginally creative solutions to their financial problems.

The players vying for EC financial markets business in the 1990s fall into at least four strategic groups: (1) British and continental European merchant banks; (2) evolving investment banking units of European universal banks; (3) non-European full-service investment banking firms; and (4) an array of niche players. Internationally, each of these strategic groups has had to adapt to many of the changes in various markets over the past decade or so—changes that transformed what had been, not much earlier, an oligopolistic set of service industries fragmented along product and country lines into a highly competitive, performance-oriented economic sector, where there are very few constants and nothing can be taken for granted.

Financial integration in the EC will clearly affect the performance of financial institutions based in the community and those based outside, especially in the United States and Japan, hoping to capture a significant share of business within and linked to the unified financial market. Restructuring of the EC banking and finance industry is proceeding at a rapid pace, marked by the search for economies of scale and scope on the part of European players through domestic and cross-border and cross-sector mergers and acquisitions as well as strategic alliances. The jury remains out on the value of such alliances (for example, Matuschka–Nomura–General Electric, Westdeutsche Landesbank–Standard Chartered, Banco Santander–Royal Bank of Scotland) as a viable response to the emerging competitive challenges posed by the EC market. Bankers have never been very good at sharing profit opportunities, except on a deal-by-deal basis, unless it is crystal clear to all parties that the whole greatly exceeds the sum of the parts. Even then there are strong incentives to end-run the alliance. Strategic alliances in the 1990s, in the EC as elsewhere, probably have to be contemplated with the view that they have finite lives and are subject to constant review.

The major Japanese houses, banks as well as securities firms, are now well established in the EC and expect to capture a large share of EC-Japan business and make increasing inroads on credit and securities business in the internal market, again backed by their core financial strength and staying power. U.S. institutions present a mixed picture, with consolidation and withdrawals from some of the traditional EC commercial banking markets contrasting with significant successes in specific capital markets and financial advisory activities.

Of the three groups, the Japanese seem to have the clearest strategic positioning, aided by their late arrival and absence of excessive baggage from the past. American and European banks and securities firms present a heterogeneous picture, ranging from the strategic clarity of Deutsche Bank and Morgan Stanley at the one extreme to the muddled image of National Westminster and Chase Manhattan at the other. In this context the need for staying power is an important consideration, both to develop franchises in the established as well as the developing areas of the market and to weather the inevitable storms of unprofitability. Successful institutions will have to master the strategies that have long characterized the most competitive financial markets—targeting new issue business, perfecting hedging tactics, building distribution capabilities, developing new products, and strictly managing costs. They will have to be aggressive, innovative, and efficient. As consolidation into a single, large regional market occurs, it will be expertise, not national monopolistic advantage, that will mark the leaders.

Competitive Positioning of U.S. Institutions. An array of factors will determine the prospective role of United States–based financial firms in the integrated EC market and their ability to compete globally with players home based in the community, Switzerland, Japan, and elsewhere.

Different savings and credit-use patterns. Given historically thin U.S. savings patterns relative to those in Europe and Japan, American financial institutions carry an inherent competitive disadvantage in tapping into the savings end of the international flow-of-funds spectrum (since they rely relatively more heavily on funding themselves in costly wholesale markets, as against cheaper retail deposits). Although they have always been good at wholesale funding and institutional placement of securities, this pattern partially cedes the usually larger wholesale-to-retail margins to foreign players (universal and commercial banks, insurance companies, and securities firms). Given a continued strong U.S. spending and antisavings bias, however, U.S. institutions have an advantage in retail lending and origination of asset-backed securities, agency securities, and so on that can be of interest to investors in Europe and Japan as well as to domestic investors. That is, global flows of funds rooted in saving and spending patterns may give an inherent retail comparative advantage to U.S. institutions at the borrower end of the spectrum and to foreign-based institutions at the savings end of the spectrum. The question then is whether U.S. institutions can more easily get close to the savers abroad or whether foreign-based institutions can more easily get close to the users of credit in the United States.

Notwithstanding the deregulatory and integrative initiatives under way, both European and Japanese institutional investors continue to favor the United States over Europe—citing continued fragmentation of the European markets, their lack of disclosure and transparency, and their poor settlement procedures. They have been pessimistic (or conservative) in their assessments of the success of the changes described here. Once such European inadequacies are resolved in the 1990s, however, foreign portfolio investment that flowed to the United States in the 1980s will find an attractive alternative in the EC. Such redirection in international financial flows would certainly have an adverse effect on the relative position of the United States in international financial markets.

Capitalization. The BIS risk-based capital accords will do much to level the international playing field with respect to book capital. But U.S. institutions continue to be seriously disadvantaged by poor market capitalization. This means that foreign-based institutions can easily and quickly undertake transactions and make strategic moves that are impossible or difficult for their U.S. competitors.

Credit standing. With the extinction of AAA-rated U.S. bank holding companies and securities firms, a premier credit rating has become a designation reserved for nonfinancial corporations and non-U.S. financial institutions. This decline in credit standing is an obvious competitive millstone for funding costs and one that is increasingly used as a competitive marketing weapon as well. The question here is how quickly U.S. institutions can digest the relics of the past (for example, less-developed country exposures and impaired real estate loans) without taking on any new ones (such as highly leveraged corporate deals) in order to reclaim credit standing that is on a par with the best of their foreign competitors.

Human resources. U.S. financial institutions continue to be relatively attractive to some of the best and brightest professionals domestically and internationally—helped by a relatively open and inclusive culture as compared with German or Japanese competitors, for example. This competitive advantage may be more durable than some others. Nevertheless, new financial skills will be required in the international context of the 1990s—skills that many U.S. institutions do not now have. The pace of change and an increasing knowledge content of financial innovations (and risk control) will place far higher demands on those performing on the front lines. The securities sales and trading, new issue, and financial advisory skills required in the emerging EC market, as elsewhere, will continue to place a heavy responsibility on the banks and securities firms for recruitment, training at the cutting edge of financial technologies, and management development and succession planning. Critical will be the development of true "decathlon players" in the various sales forces. Equally important, there must be a much more performance-oriented attitude ingrained in the people on the front lines—including an open, global view, strong peripheral vision, lateral thinking, and a willingness to accept new ideas.

Operating costs and risk management. What evidence there is suggests that U.S. financial institutions have relatively good control over cost structures. Excess costs due to overmanning and inflated expenses seem to have been driven out of many financial institutions in both commercial and investment banking. Similarly, most U.S. institutions have a better handle on position-risk (as opposed to credit-risk) management than their international competitors, in part because of their arguably greater exposure to financial volatility and better understanding of risk management techniques. The first of these may be a relatively durable advantage, since social legislation makes it more difficult to adapt employment-related costs to changing markets in many environments abroad—especially in the EC—than in the United States. The second is probably a temporary advantage, as foreign-based institutions, assisted by consultants, catch up with U.S. risk management techniques.

Economies of scale. Empirical evidence from U.S. banking experience has generally suggested that economies of scale in financial services flatten out at sizes well below some of the larger international competitors that exist today (Clark 1988). Nor does there appear to be much evidence that U.S. financial institutions with international aspirations suffer significantly from size deficiency. Recent evidence from Europe, however, suggests that economies of super scale may well be achieved by very large financial institutions (megabanks), such as the universal banking institutions of Germany and Switzerland. Still, size brings with it a potential for complexity and inertia that can be a serious disadvantage in dynamic financial markets.

Economies of scope. Residual constraints on domestic banking and securities activity and market-interpenetration barriers, especially with respect to the insurance industry, limit the development of true United States–based universals. If scope and cross-selling (as well as super-scale) benefits are indeed significant, this may constitute a competitive disadvantage with respect to the European universals, both within the unified EC market and globally.

Financial innovation. U.S. financial institutions continue to turn in world-class performances with respect to financial innovation on the product side, ranging from new forms of securitization and financial repackaging to embedded options and futures. The same is true with respect to process technologies, including state-of-the-art applications in information and transactions processing. These have largely been driven by the extremely competitive character of the U.S. domestic financial services industry. The half-life of many financial technologies is short, however, and may be getting shorter, so that sustained competitive advantage depends on a continued stream of innovations.

Staying power. U.S. financial institutions have earned a reputation in some international markets and with some groups of clients as fair-weather bankers with relatively little tolerance for even temporarily adverse market conditions or financial problems of clients. Especially in Europe and Japan they are regarded as excessively transactions oriented as opposed to relationship oriented, taking the relatively short-term view that they can abandon markets or clients in tough times and regain easy access through competitive products and pricing when things improve. Credit lines are valuable options to borrowers, and implied lines are even more valuable (and free)—banks that cannot make credible that doing business with them carries such implied lines may suffer losses of market share.

Lack of staying power is resented and derided in some environments, including parts of Europe, to the point where clients are willing to pay a bit more or accept marginally inferior quality for financial services supplied by institutions that are considered more reliable. The perceived lack of staying power may be linked to the fact that many U.S. banks have indeed retreated from international markets under competitive pressure. Those remaining will have to establish their reputation through the credibility of their institutions, not their nationality. U.S. financial institutions, after deregulation, have enjoyed few excess returns that could permit financial cross-subsidization. Competitors from countries whose financial markets have been cartelized or highly regulated, with fixed commissions or deposit ceilings, can behave quite differently in this respect—to the point of engaging in the financial equivalent of dumping.

Adaptability. Organizationally, the adaptability of U.S. financial institutions to changing competitive conditions appears to be relatively good, conditioned by the need to adapt actively at home. It is nevertheless quite uneven among individual institutions, although such differences (for example, Citicorp versus Chase versus Bankers Trust) have made themselves felt fairly quickly in the relative standing of individual institutions. This ability will become more valuable in the future. Aspects of organizational structures have to be reexamined so that they can be bent to operational necessity more quickly and opportunistically.

Adaptability may be the most underrated quality for competitive performance in the financial markets of the 1990s, in the EC as in the United States, Japan, and elsewhere. To be a significant force in international investment banking in particular, managements must become accustomed to the fact that this will always be an inherently unstable business, with profit opportunities appearing and disappearing across the principal business segments. It is also a business prone to tensions among origination, trading, and distribution functions. Both these characteristics will place a premium on the vision, continuity, and diplomacy of senior management.

In addition to tensions that arise among the various functions in the securities business, even greater potential tensions reside in universal wholesale banking. It is yet to be seen whether such institutions—as opposed to those with a narrower focus, "lighter" infrastructure, more opportunistic behavior, and more direct links between individual effort and reward—can become major players in international investment banking in particular.

The Role of Public Policy

The economic and financial reconfiguration of Europe is a major potential contribution to the further development of globalized financial markets. Underlying everything is the wave of European economic restructuring that has already begun and that will create attractive business opportunities for credit institutions as well as securities firms and investment banks. Added to this is the even more dramatic economic restructuring of Eastern Europe, which will gain momentum slowly and create major potential pitfalls but will certainly be closely linked to the EC. These developments will place substantial demands on European capital markets, creating a need for greater financial capacity. Traditional European relationship banking will be eroded by the competitive pressure, and the deepening and increased efficiency of secondary markets will lead to a greater willingness on the part of European financial institutions to trade their portfolio holdings and stimulate the market for corporate control.

The range of financial alternatives facing corporate and institutional customers in the EC is already broad and will continue to grow, eroding the advantages of any single market and placing a premium on creative, opportunistic solutions to client financings. Similarly, the range of alternatives facing institutional investors and their willingness and ability to use them will broaden as well, although international investment patterns will continue to differ significantly among countries. Institutional business will gradually supplant private client business, making it imperative for banks and securities firms to capture institutionalized financial assets. And clients will increasingly become competitors—increasing numbers of companies and institutions will invest in sophisticated treasury capabilities sufficient to do for themselves what commercial and investment banks used to do for them—and some will develop the ability to sell financial services to third parties.

The restructuring process in the most competitive national and international environments will affect the securities industry as it has in the past affected the commerical banking industry. There will be wider use of private placements, increasingly mechanized trading, automated new issues of certain kinds of securities, and sophisticated transactions-based remote access to retail investor clients through electronic or other links. Retail cross-selling of banking, investments, insurance, and other financial services (what the Germans call *allfinanz*) will characterize an increasing number of players, and there will be a continued movement toward cashless transactions.

U.S. and Japanese players will make renewed efforts to gain market share in Europe against their local rivals. The financial environment in Europe will thus become hypercompetitive as it goes through four revolutions simultaneously: (1) disintermediation (banking and securities sectors); (2) geographic interpenetration (according to the EC directives); (3) sectoral interpenetration (for example, banking-insurance); and (4) penetration of Japanese and U.S. players on all fronts. Developments will favor financial institutions home based in particular countries as (1) the markets become more integrated and competitive, favoring flexible, low-cost suppliers; (2) a separation evolves between truly global, regional, and niche players, each of which can find useful roles to perform; and (3) domestic clients in most banks' home countries, both borrowers or issuers and investors, are increasingly solicited by powerful foreign houses.

In their impact on U.S. financial institutions, public policies play a pivotal role in two ways. First is the question whether a truly level playing field will emerge in the EC, on which the competitive advantages and disadvantages of internal and non-EC (specifically U.S.)

players are fully reflected in competitive performance. Second is the question whether U.S. domestic financial regulation provides an environment conducive to competitive success in rapidly developing foreign markets such as the EC.

The Issue of Reciprocity. Both the EC Second Banking Directive and the draft Investment Services Directive contain reciprocity provisions with respect to non-EC banks and securities firms, which define how U.S. and other non-EC players will be allowed to participate in the integrated financial market.

The *Oxford English Dictionary* defines reciprocity as "mutual or correspondent concession of advantages or privileges, as forming the basis for the commercial relations between countries." Two versions of reciprocity can be applied to the financial services sector (Walter 1985a). One might be termed reciprocal national treatment, under which financial institutions from one country are afforded treatment identical to that afforded domestic institutions in host countries. The other is mirror-image reciprocity, whereby financial institutions' activities in host countries are strictly limited to host-country institutions' activities in the home country.

In practice, although mirror-image reciprocity is often espoused as the most equitable standard, in the financial services sector it is neither feasible nor desirable. In the EC context it would require that governments apply a different regulatory framework to each home country and class of foreign-based financial intermediary, with the class of each firm determined by the nationality of the majority of its owners. Such pitfalls make it virtually impossible to administer mirror-image reciprocity and have prevented even the most reciprocity-oriented countries from adhering strictly to such a policy—although many include reciprocity in their consideration of other factors related to the entry and operations of foreign-based financial institutions.

In drafting the International Banking Act of 1978, for example, the U.S. Congress in effect rejected mirror-image reciprocity in favor of a unilateral national treatment standard, putting foreign-based financial institutions on essentially the same competitive footing as domestic institutions (although some grandfathered foreign-based institutions retained better than national treatment). To have applied the concept of reciprocity in its strictest sense would conceivably have required thirty-three different policies covering foreign banks from the thirty-three countries represented in the United States at the time. Such a policy would necessarily have been largely reactive and would have resulted in an incoherent amalgam of petty regulations entirely inconsistent with the objectives of equity and efficiency of the American financial system (see U.S. Department of the Treasury 1984).

The U.S. debates on reciprocity viewed it as essentially producer oriented and protectionist, since its frame of reference is largely biased toward the suppliers of financial services rather than the benefits to consumers and users of maximum financial services competition. Nevertheless, the United States in recent disagreements with Japan on matters such as primary dealer status for Japanese securities firms has appeared to drift from essentially unilateral national treatment toward reciprocal national treatment.

Meantime, the initial interpretation of EC reciprocity provisions in both the draft banking and the investment services directives suggested mirror-image reciprocity, although later interpretations shifted toward reciprocal national treatment, which clearly better serves the interests of liberal capital markets (Group of Thirty 1989). In preparation for implementing the Second Banking Directive and in discussions of the draft Investment Services Directive, the EC Commission explicitly chose to subordinate the concept of reciprocity to the concept of national treatment, while making clear that the community intends to retain the principle of reciprocity as a lever in international negotiations in the financial services sector.

Non-EC banking and securities firms, once authorized to do business in one of the member states through a branch or subsidiary, will likewise be treated as indigenous credit institutions or investment firms, subject to equal treatment with competitors home based in any of the EC countries. Initial authorization, however, presupposes that all banks and investment firms based in any EC country receive full national treatment in the foreign institution's home country and are not subject to any form of discrimination. The reciprocity provisions of both the Second Banking Directive and the draft Investment Services Directive also contain a good deal of discretion on the part of the commission, which is charged with conducting periodic audits of conditions faced by EC players abroad.

The issue remains potentially explosive, since a financial institution from a non-EC country would be excluded from the entire community banking or securities market if its home country were found to discriminate in any respect against firms from any EC member country. This could lead to retaliation, the home country concerned possibly excluding from its markets firms from all EC members. The reciprocity provisions have also been criticized on the grounds that they could be used to prevent mergers and acquisitions of financial institutions in the EC and thereby impede a necessary restructuring of the financial services sector with foreign participation. The problem is to some extent defused, however, by grandfathering provisions that exempt from exclusion any financial institution established in the EC by the end of 1992. This covers a large number of American institutions in particular, some of which have been established in Europe longer than many European institutions. Japanese institutions, which are less well placed and more vulnerable, have rapidly increased their presence in the EC to fall comfortably under the grandfathering provisions (Walter and Smith 1990).

In addition, the continuing Uruguay Round of trade negotiations under the auspices of the General Agreement on Tariffs and Trade (GATT) may well have an influence (Feketekuty 1987). Financial services are included here for the first time, "national treatment" being the sector's equivalent of the GATT most-favored-nation principle. This implies equality of opportunity in market access, including the right to establish a viable commercial presence no less favorable than that accorded to local firms—as opposed to treatment no less favorable than that accorded to foreign firms in the applicant's home country (GATT 1986). Still, it seems unlikely that the GATT negotiations on services will be completed before the EC banking and investment services directives go into effect, by which time the commission will certainly have finished its reviews of reciprocity afforded EC institutions in other countries and been compelled to take a stand on the matter in compliance with the two directives.

U.S. Domestic Financial Regulation. The prospects for EC financial integration should do much to accelerate the pace of U.S. and Japanese reforms of laws and regulations that have prevented banks from competing with investment banking services and vice versa and both from competing in insurance.

The U.S. regulatory structure with respect to financial institutions may be among the worst of any major home country of competitive financial institutions. The maze of regulatory and cross-regulatory jurisdictions continues to amaze and delight foreign competitors—particularly since it significantly hampers the competitive performance of U.S. institutions abroad, gives foreign players a competitive edge in the domestic market, and fails to come to grips with the really serious financial stability problems, all at the same time.

No less puzzling to foreigners is congressional lack of interest and policy paralysis in the face of significant erosion in competitive potential for one of the remaining strong U.S. export industries. Pessimists see at least parts of the U.S. financial services sector as the automobile or steel industry of the 1990s, except this time dragged down by regulatory lags and the low U.S. savings rate (rather than errors and omissions within the industry itself). The issues include residual Glass-Steagall restrictions, barriers to banking-insurance cross-penetration, geographic restrictions, and the like—all of which inhibit the development of truly competitive United States–based financial institutions. Desirable regulatory changes benefiting the competitive performance of U.S. financial services firms in the EC will be of the kind that allow various players to compete in one another's markets on the basis of a level playing field and that permit the creation of American universal banks if competitive conditions require it. Without a significant and coherent reordering of the U.S. financial regulatory system, long overdue, the EC initiatives will help erode the competitive position of American financial institutions and markets.

References

Aliber, Robert Z. 1984. "International Banking: A Survey." *Journal of Money, Credit and Banking* (November).

Arthur Andersen and Co. 1989. *European Capital Markets: A Strategic Forecast*. London: Economist Publications.

Bailey, Elizabeth E., and Ann F. Friedlander. 1982. "Market Structure and Multiproduct Industries." *Journal of Economic Literature* (September).

Bank for International Settlements. 1986. *Recent Innovations in International Banking*. Basel: Bank for International Settlements.

Baumol, William J., J. Panzar, and R. Willig. 1982. *Contestable Markets and the Theory of Industry Structure*. New York: Harcourt Brace Jovanovich.

Begg, David, and Charles Wyplosz. 1987. "Why the EMS? Dynamic Games and the Equilibrium Policy Regime." In *Global Macroeconomics, Policy Conflicts, and Cooperation*, ed. R. Bryant and R. Portes. London: Macmillan.

Bertrand, Olivier, and Thierry Noyelle. 1986. "Changing Technology, Skills, and Skill Formation: The Policy Implications of the OECD/CERI Comparative Study of Financial Service Forms." Paris: OECD (mimeo.).

Bloch, Ernest. 1989. *Inside Investment Banking*, 2d. ed. Homewood, Ill.: Dow Jones Irwin.

Bryant, Lowell L. 1987. "Capital Guidelines Could Weaken Banks." *Wall Street Journal*, April 23.

Buchan, David. 1990. "Brussels Struggles to Balance Power at Top of Planned Eurofed." *Financial Times*, May 17.

Buchan, David, and Tim Dickson. 1989. "Commission Tax Proposal Meets Hostile Reception." *Financial Times*, February 2.

Caves, Richard, and Michael Porter. 1977. "From Entry Barriers to

Mobility Barriers: Conjectural Decisions and Contrived Deterrence to New Competition." *Quarterly Journal of Economics* (May).

Clark, Jeffrey A. 1988. "Economies of Scale and Scope at Depository Financial Institutions." *Federal Reserve Bank of Kansas City Economic Review* (September/October).

Cooper, Kerry, and Donald R. Fraser. 1986. *Bank Deregulation and the New Competition in Financial Services.* Cambridge, Mass.: Ballinger.

Crane, Dwight B., and Samuel L. Hayes III. 1982. "The New Competition in World Banking." *Harvard Business Review* (July–August).

Dermine, Jean, ed. 1990. *European Banking in the 1990s.* Oxford: Basil Blackwell.

Dornbusch, Rudiger. 1988. "The European Monetary System, the Dollar, and the Yen." In *The European Monetary System*, ed. F. Giavazzi, S. Micossi, and M. Miller. Cambridge: Cambridge University Press.

EC Commission. 1988a. *Proposal for a Council Directive on Investment Services in the Securities Field.* Brussels: Commission of the European Communities, COM(88) 778–SYN 176, December 16.

———. 1988b. *Proposal for a Second Council Directive on the Laws, Regulations, and Administrative Provisions Relating to the Taking-up and Pursuit of the Business of Credit Institutions.* Brussels: Commission of the European Communities, COM(87) 715, February 16.

Feketekuty, Geza. 1987. "International Trade in Banking Services: The Negotiating Arena." Washington, D.C.: Office of the United States Trade Representative (mimeo.).

Fieleke, Norman S. 1977. "The Growth of U.S. Banking Abroad: An Analytical Survey." In *Key Issues in International Banking.* Boston: Federal Reserve Bank of Boston.

General Agreement on Tariffs and Trade. 1986. *Ministerial Declaration on the Uruguay Round.* Geneva: GATT.

Giavazzi, Francesco, and Alberto Giovannini. 1989. *Limiting Exchange Rate Flexibility: The European Monetary System.* Cambridge, Mass.: MIT Press.

Gray, H. Peter, and Jean M. Gray. 1982. "The Multinational Bank: A Financial MNC?" *Journal of Banking and Finance* (March).

Group of Thirty. 1989. *Reciprocity and the Unification of the European Banking Market.* New York: Group of Thirty.

Grubel, Herbert G. 1977. "A Theory of Multinational Banking." *Banca Nazionale del Lavoro Quarterly Review* (December).

Hayes, Samuel L. III, A. M. Spence, and D. v. P. Marks. 1983. *Competition in the Investment Banking Industry.* Cambridge, Mass.: Harvard University Press.

Hindley, Brian, and Alasdair Smith. 1984. "Comparative Advantage and Trade in Services." *World Economy* (June).

International Monetary Fund. 1989. *The European Monetary System in the Context of the Integration of European Financial Markets*. Washington, D.C.: International Monetary Fund.

Kallberg, Jarl S., and Anthony Saunders. 1986. "Direct Sources of Competitiveness in Banking Services." New York: Salomon Brothers Center for the Study of Financial Institutions. (mimeo.).

Kane, J. Edward. 1987. "Competitive Financial Reregulation: An International Perspective." In *Threats to International Financial Stability*, ed. R. Portes and A. Swoboda. London: Cambridge University Press.

Khoury, Sarkis J. 1980. *Dynamics of International Banking*. New York: Praeger.

Levich, Richard M. 1988. "Financial Innovation in International Financial Markets." In *The United States in the World Economy*, ed. M. Feldstein. Chicago: University of Chicago Press.

Levich, Richard M., and Ingo Walter. 1988. "The Regulation of Global Financial Markets." In *New York's Financial Markets*, ed. T. Noyelle. Boulder, Colo.: Westview Press.

———. 1989. "Tax Policy and Regulatory Drag in the Development of Financial Centers," in Horst Siebert ed., *Reform of Capital Income Taxation*. Tübingen: J. C. B. Mohr/Paul Siebeck.

Mastropasqua, R., et al. 1988. "Intervention, Sterilization, and Monetary Policy in EMS Countries (1979–1987)." In *The European Monetary System*, ed. F. Giavazzi, S. Micossi, and M. Miller. Cambridge: Cambridge University Press.

McKenzie, George W. 1976. *Economics of the Eurodollar Market*. London: Macmillan.

Morgan Guaranty Trust Company. 1986. "America's Banking Market Goes International." *Morgan Economic Quarterly* (June).

Murphy, Paul. 1988. "The Same Old Ball Game." *Banker* (December).

Neu, C. R. 1986. "International Trade in Banking Services." Paper presented at a NBER/CEPS Conference on European–U.S. Trade Relations, Brussels, June (mimeo.).

Newman, H. 1978. "Strategic Groups and the Structure-Performance Relationships." *Review of Economics and Statistics* (August).

Office of Technology Assessment, U.S. Congress, 1986. "International Competition in Banking and Financial Services." Washington, D.C.: OTA, July (mimeo.).

Organization for Economic Cooperation and Development. 1983. *Trade in Services in Banking*. Paris: OECD.

Page, Daine, and Neil M. Soss. 1982. "Some Evidence on Transnational Banking Structure." In *Foreign Acquisitions of US Banks*. Washington, D.C.: Office of the Comptroller of the Currency, U.S. Department of the Treasury.

Panzar, John C., and Robert D. Willig. 1981a. "Economies of Scope." *American Economic Review* (May).

Pastre, Olivier. 1981a. *Multinationals: Banking and Firm Relationships*. Greenwich, Conn.: JAI Press.

———. 1981b. "International Bank-Industry Relations: An Empirical Assessment." *Journal of Banking and Finance* (March).

Pecchioli, R. M. 1983. *Internationalization of Banking*. Paris: OECD.

Roussakis, Emmanuel, ed. 1983. *International Banking*. New York: Praeger.

Russo, Massimo, and Giuseppe Tullio. 1988. "Monetary Policy Coordination within the European Monetary System: Is There a Rule?" In *The European Monetary System*, ed. F. Giavazzi, S. Micossi, and M. Miller. Cambridge: Cambridge University Press.

Sagari, Sylvia B. 1986. "The Financial Services Industry: An International Perspective." Doctoral diss. Graduate School of Business Administration, New York University.

Saunders, Anthony, and Ingo Walter. 1987. "International Trade in Financial Services: Are Bank Services Special?" Paper presented at a Symposium on New Institutional Arrangements for the World Economy, University of Konstanz (mimeo.).

Schinasi, Garry J. 1989. "European Exchange Rate Management and Monetary Reform: A Review of the Major Issues." Board of Governors of the Federal Reserve System, *International Finance Discussion Papers* (October).

Securities and Exchange Commission. 1988. Securities Act of 1933, Rule 144A and Amendments to Rule 144 and 145, *Federal Register*, 53 F. R. 44016, November 1.

Smith, Roy C., and Ingo Walter. 1990a. "Economic Restructuring in Europe and the Market for Corporate Control." Paper presented at a conference on Economic Restructuring in Europe, INSEAD, Fontainebleau, France, May 10–11.

———. 1990b. *Global Financial Services*. New York: Harper and Row.

Teece, David J. 1985. "Economies of Scope and the Enterprise." *Journal of Economic Behavior and Organization* (March).

Tschoegl, Adrian E. 1981. *The Regulation of Foreign Banks: Policy Formation outside the United States*. New York: Salomon Brothers Center for the Study of Financial Institutions, New York University.

———. 1983. "Size, Growth, and Transnationality among the World's Largest Banks." *Journal of Business* 56, no. 2.

U.S. Comptroller of the Currency. 1982. *Foreign Acquisition of US Banks: Motives and Tactical Consideration*. Washington, D.C.

———. 1984a. *A Critical Evaluation of Reciprocity in Foreign Bank Acquisition*. Washington, D.C.

———1984b. *US Banks' Loss of Global Standing*. Washington, D.C.

U.S. Department of the Treasury. 1979 (updated in 1984). *Report to the Congress on Foreign Government Treatment of U.S. Banking Organizations*. Washington, D.C.

Walter, Ingo. 1985a. *Barriers to Trade in Banking and Financial Services*. London: Trade Policy Research Centre.

———. 1988. *Global Competition in Financial Services*. Cambridge, Mass.: Ballinger—Harper and Row.

———. 1990. *The Secret Money Market*. New York: Harper and Row.

Walter, Ingo. ed. 1985. *Deregulating Wall Street*. New York: John Wiley and Sons.

Walter, Ingo, and H. Peter Gray. 1983. "Protectionism in International Banking." *Journal of Banking and Finance* (December).

Walter, Ingo, and Roy C. Smith. 1990. *Investment Banking in Europe: Restructuring for the 1990s*. Oxford: Basil Blackwell.

Wellons, Philip A. 1987. *Passing the Buck: Banks, Government, and Third World Debt*. Cambridge, Mass.: Harvard Business School Press.

Wyplosz, Charles. 1990. "Macroeconomic Implications of 1992." In *European Banking in the 1990s*, ed. Jean Dermine. Oxford: Basil Blackwell.

Yannopoulos, George N. 1983c. "The Growth of Transnational Banking." In *The Growth of International Business*, ed. Mark Casson. London: George Allen and Unwin.

7
German Banking and Monetary Policy

Anthony Saunders

Momentous changes are under way that will directly affect the future shape of the European financial system. The passage of the Single European Act in December 1985 foreshadows a fully integrated internal capital market for European Community (EC) member countries by December 1992. Indeed, a major step was the removal by Italy and France of the remnants of their foreign exchange controls, in July 1990.

This chapter analyzes the future implications of these developments from the perspective of one country, West Germany, and on *two* specific issues: (1) its central bank and monetary policy and (2) its banking system. Will, for example, the independence of the Bundesbank be preserved, or will its powers be gradually subsumed as the recommendations of the Delors report (1989) come into effect? How will West-East German monetary, economic, and political union affect the prospects for wider European monetary union? Will the large German universal banks prosper in a more freely competitive European banking system, or are there competitive pressures that will limit their growth? These and other issues are examined below.

In the next section the current structure of German monetary policy—its targets, instruments, and strengths—is described. The effects of the Delors proposals on this structure and in particular the plan for a three-stage process, moving from the current European Monetary System (EMS) of managed exchange rates toward a fully integrated European central banking system with a single European central bank and single currency, is then discussed. Then the recent developments in East Germany and their impact on German monetary policy and European monetary union are evaluated. In the next section the prospects for German banks in a single European market for banking and financial services are analyzed. In particular, what are the prospects for the large (big three) German universal banks?

Will they become dominant pan-European banks, or will they be forced back on the defensive into a fortress position within the German market? The final section is a summary and conclusion.

German Monetary Policy

The institutional structure and history of German monetary policy over the past two decades have been extensively described in recent papers by Trehan (1988), Neumann (1988), Dudler (1985), Sibert and Weiner (1989), and Kahn and Jacobson (1989). The German monetary policy process is reviewed briefly here.

Independence. The 1957 Bundesbank Act charges the central bank with the primary task of ensuring a stable value to the currency. In undertaking this task the Bundesbank was given considerable independence from the executive arm of government (the governor and directors are appointed for periods of eight years). And, although members of the executive arm can sit in on Bundesbank meetings and place items on the agenda, they are given no voting powers at all.

Final Targets of Policy. The primary target of the Bundesbank has been to achieve a low rate of inflation given the underlying growth in real production. In recent years the tolerated rate of inflation has been increasingly lowered. Thus in 1988 a 3–6 percent growth in money target was predicated on an expected 2 percent growth in real output and a "tolerated" 2 percent increase in the price level (see Kahn and Jacobson 1989). In the 1980s, the Bundesbank appears to have been very successful in lowering the inflation rate, often at the expense of rising unemployment. For example, while the inflation rate has trended downward to the 2–3 percent range, unemployment has risen, exceeding the 8 percent level since 1983. Unlike certain other countries that have attempted to follow "time-inconsistent" policies—by increasing the inflation rate so as to reduce real wage rates and unemployment in the short run, at the expense of increased future inflation, future increases in unemployment, and loss of central bank credibility—the Bundesbank has appeared to be willing to tolerate unemployment rates even in the 9–10 percent range. This unemployment cost has enhanced its reputation as an inflation-fighting central bank.

While price-level stability appears to have been the preeminent objective of monetary policy, the Bundesbank has from time to time taken actions to correct or offset exchange rate movements. It is important to differentiate between its "binding" commitments to the

EMS, which pegs the currencies of the EC to one another through the European currency unit (ECU), and its commitments to managing fluctuations in the deutsche mark–dollar exchange rate. Basically, the EMS permits bilateral exchange rate fluctuations (or bands) of 2¼ percent for each pair of currencies (for example, mark–French franc) with the exception of the United Kingdom and Italy, which have wider 6 percent currency bands. Under the EMS as constituted since March 1979, each central bank, for each bilateral exchange rate, has an obligation to take action in the foreign exchange market when currencies hit the top or bottom of their permitted fluctuation bands. Hence, if the mark is appreciating against the French franc and hits its upper fluctuation band, the Bundesbank should buy francs and sell marks, the Bank of France undertaking similar actions. Under such a *symmetry* of response, German money supply would expand, potentially at the expense of domestic price stability unless sterilized domestically, while the French money supply would contract.[1]

In actual practice, however, Giavazzi and Giovannini (1988) find that the EMS has generally exhibited *asymmetric* rather than symmetric adjustment response. Specifically, central banks of weaker currencies (such as the French franc) have often sought to stabilize their currencies before the limits of the fluctuation bands are reached. This has occurred despite the persistence of exchange controls in some of these countries. In contrast, the Bundesbank as the strongest currency in the EMS appears never to have intervened within the fluctuation bands (Giavazzi and Giovannini 1988). In addition, weaker currencies have often been subject to speculative pressures (that is, that they adjust their central exchange rates), which have been reflected in higher relative Euro–interest rates for these currencies. This *asymmetry* of adjustment, both in frequency of intervention and in interest rate levels, aligned with the Bundesbank price stability success at home, has resulted in the popular view that the mark is the anchor of the EMS and the EMS itself is really a greater deutsche mark *area*. See, for example, Giavazzi and Giovannini 1988, p. 254:

> Once an asymmetric regime has taken shape, a system of mutual exchange develops between the large and the small countries, which tends to keep the regime together. The benefits to the large country come from the fact that it need not worry about external shocks, as the adjustment is done by the small countries: it can therefore direct its policy instruments to the objective of internal stability. This is why its currency becomes the nominal anchor of the system.

Some support for this view can be found in the gradual reduction in EMS countries' inflation rates toward the German rate in the relatively stable exchange rate period of April 1983 to December 1987 (see table 7-1).

The view that the EMS is a greater deutsche mark area is not without contention. For example, de Grauwe (1989) has argued that capital controls in France, Italy, and Belgium have partially insulated these countries (and in particular their domestic interest rates), and Belognia (1988) notes that the other (noninflation) macrovariables in table 7-1 still show considerable divergences.

With respect to the mark-dollar exchange rate the Bundesbank has been more interventionist minded. This is due to the importance of the United States as a trading competitor and the rivalry between the dollar and the mark as reserve currencies. Such concerns were particularly acute during the rapid appreciation of the dollar in the period before 1985 and its rapid depreciation since. This has at times resulted in stabilizing (and occasionally coordinated) intervention even at the expense of domestic monetary policy objectives. A good example was 1987, when appreciation of the mark called for monetary ease and inflation for monetary tightening (see Kahn and Jacobson 1989). Nevertheless, in general the dollar-mark exchange rate appears to be very much a secondary policy objective of the Bundesbank when compared with price stability.

Intermediate Targets. Until recently the Bundesbank has used the central bank money (CBM) stock as its intermediate target of policy. It has done this by *publicly* announcing annual targets since 1974–1975, the first central bank to do this. The CBM aggregate is very close to the broad money aggregate M_3 except that the transactions components of M_3, currency and demand deposits, are given a higher weight than the savings components.[2] Since January 1988, however, the Bundesbank has switched to targeting M_3, reputedly because CBM became more unstable after a sudden rise in currency demand.

In table 7-2, reproduced from Kahn and Jacobson (1989), the success of the Bundesbank in meeting its targets is shown. The Bundesbank has fallen outside its target growth rate or range nine of fourteen times over the 1975–1988 period. This has occurred despite its success in suppressing innovations, such as money market mutual funds, that may affect the stability of the German money demand function. These sizable deviations are also consistent, however, with the Bundesbank's retaining a considerable degree of *discretion* in pursuing its monetary growth targets.

Operating Targets. With M_3 (or CBM) as its intermediate policy target, day-to-day operations concentrate on affecting conditions in the money market (or the market for bank reserves). Because the Bundesbank uses a lagged rather than a contemporaneous system of reserve accounting, it has chosen the cost rather than the volume of bank reserves as its target. That is, it has chosen interest rate operating targets.

Instruments. Two major instruments used by the Bundesbank to affect the cost of reserves in the money market are repurchase agreements (RPs) and the Lombard rate. The use of RPs has been particularly prevalent since 1984. Neumann (1988), for example, estimates that since then between 20 and 50 percent of the changes in the money base have been due to central bank RP transactions with the banking system. The Lombard rate is the cost of lender-of-last-resort loans (discounting bills) from the central bank. This rate usually lies above market rates; thus borrowing at the Lombard rate imposes a penalty on commercial banks. Moreover, the Lombard rate is viewed as a signal of the Bundesbank's monetary policy stance; hence a rise in the Lombard rate is viewed as a tightening of monetary policy by the Bundesbank and usually leads to an increase in other money market interest rates. From time to time the Bundesbank will also switch public sector deposits into and out of the banking system as a fine tuning device to affect the banking system's liquidity.

Note that the Bundesbank has managed to achieve relative price stability *despite* adopting an operating regime of lagged reserve accounting–interest rate targeting reminiscent of that *abandoned* in the United States in October 1979 (in favor of a regime based on nonborrowed reserves) in the face of rising U.S. inflation.

The 1990s

The Single Market and the Delors Plan. The signing of the Single European Act in 1985 created the impetus for a single market for Europe by 1992, that is, a market with full mobility of labor, capital, goods, and services across national borders. Such a market will have profound effects on German monetary policy and, in particular, on the ability of the Bundesbank to conduct an independent monetary policy as financial markets become more integrated and the momentum builds for central banks to coordinate their monetary policies, beyond what is required for the EMS, as a first stage toward eventual monetary union and the creation of a European central bank on the lines envisaged by the Delors report (1989).[3] We look first at the implications of capital market integration for German monetary policy and then at the implications of the Delors report.

Integrated Capital Markets. The elimination of barriers to capital

TABLE 7-1
MEAN VALUES OF MAJOR ECONOMIC INDICATORS, 1975–1987

Country	Period	Money growth (M1)	Inflation (CPI)	Short-term Interest Rates	Growth of Industrial Production
Exchange rate mechanism					
Belgium	2/75–2/79	6.72[a]	6.77*	5.93*	6.18
	4/83–12/87	5.79[b]	3.36*	7.51*	2.82[b]
Denmark	2/75–2/79	13.70	8.72*	11.67*	4.19
	4/83–12/87	17.13[b]	4.70*	10.11*	5.19[b]
France	2/75–2/79	10.96	9.08*	8.25*	3.79
	4/83–12/87	8.65[b]	4.75*	9.84*	1.42
Germany	2/75–2/79	10.75	3.72*	3.85*	3.11
	4/83–12/87	6.54	1.24*	4.84*	2.99
Italy	2/75–2/79	18.00*	13.95*	12.84*	14.22
	4/83–12/87	11.64*[c]	7.35*	14.95*	3.13[b]
Netherlands	2/75–2/79	10.35	6.21*	5.45	2.57
	4/83–12/87	6.00	1.43*	5.72	2.85
Ireland	2/75–2/79	19.98*	n.a.	n.a.	7.18
	4/83–12/87	7.50*	n.a.	n.a.	8.55

Non-ERM				
United Kingdom	2/75–2/79	15.71	13.69*	9.46	2.75
	4/83–12/87	17.22[b]	4.59*	9.98	3.20
United States	2/75–2/79	6.79	6.96*	6.23*	6.61
	4/83–12/87	8.85	3.46*	8.15*	5.23
Canada	2/75–2/79	7.76*	8.16*	8.53[d]	4.09
	4/83–12/87	17.35*[b]	4.11*[b]	9.44	7.16[b]
Japan	2/75–2/79	10.01	6.35*	6.70*	6.23
	4/83–12/87	5.39	1.27*	5.39*	5.88
Austria	2/75–2/79	7.87	5.30*	n.a.	3.53
	4/83–12/87	5.81	2.71*	3.72	3.32[b]
Norway	2/75–2/79	10.01	7.92	8.40*	6.20
	4/83–12/87	14.39[e]	6.50	12.89*[e]	12.24
Sweden	2/75–2/79	12.24	9.50*	8.10*	−2.69
	4/83–12/87	4.09[b]	5.88*	11.23*	4.73
Switzerland	2/75–2/79	10.39*	1.84	1.62*[f]	n.a.
	4/83–12/87	1.61*[b]	2.02[b]	3.00*	n.a.

NOTE: All data are monthly. Asterisks denote that values are statistically significant at the 0.05 level. n.a. = not applicable.
a. Data begin in 1976.02.
b. Data end in 1987.09.
c. Data end in 1987.06.
d. Data begin in 1978.05.
e. Data end in 1986.12.
f. Data begin in 1975.09.
SOURCE: *International Financial Statistics*, International Monetary Fund, 1988.

TABLE 7-2
West German Money Growth, Target and Actual, 1975–1989
(percent, annual rates)

	Target	Actual
1975	8.0	10.0
1976	8.0	9.2
1977	8.0	9.0
1978	8.0	11.4
1979	6.0–9.0	6.3
1980	5.0–8.0	4.9
1981	4.0–7.0	3.6
1982	4.0–7.0	6.1
1983	4.0–7.0	7.0
1984	4.0–6.0	4.6
1985	3.0–5.0	4.5
1986	3.5–5.5	7.7
1987	3.0–6.0	8.1
1988	3.0–6.0	6.8
1989	5.0	—

NOTE: From 1975 to 1987 the Bundesbank targeted central bank money (CBM), a weighted average of the components of the broad monetary aggregate M_3. In 1988 and 1989 the Bundesbank targeted M_3 growth rather than CBM growth because of distortion in CBM growth. Precise definitions of the monetary aggregates and the reasons for switching target variables are provided in the discussion on the choice of a monetary aggregate to target.
SOURCE: Kahn and Jacobson 1989.

flows between EC countries will increase the rate sensitivity and size of German capital flows. In particular, the greater the scope left or allowed for exchange rate adjustments within the EMS, the larger will be speculative cross-border capital movements among EC countries. To prevent destabilizing effects, the integration of capital markets will probably require greater coordination of monetary policy and interest rate policy. That is, if EC central banks wish to minimize or reduce the frequency with which they adjust their bilateral exchange rates or to reduce the size of permitted fluctuation bands, more frequent and coordinated interventions in the foreign exchange market will be required. This suggests a more *symmetric* burden of adjustment to balance-of-payments disequilibriums than has been present under the relatively asymmetric current system. In the near future stemming capital outflows from a deficit country may require *both* the weak country's *raising* interest rates and the Bundesbank's *lowering* interest rates, in addition to greater intramarginal foreign exchange intervention. In that case the EMS will no longer be (if it ever was) a greater mark area.

In addition to the increased size and sensitivity of potentially destabilizing capital movements, the single market will also prevent the Bundesbank from stifling innovations that might destabilize the German demand-for-money function. The Second Banking Directive of September 1988 (approved in June 1989), under its principal of mutual recognition, will mean that banks located in countries where a particular financial innovation is permitted have the ability to cross-sell this product innovation outside national borders. As a result innovations such as checkable money market funds in both marks and foreign currencies will compete directly with domestic bank deposits. Given the experience in the United States with the introduction of negotiable order of withdrawal (NOW), Super-NOW, and money market accounts (MMAs), the demand for narrow money is likely to become unstable, as will M_3 unless such new innovations are incorporated in a revised definition of the money supply, as in the United States. The effect of such destabilizing innovations on money demand and velocity will be to make it more difficult for the Bundesbank to attain its monetary targets.

The Delors Report and Monetary Union. The publication of the Delors report in April 1989 has created a great deal of attention and controversy regarding its future implications for the EMS in general and the role of German monetary policy in particular. The Delors report envisages a three-stage process toward achieving full economic and monetary union (EMU) in Europe.

Stage 1. Stage 1 involves greater strengthening of policy coordination among national policy makers both in the central banking (monetary) field and also in the budgetary-fiscal field, the objective being to achieve greater symmetry in economic performance among countries. Important milestones along the path to completion of stage 1 are (1) abolition of all control on intra-EC capital movements, (2) membership of all countries in the EMS, (3) the removal of remaining impediments to the private use of the ECU, and (4) a gradual pooling of foreign reserves for intervening and stabilizing bilateral exchange rates. It is proposed that Stage 1 be completed by the end of 1993.

Stage 2. Stage 2, beginning in 1994, is seen as involving an even greater degree of monetary policy coordination among central banks, leading to the eventual creation of a European System of Central Banks (ESCB), that is, a single European central bank that oversees a common EC monetary policy. While exchange rate adjustments are

TABLE 7–3
THE EUROPEAN SYSTEM OF CENTRAL BANKS (ESCB)

Mandate and Functions
- The ESCB would be committed to price stability.
- It would support economic policy set by competent community bodies.
- It would be responsible for monetary policy, exchange rate management, and maintenance of the payment system.
- It would help coordinate activities of bank supervisory bodies.

Policy Instruments
- Various policy instruments would be available to the ESCB to conduct central banking operations in financial and foreign exchange operations and to exercise regulatory powers.
- The system could buy and sell government securities on the market.

Structure and Organization
- The ESCB would have a federative structure.
- The ESCB council would formulate and implement decisions on monetary policy.
- The ESCB would have a board to monitor monetary developments and oversee implementation of common monetary policy.

Status
- ESCB council would be independent of national governments and community authority; council members would have appropriate security of tenure.
- The ESCB council would prepare an annual report for the European Parliament and the European Council.
- Administrative supervision of the system would be independent of community bodies.

SOURCE: Committee for the Study of Economic and Monetary Union 1989.

not ruled out, greater emphasis is placed on coordinated fiscal and regional policies to achieve balance-of-payments adjustments among member countries.[4]

Stage 3. In the final stage all bilateral exchange rates would be firmly and irreversibly fixed, thus eliminating any residual degree of national monetary independence. The ESCB would determine overall EC monetary policy, and national central banks would be delegated the agency function of carrying out the policies of the ESCB (see table 7-3).

Eventually national currencies would be replaced by a single

European currency (potentially the ECU). At the end of the third and final stage there would be a single fully integrated European capital market, a single European central bank, and a single European currency.

Problems and Issues

The main body of the Delors report runs to no more than forty-two pages (although it has extensive appendixes of background papers)—little wonder that a number of issues and problems are left very vague and imprecise. Some of the major issues and problems the Delors report raises, in the context of West Germany and West German monetary policy, are discussed here.

Fiscal and Budgetary Policy Coordination. Considerable stress is given in the report to the requirement that under EMU member countries must coordinate all aspects of their economic policies. While it is quite reasonable and logical that countries cannot pursue independent monetary policies under increasingly fixed exchange rates, as under the stage 1–stage 3 scenario, the Delors plan goes beyond monetary policy coordination to include fiscal and regional policy coordination as well. Theoretically, at least, exchange rate systems in which exchange rates are fixed (such as the gold standard) do not require fiscal policy coordination or centralized control as long as national central banks are sufficiently independent to prevent a country's government from monetizing its budget deficit.[5]

The fear of deficit monetization, however, does not appear to be at the core of the argument for increased fiscal and budgetary policy coordination. Rather, it is the belief that even if deficits are financed by bonds, capital markets will not act to discipline high debt (borrowing) countries sufficiently. Specifically, it is feared that movement toward EMU may result in a free-rider advantage for certain high-deficit errant countries. If investors rationally believe that, in an EMU, strong countries will not allow weaker countries to go into default on their debt obligations, this will result in a supply of implicit cross-national default guarantees from strong to weak countries. While this may mean that borrowing costs (risk premiums) are lower for weaker countries such as Greece, for strong countries like Germany the cost of borrowing is likely to increase—since the risk premiums on West German debt will reflect not only the sovereign risk associated with German budget deficits *but* also a set of conjectural implicit guarantees against debt default by weaker countries. This is a problem reminiscent of the (risk) moral hazard problems arising from mispriced (underpriced) guarantees in the U.S. thrift industry. If, indeed, investors believe that such a set of implicit guarantees exists, it would be in the *best interests* of the stronger countries, such as West Germany, to cap or constrain the deficits of weaker countries.[6]

A closely related reason why strong countries may prefer to cap the deficits of weaker countries is that by joining the EMS and the EMU and giving up a considerable degree of independence over their inflation rates—and eventually their currencies—weaker countries may lose considerable seigniorage rights. Indeed, in a recent study Grilli (1989) showed that for countries like Greece, Italy, and Ireland seigniorage provided a significant part of public financing.[7] Loss of such seigniorage creates incentives for weaker countries to meet the shortfall by increased debt issues.[8]

In addition to greater fiscal policy coordination the Delors report advocates a greater regional policy coordination than at present. But the amount of regional policy coordination needed to solve EC regional payments imbalances (for example, transfer payments and direct investment) depends on the degree to which the EC is an optimal currency area.

Optimal Currency Area. In a stage 3 regime, of either irrevocably fixed exchange rates or a single European currency, regional balance-of-payments imbalances may prove a very difficult and costly problem for the stronger countries to resolve. In an idealized optimal currency area, labor and capital are sufficiently mobile so that, with high demand for one region's output and low demand for another's, labor and capital will flow toward the high-demand region. To the extent, however, that factors such as labor are not very mobile because of language, cultural, and skill differences, demand imbalances will lead to increased inflationary pressures in areas of high regional output demand, such as the Western part of Germany. Given the current heterogeneity among EC national labor forces, it is not unreasonable to expect a significant degree of labor immobility at least in the short run. In that case, to correct regional trade imbalances may require very significant transfer payments and investment from the stronger EC countries to the weaker countries. Private capital flows and investment may partially solve the problem—to the extent that the return on capital is higher in weaker EC countries—but there is no empirical evidence that this is the case. Moreover, labor mobility from the weak regions may be reduced by the extension of German-style social welfare and unemployment programs to all EC countries as part of EMU. Further, in a recent paper Bertola (1989) argues that, for risk-averse labor, a fixed exchange rate regime implies greater intercountry real income uncertainties, which may also inhibit labor's incentive or option to migrate from weak-demand regions.

In sum, the EMU may prove very costly to Germany over and above any loss of monetary sovereignty. Specifically it may involve (1) some loss of fiscal independence over the size of its deficit, (2) some increased cost of funding that deficit, and (3) increased transfer payments to weak regions (including East Germany) in the absence of exchange rate adjustments. Indeed it is unclear whether, on a cost-benefit basis, such costs outweigh the supposed benefits of EMU, such as (1) increased trade flows due to the absence of exchange rate risk, (2) lower transaction costs or savings from bilateral currency conversions, and (3) greater power as a collective economic force relative to Japan and the United States. This is especially so since there is *no* overwhelming evidence to show that lower variability in exchange rates actually encourages trade flows.

Other Issues

While losing autonomy over fiscal and regional policy is of concern to Germany, of equivalent, if not greater, concern is the effect of the loss of full monetary sovereignty on German inflation. This concern has articulated itself into a policy stance favoring a cautious or *conservative* approach toward implementing the Delors recommendations. A number of interrelated concerns underlie this preference for a go-slow approach.

Commonality of EC Objectives. Stage 1 of Delors envisages increasing cooperation among the twelve central banks of the EC. Currently, formal cooperation is confined to the regular meetings of the existing Committee of Central Bank Governors. By stage 2 it is envisaged that this committee will evolve into the ESCB, with centralized control over EC monetary policy. As noted earlier, Germany has always placed great emphasis on price stability as the primary objective of monetary policy, often to the detriment of employment. By contrast, a number of high-inflation countries (for example, Greece, Italy, and Spain) appear to have followed so-called time-inconsistent policies, tolerating high and rising inflation rates to generate short-term gains in employment, often at the expense of even higher future rates of inflation (and inflation expectations) and future increases in unemployment. Consequently, if some governments for short-term political or electoral reasons place greater weight on objectives other than price stability and the central banks of these countries *are not* sufficiently independent of their governments, these factors may be reflected in pressure on the ESCB for a higher monetary growth rate than warranted by the underlying growth of EC real output.

There are grounds for believing, however, that time-inconsistent policies will become increasingly costly for errant countries and that fears of an inflationary bias or drift to the European monetary growth rate will be unfounded. One reason for this is that as exchange rates become more fixed in stage 1 and stage 2, those countries still pursuing greater than average monetary expansions and inflation rates will produce high and uncompetitive *real* exchange rates, with the result that any short-term employment gains are more than likely to be offset by losses in trade and employment related to trade. As a result it is arguable that all members of the EC will have an incentive to lock their monetary growth (inflation) rates to the country with the lowest inflation rate in the EC. In that case inflation rates will converge to the German rate, and the Bundesbank fears of an inflationary drift to EC monetary policy will not materialize.

Voting Powers and Independence. Many of the institutional details regarding the organizational structure of the proposed European central bank have been left unresolved. Two important questions are (1) the distribution of voting power among members of the ESCB and (2) the independence of the ESCB from both national governments and the EC Commission in Brussels. Clearly, Germany would prefer that voting power reflect the economic importance of the country. Under virtually any economic criteria, for example, gross national product or reserves, this would give the Bundesbank the most votes, although whether the other eleven countries would agree is problematic. A more thorny issue is the independence of the ESCB from Brussels. Even if it is independent of the twelve national governments, it may still come under some political pressure from Brussels. This is because if, as planned, fiscal (budgetary) policy becomes increasingly centralized at the commission level, pressure is likely to be placed on the ESCB for Brussels to have a say on monetary policy measures so as better to coordinate community-wide fiscal and monetary policies. Because of this an ESCB dominated by the Bundesbank, which has a strong commitment to price stability, may be better able to resist such pressures than an ESCB where power is diffused among all twelve members.

The Optimal Evolutionary Path of a European Central Bank and a European Currency. *Delors versus the British view.* The Delors scenario assumes a gradual and coordinated evolution of a European central bank and a single currency after the locking of fixed exchange rates in stage 3. At some preannounced date national currencies would be replaced by a European currency (for example, the ECU), that is, a "big bang" approach to the introduction of a single European-wide transactions medium. As a result national currencies, such as the mark, would *irreversibly* disappear.

An alternative plan for the emergence of a single European currency has been proposed by the British Treasury (H.M. Treasury 1989). The British plan is based on the notion of competing currencies and the belief that under currency competition good currencies drive out bad—a reversal of the traditional Gresham's law of currency competition. Under one version of the British plan national currencies of the EC would be allowed to circulate freely in all twelve EC countries. More important, any currency could legally be used for transactions purposes. In such a world, where many currencies could be used for transactions, the currency with the most stable *value* should become the dominant medium of exchange; that is, good money drives out bad money. In all probability the currency that would win this competition would be the mark, with the citizens of the other eleven EC countries voluntarily accepting Bundesbank monetary sovereignty. If this is the outcome, Goodhart (1989) has suggested that members of the eleven other central banks might then be co-opted onto the board of the Bundesbank, although its German members would retain the dominant voting interest. As a result the Bundesbank would become *the* European central bank, with the Bank of England, the Bank of France, and so on being relegated to strictly supporting roles.

One problem with this plan is that it is unclear that the mark or a good money would win such a competition. Specifically, under irreversible fixed exchange rates, weak countries (such as Spain) may pursue high-interest-rate policies. Under such circumstances, with no risk of exchange losses, a significant proportion of wealth holders might prefer to hold their transaction balances in high-rate-yielding currencies, in which case the traditional form of Gresham's law might prevail.

Parallelism versus Delors. A variant of the British competing currency plan, directly rejected in Delors, is the so-called parallel approach. This would require an activist stance by the ESCB toward generating a dominant position of the ECU among competing national currencies; that is, the ECU would gradually take over from national currencies as the transactions medium or EMU (European Monetary Unit) rather than having a big bang introduction as proposed by Delors. The parallel approach requires the ESCB to start issuing fiat ECUs in the twelve EC countries in direct competition with the national currencies, so that in each of the twelve countries there would be *two* competing currencies (rather than twelve as under the earliest British version of the competing currencies plan).

Delors and others, however, have seen a number of problems with the parallel approach. First, since the ECU is a basket of currencies, its value, by definition, cannot be more stable than the strongest (lowest-inflation) country, that is, Germany. Second, with the recent addition of higher-inflation countries, such as Greece, Portugal, and Spain, to the EC, the redefinition of the ECU in September 1989 to include these currencies may enhance concerns about its stability. Third, allowing an *additional* currency to be autonomously introduced into circulation in each country might be inflationary unless sterilized by backing the ECU note issue with local currency bonds or bills (see Wood 1989).

Despite these arguments, the parallel approach has one very strong advantage over the Delors approach. Specifically, with a Delors big bang introduction of a single European currency, the European central bank would possess little or no information regarding the European public's money demand function for the new single currency (see Wood 1989). That is, it might face considerable uncertainty regarding its interest and income elasticities as well as its stability properties. Without such prior knowledge or data, considerable monetary control errors might be made, and it would be very difficult for the ESCB to deliver price stability. At the very least the parallel approach would allow the central bank to discover the ECU money demand function over a lengthy period.

East Germany and West Germany

The recent developments in Eastern Europe and, in particular, those in East Germany may significantly alter the ultimate shape of monetary union, West Germany's role in that union, and the likely time scale for eventual monetary union. The major unknown (at the time of writing) is the eventual impact of unification on the German budget deficit, monetary growth and inflation. Indeed, the German government has already put aside $115 billion in a "German Unity Fund" to cover the cost of unification. Reflecting this reunification effect is the fact that German bond rates are now close to 10 percent while both the money supply and inflation are heading upward. Such effects may well work to weaken the anchor role of the mark in the EMS and strengthen the relative position of countries like France and the United Kingdom. For example, the United Kingdom government (especially Margaret Thatcher) has argued that the events in the East have largely made stages 2 and 3 of the Delors plan redundant.

Commercial Banking

In this part of the chapter I look at the likely effect of the single market and the Second Banking Directive on the growth and strate-

TABLE 7-4
THE INSTITUTIONAL STRUCTURE OF THE GERMAN BANKING SYSTEM

	Number of Reporting Banks, End of 1987	Volume of Business (billions of deutsche marks)
Commercial banks	314	875,782
Big banks	6	324,281
Regional and other commercial banks	157	425,541
Branches of foreign banks	59	69,846
Private bankers	92	56,114
Savings banks	598	1,400,595
Central and regional giro institutions	12	588,659
Savings banks	586	811,936
Credit cooperatives	3,487	641,410
Central and regional institutions	7	173,041
Credit cooperatives	3,480	468,369
Mortgage banks	38	523,491
Private mortgage banks	27	337,498
Public mortgage banks	11	185,993
Special functions banks	16	251,561
Postal giro and savings banks	15	55,957
All categories of banks	4,468	3,748,796

SOURCE: Deutsche Bundesbank and Rudolph 1989.

gies of German banks into the 1990s. I discuss the current standing of German banks vis-à-vis other European banks and the special nature of universal banking as practiced in Germany. I also look at the potential offensive (abroad) and defensive (at home) strategies German banks are likely to adopt to survive successfully the single market of the 1990s.

German Banking. Table 7-4 shows the institutional structure of the German banking system. It is divided into four quite distinct groups: commercial banks, savings banks, credit cooperatives, and mortgage banks.

Two immediate observations are (1) the very large number of banking institutions (4,468) and (2) the relatively low concentration ratio of bank assets—specifically, the six biggest commercial banks (which include the three giants: Deutsche Bank, Dresdner Bank, and Commerzbank) have only an 8.65 percent share of total banking assets and a 37.1 percent share of commercial bank assets.

Table 7-5 shows the relative standing of the major German banks measured by asset size, deposits, capital, and pretax earnings relative to their European counterparts at the end of 1988.[9] Measured by asset size, Deutsche Bank is the fifth, Dresdner Bank is the seventh, Commerzbank is the twelfth, and West Deutsche Landesbank and Bayerische Vereinsbank are respectively the fourteenth and fifteenth largest banks in Europe.

Unlike the banking systems of the United States, Japan, and some other European countries, the German banking system exhibits a much lower degree of separation between banking and other financial services (such as investment banking and insurance) and between banking and commerce. That is, along with the systems of France, Italy, the Netherlands, and Switzerland, the German banking system is a universal banking system with nonbank activities and services produced and marketed in-house, that is, within the bank. By comparison, banking activities, where permitted, in the United States, the United Kingdom, Belgium, Canada, and Japan are undertaken either by a separate subsidiary of the bank or, as in the United States, by a separate subsidiary of the holding company (see table 7-6).

The organizational structure of a universal bank offers a number of potential advantages in selling financial services. This is especially so in the German case where, apart from offering the usual banking products in-house, the large German banks actively participate in the management and control of commercial firms through their direct and proxy equity holdings, in the issuing and trading of stocks and bonds (investment banking), and more recently in the direct sale of life insurance products at the retail level.[10] Thus the concept of large German banks as *allfinanz* companies or financial conglomerates is generally an accurate description (although Dresdner and Commerzbank are less universal both in products offered and geographically than Deutsche Bank). This universal banking structure, in turn, should put them in a good position to exploit the single market.

Specifically, the Second Banking Directive issued in January 1988 and approved in June 1989 (*Financial Times*, June 21, 1989) by the finance ministers of the EC adopted a concept of a single banking license covering an agreed list of activities (see table 7-7), to which has recently been added financial advice, allowing banks to participate in long-term shareholding of nonfinancial companies—subject to a cap on that participation.[11] Moreover, banking activity supervision will be predominantly the responsibility of the home country, that is, the country in which the bank applies for its license, so that

TABLE 7-5: GERMAN BANKS AMONG EUROPEAN TOP FIFTEEN, 1988
(millions of U.S. dollars)

Bank	Assets	Deposits	Capital	Pretax Earnings
1. Banque Nationale de Paris	197,014	160,585	5,208	876
2. Barclay's	189,334	155,846	14,862	2,517
3. Crédit Lyonnais	178,931	150,666	5,578	811
4. National Westminster	178,473	144,974	10,760	2,546
5. Deutsche Bank	171,511	156,086	6,486	1,823
6. Société Générale	145,704	124,769	4,074	863
7. Dresdner Bank	129,525	121,180	4,301	624
8. Compagnie Financière de Paribus	121,654	80,939	5,325	929
9. Union Bank of Switzerland	110,893	93,848	6,723	729
10. Swiss Bank Corporation	102,589	89,665	6,062	624
11. Midland Bank	100,830	83,546	5,498	1,254
12. Commerzbank	100,769	96,354	3,185	484
13. Lloyd's Bank	93,783	82,971	5,202	1,722
14. West Deutsche Landesbank	92,760	85,927	2,335	212
15. Bayerische Vereinsbank	91,620	86,042	2,290	386

Key ratios for the Three Grossbanken (percent)

	Asset growth ($) 1987–1988	$\frac{D}{A}$	$\frac{C}{A}$	$\frac{\Pi}{A}$
Deutsche Bank	1.5	91	3.78	1.06
Dresdner Bank	−0.7	93.6	3.32	0.48
Commerzbank	−0.46	95.6	3.16	0.48

Deutsche Bank versus Top British and French Banks (percent)

	Asset Growth ($) 1987–1988	$\frac{D}{A}$	$\frac{C}{A}$	$\frac{\Pi}{A}$	$ exchange rate 1987–1988
Deutsche Bank	1.5	91	3.78	1.06	+2.3
Banque Nationale de Paris	7.85	81.5	2.64	0.44	+0.9
Barclay's	14.27	82.31	7.8	1.33	+8.6

D/A = deposit-asset ratio; C/A = capital-asset ratio; Π/A = return on assets
SOURCE: Institutional Investor, June 1989.

TABLE 7-6
PREDOMINANT FORM OF FINANCIAL SERVICE INTEGRATION
IN THE G-10 COUNTRIES

	Expanded Bank Powers[a]	Nonbank Subsidiary of Bank[b]	Common Holding Company[c]	Degree of Integration of Banking and Securities Services[d]
Universal systems				
France	X			High
Germany	X			High
Italy	X			High
Netherlands	X			High
Switzerland	X			High
Blended systems				
Belgium		X		High
Canada		X		High
Japan		X		Low
United Kingdom		X		High
United States			X	Low

a. Single "universal" banks directly provide in-house all banking and securities services.
b. The typical form of integration is for banks to have wholly owned nonbank financial subsidiaries.
c. A single holding company typically has significant ownership interests in both banks and nonbank financial firms.
d. Either through expanded in-house powers or through institutional affiliations.
SOURCE: Federal Reserve Bank of New York, *Quarterly Review* (1987).

German banks' activities will be supervised principally by the Bundesbank even when they operate in the eleven other countries.[12]

Given this situation, German banks wishing to expand their European activities may further exploit their universal banking advantages, such as the following:

Relationship banking. To the extent that German nonfinancial corporations acquire other nonfinancial firms abroad as part of the expected restructuring of European industry toward larger organizations, German banks will be able to extend the geographic range and scale by which they can *cross-sell* the vast array of their *allfinanz* products and services based largely on their strong domestic links

TABLE 7-7
PERMISSIBLE BANKING ACTIVITIES UNDER EUROPE 1992

Deposit taking and other forms of borrowing
Lending (including consumer credit, mortgage lending, factoring and invoice discounting, and trade finance)
Financial leasing
Money transmission services
Issuing and administering means of payment (credit cards, travelers' checks, and bankers' drafts)
Guarantees and commitments
Trading for the institution's own account or for the account of its customers in (1) money market instruments (such as checks, bills, and certificates of deposit), (2) foreign exchange, (3) financial futures and options, (4) exchange and interest rate instruments, and (5) securities
Participation in share issues and the provision of services related to such issues
Money brokering
Portfolio management and advice
Safekeeping of securities
Credit reference service
Safe custody service

SOURCE: Bennett and Hakkio 1989.

and ties with German nonfinancial corporations.

Economies of scale. To the extent that there are economies of scale from a pan-European growth in financial services output—the Cecchini report (1988) estimated an increased demand for financial services amounting to some 22 billion ECU—the larger German banks should benefit. It should be noted, however, that few studies have found significant economies of scale in U.S. banking. Nevertheless, one obvious cost economy will be the savings from needing to apply for only *one* banking license rather than twelve, if a bank wishes to expand into all the countries of the EC.

Economies of scope. Given the very diverse range of services offered by the large German banks, their expansion into the European market should give them enhanced potential to extend cost savings through further exploiting any economies of scope (again, however, U.S. studies are divided on the size of the potential cost savings from economies of scope).

Risk diversification. Currently German banks' nonfinancial firm equity holdings are heavily concentrated in the German automobile

TABLE 7-8
DEUTSCHE BANK'S EXPANSIONS

Britain: Number 3 Eurobond underwriter in 1988; owner of Morgan Grenfell, the London brokerage-merchant bank.
Italy: Bought Bank of America's Italian operations in 1986, getting 100 branches with $3.1 billion in assets.
Portugal: Took full control in 1988 of MDM Sociedade de Investimento S.A., a Lisbon investment bank.
Spain: Acquired majority control in 1989 of Banco Commercial Transatlantico, a middle-market bank.
Netherlands: Took full control in 1988 of H. Albert De Bary and Company, an Amsterdam bank specializing in trade financing.

SOURCE: *New York Times,* July 30, 1989.

and manufacturing industry; for example, Deutsche Bank owns 28 percent of the stock of Daimler-Benz. The single European market will allow them to diversify geographically and industrially. Moreover, their ability to cross-sell across national borders will probably lead to their earnings' becoming more diversified (for example, slow growth in loan business or investment banking business in Germany could be offset by fast growth in such activities in Spain). As long as the demands for bank products are imperfectly correlated among the EC countries, there will be gains from diversification.[13]

Offensive and Defensive Strategies for the 1990s

Offensive. Given these potential advantages, will the big three and other German banks take a major share of the forecasted growth in the demand for financial services (22 billion ECU according to the Cecchini report)? In analyzing this question it is important to differentiate the likely strategy of Deutsche Bank from that of either Dresdner or Commerzbank. Indeed, Deutsche Bank has openly announced its intention to become one of the few truly global banks in the world, competing alongside Citicorp and the Japanese city banks.

As the initial phase of this planned strategy, Deutsche Bank has already acquired a number of European financial firms (see Table 7-8). Commerzbank and Dresdner Bank seem to have a far less aggressive strategy. Commerzbank, for example, has chosen to approach 1992 largely through cooperative or joint ventures with Credit Lyonnais, Banco di Roma, and Banco Hispano Americano. For German banks seeking an offensive strategy, in which markets will the best opportunities lie?

Wholesale banking. The markets for Euroloans and Eurodeposits are already extremely competitive, since their growth has been largely unencumbered by national regulations. Indeed, regulatory avoidance has been a major factor driving their growth. Because of this, margins are already small, and competition is global.

The middle market for bank services. An area that may prove to involve the fiercest competition is that for the business of medium-sized European companies, or the so-called middle market. In recent years the middle market has been discovered by the large U.S. money center banks, with Chemical and others developing considerable expertise in this area. In addition, U.S. banks' experience of trying to arbitrage away the effects of interstate banking restrictions has given them considerable advantages in dealing with treasury management and geographic consolidation of funds, a problem likely to be faced by middle-market European firms as they merge, restructure, and grow in the single market. This suggests that while the middle market is likely to produce new business opportunities, Deutsche and the other large German banks may find it difficult to hold off competition from U.S. banks.

This competitive threat may create renewed incentives and pressures, from German and other European banks, on the EC Commission and national governments to adopt a more conservative interpretation of the reciprocity provisions pertaining to foreign banks seeking European banking licenses. Indeed, the potential for different interpretations of the reciprocity provisions in the Second Banking Directive has caused considerable concern among U.S. policy makers and bankers.

One interpretation of reciprocity, which would have a major adverse effect on non-EC banks seeking to gain a Eurobanking license, is the concept of mirror image national treatment. Under this interpretation of reciprocity, licenses would be granted only to banks from countries who adopt (or have adopted) the same liberal bank activity provisions inherent in the Second Banking Directive. Since universal banking is the acceptable mode under this directive, this interpretation could cause both U.S. banks and Japanese banks considerable entry problems. This is specifically because the Glass-Steagall Act in the United States and Code 65 in Japan still require separation of commercial from investment banking activities while the 1956 Bank Holding Company Act and the 1987 Competitive Equality Bank Act in the United States have sought to separate commercial banking activities from nonfinancial activities. It would then appear that neither U.S. nor Japanese banks could satisfy these strict reciprocity provisions unless the United States and Japan changed their domestic banking laws to satisfy EC universal banking provisions.

In recent months European policy makers have gone to great lengths to reassure U.S. policy makers and bankers that this is not their interpretation of national treatment reciprocity, in particular, that their concept of national treatment reciprocity is similar to that implied by the U.S. International Banking Act of 1978 (see *American Banker*, October 24, 1988, p.6). Under this alternative interpretation of reciprocity, banks from non-EC countries would be allowed access to a European banking license as long as EC banks entering into non-EC markets were treated and regulated on the *same terms* as domestic banks. Nevertheless, despite such reassurances the recent banking directive appears to have been left purposefully vague, possibly so that it can be used as a potential lever by German and other European banks if the non-EC competitive threat becomes too intense.

Retail banking. A third potential area for offensive activity expansion by German banks lies in the retail banking markets of the EC. The Cecchini report indicated a wide disparity in the pricing of retail and other banking services among European markets (see table 7-9). Banks in countries such as Spain appear to be earning considerable rents on their retail business. Entering the retail banking market of another country, however, is likely to be prohibitively costly since many of these countries already have too many retail banks. In addition, to engage in full-service retail banking would require the new entrant to pay the often excessive fixed costs of entry, such as membership of domestically owned or controlled retail check clearing and/or automatic retail payment (giro) systems.[14]

An alternative to direct *de novo* entry would be for a bank such as Deutsche Bank to acquire a large retail bank in another EC country. Traditionally, European governments have been sensitive to the idea of foreign ownership and control of their largest domestic retail banks. For example, the Bank of England has set a limit of 15 percent on the share of foreign ownership of a domestic clearing bank, and similar restrictions apply in Spain and Italy. Moreover, the number of potential takeover targets is quite small. Specifically, the *Banker* (June 1989) estimated that 93 of the 162 largest banks in Europe were either state or quasi-state firms. Of the 69 "private sector" banks, just over 40 were viewed as potentially viable targets (see table 7-10). Because of the small number of potential targets the cost of acquisition (the price-to-book ratio) may be extremely high. Finally, foreign bank entrants (either *de novo* or by *acquisition*) face strong cultural, language, and technological barriers to integrating foreign retail networks into the domestic banking organization.

Given such cost considerations, a more likely scenario is that Deutsche Bank and other German banks will not seek to engage in full-scale Euro–retail banking but will rather pick a few select targets for acquisition (to gain a foothold in these retail markets) and sell other retail products through joint ventures in the areas of financial service delivery, risk management, and securitization.

Investment banking and other nonbank financial services. Perhaps the greatest benefit to the German universal banks from the creation of a single European capital market will come from the increased provision of investment banking and other nonbank services, such as

- *Mergers and acquisitions.* While the interbank takeover market is likely to be small, the single market is likely to lead a considerable degree of conglomorate corporate restructuring, including mergers and acquisitions. Those banks that have developed significant skills in identifying targets and organizing raids will be in great demand. In all probability U.S. banks and the British merchant banks will capture a large share of this market. Nevertheless, a growing tendency (already observed) is for acquirer and targets to employ teams of advisers including *at least one* domestic bank. Thus, while a German acquirer may employ five investment bankers to provide merger and acquisition advice, one of these is likely to be among the big three universal banks. That is also likely to occur for German targets seeking defensive strategies or the best price.
- *The Euroequity markets.* In the past few years there has been a rapid growth of the Euroequity market—technically the issuing and trading in shares of domestic companies outside national boundaries. A large component of the estimated $15 billion size of the Euroequity market has been due to privatization of public corporations in the United Kingdom and France. In addition, there has been a growing tendency to cross-list shares on the exchanges of other countries. Both trends create a broader and more liquid market for equities. One likely trend in the 1990s will be for some European exchanges to disappear or even merge as competition for new and existing firms' listings intensifies. Stock markets that are already heavily computerized and "off the floor," such as London with its Stock Exchange Automatic Quotation system and large existing volume, will be at a considerable advantage. Assuming that settlement systems can be homogenized (for traders), one likely result will be the emergence of one dominant over-the-counter Euroexchange, modeled on NASDAQ/SEAQ (National Association of Security Dealers Automatic Quotes/Stock Exchange Automatic Quotation), that will be pan-European, with smaller regional or national exchanges taking care of

TABLE 7-9
DIFFERENCES IN PRICES OF STANDARD FINANCIAL PRODUCTS COMPARED WITH THE AVERAGE OF THE FOUR LOWEST NATIONAL PRICES FOR EIGHT EC COUNTRIES
(percent)

Standard service	Description	Belgium	Germany	Spain	France	Italy	Luxembourg	Netherlands	United Kingdom
Consumer credit	Annual cost of consumer loan of 500 ECU; excess interest rate over money market rates	−41	136	39	n.a.	121	−26	31	121
Credit cards	Annual cost assuming 500 ECU debit; excess interest rate over money market rates	79	60	26	−30	89	−12	43	16
Mortgages	Annual cost of home loan of 25,000 ECU; excess interest rate over money market rates	31	57	118	78	−4	n.a.	−6	−20
Letters of credit	Cost of letter of credit of 50,000 ECU for three months	22	−10	59	−7	9	27	17	8

Service	Description								
Foreign exchange drafts	Cost to a large commercial client of purchasing a commercial draft for 30,000 ECU	6	31	196	56	23	33	−46	16
Travelers' checks	Cost to a private consumer of purchasing 100 ECU worth of travelers' checks	35	−7	30	39	22	−7	33	−7
Commercial loans	Annual cost (including commissions and charges) to a medium-size firm of a commercial loan of 250,000 ECU	−5	6	19	−7	9	6	43	46

NOTE: The figures show the extent to which financial product prices, in each country, are above a low reference level. Each of these price differences implies a theoretical potential price fall from existing price levels to the low reference level.
SOURCE: Cecchini 1988.

TABLE 7-10
POTENTIAL BIG BANK TARGETS

Location of Europe's Top Banks	No. of Acquisition Targets	Bank and Status	Asset Size 1987 ($ million)	European Ranking
Belgium (3)	0	—	—	—
Denmark (6)	4	Privatbanken (CB)	15,871	86
		Provinsbanken (CB)	9,447	116
		Andelsbanken Danebank (CB)	7,861	128
		Jyske Bank	7,601	131
France (9)	5–6	Banque Indosuez (CB)	47,775	36
		Al Ubaf Banking Group (CB)	14,351	92
		Sovac (FH)	7,204	135
		Eurobank (CB)	6,373	140
		Banque Sudameris (CB)	5,104	157
		Banque de Neuflize (CB)	5,100	158
Germany (West) (8)	5–6	Bayerische Hypotheken (CB)	79,851	20
		BHF Bank (CB)	19,109	75
		Westfalenbank (CB)	14,754	91
		Vereins and Westbank (CB)	11,649	101
		Industriekreditbank (SB)	10,612	109
		Sal Oppenheim (MB)	7,995	127
Greece (1)	0	—	—	—
Ireland (2)	0	—	—	—
Italy (7)	7	Banca Nazionale dell' Agricoltura (CB)	22,361	66
		Banco di Santo Spirito (CB)	19,793	71
		Nuovo Banco Ambrosiano (CB)	17,882	80

		Credito Romagnolo (CB)	11,367	104
		Mediobanca (CB)	10,828	107
		Banca Cattolica del Veneto (CB)	8,875	121
		Banca San Paolo Brescia (CB)	5,436	149
Luxembourg (5)	5	BCCI (CB)	17,505	81
		Banque Internationale à Luxembourg (CB)	11,376	103
		Banque Générale du Luxembourg (CB)	10,311	112
		Kredietbank Luxembourgeoise (CB)	8,235	124
		BAII Group (MB)	5,200	156
Netherlands (3)	0	—	—	—
Portugal (1)	0	—	—	—
Spain (7)	5	Banco Hispano Americano (CB)	30,866	50
		Banco Español de Credito (CB)	30,797	51
		Banco Popular Español (CB)	16,617	84
		Banco de Sabadell (CB)	5,380	151
United Kingdom (15)	11	Standard Chartered (CB)	55,649	32
		Royal Bank of Scotland (CB)	31,159	47
		TSB Group (CB)	29,462	54
		Bank of Scotland (CB)	19,480	73
		Kleinwort Benson (MB)	15,025	89
		Morgan Grenfell (MB)	11,102	105
		Gerrard & National (DH/FH)	7,808	129
		Scandinavian Bank (CB)	5,858	146
		SG Warburg (MB)	5,412	150
		Hambros (MB)	5,100	159
		Schroders (MB)	5,091	160

NOTE: CB = commercial bank; MB = merchant bank; SB = specialist medium- and long-term finance bank; FH = finance house; DH = discount house.
SOURCE: *Banker* (January 1989).

smaller local firms and less frequently traded issues. Such a pan-European over-the-counter market would probably rival, both in market capitalization and in volume, Tokyo and the New York Stock Exchange.

Trends toward increased growth in Euroequity markets and trading should directly benefit the large German banks, whose earnings are currently depressed by the relatively small size and depressed volumes on the Frankfurt exchange. Indeed, their experience as major traders and market makers in the German equity market, backed by their considerable capital, would make them formidable players in any future Euroequity market.

- *Eurobonds.* In 1988 the total volume of Eurobond issues was $219 billion, of which Euro–deutsche mark issues had a 10.9 percent share (third largest after the U.S. dollar and the Swiss franc), and ECU-denominated bonds had a 5.4 percent share (sixth largest). As national borders and regulations break down, the differences between the national bond markets and Eurobond markets are likely to erode, with a considerable degree of reintegration taking place between these markets. Depending on the path toward full monetary union, either the mark or the ECU will probably garner a larger and larger share of Eurobond issues at the expense of other Eurocurrencies. This should benefit Frankfurt in its competition with London to become the primary European securities market and the big three German banks, which are major underwriters of mark bonds.
- *Investment funds.* Table 7-11 shows the dramatic growth in German investment fund management between 1980 and 1988. Accounting for two-thirds of the securities-based general funds and half of the specialized funds are the big three German banks. The Second Banking Directive opens up all the EC markets to German fund managers. Moreover, regulatory requirements—especially for investors' protection—are less burdensome than those imposed on German fund managers. This should provide considerable incentives for the big three to expand into the pan-European fund management field.

Defensive Strategies. While the big three banks seek to expand abroad, there is little doubt that they will come under threat at home. Moreover, even before the single market really gets under way, German banks are facing a shrinking share of the German savings market. For example, the share of bank deposits in total savings has declined from 56 percent in 1970 to 49 percent in 1987. One reason for the decline is the low deposit savings rates paid by German banks. Another has been increased competition for savings from the large

TABLE 7-11
GERMAN INVESTMENT FUNDS, 1980–1988
(billions of marks)

Sales	1980	1984	1985	1986	1987	1988
General funds[a]	−1.2	4.2	8.3	12.9	14.8	20.7
Bond-based	−0.5	4.5	8.5	12.1	11.0	17.9
Share-based	−0.9	−1.1	−1.0	−0.5	0.8	0.6
Real estate	0.2	0.8	0.7	1.3	3.0	2.2
Special funds[b]	2.2	4.6	7.4	12.3	17.1	15.6
Foreign funds[c]	−0.1	−0.1	−0.1	−0.1	0.4	11.6
Total	1.0	8.7	15.5	25.1	32.2	47.9
Market share (%)[d]	1.5	8.8	12.7	18.5	24.8	39.7
Total fund assets	47.1	80.1	106.2	130.6	147.3	191.7
Number of funds	605	786	885	1,065	1,275	1,507

a. Open to the general public.
b. For institutional investors.
c. Residents' net purchases of foreign funds.
d. % of total amount raised in the securities markets.
SOURCE: *Banker* (May 1989).

TABLE 7-12
WEST GERMAN HOUSEHOLD SAVINGS, 1970–1987

	Total Holdings End-Year (%)			New Investment (%)
	1970	1980	1987	1987
Life insurance	16	17	21	30
Company pension schemes	7	7	8	7
Securities—fixed-interest	9	13	15	20
—shares	5	2	2	3
Building and loan savings plans	8	7	5	−2
Bank deposits	56	53	49	42

SOURCE: *Banker* (May 1989).

German insurance companies, mainly with savings-linked life insurance contracts, helped by the general aging of the German population (see table 7-12). To counteract this competition, Deutsche Bank recently announced that it would offer its *own* insurance products through its 1,400 branches, and in March 1989, Dresdner formed a joint venture with Allianz, the largest German and European insurance company. Dresdner will sell life insurance written by Allianz, while Allianz will sell Dresdner home and consumer finance loans.

With the opening up of the single market, however, there must be a very high probability that Metropolitan Life, Equitable, and other non-German life insurance giants will also seek to enter the lucrative German market to the extent that they can overcome any residual restrictions on contract types and policy holder payouts that currently define the market.

German banks' deposit base will also come under threat from foreign bank entrants (both EC and non-EC). For example, American Express Bank in Germany recently captured mark deposits by offering higher interest rates even though it had *no* branches. Moreover, foreign banks have been traditionally hampered from expanding in Germany by the high telecommunications costs and restrictions on private (proprietary) wire networks imposed by the Deutsche Bundespost (this is also reflected in Germany's having one of the lowest ratios of automatic teller machines per head among major Western countries). As part of the single market, local telecommunications monopolies and restrictive barriers will be eroded and private sector proprietary networks encouraged (see the Cecchini report 1989), making it far easier for highly technically efficient banks, such as Citicorp, to compete.

A third area of competition for German bank deposits is likely to come from U.S.-style money market mutual funds, that is, checkable accounts whose returns and market values are linked to returns on underlying money market instruments such as Treasury bills. Historically the Bundesbank has discouraged the growth of mark-denominated money market funds, its concern being that such innovations will affect the stability of money demand and make monetary policy targets more difficult to attain. Such moral suasion is unlikely, however, to work in the single market of the 1990s.

A fourth area of competition is likely to be credit cards. While the large German banks do offer credit card products such as the Mastercard franchise, a predominant form of payment has been the debit card. As consumer experience has shown in the United States, given a free and competitive choice the convenience user prefers credit cards (because of the float), while for the nonconvenience user only credit cards, by definition, provide a line of credit. Moreover, a greater availability of foreign credit cards (such as by Barclay's, the major European purveyor of Visa) is likely to erode the check and the checking account as the predominant means of payment in Germany. Thus German banks will have to be more aggressive suppliers of credit cards as a defensive mechanism against deposit base erosion.

A fifth area of foreign competition is likely to arise in the German market for retail housing finance. This is because in Germany the retail housing finance sector is severely compartmentalized among mortgage banks, savings banks, and *Bausparkassen*. These banks usually grant mortgages for relatively short periods (often 7–10 years) and require very large down payments. As a result, unless these banks adjust, the longer-term (up to thirty years) and more flexible products offered by U.K. and U.S. banks will be very competitive and could take a sizable share of this market.

Summary and Conclusions for Commercial Banking

In the 1990s we may expect Deutsche Bank to emerge as one of the few pan-European and pan-global universal banks having some presence either through acquisition or joint ventures in all the countries of the EC. Commerzbank and Dresdner Bank, however, are likely to become Euroregionals or superregionals, selecting a few European markets and products on which to base their international presence while building up their strength at home. Moreover, as a financial center with a very large savings base and an anchor currency, Germany is likely to face a very strong foreign entry push. Four areas where competition will be particularly strong are insurance, money market mutual funds, credit cards, and retail housing finance. As a result German banks will be increasingly pushed to create new products and offer competitive rates on deposits to fend off such competition. Given the strong relationship content and ties in German universal banking, however, there must be a strong probability that they will survive this new competitive threat relatively intact.

References and Bibliography

Andrews, S. 1989. "Banks' Winning Gambits for 1992." *Institutional Investor* (June).

Belognia, M.T. 1988. "Prospects for International Policy Co-Ordination: Some Lessons from the EMS." *FRB of St. Louis Quarterly Review* (July/August).

Bennett, T., and C. S. Hakkio. 1989. "Europe 1992: Implications for U.S. Firms." *Economic Review*, FRB of Kansas City (April): 3–17.

Bertola, G. 1989. "Factor Mobility, Uncertainty, and Exchange Rate Regimes." In deCecco and Giovannini, eds., *A European Central Bank*. Cambridge University Press, Cambridge, U.K.

Carraro, C. 1989. "The Tastes of European Central Bankers." In deCecco and Giovannini, eds., *A European Central Bank*. Cambridge University Press, Cambridge U.K.

Ceasar, R. 1986. "German Monetary Policy and the EMS." Paper presented at the SUERF Colloquium, October 9–11.

Cecchini, P. 1988. "1992: The Benefits of a Single Market." Hampshire, England: Gower Press.

Centre for Monetary and Financial Economics. 1989. "The Separation of Finance and Industry and Comparative Analysis." Milan, March 10.

Committee for the Study of Economic and Monetary Union (Delors Committee). 1989. *Report on Economic and Monetary Union in Europe.* Luxembourg.

Cumming, C. M., and L. M. Sweet. 1987/88. "Financial Structure of the G-10 Countries: How Does the United States Compare?" *FRB of New York Quarterly Review* (Winter): 14–25.

deCecco, M., and A. Giovannini, eds. 1989. *A European Central Bank.* Cambridge University Press, Cambridge, U.K.

de Grauwe, P. 1989. "Is the European Monetary System a DM-Zone?" CEPS Discussion Paper no. 297. London.

"Deutsche Bank's Bigger Reach." 1989. *New York Times,* July 30 (Section 3).

Dudler, H. J. 1985. "Changes in Money Market Instruments and Procedures in Germany." Paper presented at BIS Basel, November 7–8.

Edison, H. J., and E. Fisher. 1989. "A Long-Run View of the European Monetary System." FR Board of Governors, International Finance Discussion Paper no. 339, January.

Giavazzi, F., and A. Giovannini. 1988. "Models of the EMS: Is Europe a Greater Deutschemark Area?" Mimeo.

Giavazzi, F., and M. Pagano. 1986. "The Advantage of Tying One's Hands: EMS Discipline and Central Bank Credibility." CEPS Discussion Paper no. 135, October.

Goodhart, C. 1989. "The Delors Report: Was Lawson's Reaction Justifiable?" *LSE Financial Markets Group,* S.P. no. 15.

Grilli, V. 1989. "Seigniorage in Europe." In deCecco and Giovanni, eds., *A European Central Bank.* Cambridge University Press. Cambridge, U.K.

H. M. Treasury. 1989. "An Evolutionary Approach to Economic and Monetary Union." London.

Institutional Investor. 1989. "Ranking the World's Largest Banks" *Institutional Investor* (June) 217–40.

Kahn, G., and K. Jacobson. 1989. "Lessons from West German Monetary Policy." Mimeo.

Keating, G. 1989. *Perspectives on the Delors Report.* CSFB, London. September.

Leigh-Pemberton, R. 1989. "The Future of Monetary Arrangements in Europe." *Bank of England Quarterly Bulletin* (August): 368–87.

Lewis, S., and W. Vincent. 1989. "Deutsche Bank–Life Assurance Venture Could Prove a Success." Salomon Brothers *European Equity Research* (March 17).

———. 1988. "Deutsche Bank—Strategic Perspective." Salomon Brothers, *European Equity Research* (September 15).
———. 1988. "The West German Universal Banks." Salomon Brothers, *European Equity Research* (February 16).
Molyneux, P. 1989. "Big Fish, Little Fish." *Banker* (January): 38–39.
Muehring, K. 1989. "The Struggle to Save 1992." *Institutional Investor* (May): 287–91.
Neumann, M. J. 1988. "Implementation of Monetary Policy in Germany." Paper presented at Conference on Monetary Aggregates, FR Board of Governors, Washington, D.C., May 26–27.
Rudolph, B. 1989. "Capital Requirements of German Banks and the EEC Proposals on Banking Supervision." Paper presented at the Salomon Brothers Center Conference on European Banking after 1992, April 13–14.
Sibert, A., and S. E. Weiner. 1989. "Maintaining Central Bank Credibility." *Economic Review*, FRB of Kansas City (September/October).
Smith, A. H. 1989. "A Truly International Securities Market." *Banking World* (May).
Steinherr, A., and C. Huveneers. 1989. "Universal Banking: A View Inspired by German Experience." Paper presented at the Centre for Monetary and Financial Economics, University of Bocconi, Milan, March 10.
Trehan, B. 1988. "The Practice of Monetary Targeting: A Case Study of the West German Experience." *Economic Review*, FRB of San Francisco (Spring): 30–43.
Wegner, M. 1989. "The EMS: A Regional Bretton Woods or an Institutional Innovation." In H. J. Vosgerau, ed., *New Institutional Arrangements for the World Economy*. Berlin: Springer-Verlag: 89–122.
Whitehead, D. D. 1988. "Moving toward 1992: A Common Financial Market for Europe." *FRB of Atlanta Economic Review*. (December): 42–49.
Wood, G. 1989. "One Money for Europe?" *Journal of Monetary Economics*.
Wyplosz, C. 1989. "Macroeconomics Implications of 1992." Paper presented at the Salomon Brothers Center Conference on European Banking after 1992, April 13–14.

8
Fiscal Harmonization in the European Community

G. K. *Shaw*

A Conceptual Framework and the Leading Issues

Let us represent the welfare of any member country of the European Community (EC) as a function of the efficiency gains to be anticipated from tax harmonization together with the loss of sovereignty involved in the very process of harmonization. Then we may write

$$W = W(E,S)$$

for all member countries, where E stands for efficiency gains and S for sovereignty loss. The total change in welfare for any one member can therefore be expressed by the total differential:

$$dW = \frac{\delta W}{\delta E} \cdot dE + \frac{\delta W}{\delta S} dS$$

which can be positive or negative. For the community as a whole, however, there must be a net welfare gain associated with fiscal harmonization; otherwise there would be no justification for such programs. Thus we may write

$$\sum_{i=1}^{n} dW_i \geq 0 \qquad (1)$$

Expression 1 implies that compensation is possible for any one member country suffering a net welfare loss in consequence of fiscal harmonization. The issue of whether compensation actually *has* to be paid to generate a net Pareto improvement is not one that need detain us here. The fact is that under existing arrangements compensation

---

This chapter has benefited from suggestions by Mark Perlman, detailed and critical comments from Carl Shoup, and the perceptive insights of my commentator, Leon Gordon of the EC Commission. Linda Waterman is responsible for numerous improvements in style and exposition.

FIGURE 8–1
THE ECONOMICS OF TAX HARMONIZATION

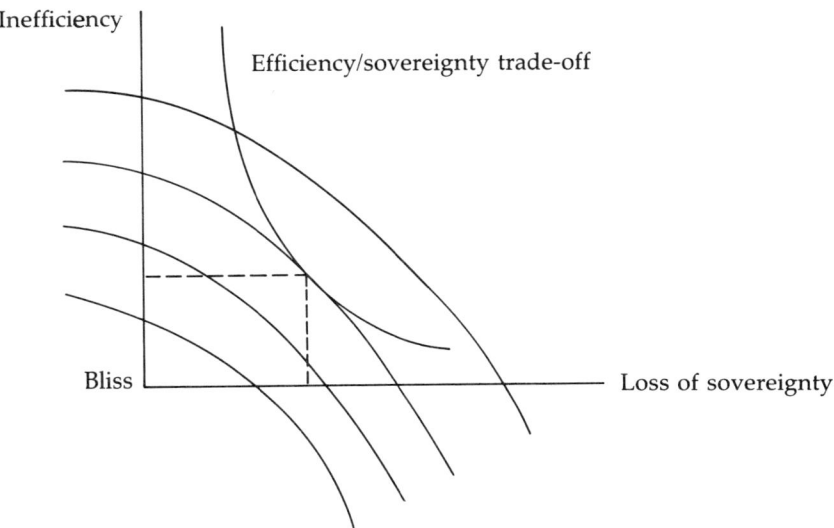

would be paid, since in fiscal matters all member countries retain a power of veto. Consequently, no measure of fiscal harmonization would be accepted by any one member state suffering a welfare loss in consequence, in the absence of compensation.

Given this framework, the question of fiscal harmonization reduces to a simple exercise in constrained maximization. We wish to maximize the function

$$W^* = W(E,S) + \lambda_1(\ ) + \lambda_2(\ ) + \lambda_3(\ )$$

etc., where $\lambda_1, \lambda_2, \lambda_3$, etc., refer to the multiple constraints emanating from the member countries. These may, for example, impose limits on the extent of revenue loss, budgetary deficit, or unemployment stemming from proposed measures of fiscal harmonization. Taking partial derivatives with respect to E, S, $\lambda_1, \lambda_2, \lambda_3$, etc., setting to zero, and solving the resulting system of simultaneous equations provides us theoretically with the constrained optimum. In diagrammatic terms what is involved, given the efficiency/sovereignty trade-off, is securing the highest attainable indifference curve (that is, closest to the origin). This analysis is portrayed in figure 8–1.

Of course, this is to beg the question of how the welfare ordering

TABLE 8-1
Members of the European Parliament

Country	Votes
Belgium	24
Denmark	16
France	81
Greece	24
Ireland	15
Italy	81
Luxembourg	6
Netherlands	25
Portugal	24
Spain	60
United Kingdom	81
West Germany	81
Total	518

Source: Hitiris 1988.

is determined. Presumably, we have to assume that some democratic process working through the European Parliament is able to express a consistent pattern of preferences. Without entering into the objections raised by welfare theorists, voting paradoxes, impossibility theorems, and so forth, it is worth noting that voting powers possessed by the member countries are by no means equal. Table 8–1 indicates the relative voting powers of the member countries, although it should be emphasized that there is no guarantee that the members of any one country will vote together on any particular issue. Finally, it may be worthwhile to note that from a purely pragmatic standpoint the various committees and agencies of the EC Commission dealing with harmonization issues are of necessity working in a large measure of isolation. That is to say, the committee dealing with corporate income taxation is largely divorced from that concerned with the harmonization of value-added tax (VAT). This, of course, is inevitable if progress is to be made. Nonetheless, it does mean that committees are working on harmonization proposals on the tacit assumption that first-best conditions are being met elsewhere. This, of course, need not be the case. It may well be that the appropriate measure of corporate income tax harmonization is not independent of the progress of harmonization proposals in respect of the social security system. At the end of the day, certain second-best adjustments may be called for.

In pragmatic terms the most important areas of required fiscal

TABLE 8-2
TAX REVENUES OF EC MEMBER STATES, 1986

	U.S. Dollars per Capita	Percentage of GDP
Belgium	5,302	45.4
Denmark	8,151	50.6
France	5,802	44.2
Greece	1,461	36.7
Ireland	2,781	40.2
Italy	3,798	36.2
Luxembourg	6,540	42.4
Netherlands	5,483	45.5
Portugal	968	32.4
Spain	1,798	30.4
United Kingdom	3,762	39.0
West Germany	5,484	37.5
Total	4,278	40.0

SOURCE: OECD 1988, tables 3, 34.

harmonization arise in those markets that reveal the greatest degree of integration. These are the markets for goods and services on the one hand and the market for capital on the other; in contrast, the labor market is relatively unintegrated owing to cultural, social, and language barriers to labor mobility. There is consequently less concern with, and less need for, measures of tax harmonization in respect of employment incomes.[1]

In the absence of harmonization in integrated markets, the prospect arises of resource misallocation in production, consumption, and investment decisions. If *posttax* decisions in these areas differ from *pretax* decisions, then *prima facie* there is evidence of tax-induced distortion generating potential inefficiencies. Clearly, one way to overcome such distortions would be to adopt a completely uniform fiscal system throughout the community. But, as Smith (1990) has rightly emphasized, such uniformity should not be the objective of policy. There are all sorts of perfectly valid reasons—social, political, and economic—why countries will choose differing levels of taxation. (Table 8–2, taken directly from Smith 1990, illustrates this point.) In light of these considerations, the imposition of such uniformity would be welfare decreasing. Rather, the objective should be to try to minimize the tax-induced distortion in critical areas while minimizing the impact on member states' revenues and social policy aims. This, of course, is precisely the approach outlined in the constrained maximization model detailed above.

Having outlined, albeit briefly, a conceptual framework, can we identify the leading issues? These appear to be three in number:

1. Why is there a need for fiscal harmonization in the light of 1992?
2. What are the prospects of attaining the required degree of harmonization by the end of 1992?
3. Finally, what are the probable consequences of failing to achieve the requisite degree of fiscal harmonization?

With regard to the first issue, the major reason for measures of fiscal harmonization within an integrated Europe has already been stated. Elementary economic theory teaches us that once trade barriers and tariffs are dismantled, significant differences in the taxation of goods and services will distort international trade and fair competition. Likewise, significant differences in the treatment of corporate and dividend income will influence the allocation of capital investment while also raising the prospects of tax fraud and evasion. Such tax-induced distortions imply real costs in the form of efficiency losses, implying lower growth rates, lower employment, and ultimately lower community welfare.

Thus far these costs have largely been avoided (although others have been incurred in consequence), simply because the degree of economic integration has been so limited. Differences in indirect taxation of goods and services, for example, have been negated by compensating border tax adjustments. With respect to the allocation of investment, restrictions on the free movement of capital, particularly those stemming from exchange controls, have served to minimize the potential misallocation of capital arising from tax differentials.

Now, however, we are faced with the prospect of 1992 and the creation of the single market, when all twelve member countries will in effect agree to act as one economic unit. Border fiscal controls are to be abolished, and all restrictions on the free movement of capital (and labor) will be eliminated—hence the need for measures of fiscal harmonization to avoid major efficiency losses. This is the challenge of the single market.

Of course, it is possible to argue that positive fiscal harmonization proposals are not required because the market process will ultimately generate an efficient solution. High-tax countries, it is argued, will find strong incentives to reduce their levels of taxation as they experience revenue losses and unemployment stemming from the practice of cross-border shopping and the flight of capital. In this way competition will inevitably force a certain measure of convergence, thus countering efficiency losses. The prospect of a market-oriented solution, however, is not one that commends itself to most observers, for bargaining strengths differ considerably among the member countries. In particular, smaller countries are likely to benefit considerably from policies of tax reduction by inducing inflows of economic activity that more than counter lower revenues obtained from the taxation of domestic residents. The outcome of a competitive free-for-all tax-cutting program is unlikely to be consistent with the true needs of the community. At the very least, it appears essential to reach agreement on *minimum* rates of taxation.

This leads into the second major issue identified above. What are the chances that the required degree of fiscal harmonization will be in place by the end of 1992? Regrettably, all the indications suggest that progress will be relatively modest and that the creation of the single market will occur without the degree of fiscal harmonization necessary to prevent serious misallocation of resources and distortion of international trade flows. Here the fundamental stumbling block remains the power of veto, which each country retains in matters of fiscal harmonization. Unanimity is required for any positive change. When one considers the sheer diversity of the twelve member countries in their national characteristics, stage of development, degree of industrialization, and so forth, the prospect of agreement looks distinctly remote. This negative conclusion is reinforced when one considers that the member countries have different timetables for national election; at any given time it seems almost inevitable that there will be at least one member country with an interest in postponing a harmonization measure that is perceived with suspicion by the electorate.

Moreover, there is little prospect that the power of veto will be readily surrendered. On the contrary, all the indications are that it will be zealously guarded, especially since autonomy in monetary matters and monetary policy is being progressively eroded. The establishment of the European Monetary System (EMS) and the exchange rate mechanism, the abolition of exchange rate controls, the proposal for the creation of a European central bank, and ultimately the creation of one uniform currency place a premium on the retention of sovereignty in the sphere of fiscal policy for any member country desirous of pursuing an independent macroeconomic policy.

Apart from the purely conceptual issues discussed above, the historical experience is not encouraging. Indeed, while there can be no doubting the revived enthusiasm for the creation of the single market, one must question whether the political will exists for major programs of fiscal harmonization. The fact remains, for example, that draft directives on corporate tax harmonization prepared some twenty years ago have not been adopted. Indeed, many proposals have never even been debated by the European Parliament. The Treaty of Rome contains no commitment to the harmonization of direct taxes, and no measure of any substance involving corporate income tax harmonization has been enacted.

In addition, it is necessary to measure the intransigence of the British government. The Conservative administration is generally regarded as less than enthusiastic about the ultimate goal of European union. It has avoided full membership in the EMS, has expressed its opposition to the creation of a European central bank and the adoption of a common currency, and has indeed questioned the need for any concerted program of sales and corporate tax harmonization. It seems clear, for all the platitudes and expressions to the contrary, that the Conservative leadership is opposed in principle to the very concept of harmonization, which implies detailed controls, dictated by the EC Commission and running counter to the free market philosophy espoused by the former Thatcher administration.

It is recognized that tax regimes will need to converge in a more integrated Europe, but this is seen as being the natural outcome of a market-oriented competitive process and not the result of a concerted program of harmonization per se. The advantages of a free market solution to the problem include not only greater allocative efficiency but also retention of national sovereignty—an issue of considerable emotive concern to the present government. The British intransigence, demonstrated by the willingness of the British government to refuse a proposition acceptable to all other members, has set an unfortunate precedent. Other countries (for example, Denmark and Luxembourg), emboldened by Britain's stance, are now asserting their independence.

Nor is it possible to ignore the macroeconomic implications of fiscal harmonization. There appear to be three major issues involved here. First of all, possible employment consequences stem from harmonization. If Spain, Greece, and Portugal, for example, were compelled to impose substantial taxes on wine as required by the commission's proposals, it seems inevitable that unemployment among marginal producers would result. Second, there are serious revenue implications for countries with high indirect taxes. In particular, current proposals suggest significant revenue losses for Denmark and Ireland, which may necessitate unwelcome and politically difficult adjustments in the rate of direct taxation. Finally, there is the problematic position of the United Kingdom, where, under current proposals, substantial increases in VAT taxation would be offset by wide-ranging reductions in excise levies on alcohol and tobacco. The net effect would appear to increase the burden of taxation on the lower paid, especially if the zero rating of VAT were to be eliminated, and would be widely condemned as being regressive, as well as giving offense to the increasingly influential health lobby.

Finally, it is questionable to what extent the recent traumatic events in Eastern Europe, will impinge on the progress to European union. It seems likely that they will generate calls for caution. Participants will want to gauge the strength of the new economic and political alliances now emerging before committing themselves to irreversible positions. In particular, the reunification of the two Germanys is likely to impose financial constraints on West Germany. It is conceivable that the West German position might become less enthusiastic about current proposals for immediate monetary union.

When consideration is given to all these factors, it appears unlikely that major fiscal changes will be enacted in the short term. What then are the consequences of failure to achieve the requisite degree of fiscal harmonization? This is the third major issue identified above and arguably one of the more difficult to resolve. A number of outcomes appear to be possible. Inevitably, there would be efficiency losses in the short term. How substantial or persistent these would be is a matter of conjecture. Member countries may well soon perceive these self-imposed costs and take steps to eradicate them. This, after all, has been the experience with the much maligned Common Agricultural Policy, which over time has eliminated the worst excesses of overproduction.

There remains, however, another, less optimistic scenario. In the absence of agreement, member countries might be tempted to engage in competitive tax cutting to benefit domestic producers, protect employment levels, and encourage external capital investment. As the experience of Luxembourg well demonstrates, cross-border shopping is a phenomenon responsive to tax differentials.[2] If such competitive behavior should emerge on any extensive scale, it will inevitably run counter to the fiscal needs of an integrated Europe. Moreover, it appears inevitable that such behavior will be accompanied by a gradual shift of the burden of taxation away from the owners of capital toward the owners of labor services. This follows from the fact that capital is the mobile factor, far more responsive to tax inducements than labor. Indeed, it is not impossible that such a development could foreshadow the ultimate abolition of the corporate income tax as a separate tax within the EC.

There is perhaps some consolation for the United States in this prognosis of failure to reach agreement on required measures of fiscal harmonization. It is unlikely, in the absence of agreement, that discriminatory fiscal measures will be adopted against third countries. Although the single market may contain shades of anti-American, anti-Japanese, and generally protectionist sentiment, it is unlikely that they will find expression in discriminatory fiscal changes.

Finally, it should perhaps be emphasized that the focal point of this paper is the question of tax harmonization. This appears to be the dominant fiscal issue in the context of 1992. From a longer-term perspecitve, however, it is arguable that the more important issue will be the need to harmonize expenditure programs in the light of long-term demographic changes and the anticipated rise in the dependency ratio confronting the EC.

European Integration—An Overview

Introduction. The EC Commission's White Paper on the completion of the Internal Market (COM 85 310 final, sometimes referred to as the Cockfield report), accepted in June 1985 and followed by the Single European Act later the same year, represents a remarkable achievement in the movement toward European integration. The clear commitment to the creation of an internal market devoid of fiscal frontiers combined with the acceptance of the principle of majority voting on matters of harmonization generally (though not on matters fiscal) can only be construed as a giant step forward toward the goal of European union.

This success is all the more remarkable in the light of the prevailing economic conditions and the apparent failure of the EC to achieve substantial benefits in matters of common policy. The acute recession and high European unemployment that characterized the 1970s and the 1980s were accompanied by the adoption of protectionist nontariff barriers, by massive state aid to ailing sectors, by market fragmentation, and by an industrial performance that could no longer claim to be competitive with the high-technology growth sectors of Japan and the United States. Moreover, economic failure had been accompanied by political disagreements and failure to agree on the community-wide budget, on membership of the EMS, or on how to end an absurdly wasteful and extremely expensive agricultural support policy. To all intents and purposes, the EC was in both economic and political disarray by the early 1980s.

Yet, paradoxically, this lamentable failure provided the spur to an extremely wide-ranging and ambitious program of unification. It was as if awareness of Europe's failure to be competitive in world markets generated the perception of the benefits to be obtained from the creation of a single market economy. Such a perception was undeniably influenced by the appearance of the Cecchini report (see Cecchini 1988), the outcome of an unprecedented research program launched by the EC Commission vice-president, Lord Cockfield. What this report did was to provide the foundation for a quantitative appraisal of the costs of European fragmentation and of the benefits to be gained by European union in contrast to the qualitative and largely subjective judgments then prevailing. The total potential gain to the community as a whole to be derived from the completion of the internal market was estimated to be 200 billion European currency units (ECU) in 1988 prices or approximately 5 percent of the community's gross domestic product. These gains stemmed principally from reduced prices to consumers, reduced costs to producers, and the realization of unexploited economies of scale in both private and public sectors as well as an increase in international trade with nonmember countries.

From the very earliest days, the founding fathers of the EC adopted the view that trade liberalization within the member states would need to be accompanied by other measures of harmonization if it were to succeed in maximizing community-wide benefits. That is to say, from the outset European integration was conceived of at its minimalist level in terms of a common market approach permitting the free movement of the factors of production, as opposed to a customs union approach concerned solely with the harmonization of tariffs.

Theoretically, the expectation was that both labor and capital would migrate from regions of low wages and profits, exploiting the principles of comparative advantage, in the search for their most productive outlet. In the process wage and profit differentials would be narrowed, output and growth increased, and economic welfare maximized. It was fully recognized, however, that differences in tax rates on goods and services or on different forms of economic activity could seriously interfere with the indicated optimum allocation of resources. There was thus a perceived need for a substantial measure of fiscal harmonization to avoid inefficient trade and factor flows. The idealists among the early "Europeans" looked on the required harmonization of fiscal regimes as a first step toward the goal of an eventual economic union enjoying common institutions and a common currency. The skeptics, of whom there were and still are many, viewed the prospect of a united Europe as largely a pipe dream, yet nonetheless accepted that there were substantial benefits to be enjoyed by sovereign national states through policies of greater trade liberalization accompanied by the requisite degree of fiscal harmonization.

This, then, was the background to the search for first principles of tax and fiscal harmonization. Today, more than thirty years on, there is a substantial and burgeoning literature on the subject, and we possess a far greater understanding of the principles and issues involved.[3] Yet controversy still remains concerning both the degree of harmonization required for the establishment of efficient production and consumption patterns on the one hand and the consequences and implications of agreed harmonization measures on the other. It is to these questions that this paper is principally addressed, in the light of the commitment to the creation of a single market devoid of fiscal frontiers by the end of 1992. Specifically, our concern will be with the following issues:

- What are the revenue implications of fiscal harmonization for the member states?
- What are the microeconomic effects of tax changes on factor mobility and the location of industry?
- What are the macroeconomic effects of fiscal harmonization on economic growth, employment, and price stability?
- What are the implications for the composition of the tax mixture and the progressivity or regressivity of the tax-benefit structure?
- What are the implications for the trading relationships maintained with outsiders, in particular with the United States and Japan?

The Scale of the Problem. In addressing the issue of harmonization it is usual to focus attention on indirect taxation and in particular on excise duties, where the largest differences manifest themselves. It is important to note, however, that many other aspects are involved, some of which are not easily quantified. Government subsidies to nationalized industries, for example, particularly in the transportation and communication sectors, may constitute sizable hidden subsidies to the export sector of a member state. In the same vein differing public procurement policies within the member nations may confer selective benefits on certain industries or sectors that may impede the most efficient allocation of resources.

At the same time certain expenditures undertaken within any one member country may confer benefits on all member states. This raises the issue of how provision is to be financed. Finally, the question of fiscal harmonization is not one that can be pursued independently of the issue of administrative efficacy or of the scope for tax evasion and avoidance or indeed of the entire climate of fiscal compliance, which differs substantially among heterogeneous member nations.

Indirect taxes. In the early days of the theory of economic integration it was widely assumed that the acceptance of a single market and the abolition of fiscal frontiers would necessitate the termination of the destination principle of indirect taxation and its replacement by origin-based taxes. In the former case taxes imposed on exports are rebated in full upon export; the rates of tax prevailing on like goods in the country of destination are then imposed upon import. Accordingly, goods compete on equal footing in both domestic and export markets regardless of differences in national indirect tax rates. No artificially tax-induced distortion arises to deny the principle of comparative advantage, but a cost is imposed—namely, the maintenance of fiscal frontiers.

The maintenance of such fiscal frontiers was considered necessary to refund taxes on exported produce while imposing taxes on imports. (It is only comparatively recently that consideration has been given to the possibility of making such border tax adjustments while abolishing fiscal frontiers.) The costs associated with the maintenance of fiscal frontiers, including the delays and bureaucracy entailed, have been estimated at some 5 to 7 percent of the value of all goods traded between community members each year. Moreover, the abolition of fiscal frontiers is looked on as being desirable because of the psychological impact it would have in the drive toward European unity.

The destination principle, when fairly applied, enjoys the advantage of treating imports and domestically produced goods alike. Moreover, since the fiscal revenues accrue to the country of final consumption, it permits tax rate changes to be made in the light of prevailing macroeconomic policy needs and thus contributes to stabilization goals. The constraint on the degree of tax autonomy appears to lie in the scope and incentives provided by the prospect of cross-border shopping. Transportation costs, however, including the cost of time and inconvenience, would limit the allocative distortions, and U.S. experience suggests that differences in the rate of local sales taxation of 4 to 5 percent have but minor impact on locational decisions.

In contrast, under the origin principle of taxation, there is no rebate of tax on exported products, nor is there any tax imposition on imported goods. Goods are simply taxed at the rate applicable in their country of origin, and accordingly border controls or border tax adjustments are not needed. It was for this reason initially that adoption of the origin principle was seen as the key to the removal of fiscal frontiers. Clearly, however, such a system of taxation poses a considerable danger of resource misallocation in both production and consumption decisions unless effective tax rates are substantially harmonized. With no restrictions imposed on factor movements, producers would have a tax-induced incentive to locate in low-tax countries regardless of the conditions of comparative advantage, and equally consumers would be offered a tax-induced incentive to prefer products emanating from low-tax countries.[4]

Hence a dual philosophy emerged: that the abolition of fiscal frontiers would require adoption of the origin principle of taxation and that under such a system considerable harmonization of tax rates would be required to prevent serious misallocation of resources.[5] The origin principle of taxation was seen to possess the overriding advantage of permitting the abolition of fiscal border controls and allowing the transition toward a single market economy. The need to harmonize rates, however, implies a loss of autonomy and a decrease in the degree of freedom in macroeconomic policy formation.

Moreover, it carries obvious revenue implications in that countries with high indirect taxes would be compelled to reduce their rates of tax and seek alternative revenue sources, implying a change in the composition of the tax mixture that may not be administratively or politically feasible. It is because of these drawbacks that considerable attention was accorded to a seminal paper by Cnossen (1983) that first proposed the radical step of maintaining the destination principle of taxation while abolishing border fiscal controls. This proposal has exercised considerable influence on subsequent progress toward a single market and has raised the issue of just how much harmonization of indirect taxes will be required to meet the objective of the single market without generating undue trade distortion. This turns out to be a decidedly complex issue and one that we shall examine in some considerable detail.

The principal forms of indirect taxation within the EC consist of a general form of sales tax, the VAT, and a number of specific excise duties, particularly on alcohol, petroleum products, and tobacco. The VAT is a broad-based tax extending through to the retail stage; accordingly it is highly significant in revenue generation. Currently it provides approximately 17 percent of all tax revenues in the EC, being in some states the single most important source of revenue.

Although substantial agreement has been reached on the definition of the tax base, considerable differences emerge with regard to tax rates, reflecting differences in equity stances. Thus, for example, in both the United Kingdom and Ireland the practice of zero rating goods deemed to be essentials (food, children's clothing, public transportation, and the like) is widespread, while France, Belgium, and Italy impose a higher rate of VAT on goods deemed to be luxuries (including jewelry, furs, and perfume).[6] Clearly, harmonization carries implications for income distribution as well as for the macroeconomy.

Nonetheless, considerable progress toward greater uniformity is being achieved. Initially, the commission proposed two broad bands of VAT taxation with rates of 4 to 9 percent for goods deemed necessities and rates of 14 to 20 percent for all other goods and services. Such a plan, if realized, together with the commitment to terminate exemptions and zero-rated goods, would have implied a considerable convergence toward the principle of harmonization if not of uniformity in sales taxation.[7]

Arguably, greater difficulties remain in relation to excise duties. Again, wide disparities exist in the rates of excise duty, and any discretion in the rates of permitted excise taxation would be compounded by the permitted margin for VAT since the latter is levied on the price of goods inclusive of excise duty. Consequently, having determined the permissible range of variation for VAT, it is essential that reasonably stringent harmonization be achieved in excise taxation.

One major problem arises from the fact that goods subject to excise taxation often face highly inelastic demand conditions and have been singled out for taxation primarily because of their revenue-raising potential. Accordingly, any harmonization program could generate severe budgetary impacts for the member states. Thus far, apart from a limited agreement on tobacco taxation involving the combination of a specific per unit and percentage retail sales tax with fairly broad bands of tax, little progress has been achieved.

Direct taxes. The harmonization of direct taxation produces particular problems of analysis since much depends on differing assumptions of tax incidence. Conventionally it is assumed that direct taxes—that is, personal income taxes, including national insurance contributions, and corporation income taxes—are borne by the person or body on whom they are imposed. If this is the case, it follows immediately that failure to harmonize such taxes would suggest possible misallocation in the spatial distribution of productive factors.

In the case of the personal income tax, for example, one might expect that incentives would exist for highly qualified and skilled labor to migrate to low-tax regions, while unemployed and unskilled workers might more readily migrate to countries with high social security benefits. Intertemporally, one might expect workers to express a preference for retirement in countries associated with high benefits, having worked in countries with relatively low social security contributions over their working lives. Indeed, such behavior would be consistent with utility-maximizing behavior implicit in the life-cycle hypothesis of consumption determination.

In practice, considerable differences exist in personal income tax rates and social security contributions and benefits among the member nations of the EC; yet comparatively little attempt has been made to harmonize either the tax base or the tax rates. Any attempt at harmonizing personal income tax rates would have severe repercussions on any economy desirous of pursuing an independent macroeconomic policy, and it is no doubt for this reason that such moves have been strongly resisted. This is of particular significance because of the rapid increase in the importance of the personal income tax in the tax structure of member states. The weighted average of the income tax ratio of the member states has increased by more than 50 percent over the period 1965–1983, reflecting a host of influences, including the extension of withholding schemes for wage income, uncorrected fiscal drag, and inflation, which combined to reduce the real value of initial allowances and push taxpayers into higher tax brackets (Messere 1983).

Considerable differences exist in the effective rates of income tax applicable to the average industrial wage in the member states. At the same time, however, it appears that language and other cultural differences render labor relatively immobile, and this suggests that for the moment the misallocation of labor inputs is not a serious problem. Significantly, the personal income tax has not been included among the taxes intended for harmonization, and it now appears that a tacit agreement exists to leave this tax within the sphere of national sovereignty.[8]

More serious difficulties of resource misallocation appear to arise in the case of capital movements, where in principle the tax base is exceedingly mobile. Needless to say, as well as considering differences in tax rates, it is necessary to pay attention to differentials in the provision and timing of depreciation allowances, as well as considering differences in the tax treatment of distributed and undistributed profits. Indeed, it appears that merely harmonizing the nominal rates of corporation tax within the member states would have a comparatively minor effect in approximating effective tax rates (Bird 1987). Moreover, not only do effective rates of tax differ substantially among the member states, but also considerable differences emerge among different sectors within member states.

Nonetheless, in principle the issue is very clear. Given the free movement of capital inputs, economic theory would predict that capital would be so allocated as to make posttax rates of return equal. From a purely economic welfare vantage point, however, it is equality in the pretax rate of return that is required to maximize output. It follows that differing rates of corporate income tax among member nations can seriously interfere with the optimal allocation of resources.

Regrettably, considerable differences exist with respect to the treatment of corporate income, and comparatively little agreement has been reached on proposed reform. The scope of the tax, the tax base, differs widely among countries. The tax applies to partnerships in some cases, but not in others. Differences of opinion exist over what constitutes taxable profits. There are legal differences with respect to the measurement of capital gains and losses, the manner in which stocks and inventories are to be valued, and the way in which depreciation is to be measured. All these items are significant because they enter into the determination of net taxable income.

If there are important differences in the tax base, there are also sizable differences in the rate of tax applied, differences that are often accentuated by the granting of special concessions to certain sectors (energy conservation) and regions deemed worthy of preferential treatment. Moreover, whereas for VAT the mechanism of border tax adjustment explicit in the destination principle effectively ensures the neutrality of taxation in international trade, no such mechanism exists with regard to differences in the corporate tax burden. Indeed, it is a widely accepted principle, endorsed by the General Agreement on Tariffs and Trade (GATT) as well as by the EC Treaty, that the rebate of direct taxes imposed on corporate income should be expressly denied. If only for this reason, there is arguably greater need for measures of harmonization of corporate income taxes than of indirect taxes.

Perhaps the most contentious area of disagreement, however, rests with the treatment of distributed and undistributed profits. Broadly speaking, there are two possible approaches to this question. At one extreme the company is viewed as a distinct legal entity, quite divorced from its shareholders, despite their ownership. It is accordingly taxed on its profits, whether distributed or not, and then any distributed profits in the form of dividends are taxed again as personal income received by those shareholders. The standard objection to this system is that it entails the double taxation of dividends.

At the other extreme the separate existence of the company is denied, and it is looked on merely as a partnership of its shareholders. Under such a system any corporate tax paid is automatically credited in full against the personal tax liability of the shareholders. The majority of the countries of the EC operate a system somewhere between these two extremes, whereby a portion of the corporate tax paid is credited against personal income tax liability. It is likely, therefore, that future harmonization of the corporation tax will be along these lines. Even though the corporate income tax is a relatively minor source of revenue, however, the difficulties should not be underestimated, for the amount of corporate tax credit allowed against personal income tax liability varies enormously among the member countries—currently ranging from 15 percent to 100 percent.

Indirect Taxation—VAT and Excise Duties

The EC Commission, in advocating the abolition of fiscal frontier controls, insisted that such abolition will require changes in the structure and rates of indirect taxation. In the case of VAT, for example, a two-tier system was initially proposed, with a standard rate of tax falling between 14 and 20 percent together with a reduced rate of taxation of between 4 and 9 percent for certain goods and services. Between these ranges or bands of taxation, member countries would be free to vary their rates of tax to meet legitimate revenue needs and pursue macroeconomic policy goals. They would not be free to impose tax rates falling outside these bands, nor would they be able to determine which goods fall into each category. Finally, the current zero-rated classification of goods would be abolished.

With respect to excise duties the degree of harmonization is more stringent. Here complete uniformity in the rate of duty is proposed, but since goods subject to excise duty are also subject to VAT, again differences would arise in the total tax burden. Inevitably, in the face of opposition the commission was compelled to relax these proposals to permit greater flexibility for member states at least for an interim period.[9] Nonetheless, while pragmatism has dictated concessions, the initial proposals accurately reflect the philosophy of the commission and are probably more indicative of its long-term aims.

These proposals appear to reflect the belief that the abolition of fiscal frontiers necessitates termination of the existing system of exempting exports from domestic tax upon export. Second, they appear to reflect the view that if exports are now subject to taxation before export, then regardless of the extent and manner of any subsequent tax credit to be granted, only comparatively minor differences in tax rates are acceptable if trade and consumption distortions and tax fraud are to be avoided.

VAT—the Existing System. Assume, for purposes of exposition, two member countries, A and B, with VAT rates of 10 percent and 20 percent respectively. Assume further that an exporter in country A exports goods to country B worth $200 net of tax. Under the present

FIGURE 8–2
The Existing System of the Value-added Tax

	Export Stage	Import Stage	Retail Stage
Country	A	B	
Tax rate	10%	20%	
Exports	200		
Imports	—	200	400 + VAT
Tax levy	—	40	80–40
Total tax	Nil	40	40

system the exporter secures a tax rebate for any tax paid in country A. The importer in country B then pays VAT on the imported value at the rate of 20 percent; that is, he pays $40. This is the essence of the destination principle of taxation—goods are ultimately taxed at the rate of tax prevailing within the country of final destination regardless of where they are produced.

Suppose now that the importer transforms his purchased inputs into a product with a final selling price of $400 plus VAT. It will now retail for a total price of $480, of which $80 represents tax, $40 of which is collected at the importation stage and $40 at the final retail stage since the original import tax is now deducted as a tax credit. Notice that the final selling price before tax, $400, is determined solely by the value added by the importer to the original $200 of imports: it is unaffected by the actual rate of VAT imposed upon import because regardless of the rate it is ultimately credited against final tax liability. Schematically, the system is outlined in Figure 8-2 In this example the total fiscal yield of $80 accrues entirely to the government of country B, where the product is consumed. Such a system of taxation has a number of positive advantages:

- In any one member country, all goods, whether domestically produced or imported, pay the same rate of tax. This is achieved by virtue of the tax credit mechanism operating at the border control, whereby taxes paid before export are rebated. Effectively, exported goods are taxed at a zero rate.
- Because of this no tax-induced cost distortions influence the choice of location of the productive unit. The tax is locationally neutral. No tax incentives are provided to locate in regions other than those conforming to the natural principles of comparative advantage.
- Such a system thus permits countries to adopt widely different rates of indirect taxation and moreover to make tax changes at will without influencing optimal trade and consumption patterns. This is an important consideration for macroeconomic policy formulation and also for national sovereignty in allowing countries to pursue taxation policies with regard to other goals of social policy.
- Taxes accrue to the government of the country of final consumption regardless of where the goods were produced. This is an important distributional consideration implying, for the most part, conformity with the principle that each country should pay its own taxes.
- Fraud and tax evasion are rendered comparatively difficult. Moreover, border tax officials can operate the system with a minimum of information. It is not necessary to know, for example, either the country of origin of imports or the country of destination of exports for border officials to apply the system of compensatory taxation and rebates. Finally, of course, for exports to be zero rated they must physically leave the country of origin. The possibility that zero-rated exports will be returned to the marketplace of the country of origin having escaped all tax is thus rendered minimal.
- Finally, with such a system of taxation, in principle no incentive is provided for personal cross-border shopping, which might otherwise create difficulties in the border regions of high-tax member countries. No tax advantage can be gained by crossing the border to shop, owing to the subsequent border tax adjustment—other than in the most trivial cases of immediate consumption.[10]

These advantages are indeed considerable. The overriding drawback in the conventional view is that this system appears to rely on maintaining not only border tax adjustments but also border tax controls; this is inimical to the goal of creating a single market possessed of all the characteristics of a domestic market. This is the fundamental question that the commission has addressed: Is it possible to retain the system of border tax adjustment without simultaneously maintaining fiscal border controls?

Could not border control be dispensed with by shifting the

process of border tax adjustments to books of account of individual traders? If this question is answered in the affirmative and if it could be combined with some kind of compensatory clearing scheme to redistribute revenues, it would allow the elimination of border fiscal controls while retaining almost all the benefits of the destination principle of taxation. In so doing it would question the extent to which tax rate harmonization is required. The commission's proposals were undoubtedly influenced by a seminal paper by Cnossen (1983), which first questioned the then conventional wisdom that the abolition of fiscal border controls would require the adoption of an origin-based tax regime, which in turn would require the harmonization of tax rates.

Cnossen's contention is that border tax adjustments can be computed equally well on the basis of books of account and written records. Various schemes of adjustment could be devised, but one of the most compelling, taken from Cnossen, is outlined below. Its logical simplicity is engaging to say the least. Simply stated, exports of goods from member states would pay the VAT prevailing within the country of export—no tax rebate would be provided. But the first taxable entity in the receiving country would receive a tax credit for the full amount of foreign VAT paid. The importer would have every incentive to list the credit and submit it for repayment to his local VAT office. Thus the VAT administration in each importing member state would amass a number of such credits, which would be totaled and tabulated separately according to the country of export. Each member country would then present the tax credits to the other member states for repayment. Obviously, a community-wide clearing mechanism would evolve, with net payments being made to countries that are net exporters in their balance of trade. In effect, the principle of zero-rated export tax and tax payments being made by consumers in the country of final destination would be restored.

This is essentially the proposal adopted by the commission. To illustrate in line with the previous example, the exporter in country A would pay tax at 10 percent on the final selling price of $200 but reclaim a rebate of 10 percent on the value of his purchased inputs, which have previously been subject to domestic taxation. The VAT authorities in country A, however, have now collected a total of $20 on the ultimate export of goods to country B, since they have previously collected tax on earlier value added. Thus the importer in country B would file a tax credit to the value of $20 to his VAT authorities, who would present the tax claim back to country A for repayment. In effect, country A has exported goods carrying a 10 percent VAT burden, but through the system of credit repayment the

FIGURE 8–3
THE PROPOSED SYSTEM OF THE VALUE-ADDED TAX

		Export Stage	Import Stage	Retail Stage
Country	A		B	
Tax rate	10%		20%	
Exports	200			
Imports	—		220	400 + VAT
Tax levy	—	20	0	80–20
Total tax		20	0	60

principle, if not the practice, of zero-rated export taxation is restored. If now we assume that the importer again turns his purchased inputs into a product carrying a final selling price of $400 plus VAT, the final price will again rise to $480, of which $80 is tax. In contrast to the previous case, however, the tax paid at the retail stage is $60, since only $20 can be claimed as a tax credit owing to the lower rate of VAT in country A. Schematically, the situation is illustrated in figure 8-3.

Moreover, now $20 of the tax yield is being collected by country A even though consumption occurs solely in country B. The amount of tax diverted to country A in this manner will, of course, be greater, the greater the rate of tax in country A. This is the justification for the establishment of the clearinghouse mechanism to redistribute fiscal revenues. Without such a provision countries that have high taxes or are net exporters would, *ceteris paribus*, tend to gain revenue while low-tax countries or net importers could lose revenue. For certain countries, especially Greece and Ireland, the loss could be substantial and politically unacceptable.

In principle, therefore, the zero rating of exports is not essential to maintain consistency with the destination principle of taxation. Goods may be exported bearing the VAT of the exporting country provided the subsequent refund equals the tax already paid. The proposed system, however, raises many doubts and questions. In particular, it would require a great deal of cooperation and coordination among the various VAT regimes in the member states, unlike the present system, where essentially national tax regimes function independently.

In addition, the complexities are increased by virtue of the fact that importers would be required to reclaim tax credit at different rates depending on the source of their imports. The possibilities of tax fraud and the difficulties of adequate policing appear to be considerable. Obviously, in principle, such abuse could be subject to control; but quite apart from the amount of paperwork and bureaucracy required for the system to operate at all efficiently, Lee, Pearson, and Smith (1988) emphasize a logical difficulty in its effective enforcement. In their view national revenue authorities would be more concerned to check whether VAT had been paid on exports than to scrutinize claims for input VAT tax since the former imply net payments to member states while the latter imply a corresponding receipt. The existence of the clearinghouse mechanism would reduce the incentives to check on dubious and fraudulent claims for input VAT. This remains a troublesome feature of the commission's proposal.

Although the commission's proposals effectively retain most of the advantages of the existing system of taxation according to the principle of destination, including that of allowing disparate rates of tax, nonetheless they have called for a considerable measure of tax rate harmonization. Again, in adopting this view considerable attention is given to the possibilities of tax fraud and evasion, the incentive to fraud and evasion being greater the greater the differences in the rate of tax. The removal of border controls would reduce the amount of documentary evidence available to the tax authorities, compounding the difficulties of policing and enforcement.

Arguably, however, the need for comparative uniformity in tax rates stems more from the potential for cross-border shopping, which arises from the abolition of border controls. Sizable differences in taxation not only could imply considerable tax loss for high-tax rate countries but also could have a severe adverse impact on business and retailing activity in border regions. As Lee, Pearson, and Smith (1988) have contended, however, these are all costs imposed on the residents of countries choosing to operate high-tax regimes. They are thus self-imposed costs that do not require community interference. In this view all that is required is agreement on a minimum rate of tax to prevent a "fiscal free-for-all" with countries cutting taxes to generate border shopping. Provided that agreement is reached on minimum rates of tax, differences in VAT rates would not require community-wide agreement. It would be for each country to assess the costs and benefits of raising tax rates above the agreed minimums.

Finally, as a matter of casual empiricism, considerable differences in prices appear to coexist within the same high street without generating disastrous consequences for the traders concerned. One might question, therefore, whether the commission has been too conservative in stipulating the range for the permitted rates of VAT. Certainly, it appears that a raising of the higher rate (or indeed its outright abolition) of the proposed standard rate of VAT would remove some of the pressures on high-tax countries without threatening the underlying economic basis of the single market economy.[11]

Excise Taxation. If the abolition of fiscal border controls generates difficulties and necessitates changes in the operation of VAT, the difficulties are compounded in the case of excise duties, which apply mainly to alcohol, tobacco, and mineral oils, including petroleum products. In general the issues raised are more complex for the following reasons:

• Greater diversity exists within the member countries in the administration of excise duties than of VAT. For VAT a common uniform system has been agreed to and to a large extent attained with respect to the definition of the tax base, methods of assessment, permissible allowances, and so forth. In contrast, for some countries adoption of a common excise duty system will mean a considerable administrative upheaval.

• The excise duty is levied at only one stage in contrast to the VAT. This eliminates the cross-checking of tax payments, which acts as an important source of control in the case of VAT. Moreover, simple audit controls would probably be insufficient to enforce compliance with the tax law, solely because of the higher rates of excise duty (see next item).

• Much higher rates of taxation apply in the case of excises—and more pertinently the differences in the rates of tax tend to be significant among the member countries. Sizable differences in tax rates increase the appeal of tax fraud and tax evasion and make personal cross-border shopping much more attractive, once border fiscal controls have been abolished. This is particularly true for alcohol and tobacco products, which are relatively nonbulky and readily transferable. These considerations tend to support the commission's contention that a greater degree of fiscal harmonization is required of excise duties than of VAT.

The existing system. Bonded warehouses: In this system of control, favored by the United Kingdom among others, the bonded warehouse permits goods to be stored net of tax. On leaving the warehouse for retail sale, they are subject to excise duty. Clearly, such a system has the advantage of minimizing the period between tax payment and eventual sale (an important consideration for importing and producing companies in the case of highly taxed goods), but its effective enforcement depends on careful policing and supervision by the customs officials involved. In particular, since exported products are zero rated before export, it is essential that officials monitor the movement of goods to and from the bonded warehouses and guarantee that such goods do actually leave the country. It is also essential that they possess the right of access to bonded warehouses and production units at all times. Obviously, effective control is easier for products that are imported (tobacco in the United Kingdom) or for goods where economies of scale make for substantial concentration of production (as in cigarette manufacture).

Tax stamps: The alternative approach depends on the use of tax stamps or other identifying physical markings to signify that excise duty has indeed been paid. This approach is especially popular for tobacco products, not only in the EC but also in other countries, including the United States and many third world countries. One advantage of such a system is that different markings can denote different rates of duty according to preferential treatment granted to certain consumers while still providing a means of enforcement and control.

Of these two approaches, the EC Commission, again apparently influenced by Cnossen's celebrated paper, has opted for a system of linked bonded warehouses to supervise excise taxation throughout the community. Under such a system exported goods would be zero rated, allowing them to be transferred to a bonded warehouse in another member country without taxation until the time for retail sale. Presumably, upon retail sale and taxation they would enjoy unrestricted right of movement throughout the community. Indeed, once fiscal border controls have been abolished, it would be extremely difficult to restrict such movement. This consideration would tend to reinforce the commission's call for uniformity of excise duty rates of tax to minimize the potential for tax fraud and evasion.

Even if this were to be conceded in principle, however, one must question whether the commission has been too sanguine in proposing rate approximation given the markedly different rate structures now prevailing. Rate differences reflect a host of influences, most notably differences in social policy and the desire to protect certain politically important producer groups. The revenue implications are also daunting. A potential problem arises with respect to the distribution of tax revenues. Again, this is an important point raised by Lee, Pearson, and Smith (1988). Economies of scale might dictate the advantages of centralizing production and warehousing facilities once fiscal border controls are dispensed with. Revenues would then accrue to the countries of location of these production and warehousing facilities, not to the countries of consumption in the absence of any clearinghouse mechanism.

Harmonization of Indirect Tax Rates—Current Proposals. *Value-added taxation.* The commission has adopted a pragmatic approach to the question of the harmonization of indirect tax rates; it is proposing rate approximation on the basis of averaging existing rates of taxation within the member states. This crude and essentially politically expedient approach has little underlying economic rationale and implies revenue losses for states having high indirect taxes and revenue gains for countries having comparatively low indirect taxes.[12] In the same way, in advocating a standard rate of 14 to 20 percent together with a reduced rate of 4 to 9 percent for certain categories of commodities and services, the commission has proposed a two-tier system of VAT. Again, such a two-tier system appears to reflect a pragmatic compromise that is considered politically acceptable given existing practice.

On purely efficiency grounds a single uniform rate of VAT applying to all goods and services without exception would be allocationally superior and would also possess the virtue of being easier to administer. Only one country (Denmark), however, now operates such a single uniform rate of tax while the others operate either two or three tax rates according to the nature of the goods concerned. In particular, the United Kingdom has a zero rate of tax on many goods deemed essentials, and in an important paper Davis and Kay (1985) estimated that such zero-rated goods accounted for approximately 30 percent of British consumer expenditure. Clearly, any attempt to subject these products to the standard rate now prevailing would have severe distributional repercussions stemming from the significant price effects. Indeed, even subjecting such goods (which include foodstuffs, books and newspapers, and passenger transportation services) to the proposed minimal 4 percent levy would be viewed as seriously regressive in that such goods form a more significant fraction of consumer spending of the poorer households. Moreover, children's clothing, currently zero rated in the United Kingdom, is not to be included in the reduced rate band according to present

TABLE 8-3
VALUE-ADDED TAX RATES IN EC MEMBER STATES, 1987

	Standard Rate	Increased Rate	Scope of Zero Rate
Belgium	19	25, 33	Newspapers
Denmark	22	—	Newspapers, large ships and aircraft
France	18.6	33.5	—
Greece	18	36	—
Ireland	23	—	Wide range of items
Italy	18	38	Newspapers and some minor items
Luxembourg	12	—	—
Netherlands	18.5	—	—
Portugal	16	30	Basic foods, newspapers, medicines
Spain	12	33	—
United Kingdom	15	—	Wide range of items
West Germany	14	—	—

SOURCE: Lee, Pearson, and Smith 1988.

proposals and thus would be subject to the standard rate of VAT. Existing rates of VAT for the member countries are shown in table 8-3; indirect taxes as a whole for eight member nations are given in table 8-4.

Clearly, the commission's proposals imply that Spain and Luxembourg would be compelled to raise their standard rate of VAT while Denmark and Ireland would be compelled to reduce theirs. The remaining member states could retain their existing standard rates of VAT, and some countries, particularly France, West Germany, the Netherlands, Spain, and Portugal, could retain their reduced rates as well. The higher rates would be abolished, but since these refer to a limited range of goods, the revenue effects are unlikely to be substantial.

The United Kingdom would be able to retain its existing standard rate of tax but would be compelled to terminate its zero rate of duty over a wide range of goods, and thus the overall importance of the VAT would be increased. Interestingly, Ireland would be compelled to reduce its lower rate of tax in addition to its standard rate. The revenue implications of these changes are not insignificant; however, rather than examine them in detail at this juncture it seems preferable to delay detailed analysis until we have examined the implications for excise duties. From the purely macroeconomic point of view, it is the

TABLE 8-4
INDIRECT TAXES IN THE PUBLIC FINANCES OF EIGHT EC MEMBER STATES, 1984
(billions)

	Belgium (FB)	Denmark (Kr)	France (FF)	West Germany (DM)	Ireland (£)	Italy (Lire)	Netherlands (HFl)	United Kingdom (£)
Revenues from VAT	329	55.3	381	110	1.37	38,200	28.3	18.0
Excise duty on alcohol	17	5.7	12	6	0.38	500	1.8	3.9
Excise duty on tobacco	30	6.4	15	14	0.28	4,200	2.1	4.0
Excise duty on mineral oils	53	5.6	69	24	0.40	13,000	4.0	5.9
Other indirect taxes	59	19.7	73	17	0.38	8,600	6.9	4.1
Total indirect taxes	487	92.8	551	172	2.80	64,500	43.1	35.9
Indirect taxes as percentage of total tax receipts	23	35	28	26	44	25	24	29
Indirect tax receipts as percentage of GDP	11	17	13	10	17	9	11	11

SOURCE: Lee, Pearson, and Smith 1988.

TABLE 8-5
EXCISE DUTY ON ALCOHOLIC DRINKS IN EC MEMBER STATES, 1986
(ECU)

	Spirits per Bottle	Still Wine per Liter	Beer per Liter
Belgium	3.76	0.33	0.13
Denmark	10.50	1.57	0.71
France	3.45	0.03	0.03
Greece	0.14	0	0.10
Ireland	8.17	2.79	1.13
Italy	0.69	0	0.17
Luxembourg	2.53	0.13	0.06
Netherlands	3.89	0.34	0.23
Portugal	0.74	0	0.09
Spain	0.93	0	0.03
United Kingdom	7.45	1.54	0.68
West Germany	3.52	0	0.07
Proposal[a]	3.81	0.17	0.17

a. EC Commission proposal
SOURCE: Lee, Pearson, and Smith 1988.

total revenue change in indirect taxation that is relevant, and here we might well expect some countervailing influences.

Excise duty taxation. Paradoxically, even though excise duties amount to merely half the revenue obtained from VAT, greater difficulties, both political and economic, are involved in their proposed harmonization. This, of course, reflects the fact that the VAT is a general tax in contrast to the excise duty, which to all intents and purposes applies to five major products—tobacco, wine, beer, spirits, and hydrocarbon oils. Moreover, the manner in which excise duty taxation has evolved over the years reflects protectionist sentiment within the member states, each seeking to benefit its own domestic producers. In particular, for alcoholic beverages, which presumably are competitive substitutes, there are clear indications of tax policies designed to tax domestic producers at a lower rate than that applied to imported products. Table 8-5 details the widely different rates of excise taxation on alcoholic drinks pertaining within the member states.

Again, the commission's proposals reflect a perception of what is politically feasible, given existing practices, rather than an attempt to design a rational system of alcohol product taxation. Thus, given that the taxation of spirits is considerably higher than that of either wine or beer (in terms of alcoholic content), this is accepted as a constraint dictating the nature of rate approximation. Thus it is proposed that spirits be taxed on alcoholic content at a rate reflecting the average excise duty now pertaining in the member states. As table 8-5 illustrates, this would involve substantial reductions in the rate of duty for Denmark (64 percent), Ireland (53 percent), and the United Kingdom (49 percent). In contrast, there would be colossal percentage increases for Spain, Portugal, Italy, and Greece and negligible consequences for Belgium, the Netherlands, and to a lesser extent France and West Germany.

Beer is also to be taxed in accordance with alcoholic content, though at a substantially reduced rate of tax as compared with the taxation of spirits, again reflecting historical trends and perceptions of equity. In contrast, the taxation of wine is to be by volume only, with the net effect that a liter of wine would bear the same fiscal burden as a liter of average strength beer. As Lee, Pearson, and Smith (1988) convincingly argue, no clear rationale emerges for establishing such a relationship given that the alcoholic content of equal quantities of wine and average strength beer differ; presumably, they are deemed to compete on a volume basis from the vantage point of the potential consumer. As in the case of spirits, the proposals for beer and wine would imply substantial tax reductions for Denmark, Ireland, and the United Kingdom. For the United Kingdom and Denmark the rate of duty on beer would fall by approximately 75 percent while the rate of duty on wine would decline by almost 90 percent. For Ireland, the corresponding reductions in the rates of duty would be on the order of 85 percent and 94 percent.

Other countries would be faced with corresponding increases. The wine-producing countries of Greece, Italy, Portugal, Spain, and West Germany, which do not tax still wine, would be compelled to introduce the tax, and the other major wine producer, France, would be required to increase its duty more than fivefold. Given the magnitude of these proposed changes and their implications not only for national revenues but also for other aspects of social policy, it is difficult to believe that approximation will occur by the end of 1992—since member countries still retain the right of veto in matters of fiscal harmonization.

The commission was ultimately compelled to recognize the logic of this position and grant revised proposals giving greater flexibility in place of absolute harmonization. In particular, alcohol and tobacco have been given minimum rate targets that individual countries may exceed if they wish in line with their revenue needs and health and social policies. Yet without substantial harmonization it is difficult to imagine the abolition of fiscal frontiers without creating the conditions conducive to considerable cross-border shopping and possibilities of tax fraud and evasion.

With regard to other excisable products the picture is more promising. Indeed, for tobacco products there has been a considerable measure of agreement on the structure of taxation. Thus it has been agreed that the taxation of cigarettes should take the form of a combined specific tax together with an ad valorem tax as a percentage of the retail price. Moreover, the commission has stipulated that the ratio of specific to total tax should lie between 5 and 55 percent. This ratio is of considerable importance to the competitiveness of national markets. The greater the ad valorem component in the overall fiscal burden, the greater is the price advantage afforded to lower-quality cigarette producers; whereas the greater the specific component, the more the better-quality products will dominate. As table 8-6 clearly shows, this ratio varies widely among the member countries, reflecting attempts to provide a hidden form of protection to domestic producers.[13]

To consider but one example, both Italy and France favor ad valorem taxation—not surprisingly since they both use home-grown tobacco, which is subsidized under the Common Agricultural Policy. In contrast, the United Kingdom relies on more expensive imported tobaccos, produced without subsidy. The adoption of ad valorem forms of tobacco taxation thus serves to widen the absolute price differences between domestically produced and imported tobacco.

Once again the commission has favored a pragmatic compromise solution by moving in favor of averaging existing practices, despite the overwhelming theoretical advantages favoring specific taxation. This is ably demonstrated by Kay and Keen (1982, 1987). Thus under the commission's proposals the total ad valorem component would lie between 52 and 54 percent of the retail selling price, while the specific tax component would total 0.39 ECU per packet of twenty. Although tobacco product prices vary substantially throughout the member countries of the EC, the differences are in large measure to be explained by differences in quality. As illustrated in table 8-6, a considerable degree of uniformity already exists in the more important tax–retail price ratio.

With regard to the taxation of hydrocarbon oils, especially petrol and diesel fuel, the proposed harmonization is relatively far easier to enact. With regard to petrol, for example, the commission is proposing a simple specific duty representing the unweighted average of existing rates of taxation throughout the community.[14] With regard to the taxation of diesel fuel, harmonization is proposed on the basis

TABLE 8-6
CIGARETTE TAXATION IN EC MEMBER STATES, 1986

	Specific Excise (ECU)	Ad Valorem Excise (including VAT) (%)	Ratio of Specific to Total Tax (%)	Total Tax per Packet (ECU)	Retail Price (ECU)	Proportion of Tax in Price (%)
Belgium	0.05	66	5	0.87	1.24	70
Denmark	1.52	39	55	2.76	3.16	87
France	0.03	71	5	0.51	0.68	75
Greece	0.01	58	5	0.26	0.43	61
Ireland	1.00	35	53	1.88	2.54	74
Italy	0.03	69	5	0.73	1.02	72
Luxembourg	0.03	64	5	0.65	0.96	67
Netherlands	0.24	54	25	0.97	1.36	72
Portugal	0.04	63	9	0.59	0.73	69
Spain	0.01	35	12	0.12	0.31	39
United Kingdom	0.96	34	55	1.76	2.35	35
West Germany	0.52	44	40	1.29	1.77	73
Proposal[a]	0.39	52–54				

a. EC Commission proposal
SOURCE: Lee, Pearson, and Smith 1988.

TABLE 8-7
EXCISE DUTY ON MOTOR FUEL IN EC MEMBER STATES, 1986
(ECU per liter)

	Four-Star Petrol	Diesel Oil
Belgium	0.25	0.12
Denmark	0.46	0.19
France	0.39	0.19
Greece	0.42	0.12
Ireland	0.38	0.29
Italy	0.53	0.12
Lux.	0.20	0.10
Neth.	0.29	0.08
Portugal	0.41	0.18
Spain	0.20	0.03
United Kingdom	0.31	0.26
West Germany	0.24	0.20
Proposal[a]	0.34	0.18

a. EC Commission proposal.
SOURCE: Lee, Pearson, and Smith 1988.

of the weighted average of existing rates of duty to minimize the revenue losses. Details are presented in table 8-7. In the majority of cases the implications for member states would not be traumatic, with revenue losses on petrol taxation being offset in part by gains on diesel. Even where potential revenue losses or price effects are substantial, however, this seems to be an area where comparative uniformity in tax burdens is essential to the ideal of the single market, since any significant differences would have repercussions on industrial cost structures.

Revenue Consequences. Looking at the proposed changes in indirect taxation overall, one can identify three countries where the consequences would be dramatic and politically contentious. For Denmark and Ireland the revenue losses would be substantial and would, a priori, signify the need for greater reliance on direct taxation. For the United Kingdom the revenue implications are less acute because the reduction in excise taxation would be more than offset by the required increase in VAT taxation. But by the same token the political consequences of subjecting food, children's clothing, and basic passenger transportation services to taxation while substantially decreasing the taxation of spirits, wine, beer, and tobacco products would be at best embarrassing, most probably regressive, and certainly guaranteed to upset the increasingly influential health lobby.

Before examining these issues in any detail, it is necessary to point to the difficulties implicit in any attempt to quantify the revenue consequences. It is clearly inadequate to apply the proposed rates to the existing tax base because changes of such magnitude are bound to generate substantial changes in consumption patterns. What is required is a detailed knowledge concerning the elasticity of demand for specific goods. But simply because the proposed changes are of such a magnitude, little empirical evidence can be invoked to provide reliable guidance. Estimates derived from the experience of annual budgetary changes in indirect taxation are of limited value because their scale is minuscule in comparison with what is now proposed. No chancellor of the exchequer, for example, has previously embarked on a 75 percent decrease in the taxation of beer. Moreover, it is necessary to determine exactly how any given tax change will translate into the corresponding price change. Symmetry as between the effects of tax increases and tax decreases cannot be assumed. Whereas producers will try to pass tax increases forward in price rises to the consumer, substantial tax cuts are likely to provide the opportunity for clandestine increases in profit margins. Finally, of course, the question is raised whether such substantial tax-induced price changes will induce money illusion on the part of the consumers.[15]

Nor can one ignore the macroeconomic implications. Tax-induced price changes will inevitably have repercussions on national wage bargaining. The change in the tax composition is in itself an important determinant of the macroeconomy, with the conventional wisdom pointing to the greater deflationary impact of indirect taxes. In addition, there are employment effects to consider. Much of the proposed harmonization will reduce the degree of protection previously accorded to domestic producers through the fiscal system. Such will be the case in respect of the tobacco producers in France and Italy and likewise of previously untaxed wine growers in the wine-producing countries. This loss of protection is unlikely to leave employment levels unaltered. It is, of course, true that compensating changes may occur in their traditional export markets, but there can be no guarantee that such changes will cancel each other out. Harmonization is proceeding primarily by averaging, without weighting, existing rates of tax. No attempt is being made at maintaining existing expenditure patterns.

In short, the proposed measures of fiscal harmonization will undoubtedly exert macroeconomic effects of unknown degree, which in themselves will carry further consequences for fiscal revenues. Finally, of course, changes in the tax mixture and in the rate of VAT

TABLE 8-8
REVENUE CONSEQUENCES OF FISCAL APPROXIMATION ASSUMING
UNCHANGED SPENDING PATTERNS

	As % of Indirect Tax Receipts	As % of Total Tax Receipts
Belgium	3	0.7
Denmark	−27	−9.5
France	−6	−1.7
Ireland	−10	−4.4
Italy	−3	−0.8
Netherlands	6	1.4
United Kingdom	2	0.6
West Germany	6	1.6

SOURCE: Lee, Pearson, and Smith 1988.

carry important implications for the degree of automatic stabilization incorporated in the tax system. What this amounts to is that the changes proposed by the commission are unlikely to be neutral in their macroeconomic impact even if compensating changes in revenues are made elsewhere. Granted these caveats, which render any attempt at precise estimation extremely suspect, it is of interest to highlight the following three cases suggested by table 8-8.

Denmark. The revenue consequences of the proposed harmonization appear to be the most serious for Denmark. Indirect taxation accounts for some 35 percent of all fiscal revenues. Under existing proposals Denmark would be compelled to reduce its rate of VAT from 22 percent to 20 percent. In addition, of course, for a number of products it would have to replace its current 22 percent rate by the maximum permitted 9 percent rate in the reduced rate category. Moreover, this loss of VAT would be reinforced by a substantial loss of excise duty. Apart from Italy, Denmark has the highest levy of duty on petrol in the EC. Moving to the arithmetical average as presently proposed would imply a substantial loss of duty; moreover, such a loss would be compounded, if only minimally, by the enforced reduction in the taxation of diesel fuel. Similar reasoning applies in the case of tobacco and alcohol. Denmark has the highest rate of taxation of cigarettes (tax expressed as a percentage of retail price), and it will be compelled to make substantial reductions if the commission's proposals are put into practice. Again it has the highest rate of duty on spirits and beer and is second only to Ireland in the taxation of wine. At the time of writing no precise econometric exercise has been carried out to determine the revenue consequences.

Applying the proposed changes to the tax base as it was in 1984, however, and assuming that no change would occur in expenditure on the taxed goods in consequence of the suggested tax changes, Lee, Pearson, and Smith (1988) conclude that indirect tax receipts would fall by a staggering 27 percent, or almost 10 percent of total tax revenues.

These estimates, of course, are grossly overstated, as the authors fully acknowledge. Such substantial tax reductions would inevitably lead to price decreases, inducing a countervailing increase in the quantities consumed. Nonetheless, what empirical data there are suggest overall price inelasticity with the possible exception of transportation services, and it would seem inevitable that compensating increases in the rate of direct taxation would be called for. It is instructive to note that Denmark has been one of the most insistent advocates of the view that the abolition of fiscal frontiers need not require tax rate harmonization, and it will be interesting to see to what extent one of the smaller partners of the EC is prepared to defend this position even to the point of veto.

Ireland. Remarkably similar arguments apply to Ireland. It has the highest rate of VAT in the EC (at 23 percent) and will be compelled to reduce this to 20 percent. In addition, it will be compelled to cut its reduced rate from the existing 10 percent to the proposed maximum 9 percent. Very substantial reductions will be required in alcohol and tobacco taxation. The proposed reduction in petrol taxation is relatively modest, from 0.38 to 0.34 ECU per liter (four-star petrol), but again this is reinforced by the proposed reduction in diesel fuel taxation from 0.29 to 0.18 ECU per liter.

The significance of indirect tax reduction is emphasized by the fact that indirect taxes now account for some 45 percent of all fiscal revenues. Some evidence suggests that this reliance on indirect taxes reflects the existence of a substantial informal economy and the difficulties of imposing comprehensive income taxes. Nonetheless, Ireland is arguably better placed than Denmark to adjust to the proposed system. In contrast to Denmark, the estimate of Lee, Pearson, and Smith (1988), calculated on the basis of an unchanged tax base, suggests a 10 percent decrease in indirect tax receipts, which amounts to a decrease of less than 5 percent of total fiscal receipts. Again, countervailing quantity changes should reduce this figure. Nonetheless, these reductions are considerable, and again the question whether Ireland will countenance acceptance of the proposed changes has to be posed. If it chooses not to adhere to the commission's proposals, the lack of a common border with most other member states and the significant transportation costs involved appear to grant it considerable leeway in maintaining rates above the theoretical maximums.

The United Kingdom. The situation of the United Kingdom differs sharply from that of either Denmark or Ireland in that the proposed changes in indirect taxation largely cancel out in their revenue effects. That is to say, the substantial rise in VAT and relatively steep increase in petrol excise duty will be substantially offset by the reduction in the taxation of alcohol and tobacco products. Consequently, the major issues that arise in the United Kingdom from the proposed harmonization measures turn more on the distributional consequences on the one hand and the impact on the consumption of products possessed of substantial external costs on the other.

Fortunately, a considerable amount of work has already been completed in determining the revenue consequences and analyzing the distributional implications. See, in particular, the studies of Lee, Pearson, and Smith (1988), Lee and Pashardes (1988), and Symons and Walker (1989). These studies are extremely sophisticated in their approach. Following on the seminal Almost Ideal Demand System (AIDS) approach of Deaton and Muellbauer (1980a), they allow for considerable interdependence in the consumption patterns of competing goods. Thus, for example, significant decreases in the duty on wine may so stimulate consumption as to depress the consumption of beer and decrease tax revenue from the latter accordingly. Likewise, tax changes generate wealth effects that will exert spillover effects on the consumption of taxable goods that are not themselves subject to tax rate change. Indeed, the great virtue of these models is that, invoking cross-sectional data in the comprehensive family expenditure surveys, they attempt to demonstrate the way in which a change in the price of any one broad commodity group will impinge on the consumption of all other commodities. Thus they are grounded in the traditional axioms of rational consumer theory and fully allow for relative price and income effects. They do not attempt, however, to take account of any macroeconomic repercussion that might be expected from consideration of wage-price spirals, budgetary deficits or surpluses, exchange rate movements, and so forth.

Broadly, these studies draw similar conclusions. Lee, Pearson, and Smith (1988) conclude that expenditures on alcoholic beverages would increase substantially, offsetting by some 50 percent the revenue loss that would occur if quantities remained unchanged. In the same vein, the 20 percent increase in the taxation of petrol would be offset in part by substantially reduced consumption. These findings illustrate dramatically the dangers and limitations in attempting to apply the proposed tax rate changes to an unchanged tax base for the purposes of revenue calculations. The authors estimate the net increase in indirect tax revenues to be on the order of £0.8 billion.

In like manner Symons and Walker (1989) demonstrate the high price elasticities associated with the consumption of alcoholic beverages. In addition, they point to significant cross-price elasticities between alcohol and the price of fuel—an increase in the price of fuel promoting an increase in beer and wine consumption. Overall, they point to an increase in indirect tax revenues on the order of £0.49 billion per year. But when using family expenditure survey data corrected for discrepancies with national income accounts data, particularly for the underrecording of certain items, they suggest that the additional revenue gain could be on the order of £1.08 billion. These findings are thus in general conformity with the belief of the EC Commission that the proposed system of fiscal harmonization would produce a relatively small or moderate increase in revenues for the United Kingdom.

Distributional considerations. Purely because the revenue implication for the United Kingdom are relatively small, attention, especially in political circles, is more likely to be focused on the distributional considerations. At first glance the measures look distinctly regressive. The increase in VAT would accentuate the tendency, initiated by the first Thatcher administration, to increase the indirect tax ratio at the expense of the direct.

Moreover, items classified as largely essentials, including many food items, transportation services, and the like, currently zero rated, would be subject to the minimum 4 percent rate. Indeed, children's clothing, now zero rated, would become subject to the standard rate of VAT. At the same time expensive spirits, fine wines, and imported Havana cigars would become considerably cheaper. Moreover, goods currently zero rated for VAT purposes, as might be expected, account for a much greater percentage of the expenditure of poorer households. Not surprisingly, the proposed harmonization of VAT would imply a greatly increased fiscal burden for the poorer household when expressed as increased additional tax payment as a percentage of gross income. Moreover, analysis of the total indirect tax burden by income decile shows a much greater proportional rise for the lowest income group (figure 8-4).

Caution is needed, however, before concluding that the proposed harmonization measures are necessarily regressive. In particular, terming indirect tax changes regressive or progressive without considering other changes, especially expenditure changes, may be objected to on methodological grounds. If, as seems likely, those economies experiencing gains in indirect tax revenues are also in-

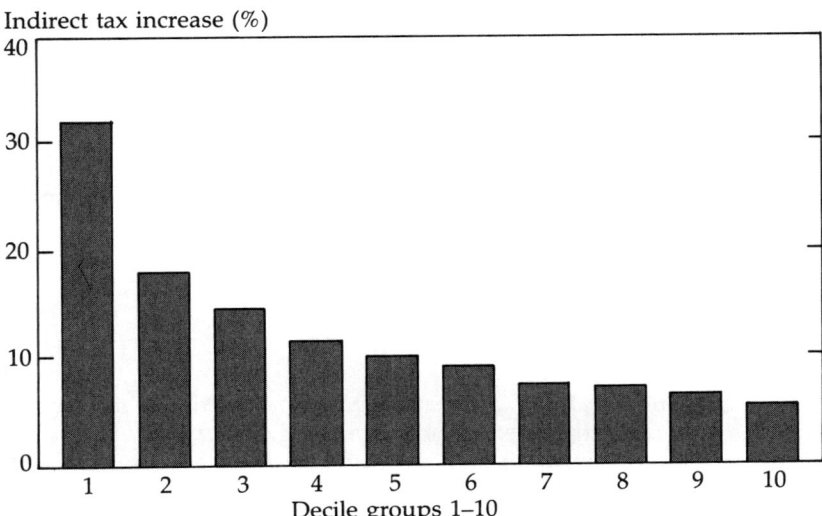

FIGURE 8-4
CHANGES IN INDIRECT TAX BURDEN BY INCOME DECILE,
UNITED KINGDOM

SOURCE: Symons and Walker 1989.

volved in increased expenditures arising from harmonized social security programs, which may be expected to benefit the poor and the unemployed, the resulting outcome may be far less clear-cut. Indeed, there appears to be considerable justification for linking the two sets of proposals to overcome a possible major drawback of indirect tax harmonization (Symons and Walker 1989).

Corporate Income Tax Harmonization

On completion of the single European market there will be no impediments to the movement of capital throughout the EC. What measures of tax harmonization are desirable in the light of this radical step? And what are the realistic prospects of their being achieved? In pursuing these questions we shall concentrate on two broad issues; efficiency considerations on the one hand and equity considerations on the other. In doing so we shall distinguish between direct capital investment—investment in productive assets—and financial investment or portfolio investment. After 1992 the latter is likely to dominate capital flows within the EC.

FIGURE 8-5
DIFFERENTIAL TAXATION AND CAPITAL ALLOCATION

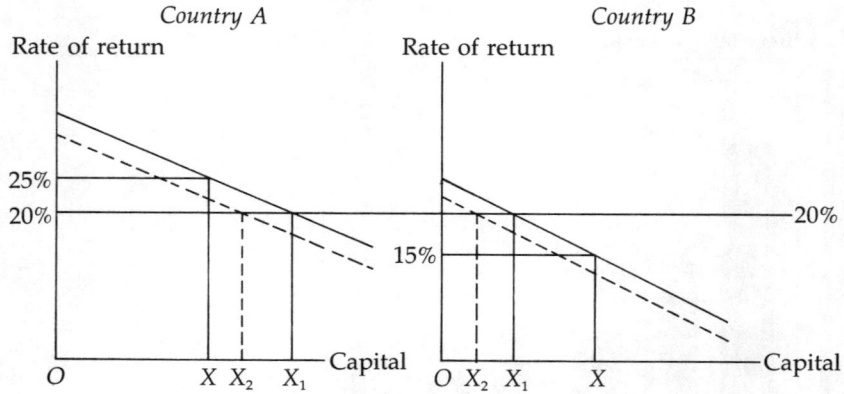

Efficiency Considerations. *Location of productive units.* The most obvious source of allocative inefficiency stemming from failure to harmonize corporate tax burdens derives from tax-induced distortions in the decisions about location. In principle the issue is very clear. Given the free movement of capital inputs, economic theory would predict that capital would be allocated to equate posttax rates of return on investment. From the vantage point of pure welfare economics, however, it is equality in the pretax rate of return that is required to maximize output. Thus differing rates of corporate income tax among member nations can seriously interfere with the optimal allocation of resources.

Figure 8-5, depicts two countries A and B before the formation of a common market. Let us assume initially that capital can be more productively employed in country A than in country B. Accordingly, a given amount of capital, say OX, will earn, let us assume, a 25 percent marginal rate of return in country A but only a 15 percent marginal rate of return in country B. Now let us allow for the free movement of capital after the formation of a common market. Capital in country B will now possess an incentive to transfer to country A and earn a higher rate of return. At the margin the first unit of capital transferred from country B will relinquish a 15 percent return but will be compensated by a 25 percent return upon relocation in country A. It follows that the combined income from capital in countries A and B considered collectively must increase. As capital is transferred from B to A, marginal rates of return will rise in country B but fall in country A. As long as the rate of return at the margin remains higher in country A, however, the process will continue, implying a net increase in the income obtained from capital. Clearly, this process will come to an end only when the marginal rate of return is equal in the two countries. The diagram illustrates this equilibrium at the rate of return of 20 percent, with the capital stock having increased by the amount $OX - OX_1$ in country A and having decreased by the equal amount $OX - OX_1$ in country B. From the reasoning above this is clearly an optimum situation. Any other allocation of capital between the two economies must imply a net decrease in the total income derived from capital.

Now let us pose the question, How would this optimal allocation be influenced by the existence of a differential rate of taxation on profits between the two economies? Conceptually, to pursue this question all we need do is to postulate the existence of a capital profits tax in one economy but not in the other. Suppose, for example, we allow for a tax in country A. For the potential investor concerned about maximizing the posttax return, the situation is akin to a parametric inward shift of the rate-of-return schedule for country A, as indicated by the hatched line, implying that the transfer of capital into country A will be curtailed by the amount $OX_1 - OX_2$.

Alternatively, consider a tax imposed solely in country B. Then again the rate-of-return schedule for country B will be shifted inward from the vantage point of any potential investor, again as indicated by the hatched line, implying an additional transfer of capital from country B by the amount $OX_1 - OX_2$. In either case the allocation of capital will differ from that deemed optimal, and income derived from capital will fall below what is theoretically attainable. Some uniformity in the treatment of corporate income taxation accordingly seems to be a very desirable feature of future fiscal harmonization programs before the implementation of the single market. If fiscal harmonization succeeds in eliminating tax-induced changes in the optimal allocative pattern, it is deemed to possess capital-export neutrality (CEN). That is to say, companies will possess an incentive to locate investment in countries that have the highest posttax return; if these differ from the countries of the highest pretax return, then the principle of CEN has been violated.

Efficiency of investment. The principle of CEN avoids distortion in the locational decision. It does not in itself, however, guarantee the most efficient use of productive capital if corporate tax burdens differ among competing firms. Ideally, investment opportunities within any one country would be exploited, initially at least, by the most efficient firm. This will tend to be the case, *ceteris paribus*, if all firms investing in a given country face the same effective tax burden. If this situation prevails, then it is said (perhaps somewhat misleadingly) to be consistent with the principle of capital-import neutrality (CIN). The principle of CIN would be violated if an investment opportunity were to be exploited by a less efficient firm solely on account of its facing a lower corporate tax burden than its more efficient competitor.

In its commitment to the creation of a single European market, the EC Commission has emphasized the need for neutrality. Companies should be free to locate, produce, and sell anywhere in Europe without their decision making's being influenced by differences in comparative tax burdens. The playing field, it is alleged, should be level for all teams from the member countries and not, as it is now, often tilted against visiting opponents. The neutrality principle, sometimes referred to as the 1992 principle, demands both CEN and CIN. What this means, in effect, is that harmonization of the corporate income tax must produce identical fiscal burdens for competing companies regardless of their source, location, or repatriation of profits. Needless to say, the 1992 principle applies only to member states. This accounts for the expressed concern that both Japanese and American business firms may face discriminatory tax treatment.

The level of investment. As we have seen, efficient allocation of resources requires harmonization to produce an equalization of corporate tax burdens for competing firms. In itself, however, this is insufficient because the precise details of the harmonization program will influence the volume of investment. This is an important point, ably demonstrated by Pearson (1989). It suggests that if the EC Commission approaches the task of corporate income tax harmonization by averaging existing rates of tax (as was its approach to the harmonization of excise duties), the result may well be suboptimal and lead to a diminution of investment activity. Averaging implies a raising of the lowest rates; while it may establish fair competition between competing firms, it can do so only by terminating certain marginal investments. Harmonization per se is a necessary but not a sufficient condition for improved allocative efficiency. In particular, harmonization programs geared to the averaging of existing rates of tax must be viewed with a good deal of caution.

Savings. The preceding argument has focused on the efficiency of productive capital investment. Similar reasoning applies to both the allocation and the volume of savings within the EC. Rationally, savings will be allocated not necessarily to their most productive use but rather to secure the highest posttax return. Differences in the tax treatment of dividends can produce distortions in the allocation of savings just as they can distort the allocation of productive capital investment.

One solution to this problem would be to levy dividend taxation according to the country of residence of the shareholder, regardless of the origin of the source of the dividend. In this case no wedge can be driven between the highest pretax return and the highest posttax return, the rate of tax being determined solely by country of residence. Such a principle not only avoids misallocation of portfolio investment but also allows the existence of differences in tax rates of dividend income among the member countries. Personal taxes will determine the posttax return on saving without interfering with the most efficient allocation of savings. Indeed, there appears to be no more reason to harmonize the rate of taxation from capital at the personal level than to harmonize personal rates of income tax. Taxation of dividend income according to country of residence may be compared with the destination principle in the taxation of commodities. Both may be looked on as protective devices that permit the continuation of differing rates of taxation without generating tax-induced distortions.

Equity Considerations. With regard to equity and assuming that we have achieved an efficient allocation of productive resources throughout the community, the main issue turns on how fiscal revenues are to be allocated among member states in a manner deemed "fair and acceptable." This is the issue of jurisdiction on which, as King has rightly emphasized (King 1989), it is arguably more difficult to secure agreement. In contrast to the efficiency arguments, where the anticipated allocative gains can in principle benefit all members of the community, here we are dealing with an essentially zero-sum game. Member governments can be expected to be especially zealous in safeguarding their sources of revenue.

The principal difficulty lies in the fact that there is no scientific basis for determining what is fair and acceptable. After 1992 it will be commonplace, for example, for British shareholders to own shares in a French company, located in Italy and producing goods for resale to West Germany. Which country or countries will have a claim to corporate tax revenue? Equally, if a French company located solely in France produces a product that is exported to all the remaining member countries, could those countries not legitimately claim that they are the source of the French company's profits and therefore entitled to a share of corporate tax revenues?

Historically, of course, the country of location of the productive unit has seen itself as the rightful taxing authority entitled to full payment of the corporate income tax liability, regardless of the country of residence of any parent company or the domicile of its shareholders. In addition, many countries have imposed a further withholding tax on dividend payments made to shareholders across national borders. And, while it has been commonplace for a country to grant a tax credit to shareholders against the corporate tax paid before the taxation of dividends, such a provision has usually been limited to shareholders residing within its own borders. Most countries are reluctant to grant tax credits when the dividends are paid to shareholders overseas, for the credit effectively amounts to a rebate of the domestic corporate tax liability with a consequent loss of domestic revenue.

In short, national governments have behaved in a manner calculated to maximize their share of a European company's tax liability. In particular, they have displayed acute suspicion of activities such as transfer pricing, when it is being invoked to transfer taxable profits to countries of lower tax jurisdiction, to such an extent that it has become impossible for research and development expenditures, undertaken centrally, to be correctly allocated to subsidiary companies.

The resultant double taxation of firms whose activities straddle many countries has been a major cause of concern for European countries. In particular, it has been seen as a particularly important factor inhibiting mergers between European companies while allowing Japanese and American companies to exploit such investment opportunities. If 1992 succeeds in achieving a measure of harmonization that takes account of these barriers to intra-European mergers, it will go a considerable way toward removing the comparative advantage currently enjoyed by American and Japanese companies.

Ideally, tax policy should be neutral between a merger of two firms within a member country and a merger of firms between member countries. In practice, in the European Community, mergers across national borders are prohibited for tax reasons even though they are probably more desirable competitively—mergers within a country being more likely to stifle competition. The tax system discriminates against European mergers in the following manner. As firms merge across borders, the percentage of domestic profits declines, and at some point domestic posttax profits become insufficient to meet shareholder dividend payments community-wide. When tax credits are limited to domestic posttax profits, this implies a steep rise in the effective tax burden. Owing to these elements of double taxation, it is not possible for European countries to take a "European view" of investment opportunities—a restriction, it may be noted, that does not apply to U.S. or Japanese investment. What is required is a comprehensive multilateral double tax agreement throughout the EC to remove this major source of distortion.

Alternatively, in attempting to resolve this very complicated issue of a fair and equitable division of corporate tax revenues, the EC might well learn from experience in the United States and Canada. In these two countries the individual states and provinces do not attempt to ascertain the precise origin of taxable profits as such. Indeed, in a highly integrated economy such as the United States it would become virtually impossible to do so. Rather, taxable income is allocated among the states according to some predetermined formula reflecting the degree of economic activity carried out within any given state. Typically this will reflect employment, the amount of capital employed, and sales activity within a given state as a fraction of the total, to determine the respective claims on the corporate tax revenues. Such a unitary approach to taxation would go a long way toward ending a major weakness of European corporate taxation.

The Current Corporate Tax System. In attempting to compare differing systems of corporate taxation, it is inadequate to look solely at differences in tax rates. What is required is a measure of the effective marginal rate of taxation that takes account also of important differences in the tax base as well as important differences in the tax system, in particular the manner in which dividends are to be treated. Fortunately, economists have developed models specifically to allow such comparisons (King and Fullerton 1984), to which we shall return. For the moment, however, let us begin by examining the actual nominal situation within the EC. To permit comparisons details of both the United States and Japan are also included.

Tax rates. Nominal tax rates are presented in table 8-9. They range from a mere 10 percent in Ireland to a maximum of 56 percent on undistributed profits in West Germany. The table also indicates the type of tax system in use, that is to say, whether countries operate a classical, split-rate, or imputation system of taxation. For shareholders generally the system of taxation is arguably more important than the tax rate, and it behooves us to present a brief description of the competing mechanisms.

Under the classical system the company is treated as a separate entity from its shareholders and taxed accordingly on its taxable profits. Dividends paid out of posttax profits and received by shareholders are then treated as any other form of personal income and subject to personal income taxation. In effect, dividends are subject to a form of double taxation. Under such a system, if interest payments are tax deductible, debt finance tends to be favored over equity finance. Split-rate systems of taxation differ in that a lower rate of taxation is applied to the proportion of profits that is distributed.

TABLE 8-9
NATIONAL TAX RATES FOR VARIOUS COUNTRIES, 1988

	National Tax Rate	Type of Tax System	Imputation Rate[a]
Belgium	43	Imputation	33.3
Denmark	50	Imputation	20
France	42	Imputation	33.3
Greece	44	Imputation	44
Ireland	10	Imputation	5.3
Italy	36	Imputation	36
Luxembourg	36 + 0.72	Classical	—
Netherlands	35	Classical	—
Portugal	35/47	Split rate	—
Spain	35	Imputation	9.1
United Kingdom	35	Imputation	25
West Germany	36/56	Split rate/ imputation	36
Japan	32/42	Split rate	—
United States	34	Classical	—

a. Percentage of gross dividend.
SOURCE: Adapted from Devereux and Pearson 1989.

Finally, under an imputation system, corporate taxes paid by the company are allowed as a tax credit, either wholly or in part, against subsequent tax liability of shareholders upon the receipt of dividend income. At present Italy, West Germany, and Greece operate a full (100 percent) imputational system, which eliminates the double taxation of dividend income in its entirety.[16]

The tax rates presented in table 8-9 are misleading to the extent that they ignore any additional tax burden on income from foreign sources. Many countries impose additional withholding taxes on profits when they are transferred from the source country back to the parent. Such rates can vary substantially; as indicated in table 8-10, there is very little uniformity, and they appear as a major cause of distortion in investment decisions. Moreover, income from foreign sources can be taxed yet again. That is to say, when profits are repatriated, they may be subject to taxation in the country of residence. Again, there is no uniformity. In some cases income from foreign sources may be entirely exempt from additional taxation. In others it is exempt if transferred from some countries in the EC but not from others. Some countries, which include the United Kingdom and the United States, operate a credit system. That is to say, taxes paid overseas, including any withholding taxes, are compared with

TABLE 8-10
WITHHOLDING TAX RATES FOR VARIOUS COUNTRIES, 1988

Source							Residence							
	B	Dk	F	WG	G	Ire	I	Lux	Nl	P	S	UK	Jap	US
Belgium		15	15	15	15	15	15	15	15	15	15	15	15	15
Denmark	15		0	10	30	0	15	5	0	10	10	0	10	5
France	10	0		0	25	10	15	5	5	15	10	5	10	5
Greece	25	42	42	25		42	25	42	35	42	42	42	42	42
Ireland	0	0	0	0	0		0	0	0	0	0	0	0	0
Italy	15	15	15	32	25	15		15	0	15	15	5	10	5
Lux.	10	5	5	10	15	5	0		3	15	5	5	15	5
Neth.	5	0	15	10	5	0	15	3		25	5	5	5	5
Portugal	12	10	12	12	12	12	12	12	12		10	10	12	12
Spain	15	10	10	10	20	20	15	10	10	10		10	10	20
U.K.	0	0	0	0	0	0	0	0	0	0	0		0	0
Japan	15	10	10	10	20	10	10	20	10	20	10	10		10
U.S.	15	5	5	15	30	5	10	5	5	30	30	5	10	
W.Ger.	25	25	25		25	20	25	25	25	15	25	20	15	15

NOTE: Based on repatriation of dividends to a parent owning 100 percent of the subsidiary. Withholding taxes are often higher when a lower proportion of the subsidiary is owned by the shareholder.
SOURCE: Devereux and Pearson 1989.

what the tax burden would have been had the income originated domestically. Any shortfall is then recouped in additional domestic taxation. Again some countries operate a mixed system, and in some cases income from foreign sources is partially exempted from taxation, the remainder being subject to normal rates of domestic corporate tax liability.

The tax base. Many factors enter into the determination of the tax base. In the United Kingdom, for example, capital gains are index linked for tax purposes, which is not the case in the other member countries. Far and away the most important factor, however, is the method and manner by which business firms depreciate assets. There are wide disparities in practice within the EC. Finally, inflation is of crucial importance in determining the value of depreciation allowances. If, for example, depreciation allowances are geared to historical cost figures, as is normally the case, inflation progressively erodes the real value of the allowance. As Devereux and Pearson emphasize in their influential study (Devereux and Pearson 1989), since inflation rates differ within the EC, identical tax systems would produce differences in the effective marginal tax rate. Moreover, inflation can change the relative burden of taxation. Again, to cite Devereux and Pearson, the fact that the United Kingdom possesses a more generous tax system than Spain in the absence of inflation need not necessarily imply that this will be the case if both countries experience equal inflation rates.

Effective tax rates. As indicated at the beginning of this section, *effective* marginal rates of taxation have been devised to take account of these diverse factors. The seminal paper is that by King and Fullerton (1984). Here the effective marginal tax rate is calculated as the difference between pretax and posttax rates of return that would justify investment in a marginal project. Positive marginal effective rates deter investment while negative rates (that is, subsidies) encourage investment.

Crooks, Devereux, Pearson, and Wookey (1989) have extended the analysis in a highly original way to permit comparisons of investment by EC companies when they invest in each of the other member states. This allows one to compare the effective marginal rate of tax confronting, say, a British company when it invests in West Germany with an identical investment by the same company in France, Italy, or elsewhere. The importance of this framework is that it permits a method for evaluating the extent to which any proposed reform would move the system toward greater neutrality.

Without detailing the many assumptions underlying the model

TABLE 8-11
Required Pretax Rates of Return for Various Countries

	Own Country	Investing In	Investing From	Ratio of Protection
Belgium	5.83	6.67	6.78	0.98
Denmark	7.02	7.96	6.61	1.20
France	5.75	6.33	6.70	0.94
Greece	5.55	7.59	6.97	1.09
Ireland	5.08	4.68	7.41	0.63
Italy	5.60	6.32	7.54	0.84
Luxembourg	6.19	6.74	6.69	1.01
Netherlands	6.11	6.63	6.68	0.99
Portugal	6.59	6.37	7.22	0.88
Spain	6.10	6.90	6.91	1.00
United Kingdom	6.12	6.46	6.65	0.97
West Germany	8.86	8.83	6.35	1.39
Japan	8.24	8.22	7.07	1.16
United States	5.93	6.67	6.76	0.99
Average of column	6.35	6.88	6.88	1.01

SOURCE: Devereux and Pearson 1989.

(which are of considerable importance in generating the final results), it is useful to highlight some of the more significant findings. Table 8-11 offers a summary view. Column 1 depicts the rate of return necessary to generate a posttax rate of return of 5 percent for a company investing within its home country. The second column shows the average rate of return required by companies from other countries investing within that country to secure a 5 percent posttax return. The third column shows the average rate of return required by companies from within that country when investing outside their own country.

Thus, for example, a Danish company would require a pretax return of 7.02 percent if investing within its own borders and an average 6.61 percent when investing externally, whereas companies from outside Denmark investing in Denmark would need 7.96 percent to obtain the same 5 percent posttax return. The final column expresses an index of the incentive provided by the international tax system in encouraging the movement of capital. It measures the average rate of return required when investing in a country divided by the average required rate of return when investing from that country. A measure less than 1 implies that it is cheaper for firms from other countries to invest within that country than for firms within that country to invest outside. *Ceteris paribus*, therefore, a figure less than 1 would point to the attempt to encourage capital inflows. Ireland provides a classic example of the tax system's being directed at encouraging capital inflow.

The other interesting feature deriving from the summary table concerns the comparative position of nonmember countries such as Japan and the United States. There is no real distinction between the rates of return required by Japanese and non-Japanese companies when investing in Japan. The tax system does not appear to discriminate in favor of Japanese investment. It is relatively easier, however, for Japanese companies to invest externally; a 7.07 percent posttax return is required, compared with an 8.24 percent return on domestic investment, to generate the same 5 percent posttax return. The encouragement given to Japanese external investment is reflected in recent sizable investment in Britain and the EC countries. It also goes some way to compensate on the capital account for large surpluses on the balance of trade.

With regard to the United States, the table suggests that American companies enjoy a relative advantage over outsiders when investing within the United States, the required rates of return being 5.93 percent and 6.67 percent respectively. But American companies do not appear to suffer any corresponding disadvantage when investing externally. The required rate of pretax return for American companies is in the region of 6.76 percent, which is only significantly bettered by West Germany with 6.35 percent and falls marginally below the average required rate of the group as a whole.

This naturally leads into a question of how this comparative position may be affected by progress on corporate tax harmonization. It is reasonable to assume, despite all the platitudes to the contrary, that in reaching agreement the interests of nonmember countries will be discounted. That is to say, in removing the impediments and distortion now existing among member countries, it is likely that the comparative lack of neutrality in respect to third-party investment will be increased. Indeed, this is exactly the history of the Common Market with respect to tariffs. The abolition of internal tariffs on formation of the Common Market was accompanied by a decrease in the average tariff confronting nonmember countries, but the net effect was to increase the differential and the degree of protection afforded to member nations. It is perhaps too soon to conclude, however, that the competitive position of the United States and Japan will suffer adversely, because all the signs are that any significant measure of tax harmonization within the EC remains a very distant possibility.

Progress and Prospects. Historically, the harmonization of corporate income taxation was not seen as being of major importance by the founding fathers of the EC. Indeed, the Treaty of Rome does not involve any obligation to harmonize direct tax rates; instead, the focal point is clearly directed toward removing the impediments to trade implicit in the differing systems of indirect taxation. It is for this reason that attempts to harmonize the corporate income tax have been introduced under the celebrated Article 100—a catchall provision that allows the commission powers to issue directives to "approximate" activities that "directly affect the establishment or functioning of the Common Market." The very breadth and vagueness of this provision, however, is both its strength and its weakness. It allows the commission to raise almost any issue, but at the same time it permits any one member country powers of interpretation to justify the use of its veto in matters of tax harmonization.

Given this fact, it will take a very strong political will to bring about any substantial measure of harmonization of enterprise taxation by the end of 1992. Although member countries are showing increased awareness of the importance of this issue as the single market draws near, it must be conceded that at present such a commitment is lacking; indeed, at the risk of possible exaggeration it can be argued that there is no real unanimity on the need for harmonization. This is not very far removed from the position adopted by the former Thatcher administration. Although recognizing the need for convergence of tax regimes to permit adequate competition without undue distortion, the requisite degree of convergence is viewed as being the outcome of market forces, not bureaucratic regulation and more government. To quote directly from the former British prime minister's speech of September 1988:

> The creation of a single European market by 1992 means action to free markets, to widen choice and to produce greater economic convergence through reduced government intervention.

This sentiment was echoed by the former chancellor of the exchequer, Nigel Lawson, in his Königswinter speech of the same year:

> It is by releasing, not restraining, market forces, that one best engenders the economic growth which makes it possible to fulfill the social and other objectives . . . deregulation, rather than harmonization, should be our central concern.

In brief, the British position is that the case for harmonization of the corporate tax structure has not been made and that the creation of the freer market structure after 1992 will be sufficient to bring about any requisite convergence within a sufficiently short period without adversely affecting the business community. In the face of this position by one of the more powerful and influential members of the twelve, can one seriously believe that significant agreement on corporate tax harmonization will be achieved by the end of 1992?

Quite apart from British intransigence, the history of the progress on this issue is hardly encouraging. A number of draft directives dealing with the taxation of corporate enterprise have been put forward over the past twenty years without ever being adopted. Indeed, with the passage of time and with developments in corporate income taxation generally over the years, especially in the United States, where the tax base has been substantially widened and marginal rates lowered, they have become progressively more out of date. Nonetheless, a program of corporate tax harmonization has been recently resurrected in a commission internal white paper (COM [88] 320 final July 15, 1988). This white paper, commonly referred to as the Three Tax Directives, is in effect a rehash of three earlier draft directives, as follows:

- Mergers Directive (COM [69], 5 final, Brussels, January 15, 1969)
- Parent and Subsidiary Directive (COM [69], 6 final, Brussels, January 15, 1969)
- Arbitration Procedure Directive (COM [76] 611 final, OJC 301, December 21, 1976)

None of these directives has been adopted. Indeed, no directive of any significance dealing with the taxation of corporate enterprise has ever been adopted. The history of corporate tax harmonization in the EC has been described as "long and inglorious" (Pearson 1989) and as "glacial" (Isaac 1989), the latter implying that "whilst movement can be detected it has been slow and has deposited a fair amount of detritus on the margins of its course."

Nonetheless, the commission has succeeded in identifying key areas where change is deemed to be desirable and is actively promoting agreement on these in proposing a package deal. In essence, the thrust of these proposals is directed at eliminating the tax-induced costs borne by businesses operating or cooperating across community borders that are not borne by companies operating or cooperating within any one member country. These general areas of required agreement can be identified as involving the tax base, the tax rate, and the system of taxation:

Agreement on the tax base. A common basis for defining and treating capital gains, capital losses, and the valuation of stocks is required. Here the question of index linking needs to be addressed.

A major recommendation concerning the tax base turns on the very generous treatment of losses. What is proposed is an unlimited carry-forward period for losses combined with a two year carry-back period (subsequently amended to three years by the European Parliament), but this generosity is restricted to nondistributed profits.

The most important recommendation, however, concerns depreciation. It is suggested that assets be depreciated for tax purposes at the same rates as for accounting purposes—effectively eliminating accelerated depreciation. This is an important provision, but it appears to require agreement on the definitions of useful life of alternative assets, which currently differ among the member countries. It is also proposed that depreciation be extended to buildings (contrary to current United Kingdom practice) and that straight-line or declining-balance options may be exercised at the discretion of the firm, but there are no provisions for the index linking of depreciation allowances. Agreement on these proposals would go a long way toward promoting unity with respect to the tax base.

Agreement on the tax system. Essentially, there are three potential methods of corporate income taxation, as previously outlined. The recommendation favored by the EC Commission is for a partial imputation of the corporate income tax. Although complete imputation would be more logical, this was rejected on the grounds that it would produce severe revenue losses for certain member countries. The current proposal calls for a uniform rate of corporate income tax, regardless of whether profits are distributed, which will fall between 45 and 55 percent. Any dividend distributed by a company within a member state carries with it a tax credit determined by that member state within the range 45–55 percent.[17]

An important provision embodied in the recommendation is that the cost of the tax credit shall be borne by the member state of the company distributing the dividend unless expressly excluded by bilateral agreement. This is an extremely important provision, which, if enacted, would go a long way toward meeting a major criticism of the present system, which often discriminates against cross-border investment. West Germany, for example, does not grant tax credits to nonresidents. Although it boasts a full imputational system of corporate taxation, it is limited to shareholders resident in West Germany. Such discrimination is clearly a source of distortion in the allocation of portfolio investment.

While such a provision appears to represent a major step forward, it does, nonetheless, present certain problems essentially of a technical nature. What is implied is that the tax authorities in the state where the profits were made obtain the initial corporation income tax while the tax credit is received by shareholders in the country where they reside. In the case of foreign shareholders the tax credit will be presented to the tax authorities of their country of domicile. It is clearly the intention, however, that the source country be ultimately liable for the refund. Thus what is required is for the dividend payment received by the foreign shareholder to be accompanied by a tax credit voucher, which he then presents to his own tax authorities. His own tax authorities will submit it back to the country of source for financial compensation.

Presumably, some kind of clearing bank mechanism will arise, just as in the VAT proposals. A major difference does exist between the two, however. In the case of VAT the importer has every incentive to present tax credits to his own tax authorities to obtain repayment. In the case of the corporate income tax credit, however, shareholders may possess an equally strong incentive not to disclose foreign-based income receipts. This is an important point emphasized by Pearson (1989), which implies possible revenue losses for countries where international portfolio investment becomes the norm. Finally, it is perhaps worth noting that these proposals include provision for a 25 percent withholding tax on dividend payment to deter fraud, but again this accrues to the country of source and not necessarily to the country of the shareholders' residence.

The need to eliminate double taxation is not only concerned with dividend payments to shareholders. It applies also to dividends distributed by a subsidiary company to its parent company that resides in another member state. This could be achieved either by exempting from taxation distributed profits in the country of the parent or by granting imputation of the foreign tax paid against the tax liability within the parent country. Current proposals would allow countries to opt for either of these systems.

Agreement on tax rates. If agreement can be obtained with respect to the tax base and the tax system, agreement with regard to the tax rate is relatively minor. U.S. experience has demonstrated that differing states can live with a wide disparity of corporate income tax rates. The commission's proposal, dating from 1975, was for a rate within the range 45–55 percent, which, in the light of recent tax reform in both the United States and the United Kingdom, now appears excessive. In any case the need appears to be for agreement on a minimum rate of tax to avoid a competitive free-for-all, with countries cutting tax rates in an attempt to attract investment. Once such a rate was agreed, one might question whether there is any need to impose an upper limit, on the grounds that to adopt a rate in excess of this would impose costs solely on the member country exercising this option.

Agreement on mergers. In many respects mergers are the key problem. Within the EC serious tax penalties now inhibit mergers of firms across national borders. It is easier for firms to merge within a member country than across national borders. This is not the case, for example, in the United States. There is no advantage (other than perhaps a geographical one) for a New York firm to merge with another New York firm as opposed to merging with one in Massachusetts. Within the EC adoption of the existing draft directive on mergers would not adequately deal with this problem since it would not overcome the difficulties of double taxation. In contrast, non-member countries, because of internationally negotiated tax agreements, are in a preferable position. American or Japanese companies can consider European-wide community investment strategy in a manner now denied to the members of the EC.

A Radical Solution. The EC Commission appears to be moving toward a program of harmonization of the corporate tax that involves harmonization of the tax base, agreement on tax rates, and adoption of a partial imputation system. Even if it were possible to reach agreement on these issues, which essentially amount to no less than a proposal for a single European corporate tax, the bureaucratic costs imposed on governments and the administrative costs associated with fiscal compliance by business firms and companies would be substantial. The complexities of attempting to harmonize the corporate tax regimes of twelve independent member countries that differ so substantially, not only in the nature of the tax laws on the books but also in the way in which those laws are interpreted and enforced, raises extremely daunting problems. It is unlikely that the political commitment will be forthcoming for such an ambitious program, certainly not by the end of 1992, and it is likely that individual member countries will guard their fiscal sovereignty jealously. Nonetheless, assuming that such an agreement were a feasible possibility on the political horizon, what would be an optimal solution?

What is proposed here is nothing less than the abolition of corporate income taxation within the EC. Why is there a need for the separate taxation of the income of corporate enterprise? Dividends and capital gains could continue to be taxed under the personal income tax applicable in the country of residence of the shareholder. At a stroke all impediments and distortions to the free flow of capital to its most efficient use would be eliminated. Not only would neutrality be established in respect of capital within the member countries,

TABLE 8-12
Summary Appendix: A Statistical Overview of Europe and Its Major Industrial Competitors, Various Years, 1985–2000

	EC12	B	DK	WG	G	S
Area (000's sq. km)	2,260.7	30.5	43.1	248.7	132.0	504.8
GDP 1989 (1985 = 100)		112.7	112.0	103.0	111.1	107.6	119.6
Imports (1985 = 100)		133.3	135.9	107.6	120.5	130.1	182.2
Exports (1985 = 100)		117.7	130.3	117.2	112.9	137.5	122.3
Balance of trade (1988) (M10 ECU)	14,488	946	1,741	65,403	−5,132	−14,922
Population 1988 (000's)	324,776	9,883	5,130	61,421	9,985	38,995
% of EC population	100	3.0	1.6	18.9	3.1	12.0
Population est. yr. 2000 (000's)	329,678	9,615	5,154	60,484	10,334	40,746
F/T education (000's)		1,946	947	9,455	1,727	9,122
Unemployment Sept. 1989	10.2	10.5	9.0	6.8	2.3	17.0
Industrial output 1989 (2d qtr.) (1985 = 100)		114.1	114.9	112.3	110.8	105.4	122.0
Consumer general price index 1989 (2d qtr.) (1985 = 100)		110.7	104.1	112.7	101.2	162.4	120.0
Hourly wage in industry 1989 (2d qtr.) (1985 = 100)	n.a	110.0	126.2	114.1	n.a	140.0
Mean exchange rate Sept. 1989 (1 ECU=)		43.43	8.06	2.07	176.70	130.00

TABLE 8-12 (continued)								
F	Ire	I	Lux	Nl	P	UK	US	Jap
549.0	70.3	301.3	2.6	41.8	92.4	244.1	9.372.7	372.3
111.1	112.0	114.0	116.3	110.0	118.3	113.6	113.7	117.7
130.5	125.0	133.1	125.1	126.2	190.3	136.4	136.0	152.2
115.3	137.0	118.7	128.1	121.0	135.8	111.4	158.4	114.8
−6,818	2,612	−512	946	6,910	−4,336	−31,411	−106,943	80,536
55,872	3,540	57,452	375	14,760	10,287	57,077	239,283	120,754
17.2	1.1	17.7	0.001	4.5	3.2	17.6	n.a	n.a
57,882	4,123	57,226	374	15,588	11,141	58,857	268,079	127,683
12,160	915	11,282	n.a	2,958	n.a	9,646		
11.0	17.3	16.6	1.4	6.7	6.5	6.1	n.a	n.a
115.8	145.7	123.6	126.1	104.4	119.3	106.9	114.5	118.6
108.7	109.4	116.5	101.7	100.6	133.9	113.0	110.0	101.3
116.5	124.5	122.0	n.a	n.a	176.0	132.1	110.0	n.a.
7.00	0.78	1,492.7	43.43	2.34	173.91	0.67	1.06	154.21

NOTE: B = Belgium; DK = Denmark; WG = West Germany; G = Greece; S = Spain; F = France; Ire = Ireland; I = Italy; Lux = Luxembourg; Nl = Netherlands; P = Portugal; UK = United Kingdom; US = United States; Jap = Japan. n.a. = not available.
SOURCE: European Research Press, 1990, vol. 1, pt. 1.

but equally such a regime would be perfectly neutral with respect to the capital investment of outsiders.

The immediate objection to such a proposal would turn on the loss of revenue. Member governments would simply not countenance such a windfall loss. But such an objection can be overstated. First of all, there would be no need to abolish the corporate income tax overnight. It would be sufficient upon the creation of the single market to announce that the corporate tax would be phased out over, say, a fifteen-year period to avoid major misallocations of productive venture capital.

Moreover, the resulting stimulus to investment would create growth and employment that would add to alternative revenues. Part of the revenue lost would be recouped in greater dividend and capital gains taxation. And the budgetary consequences of gradual abolition would not be as severe as one might imagine. The corporate income tax is a relatively modest source of fiscal revenues. In 1986 the corporate income tax accounted for 7.2 percent of total tax revenue raised in the EC, compared with 30.9 percent raised by VAT and excise duties (OECD 1988). It may be objected that such a move would be regressive, but this is by no means clear, not only because of the widening spread of share ownership but also because dividend taxation would remain a policy issue for independent sovereign states.

In any event it is likely that the role of corporate profit taxation will decline relatively when compared with the taxation of labor income. This is simply a consequence of the greater mobility of capital as compared with relatively immobile wage labor. After 1992, when there are no further restrictions on capital flows, capital will migrate to the lower-tax regions in the absence of complete harmonization. In addition, individual countries will have an incentive to engage in competition to attract net inward investment by cutting effective tax rates. A competitive free-for-all can be expected to shift the burden of taxation away from capital and toward labor income. What is required in post-1992 Europe is a uniform system of corporate income taxation possessed of a common tax base, tax rate, and tax system with no artificial incentives to practices such as transfer pricing or discriminatory treatment against outside third-country investment. The abolition of the corporate income tax provides the ultimate solution.

References and Bibliography

Alderson, John. 1988. "Are Border Controls Necessary?" In Bieber, Dehousse, Pinder, and Weiler 1988.

Alworth, J. S. 1988. *The Financial, Investment, and Taxation Decisions of Multinationals*. Oxford: Basil Blackwell.

Banham, John. 1989. "1992—Is British Business Ready?" *Royal Bank of Scotland Review*, no. 161 (March).

Berglas, Eitan. 1981. "Harmonization of Commodity Taxes: Destination, Origin, and Restricted Origin Principles." *Journal of Public Economics* 16, no. 3: 377–87.

Bieber, Roland, Renaud Dehousse, John Pinder, and Joseph H. H. Weiler, eds. 1988. *1992: One European Market?* European Policy Unit at the European University Institute, Florence. Baden-Baden: Nomos Verlagsgesellschaft.

Biehl, Dieter. 1988. "On Maximal versus Optimal Tax Harmonization." In Bieber, Dehousse, Pinder, and Weiler 1988.

Bird, Richard M. 1987. "Corporate-Personal Tax Integration." In Cnossen 1987.

Boadway, Robin. 1989. "Corporate Tax Harmonisation: Lessons from Canada." In Gammie and Robinson. 1989.

Boltho, A. 1989. "European and United States Regional Differentials: A Note." *Oxford Review of Economic Policy* 5, no. 2: 105–15.

Bos, Marko, and Hans Nelson. 1988. "Indirect Taxation and the Completion of the Internal Market of the EC." *Journal of Common Market Studies* 27, no. 1 (September): 27–44.

Butler, Michael. 1986. *Europe: More Than a Continent*. London: Heineman.

Cecchini, P. 1988. *The European Challenge 1992: The Benefits of a Single Market* (with Michael Catinat and Aleus Jacquemin). English ed. by John Robinson. London: Wildwood House.

Chown, John F. 1989a. *Company Tax Harmonisation in the European Community*. London: Institute of Directors.

———. 1989b. "Tax Harmonisation in Europe." In Gammie and Robinson 1989.

Cnossen, Sijbren. 1981. "Dutch Experience with the Value Added Tax." *Finanzarchiv* 39, no. 2: 205–14.

———. 1982. "What Rate Structure for a Value Added Tax?" *National Tax Journal* 35, no. 2.

———. 1983. "Harmonisation of Indirect Taxes in the EEC." *British Tax Review* 4: 232–53.

———. 1989. "How Much Tax Harmonization in the European Community?" In Gammie and Robinson 1989.

Cnossen, Sijbren, ed. 1983. *Comparative Tax Studies: Essays in Honor of Richard Goode*. Amsterdam: North-Holland.

———. 1987. *Tax Coordination in the European Community*. Series on International Taxation, no. 7. Deventer, Antwerp: Kluwer Law and Taxation Publishers.

Cnossen, Sijbren, and Carl S. Shoup. 1987. "Coordination of Value-added Taxes." In Cnossen 1987.

Commission of the European Communities. 1963. *Report of the Fiscal and Financial Committee* (Neumark Report). Brussels.

———. 1969a. *Draft Directive Concerning the Common System of Taxation Applicable in the Case of Mergers, Divisions, and Contributions of Assets Taking Place between Corporations of Different Member States.* COM (69) 5 final. Brussels, January 15.

———. 1969b. *Draft Directive Concerning the Common System of Taxation Applicable in the Case of Parent Corporations and Subsidiaries of Different Member States.* COM (69) 6 final. Brussels, January 15.

———. 1975. *Draft Directive Concerning the Harmonisation of Systems of Company Taxation and of Withholding Tax on Dividends.* COM (75) 392 final. Brussels, August 1.

———. 1976. *Draft Directive on the Elimination of Double Taxation in Connection with the Adjustment of Transfers of Profits between Associated Enterprises (Arbitration Procedure).* COM (76) 611 final. Official Journal of the European Communities (OJC) 301, December 21.

———. 1985. *Completing the Internal Market.* White Paper to the European Council. COM (85) 310 final. Reproduced in Bieber, Dehousse, Pinder, and Weiler 1988.

———. 1987. *Completion of the Internal Market: Approximation on Indirect Rates and Harmonization of Indirect Tax Structures.* Global Communication. COM (87) 320 final.

———. 1989. *Communication on the Completion of the Internal Market: Approximation of Indirect Taxes.* COM (89) 260.

Cottey, P. 1988. *Macroeconomic Policy Areas of the EEC: Towards 1992.* International Studies in Economics and Econometrics. Deventer: Klumer Academic Publishers.

Crooks, Edmund. 1989. *Alcohol Consumption and Taxation.* IFS Report Series no. 34. London: Institute for Fiscal Studies.

Crooks, Edmund, Michael Devereux, Mark Pearson, and Charles Wookey. 1989. *Transnational Tax Rates and Incentives to Invest.* IFS Working Paper Series no. W89/9. London: Institute for Fiscal Studies.

Davis, Evan, and John Kay. 1985. "Extending the VAT Base: Problems and Possibilities." *Fiscal Studies* (February).

Deaton, A., and J. Muellbauer. 1980a. "An Almost Ideal Demand System." *American Economic Review* 70, no. 3 (June): 312–26.

———. 1980b. *Economics and Consumer Behaviour.* Cambridge: Cambridge University Press.

Devereux, Michael, and Mark Pearson. 1989. *Corporate Tax Harmonisation and Economic Efficiency.* IFS Report Series no. 35. London: Institute for Fiscal Studies.

———. 1990. "Harmonising Corporate Taxes in Europe." *Fiscal Studies* 11, no. 1 (February): 21–35.
Easson, Alex J. 1988. "The Elimination of Fiscal Frontiers." In Bieber, Dehousse, Pinder, and Weiler 1988.
Economic and Social Committee. 1978. *Information Report of the Section for Economic and Social Questions of the Economic and Social Committee on Tax Harmonization* (Brussels: Fredersdorf Report).
Economist. 1989. "1992 Under Construction: A Survey." *Economist*, London, July 8.
El-Agraa, Alim., ed. 1988. *International Economic Integration*, 2d ed. London: Macmillan.
European Research Press. 1990. *European Research*, vol 1, pt. 1 (January).
Fitchew, Geoffrey. 1989. "The Single European Market and Tax Harmonisation." In Gammie and Robinson 1989.
Fredersdorf Report. 1978. See Economic and Social Committee.
Gammie, Malcolm, and Bill Robinson, eds. 1989. *Beyond 1992: A European Tax System: Proceedings of the Fourth IFS Residential Conference, Oxford 1989*. IFS Commentary no. 13. London: Institute of Fiscal Studies.
Giersch, Herbert. 1989. "Europe's Prospects for the 1990's. *Economic Papers*, no. 76 (May). Directorate-General for Economic and Financial Affairs, Commission of the European Communities, Brussels.
Guieu, Pierre, and Claire Bonnet. 1988. "Indirect Taxation and the Completion of the Internal Market of the EC." *Journal of Common Market Studies* 25, no. 3 (March): 209–22.
Helm, D., and S. Smith. 1989. "Economic Integration and the Role of the European Community." *Oxford Review of Economic Policy* 5, no. 2: 1–19.
Henderson, David. 1989. *1992: The External Dimension*. Occasional Papers no. 25. New York and London: Group of Thirty.
Hitiris, T. 1988. *European Community Economics*. Brighton: Harvester/Wheatsheaf.
HM Department of Trade and Industry. 1989. *The Single Market—The Facts*, 3d ed. London.
HM Treasury. 1988. *Taxation in the Single Market: A Market Based Approach*. London. September 8.
Institute of Economic Affairs. 1989. *Whose Europe?: Competing Visions for 1992*. IEA Readings, no. 29. London.
Isaac, John. 1989. "Corporate Tax Harmonisation." In Gammie and Robinson 1989.
Kay, J. A., and M. J. Keen. 1982. *The Structure of Tobacco Taxes in the European Community*. IFS Report Series no. 1. London: Institute for Fiscal Studies.

———. 1987. "Alcohol and Tobacco Taxes: Criteria for Harmonisation." In Cnossen 1987.
Keen, M. J. 1987. "Welfare Effects of Commodity Tax Harmonisation." *Journal of Public Economics* 33: 107–14.
———. 1989. "Pareto-improving Indirect Tax Harmonisation." *European Economic Review* 33: 1–12.
King, J. R. 1986. "On the Revenue Effects of Tax Changes." *Fiscal Studies* 7, no. 1: 51–60.
King, M. A. 1989. "Harmonisation of Taxes on Income from Capital in the European Community." Paper prepared for LSE Financial Markets Group and Institute of Fiscal Studies Joint Conference on Tax Harmonisation in Europe, October 26. Mimeo.
King, M. A., and D. Fullerton, eds. 1984. *The Taxation of Income from Capital: A Comparative Study of the United States, the United Kingdom, Sweden, and West Germany*. Chicago: University of Chicago Press.
Knocker, Simon Paul. 1990. *The European Commission's Indirect Taxation Proposals for 1992—An Evaluation*. Department of Economics Honors Dissertation. University of St. Andrews, St. Andrews, Fife.
Lee, Catherine, and Panos Pashardes. 1988. *Who Pays Indirect Taxes?* IFS Report Series no. 32. London: Institute for Fiscal Studies.
Lee, Catherine, Mark Pearson, and Stephen Smith. 1988. *Fiscal Harmonisation: An Analysis of the European Commission's Proposals*. IFS Report Series no. 28. London: Institute for Fiscal Studies.
Lodge, Juliet. 1986a. "The Single European Act: Towards a New Euro-Dynamism?" *Journal of Common Market Studies* 24, no. 3 (March): 203–23.
———. 1986b. *European Union: The European Community in Search of a Future*. London: Macmillan.
McLure, Charles E., Jr. 1989. "European Integration and Taxation of Corporate Income at Source: Lessons from the US." In Gammie and Robinson 1989.
Messere, K. 1979. "A Defence of Present Border Tax Adjustment Practices." *National Tax Journal* 32, no. 4.
———. 1983. "Trends in OECD Tax Revenues." In Cnossen, ed. 1983.
Musgrave, Peggy B. 1987. "Interjurisdictional Coordination of Taxes on Capital Income." In Cnossen 1987.
Organization for Economic Cooperation and Development (OECD). 1988. *Revenue Statistics of OECD Member Countries 1966–1985*. Paris.
Overture, Stephen Frank. 1986. *The Economic Principles of European Integration*. New York: Praeger.
Pearson, Mark. 1989. "Corporate Tax Harmonisation in the European Community." In Gammie and Robinson 1989.
Pearson, Mark, and Stephen Smith. 1988. "1992: Issues in Indirect Taxation." *Fiscal Studies* 9, no. 3 (August): 25–35.

Pelkmans, Jacques, and Peter Robson. 1987. "The Aspirations of the White Paper." *Journal of Common Market Studies* 25, no. 3 (March): 181–92.

Pelkmans, J., and A. Winters. 1988. *Europe's Domestic Market.* Chatham House Papers, no. 43. London: Chatham House.

Pinder, John. 1988. "Enhancing the Community's Economic and Political Capacity: Some Consequences of Completing the Common Market." In Bieber, Dehousse, Pinder, and Weiler 1988.

Price Waterhouse. 1988. *Corporate Taxes: A Worldwide Summary.* London: Price Waterhouse.

Ritter, Wolfgang. 1989. "Harmonisation of Taxes as a Prerequisite for a Single European Market." In Gammie and Robinson 1989.

Robson, Peter. 1987. *The Economics of International Integration,* 3d ed. London: Allen & Unwin.

Rose, Manfred. 1987. "Optimal Tax Perspective on Tax Coordination." In Cnossen 1987.

Royal Bank of Scotland. 1989. *Review,* no. 162 (June). Special 1992 ed.

Shoup, Carl S. 1953. "Taxation Aspects of International Economic Integration." In *Aspects Financiers et Fiscaux de l'Integration Economique.* Institut International des Finance Publiques. The Hague: Van Stockum.

———. 1969. *Public Finance.* London: Weidenfeld and Nicholson.

Shoup, Carl S., ed. 1967. *Fiscal Harmonization in Common Markets,* 2 vols. New York: Columbia University Press.

Sinn, Hans Werner. 1987. *Capital Income Taxation and Resource Allocation.* Amsterdam: North-Holland.

———. 1989. "Tax Harmonisation and Tax Competition in Europe." Paper prepared for LSE Financial Markets Group and Institute for Fiscal Studies Joint Conference on Tax Harmonisation in Europe, October 26. Mimeo.

Smith, Stephen. 1988. "Excise Duties and the Internal Market." *Journal of Common Market Studies* 27, no. 2 (December): 147–60.

———. 1990. *The European Community's Priorities in Tax Policy.* IFS Working Paper Series no. W90/2. London: Institute for Fiscal Studies.

Strange, Susan. 1988. "A Dissident View." In Bieber, Dehousse, Pinder, and Weiler 1988.

Symons, Elizabeth, and Ian Walker. 1989. "The Revenue and Welfare Effects of Fiscal Harmonization for the UK." *Oxford Review of Economic Policy* 5, no. 2 (Summer): 61–75.

Toulemon, Robert. 1988. "Achievement of the Single Market in Information Technology." In Bieber, Dehousse, Pinder, and Weiler 1988.

Waller, David. 1989. "A Persistent Distortion in the Post-1992 Era." *Financial Times* (London), November 3.

9
Commentaries on Part Three

A Commentary by Leon Gordon

My last visit to Washington ten years ago was as part of an exchange scheme for officials in the European Community and the United States. My brief was to examine differences in state sales taxes and corporate taxes. In return, I organized a visit by a U.S. Treasury official to look at the value-added tax (VAT) in the EC, and I still wonder whether that might not be one of the solutions to the U.S. deficit.

I should like to compliment Keith Shaw on the sound scholarship and elegant presentation of his chapter. In the time available I cannot do justice to it in its entirety. All I can do is to seek to complement the insights of an academic economist with those of an international tax official who has been privileged to work on the policy formation that went into the fiscal harmonization program of the EC. I shall confine my remarks to the field of indirect taxation.

What I should first like to do is to lay more stress than, perhaps, the paper does on the importance of the legal context in which the community has developed its tax programs. The legal basis is to be found in Article 99 of the Rome Treaty of 1957, where we find the following provision: "The Commission shall consider how the legislation of the various Member States concerning turnover taxes, excise duties, . . . can be harmonized in the interest of the common market." This provided the foundation for the first and second VAT directives of 1967 and the monumental sixth VAT directive of 1977.

What is not generally known, however, is that in these early VAT directives we were already looking far ahead to the sort of system we would eventually wish to adopt. The first directive has as one of its preambles: "whereas it is therefore in the interest of the common market to achieve such harmonization of legislation concerning turnover taxes . . . as will make it possible subsequently to achieve the aim of abolishing the imposition of tax on importation and the remission of tax on exportation in trade between Member States." Similar wording is found in the accompanying second directive and in the sixth directive.

So the system, as Professor Shaw has just described it, which was introduced in 1967, was initially conceived as a transitional arrangement, albeit one that has resulted in a common system of turnover taxation. Its transparency is a vital factor in international trade and helps to explain why the VAT has been adopted by seven countries of the Organization for Economic Cooperation and Development outside the EC. But it was essentially a transitional stage, which would eventually give way to a system that did not distinguish between domestic and intracommunity transactions.

I now direct your attention to the legal framework that has conditioned our actions under the Single European Act of 1987. Article 8a imposes on the community the obligation to complete the internal market: "The Community shall adopt measures with the aim of progressively establishing the internal market over a period expiring on 31 December 1992." This sets out very clearly what our objectives are.

To attain them we need a definition of the internal market, and here it is: "The internal market shall comprise an area without internal frontiers"—I repeat—"without internal frontiers in which the free movement of goods, persons, services and capital is ensured in accordance with the provisions of this Treaty." The whole exercise since the white paper was produced in 1985 and the internal market enshrined in the Single European Act two years later has been to design arrangements that will enable us to abolish internal tax frontiers between member states.

The Single European Act also has an important taxation provision in the form of a revised Article 99. The council is now required to harmonize turnover taxes (VAT), excise duties, and other forms of indirect taxation—"to the extent that such harmonization is necessary to ensure the establishment and functioning of the internal market within the time-limit laid down in Article 8a." Harmonization has thus been tailored to meet the specific needs and deadline of the internal market and is an integral part of the process.

So much for the legal parameters. What about the economic argument? Let us take the case of cross-border shopping. It is a highly sensitive issue in a small, densely populated part of the world like northwestern Europe. Brussels is only one hour's drive away from four other countries: West Germany, France, Luxembourg, and the Netherlands. Where market access is so easy, the need for harmonization is felt very acutely, more than Professor Shaw appears to allow for.

Luxembourg is a classic case of fiscal distortion. From the figures of consumption of alcohol per head of population, it would appear that citizens of the grand duchy do nothing but drink liquor from opening time to closing time and far into the night. The OECD figures for 1984 show, for instance, a Belgian as consuming 10.7 liters of pure alcohol per annum, a German 11.9 liters, an American 7.9 liters, and a Luxembourger a staggering 19.3 liters.

We all know why. We see the same phenomenon, the same distortion, in another product, road fuel (oil, gasoline), which is eloquently documented in the recent OECD study on consumption taxes. Luxembourg is 1/3,500 the size of the United States. Although we would not expect the consumption of road fuel to be pro rata, we would expect it to reflect disparities in geographical size. Sure enough, the United States leads with 1.53 tons of oil equivalent per head, followed by other large countries like Canada, 1.20, and Australia, 1.02. West Germany, the strongest of the European economies, consumers 0.61 tons and little Luxembourg 1.42 tons. It is absurd. Macroeconomically these figures can get lost, but because of the political and social consequences for the regions on the higher-taxing side of the border, these issues cannot be ignored.

Indeed, the situation has reached such extreme proportions on certain borders, those between Denmark and West Germany, for instance, and between Northern Ireland and the Republic of Ireland, that Denmark and Ireland require a minimum absence of forty-eight hours from their territory before one can bring back the full allowance of cigarettes and spirits. This is nothing less than a denial of citizens' economic rights under community law, which lays down how much one can bring in for personal consumption.

So things have got a bit out of hand and we need to redress the situation. We are proposing as part of the 1992 program to raise the travelers' allowances progressively until they entirely disappear by 1993. This will put pressure on countries like Denmark and Ireland that have been adopting restrictive policies to permit free movement, which is, after all, what the community is all about—free movement of persons, goods, services, and capital.

I want to devote a few words to convergence because this is a process that we have allowed for in our proposals, without relying exclusively on market forces to achieve these results. What has happened since our proposals were made in 1987? Let us start with the VAT. The Netherlands has reduced its standard rate from 20 to 18.5 percent, thus getting nearer to the center of the band proposed by the EC Commission. Ireland—a country at the very top of the VAT league, as mentioned in Professor Shaw's chapter—has just dropped its standard rate from 25 to 23 percent. In France the top rate of VAT has progressively come down from 33 to 25 percent. We have actually got an agreement in the Council of Economics and Finance Ministers on an approximation of rates, based on figures that the commission put forward in 1987.

Even in the very controversial area of excise duties, we are noticing movement toward the levels that the commission has proposed. West Germany has raised its duties on heating oil and on petrol, a politically sensitive product. It has adjusted the duty on cigarettes to conform more closely to the figures that we put forward in 1987. Ireland has halved its duty on liquid petroleum gas to get it nearer to the commission's figure. Denmark reduced its duty on petrol in two stages, so that after July 1990 it was virtually down to the German level. The difference had been so great that petrol could hardly be sold on the Danish side of that border.

Where are we now? We are in a process of continuous institutional dialogue with parliament and the council. There is growing pressure for agreement on sufficient approximation of rates—I stress approximation, not uniformity—to allow us to abolish frontiers by December 31, 1992.

The commission has amended the excise duty proposals to take account of health and environmental considerations and of the need for flexibility. We have replaced a single rate of excise duty by a rate band or, in certain cases, a minimum rate to take effect on January 1, 1993.

Finally, I must take issue with Professor Shaw over the question of the veto. It is not a practical option anymore. It is true that we require unanimous agreement, and I think we will get it. I do not see any one country taking the political risk of frustrating the wishes of the other ten or eleven, and that is the situation on the fiscal front as far as indirect taxes are concerned.

In a recent issue of the *Times*—I had to blink twice when I read this—there was even an indication, in the course of an interview with a senior customs official, that Britain might give up its practice of zero rating children's clothing. This was previously inconceivable, something Margaret Thatcher has always opposed, but maybe she is not as inflexible as she seems. I am convinced that by the end of 1992 we will have sufficient agreement on the systems of tax and the rates of tax to be able to abolish internal frontiers, allowing goods, services, and persons to move freely across them.

A Commentary by William Haraf

Ingo Walter's chapter is entitled "European Financial Integration and Its Implications for the United States." The chapter is ambitious in its scope. It covers prospects for the European Monetary System, problems of macropolicy convergence, financial integration issues from both an efficiency standpoint and a macropolicy standpoint, regulatory position and restructuring in the various European Community countries, and the implications of all that for the United States.

Clearly the issues posed by European financial integration are many and broad. Analyzing them is complicated by the often overwhelming role of politics in institutions.

In commenting on a chapter like this, it is hard to figure out where to begin. I decided to limit my comments to two areas. First, I will talk about capital flows, because that is an important issue. Second, I will talk about the efficiency aspect of financial integration, something that Anthony Saunders and Mr. Walter have already discussed to a certain extent.

It is clear that the 1992 program was intended to foster a supply-side revolution within the EC by removing remaining barriers to economic integration and cross-border competition. There is no longer any doubt that it will be successful in making EC economies much more efficient and competitive globally.

The Cecchini report estimates that the 1992 program will increase gross domestic product within the EC by 2.2 percent per year. I think that is optimistic. Nonetheless, the effects will be quite significant.

A key component of the 1992 program is the elimination of capital controls. European governments have long used capital controls to maintain exchange rates and to manage their balance of payments. The phaseout of these capital controls, more than anything else, would create a highly integrated EC market. Moreover, that phaseout is coming at a time when capital markets around the world are opening up. That adds to the significance of the movements within the EC.

The 1992 program has made the EC increasingly attractive to global investors. Stock markets are booming. Investment demand is way up. There is a flurry of mergers and acquistions. Viewing the 1992 program together with developments in the Soviet Union, Eastern Europe, and elsewhere, I believe that the 1990s will bring global changes of a magnitude seldom seen in a lifetime.

Eastern Europe and the Soviet Union have undergone the equivalent of a Chapter 11 filing. They are now trying to restructure their supply-side program and to attract capital from abroad, in large part as a result of the 1992 program and the apparent success of the EC in trying to achieve European integration.

In just the few months that we have seen the barriers to Eastern Europe come down, we have seen a large number of East-West investments in trade deals announced. Nearly $500 million has been pledged for investment by U.S. and West European companies—this in a very short time—more than 700 joint ventures in trade deals. The World Bank has recently pledged $5 billion to Eastern Europe over the next three years, and EC members have agreed to establish another multilateral lender for Eastern Europe, the European Bank for Reconstruction and Development.

The developments in Eastern Europe, however, are not an unmixed blessing from the perspective of the EC. Countries like Spain and Portugal, which figured to be recipients of substantial foreign direct investment, now fear that they will lose out to Poland, to Hungary, to Czechoslovakia.

Moreover, plans for a monetary union between East and West Germany have led to concerns about rising inflation and interest rates that will inevitably spill over to the other EMS partners. There is already talk about decoupling the French franc, the peseta, and the guilder from the deutsche mark, and no doubt progress toward full monetary union within the EC is likely to be slowed considerably by these recent developments.

Competing for capital with Europe, both Eastern and Western, will be the privatization campaigns in Latin America. The most ambitious privatization program in the world is not in Eastern Europe but in the troubled economy of Argentina. Mexico, Brazil and Venezuela are also privatizing in an effort to rebuild their economies.

The needs of countries in Eastern Europe and Latin America for capital to build infrastructure, to clean up the environment, and to build world class industrial capacity are truly massive. Competition to attract capital in the coming years will be fierce, and we could see global reallocations of capital on a very grand scale.

What does all this mean for the global economy and for the United States? First of all, we are already beginning to see a global increase in the demand for investment to implement various supply-side programs around the world. Even if these programs are fully successful (and they will not all be), it is clear that the aggregate demand effects will come first. They will show up in the form of an expansion in output in countries that are not already operating at full capacity and an upward pressure on prices and on interest rates.

The higher interest rates and the stronger dollar that we are already seeing in the United States will not, in my view, be contractionary, as some people have said. They are a symptom of the higher demand for goods and services coming from abroad, both currently and prospectively. In the near term the traded goods sector of the U.S. economy will improve, and our trade balance will decline.

Second, there will be increased financial and real sector volatility associated with some very significant unresolved issues around the world. First among them are the political and economic instability in Eastern Europe, the difficulties of harmonizing monetary and fiscal policy arrangements within the EC, and another factor, completely apart from all of those, the perceived overvaluation of Japanese asset prices, both stock market prices and land values. There is an uncertain element to this that I think will lead to more volatility in securities market prices and in exchange rate.

Third, there will be portfolio effects, global reallocations of capital. In the 1980s the United States was by far the greatest importer of capital in the world, not only from the developed countries but also from the developing world in the form of flood capital. The Reagan-led supply-side revolution made investment in the United States attractive. Capital was also attracted to the United States by our settled political and legal structures, a more or less responsible monetary policy, the relative stability of our banking system, and the depth and efficiency of our securities markets. The United States has offered the safest harbor in the world for the world's investors. We really play the role that Switzerland has been noted for in the past.

The United States has benefited enormously from these capital inflows. Now it may be Europe's turn. The supply-side program there and the elimination of barriers to capital flow mean that the EC will be very attractive to global investors. European financial markets will receive a tremendous boost from integration, particularly if the EMS remains strong in the face of the pressures coming from German reunification and the opening up of Eastern Europe. This should create a viable and attractive alternative to the U.S. market for global investors.

As a result, over the course of the 1990s the dollar may play a lesser role in the world economy, and we may lose some of the advantages of being the world's safe haven. It is unlikely that the United States will be able to attract capital in the future as it did in the 1980s, at least not without having to pay a much higher price for it.

As for Eastern Europe, Latin America, and the Soviet Union, capital will be available to those nations to the extent that professional investors that manage large pools of funds feel that the risks are justified. We have some very troubled economies. So far we have seen some apparent interest from the private sector. In addition, Western governments are anxious to facilitate the transitions of those economies to full global trading partners. But it is not clear whether they will improve their situation and whether they will retain the ability to attract capital from abroad.

Let me spend just a few moments on the efficiency aspects of financial integration. Citicorp is unique among U.S. bank holding companies in trying to build a global business. It is particularly active in the European market now. In fact, one can make the argument that it is the only pan-European bank. It is in more European countries with a sizable presence than any European bank. But most U.S. bank holding companies are retrenching from foreign markets at the same time that we are seeing a rapid expansion of foreign banks in the United States. It is truly the case that the role of the U.S. bank is dwindling in overseas markets, and there is an important question about what is going on.

In part it reflects the global macrofinancial environment that we operate in, the constellation of asset prices around the world. It is part of the process by which we import foreign capital. But it also reflects a relatively inhospitable regulatory climate in the United States, one that does not foster a healthy and globally competitive industry and that does not serve our own financial services customers very well.

We have been truly impressed with the implications of the Second Banking Directive, the opening up of capital markets within the EC. As for what that means for the efficiency of the financial sector within Europe, we can make the case that Europe is truly going to leapfrog us in the efficiency and dynamism of its financial sector.

As a corporation we at Citicorp are very concerned about our global competitive position. But the stakes are really much higher than that for the U.S. economy. The semiofficial Cecchini report, which predicted a 2.2 percent rise in GDP from the 1992 program, gets fully 1.5 percent of that from financial integration, from the erosion of barriers to capital movement and improved efficiency of financial markets within the EC.

We have to start thinking about a similar program in the United States, and it would have to be a broad one. It would involve relooking at restrictions on interstate banking, the Glass-Steagall Act, the Bank Holding Company Act. We have a long way to go to make our financial system as efficient as the European financial system of the 1990s.

A Commentary by Paul Mentré

Europe is currently crossed by two monetary currents. The first one, described in the Delors report, is the march toward the economic and monetary union of the European Community. The other, generated by the dismantlement of the Berlin Wall and its consequences, is the emergence of the monetary unity of Germany. One should use two different words, unity and union, since the objectives, the procedures, the timing of these two movements are quite different. But one should at the same time deal with them together since their economic and financial consequences are intimately related.

Two Distinct Procedures

The monetary unity of Germany and the monetary union of Europe have a common thread, their reliance on a federal structure, which may explain why they are sometimes treated in the same way. The Bundesbank embodies this federal structure. Created as a successor to the Bank für Deutscher Länder, dominated by the *Länder*, it relies also on regional central banks (the *Zentrallandesbanken*). But the monetary policy in its totality is determined and conducted by the central body. The main decisions are taken by the supervisory council, which includes the permanent directors, appointed at the federal level, and the presidents of the regional central banks, with, as a fundamental objective, the task of ensuring the stability of the German currency, the deutsche mark.

The Process of the Monetary Unity of Germany. Today it is clear that the monetary unity of Germany will be nothing else than the extension of the currency area of the deutsche mark and of the zone of competence of the Bundesbank.

As far as economic matters are concerned, uncertainties remain, too. The move from a centrally planned economy to a market economy implies the adoption of a set of legal texts organizing, among other things, private property, the protection of contracts, and the freedom of employment, wages, and prices. These legal texts may result either from the automatic consequences of the individual entry of new *Länder* into the Federal Republic of Germany or from a vote by the new East German Parliament of a law extending to East Germany the legal framework of West Germany. It may also result from a more protracted and complex negotiation between the two Germanys.

In the monetary field, however, the situation is quite clear. The deutsche mark is the symbol of German prosperity. Only its rapid introduction in East Germany can stem the flow of some 2,000 East Germans arriving daily in West Germany. The objective of the joint committees set up by Chancellor Helmut Kohl and Prime Minister Ludwig Moodrow is in this respect without ambiguity. And the pressure of daily events accelerates the timetable of its implementation.

Practically, there will be, one day, an exchange of assets denominated in East German currency (the öst mark) with deutsche marks and a conversion of price and wage contracts into deutsche marks (at conversion rates to be determined). Representatives of the eastern part of Germany will sit in the Bundesbank council, but their presence will be diluted among the presidents of all regional central banks. At the most one can conceive that, while awaiting political union, the East German central bank, the Staats bank, might be represented in the council by a number of members approximating the future number of East German *Länder*, which could give it a relative weight during the interim period. But the German monetary process is indeed a process based on a larger circulation of a preexisting currency, the deutsche mark, and on the extension of an existing central bank, the Bundesbank.

The Process of the Economic and Monetary Union of Europe. The objective of the process toward the economic and monetary union of Europe cannot, obviously, be the same. To some extent it is in fact the opposite objective. The power and international role of the deutsche mark have been conducive to a situation where, in broad terms, the relations between major third currencies (the dollar and the yen) and individual European currencies are exclusively determined by the intervention policy of the Bundesbank, conducting its interventions only in dollars, while the other European central banks intervene in deutsche marks to protect the bilateral rates vis-à-vis the deutsche mark, resulting from the parity grid, agreed under the exchange rate mechanism of the European Monetary System. This is reflected in the disproportionate share of the dollar–deutsche mark transactions in spot and forward exchange markets compared with other dollar–European currencies transactions. This is translated, in the EMS, by a kind of alignment of the policy of the other European central banks on the policy of the Bundesbank, the anchor of the system.

To a large extent the economic and monetary union of Europe is constructed as a reaction to this process. Former Chancellor Helmut Schmidt, the father of the European Monetary System, together with President Valéry Giscard d'Estaing, has repeatedly said that it was politically unsound for a national currency to be hegemonic in a common space. The partners of Germany have criticized the asymmetry of a system under which their own objectives are superseded by the objectives defined unilaterally for the strongest currency. And, with certain hesitations from the Bundesbank, the German authorities concur in the objective of a balanced economic and monetary union of Europe.

The European Council, when setting up the Delors Committee in Hanover (June 1988), when approving in Madrid (June 1989) the Delors report as the basis for further progress, and when determining in Strasbourg (December 1989) the timetable for the future works, did embrace such an approach. For the Delors report deals indeed with a European system of central banks, which means a collective institutional setting.

To achieve this goal it contemplates a first stage, without a modification of the Treaty of Rome, during which there would be a greater coordination of economic and monetary policies, abolition of exchange controls, and, if possible, entry into the exchange rate mechanism of the nonmember European currencies, that is, the escudo, the drachma, and the pound sterling.

In a second stage, resulting from an amendment to the treaty, the European system of central banks would progressively take over the definition of monetary policy, in both its internal and its external aspects, while budgetary and fiscal policies would become progressively more constrained. The convergence and the unity of policies would permit the stability of exchange rates, the reduction of fluctuation margins (presently 2.25 percent above and below bilateral central rates), and the acceptance of a subordinated role for national central banks.

The third stage would be the culmination of this evolution in the definition of immutable fixed parities, the suppression of fluctuation margins, and the progressive substitution of a common European currency, exemplified by the European currency unit, for the national European currencies.

To be sure, in this respect one can address some criticisms to the Delors report, which does not contemplate a rapid substitution process and a genuine European monetary federalism. The first stage does not include any measure in this direction, since the creation of a European Reserve Fund, jointly intervening on foreign exchange markets, and the concept of "the ECU, a parallel currency," freely circulating side by side with national currencies, have not been agreed on. The second stage seems to leave much too important a role for national central banks since the "federals" (probably five) will be in a minority position, in number and in weighted vote, against the twelve national governors, on the policy-making council. In contrast, the

Federal Open Market Committee, the policy-making organ of the U.S. Federal Reserve System, is composed of seven federal members and five regional members. Finally, the organization of the move to the third stage by a transfer of competences and the emergence of a common currency is defined only in broad and vague terms.

Those members of the European Council who were reluctant about the whole federal process have been able to use these ambiguities to put a brake on the process. For the time being the first stage took effect on July 1, 1990; it was preceded by the abolition of exchange controls in France, Italy, and Belgium, the narrowing of the Italian lira margins, and the adoption of the directives on coordination. The second stage should result from the adoption and the ratification, at an unknown date, of an amendment to the treaty, prepared by an intergovernmental conference having its first meeting in December 1990 but having no deadline for its conclusions. The third stage may or may not be included and predefined in the amendment thus negotiated in 1991.

The new panorama resulting from German monetary unity should lead to an acceleration and a sharper definition of this process. For, by their economic and financial consequences, the two movements, the monetary unity of Germany and the economic and monetary union of Europe, are indeed interrelated.

Two Interdependent Movements

The monetary unity of Germany and the monetary union of Europe have different rhythms. One cannot exclude that on July 1, 1990, the achievement of German monetary unity—a single currency—and the beginning of the first stage of a lengthy process toward the monetary union of Europe will occur simultaneously. Nobody wants the deutsche mark to become the only European currency and the Bundesbank the only central bank in Europe. It is therefore normal to see independent processes and differing timetables. But it is nevertheless to be hoped that the two undertakings respond to a common logic. Their interdependence is in fact reflected in both the economic and the financial aspects of the common European territory.

The Economic Aspects. The economic and financial weight of East Germany should not be overestimated. Its GNP amounts to 10–15 percent of the West German GNP and is inferior to the GNP of Rhineland-Westphalia, Bavaria, or Baden-Wurtemberg. Its monetary mass amounts to 6 percent of that of West Germany. To be sure, if GNP per capita (or productivity per person) were to reach, in the framework of the German economic and monetary unity, West German levels, the relative importance of the two economies would be determined by the comparative size of the population, giving a greater weight to the eastern part of Germany.

In this respect the rate of conversion between the deutsche mark and the öst mark will be of paramount importance. If a ratio of one to one is adopted for wages, as may be expected from some official statements, the East German workers will benefit from wages amounting to a third of the West German wages—plus subsidized rents—whereas the ratio of productivity lies between one-fourth and one-fifth. This would constitute a strong incentive for workers to keep their jobs in East Germany, thus stemming the flow of immigrants to West Germany. But the competitiveness of East German enterprises would not be sufficient, unemployment would increase, and West-to-East transfers for social subsidies would be necessary. If the conversion rate were two to one, competitiveness, growth, and employment would be greater, but there would be a risk of seeing a continuing exodus and a continuing increase of public expenditures in West Germany devoted to resettlement of the newcomers. Whatever the choice, it is clear that pressure will be exerted on German public expenditure, which, in addition to the new consumption and investment needs in East Germany and to the housing requirements in West Germany, will feed internal demand and expansion.

As a whole German reunification should contribute to a better economic balance within the EC. Continuing economic strength by Germany, as displayed in 1989, and a reduction of its external surplus would constitute positive factors for the stability of the EMS. But to a large extent this will depend on the way in which the new expenditures are financed. It would not be abnormal to see the EC, through its structural funds, contribute to them. How to deny to Saxony, destroyed by almost half a century of state communism, what is granted to the Mezzogiorno, to the eastern part of France, or to Wales? But then an appropriate and timely dialogue on this contribution should take place. Anyway the bulk of the cost will fall on the West German budget. To be sure, West Germany will benefit from some savings on military expenditures. But, fundamentally, a choice will have to be made between an increase in the budget deficit and an increase in taxation. For the partners of Germany, an ideal solution would be an increase in the VAT rate, a step in the direction of EC tax harmonization. But there is a risk that the road of an enlarged deficit will be chosen. With an unchanged monetary policy, this could present a risk of inflation. A tightening of the monetary policy, more plausible, would increase interest rates, already historically high, and put a progressive brake on growth within the EC. Thus the German integration and the way in which the added public expenditures that it implies are paid for are indeed subjects of common interest for all Europeans.

The Financial Aspects. By itself the insertion into the EMS of a deutsche mark benefiting from a wider area of circulation does not entail major institutional problems. The administration of the system is determined by an agreement between central banks, underwritten by the Bundesbank. The relative weight of the deutsche mark in the ECU, a basket of currencies, now a little more than 30 percent, would be increased; but since the revision of the relative weights in the ECU takes place every five years, the next one will be in 1994. It is clear, however, that the risks attached to a dominating currency will be increased.

It is therefore urgent to strengthen and develop the use of the ECU, a synthetic currency. The institutional approach envisioned in the Delors report and translated into the European system of central banks should henceforth embody an operational approach where the ECU, as a parallel or an optional currency, would fully play its role. Such is the wish of the Association for the Monetary Union of Europe, which includes large EC corporations such as Phillips, Fiat, BAT, Total, and Bosch. The association underlines that the 1993 single EC market will not bring to European firms an access to a unified market comparable to the U.S. or Japanese market if the European firms do not have the possibility to invoice, lend, and invest in a single currency throughout Europe. This will require a number of private initiatives, notably for invoicing, but many public initiatives as well, aiming, among other things, at use of the ECU in EC operations, at a merging of the private and official ECUs, and at a presence of the central banks in the ECU interbank clearing.

It is a direction in which one should engage oneself with speed and determination. There is, indeed, a risk that German industrialists and bankers could give a priority to their developments in the eastern part of Germany and, to a lesser degree, in independent East European countries at the expense of the 1993 EC single market. Already the Deutsche Bank, an ardent defender of the single market, is announcing the opening of fifteen branches in East Germany. And Volkswagen is already negotiating the restructuring of the East German automobile industry.

A new dynamic should be given without delay to the monetary integration of Europe. The monetary unity of Germany could constitute for the economic and monetary union of Europe a factor of diversion, delay, and weakness. These fears should be dissipated without delay. A concerted action is needed at the level of the European Council. Its content is known. The common political will should now express itself.

A Commentary by Patrice Vial

To a European, the conclusions of the two chapters by Ingo Walter and Anthony Saunders sound very reassuring. Mr. Walter's chapter urges the American authorities to adjust their regulations to resemble European regulations, and Mr. Saunders's chapter contends that German banks will survive the new competitive environment relatively intact.

Is there really no need to worry for European banks in the new highly competitive environment that is to take place? Though I am glad that others think we have no problem, most European bankers would tend to have, at this time, a less clear-cut conclusion. Opportunities will undoubtedly develop, but competition will be fierce.

I will comment briefly on this, first by pointing at some of the environmental changes that lie ahead for the financial system in Europe. Then, I will consider what impact these changes are likely to have on the relative competitiveness of the European financial system as compared to the American financial system.

Environmental changes are clearly creating new opportunities in European financial markets. Although it is tempting to attribute all these coming benefits to financial integration, other, very powerful factors are involved that should not be underestimated. First, there are demographic factors.

The postwar baby-boomers are now entering their forties, and Europe has many more baby-boomers, in relative terms, than does the United States. These people will increase their savings, not only because they have reached the age when people save more but because they are aware of incipient challenges to the public social security system. In ten to fifteen years, it is by no means certain that we will be able to sustain the pension level now paid to retired people. This fact will encourage people now in their forties to increase their savings and look for new financial products designed to supplement their official pensions. The market for innovative pension products is therefore growing rapidly.

A second positive demographic factor for the financial industry is the age of postwar entrepreneurs in Europe. They are now in their sixties and seventies, which means that the market for business transmission and investment banking will also be expanding. We see this happening in France, Germany, and other countries as well. The next ten years will be marked by full-fledged activity in the transmission of capital, especially with medium-sized firms, the shares of many of which are not listed on any Stock Exchange. This creates opportunities for financial intermediaries.

We must also bear in mind, in addition to these demographic factors, structural factors that are equally unrelated to financial integration. Over the past decade Europe, unlike the United States, has seen tremendous improvement in its balance-sheet structures, both in the manufacturing sector and in the financial sector. We are entering the 1990s with sound balance sheets and low debt, which was not the case in most European companies ten years ago and which stands in sharp contrast to the situation on this side of the Atlantic.

One result of this development is that many European companies are now planning to expand in ways not feasible ten years ago. This will enhance both internal and external growth prospects, thus generating a booming market for financial services in Europe.

Europe also has a much lower level of household indebtedness than the United States. Such indebtedness could be expanded, and financial services may well develop in this area.

All these factors, though independent from financial integration, will certainly be enhanced by its arrival. But even if financial integration proceeds more slowly than expected, they are here to stay. They will contribute, whatever the circumstances, to the development of the financial services industry.

Financial integration will happen, of course, sooner or later. What will it bring? First a change in the geographical pattern of financial flows. Western Europe, taken as a whole, is at equilibrium in its balance of payments, while presenting regional and local deficits or surpluses. But until now the financial fragmentation of the subcontinent has forced many of its actors—corporations, municipalities, and governments—to go abroad for financing because there was no single European market for funds. They went to the United States or elsewhere, or to offshore financial markets.

Financial integration in Europe will make it easier for European borrowers to directly meet potential European lenders. In the past, for instance, the city of Barcelona, might have gone to U.S. banks for money; in the future Barcelona will find it much easier to get money directly from Germany. This is a basic fact to understand.

We must also recognize that a lot of merger and acquisitions activity will boost Europe's investment banking position. The development of financial integration and deregulation will help Europeans find long-term maturities—which previously could be found only in offshore markets—within Europe. To sum up, all signals indicate that European financial markets will be very active in the next ten to fifteen years.

I turn now to the question of the relative competitive positions of the various contenders in this new game. We should expect to see in the financial service industry what we see in other industries. Large organizations will have a competitive advantage when it comes to production and distribution of mass products, while there may be fruitful "niches" for smaller firms in the area of more specific financial services.

Large "branded" networks will have a competitive advantage for mass distribution of standardized financial products: They will be best able to collect household deposits, extend standardized credits, and price standardized insurance products. There is no lack of candidates within European banks and insurance groups to perform this function! Western Europe is known to be "over bankerized"; well-established networks will be in a particularly good position to cater to this type of retail activity.

In the "corporate finance" business, Europe is in a contrasted situation. Some countries are very open to non-local banks; in others, as Mr. Saunders pointed out in his paper, there are strong, traditional links between local, well-established financial entities and industrial corporations. Often banks or insurance companies hold a portion of the capital of industrial companies. When it comes to counselling or financing strategic developments, the bank that is in such a position obviously has an advantage over any other outside competitors, whether from another European country or the USA.

What, then, can we conclude about the position of American banks in the European market? Traditionally, American banks have had strong points and weaker points. Their strong points are that they are very flexible and innovative and very international. They are able to maintain an international network, and they are able to attract highly skilled people. Among the weaker points is the fact that they often tend to concentrate on shorter-term profit opportunities, sometimes not bothering to build stable relationships with their corporate clients.

In the area of flexibility, European banks will probably not be as efficient as American banks in the near future. They tend to react more slowly than American banks. But on all the other points, I believe that European banks will be able to be as competitive as American banks. On the other hand, the larger "universal" European banks are probably less exposed to risk because of a more diversified asset and liability base.

Many experts would probably conclude that the market left open for American banks will be mostly the market for specialized investment advice and counsel, because that market requires a high degree of adaptability, a good ability to efficiently manage a worldwide information base, international contacts and a very effective international placement capability.

I am sure that American banks are good at all this. But I am also confident that they will find many other opportunities in the European market. Actually, American bankers in Europe seem satisfied with their prospects. Even if they have a smaller share of the market, the market itself will probably be much larger for the reasons that I have just explained. May I add that, since the financial integration will in itself create a competitive environment for financial services in Europe, we certainly see so harm and welcome having American banks being parties in this competition.

A Commentary by Norbert Walter

I agree with Anthony Saunders's assessment of the German situation, particularly his description of monetary policy, which is determined by an optimal distance from a country. If one is too close to a country, his assessment normally lacks the kind of overview one can get from a different country, from another planet.

Nevertheless, it is not fair to say that the Bundesbank can be blamed for relatively high unemployment in West Germany. It did not accept long-term unemployment because it did not accept inflation in the medium and the longer term. There are good arguments that other causes must be found to explain West German unemployment, because the deliberate decision of other countries to embark on a different policy obviously did not help to avoid high unemployment there. Therefore, I think the Bundesbank was right not to pursue time-inconsistent policies.

In periods when interest rates were increasing rapidly, of course, unemployment was jumping in West Germany. But to argue that the increase of unemployment is due to monetary policy is I believe, too simplified an argument.

A number of supply-side issues determine what has happened

to our labor market and to unemployment. We had a change over time caused by demographic factors and factors that come from intervention in our labor market. We had massive intervention in our labor market from the government side, from social legislation in particular, but from wage policies in a cartelized labor market as well. These are certainly based on the social benefit systems in our country and therefore cannot be considered a totally independent argument.

I accept that there are short-run unemployment implications of monetary policies, but I do not believe that there are long-run relationships between monetary policy and unemployment. For the longer-run developments—and we are talking about such developments here—the structural arguments explain much better what has happened to our country's unemployment.

Another question is, What will Germany lose when we have monetary integration in the European Community? Will there be a loss of monetary sovereignty? Will there be increased fiscal transfers, especially to the southern countries in the EC, when the policy instrument of exchange rates can no longer be used?

Mr. Saunders mentioned that a number of important things can be gained by monetary union. This is true not only for the consumer, for the customer, for the user of financial services. It is more than that. The producers of financial services in Europe, and in West Germany in particular, can win from developing a market that has a depth and width in line with the size of capital markets elsewhere, as in Japan, the United States, or London.

So far we have a very fragmented, a very shallow capital market in continental Europe. If we want to be players on a European scale, and even more if we want to be players on a global scale, we must overcome the parochial structure of national, if not regional, capital markets in Europe, another argument that is important in discussing monetary union.

The characteristics of stage three of the Delors report describe the functions and the priorities of a central bank in such a way that a German can hardly disagree that such a solution would be marvelous for Europe. The report stated that the objective of price stability has priority, that the bank would be independent of national governments and community authorities, that it would not lend to public sector authorities, and finally, that it ought to have a federal structure. If these principles are filled with life, what more should Germans ask for? It is against this background that I am a little more optimistic and positive about accepting what is obviously in the cards for Europe.

There is then the argument of the implication of European monetary union for fiscal transfers, the argument that there might be a free-rider advantage for certain high-deficit countries. To some extent this is correct, and the Delors report addressed the problem in a not very appropriate manner. The report suggested that we should have coordinated demand management policies in Europe.

If that were the interpretation, there would be a good argument that this is not necessary and certainly not very helpful. But to avoid the free-rider problem, there should be standards for fiscal policies in Europe such that unsolid fiscal behavior is not allowed for. To define what that is has always been difficult, and is more difficult today.

I think we could all agree that Italian fiscal behavior is not in line with sound fiscal behavior, and certainly we could agree that the governments in Belgium and Denmark have to cut down their [fiscal] deficits. But the present fiscal stance of other European countries is such that the European central authorities should not or would not need to intervene in their policies.

This holds true for the United Kingdom, a country that has a budget surplus. It holds true for the West German budget, which will have a higher deficit in the new few years due to the German unification process adding to the burden of the taxpayer in the enlarged Germany. Certainly these are not countries that would be considered free riders.

If there could be an agreement that fiscal behavior has to be in line with sound practices, this certainly would be a meaningful addition to the description of stage three of the Delors report for the European central bank system.

When we discuss monetary integration in Europe, we should not talk about issues like the behavior of Mediterranean countries. As experience has shown this can create a moral hazard problem for those countries. What we have seen over the past eight years or so is that the French government and business community, a number of other governments in Europe, as well as the citizens of these countries, have understood that policies based on money illusions and exchange rate illusions finally do not pay and that, therefore, a policy following the anchor of the deutsche mark is meaningful for the well-being of those countries. This lesson has been learned in a number of countries and is about to be learned in Italy and in Spain too. These are good reasons why we do not have to argue too extensively in this direction.

The second part of Mr. Saunders's chapter, is interesting for somebody coming from the West German banking scene. We are, of course, quite happy that we are considered to be in a relatively good position. After listening to what he summed up as the implications of Ingo Walter's paper, I am even more reassured.

There are some minor points to discuss, though. There is always a discussion of industrial holdings by West German banks. It is true that we have some holdings, but all banks in the Federal Republic hold less than 1 percent of the total share capital of all listed companies in West Germany. That is certainly not a high figure.

Relationship banking is, of course, something we are proud of. It has implications that are helpful for the development of longer-term strategies. Certainly it was helpful for companies in periods of risk; the bailout that banks have carried out in West Germany is proof of that. It obviously was an additional reason for companies to remain customers of our banks even when the fees and the margins were somewhat lower with non-German suppliers of financial services.

Concerning the European financial market 1992, there is no disagreement that the quantitative leap in the wholesale market will not affect German banks strongly because their integration in that field is already in place. The qualitative leap will be in the retail sector and in the middle market. It is the high-net-worth individuals we are aiming at, and some parts of investment banking. It is merchant acquisition, where we consider that a lot of work has to be done in the future. Our most recent acquisition, Morgan Grenfell, is an important element in our preparation for "1992." We were lucky that Morgan Grenfell was available in the market at this time. It was quite expensive, but I think it will pay off.

As to the strategies we have embarked on, of course, there would be a strategy of having retail banking all over the place. Since a number of countries in Europe are already overbanked, however, do not, for example, expect German banks or Deutsche Bank to be retail bankers in the United Kingdom. It is obvious that we would spend a disproportionate amount of money and would not gain much. We cannot start from scratch in a number of countries where we want to have a retail market because it would take too much time. Therefore, our aim is to become a European bank by acquistions in other countries.

In some countries it seems to be difficult to achieve that target. In Ingo Walter's chapter, the most important point was mentioned: the targets are very few. Particularly in France the number of targets is extremely low, so it is difficult to become a major retail banking player in that country. There is practically no private bank that could be acquired, but we are still searching the market. The French government may rethink its ideas about nationalized banks. If the result were privatizations there would be a chance to acquire a bank even in France.

There is an argument that the EC commission was not prepared to open up the European financial market to world financial services. The contention that the Second Banking Directive does not provide the necessary background for a true open market system is not too well taken. I believe that this directive and its interpretation by all parties involved, including the Americans, namely that national treatment is now being guaranteed, has found acceptance in the United States. It is strongly supported by German banks. No doubt, there are fallback positions. Of course, we hope that the United States will act accordingly and that the proposed Riegle Bill, which asks for a stricter concept of reciprocity, will not be something that upsets the Europeans again.

It is obvious that banks that want to be global players must have a competitive environment at home; otherwise they are tempted to fall asleep. Therefore, European banks and West German banks in particular are happy with the openness that results from the Second Banking Directive. I hope that West Germany, a country that has long been exposed to international competition and has had convertibility since 1958, is in a good position to weather the storm when the hypercompetition that Ingo Walter has been talking about finally takes place.

Notes

CHAPTER 1: FUTURE OF THE TRADING SYSTEM, *Brian Hindley*

1. Of course, there is also Japan. But in trade terms, Japan is the object of hostility from both the EC and the United States and is the principal potential target of a resurgent protectionism in either or both. Japan has a clear and actual interest in maintaining the GATT as a force for liberal trade policies, but it cannot effectively lead in that direction, given the attitudes of the EC and the United States.

2. One advantage lies in the number of bilateral treaties that would be required. There are 102 GATT contracting parties (CPs). For each CP to have a bilateral treaty with the other 101 would require $101 + 100 + 99 + \ldots + 2 + 1 = 5{,}151$ treaties.

3. As a matter of identity, the trade deficit, $X - M = S - I - (G - T)$, where S is saving, I is investment, and $(G - T)$ is the budget deficit of the government. Any or all of these variables might be affected by trade policy. But these effects are likely to be small, relative to the current size of the U.S. trade deficit.

Even highly sophisticated commentators sometimes give a contrary impression. Dornbusch, Krugman, and Park, for example, are usually quite clear about the relation between the trade deficit and trade policy. At the end of their pamphlet, nevertheless, their language becomes loose: "Congress and the electorate are frustrated with poor trade performance and recognize that at least in part this reflects trade restrictions abroad" (p. 38). Many things are responsible "at least in part" for U.S. trade performance. To leave open the possibility that trade policy is *primarily* responsible (a "fact" that is also "recognized" by elements of the Congress and the electorate) does not seem helpful to anyone except protectionists.

4. In fact, it is far from demonstrated. Takeuchi 1988, provides a useful survey of the evidence.

5. The United States has had historical experience of the problems created by adherence to absolute reciprocity. U.S. use of the conditional MFN clause in its nineteenth century commercial treaties had many of the effects of absolute reciprocity. In 1919, the U.S. Tariff Commission reported to Congress on "Reciprocity and Commercial Treaties." It said that:

> . . . a policy of special arrangements, such as the U.S. has followed in recent decades leads to troublesome complications. . . . When each country with whom we negotiate is treated by itself, and separate

arrangements are made with the expectation that they shall be applicable individually, claims are nonetheless made by other states with whom such arrangements have not been made. Concessions are asked; they are sometimes refused; counter concessions are proposed; reprisal and retaliation are suggested; unpleasant controversies and sometimes international friction result.

6. The situation described in this paragraph is, of course, that of the Coase theorem (Coase 1961). The gist of that theorem is that so long as property rights are allocated to *someone*, the outcome of (costless) negotiation will be an optimal allocation of resources. The allocation of property rights affects the distribution of income, not the allocation of resources.

The relevant point in the present context is that the mere fact that an action by A affects the welfare of B, does not make a good economic case for providing B with any direct right to control or influence the action of A. So long as A has the relevant property right, B can negotiate with him (and *vice versa*).

7. The United States made 195 affirmative findings of dumping in 1980–1986, (including 19 against NMEs [nonmarket economies]), and 181 affirmative findings in subsidy actions. In the same period, Canada made 140 affirmative findings in antidumping cases and 8 in antisubsidy cases; Australia made 219 affirmative findings in antidumping cases and 8 in antisubsidy cases; and the EEC made 213 affirmative findings of dumping (108 related to NMEs) and 6 in antisubsidy cases. See Finger and Olechowski (1987), Appendix 8.

8. Wolf 1989 discusses the global implications of the 1992 project.

9. After this section was written, a GATT panel ruled that the EC "screwdriver-plant regulation" is inconsistent with the GATT.

10. The U.S. Omnibus Trade and Competitiveness Act of 1988 also contains anticircumvention measures. For example, antidumping and countervailing duties can be extended to parts and components imported into the United States if the parts come from the same country as the finished product subject to antidumping duty, and the difference between the value of the assembled product in the United States and the value of the components is "small." The U.S. authorities must also consider the relation between the assembler and the exporter whose finished product is subject to dumping duties and whether the importation of parts has increased after the imposition of duties on the finished product.

U.S. law also allows the extension of an antidumping or countervailing duty when products are subsequently altered or further developed. Thus, for example, in 1983 an order made with respect to *electric* typewriters from Japan was extended to *electronic* typewriters on the basis that the electronic typewriters resembled electric typewriters with respect to appearance, use, and marketing display and thus could be considered to be merchandise of the same class or kind.

11. The document is four pages long and covers all aspects of 1992—not merely services.

12. Section 22 required the administration to impose quantitative restric-

tions or special fees whenever "any article or articles are being or are practically certain to be imported into the United States in such quantities as to render ineffective or tend to render ineffective, or materially interfere with [any U.S. farm program]."

13. On what might be hoped for from the Uruguay Round, see Wolf 1990.

CHAPTER 4: ASIAN NICs IN THE 1990s, *Raymond J. Ahearn and Anne Dibble*

1. Calculated from OECD trade statistics.
2. Preliminary 1989 data indicate that South Korean exports to the EC have declined by about 10 percent since 1988. According to some sources, this decline has been influenced by EC restrictive actions affecting more than thirty South Korean products, including VCRs, polyester yarns, videotapes, and bicycle tubes. The appreciation of the won against European currencies is another important influence. Whether these developments are the harbinger of a more restrictive EC market is uncertain. See *Trade Korea*, December 15, 1989, p. 15.
3. See, for example, chapter in 1988 MITI White Paper on Japan's trade with the rest of Asia.

CHAPTER 7: GERMAN BANKING AND MONETARY POLICY, *Anthony Saunders*

1. In actual practice the Bundesbank has usually sought to sterilize exchange rate intervention effects by domestic monetary adjustments. Thus Ceasar (1986) estimates that exchange rate interventions increased the German money base by only DM 1.8 billion between 1979 and 1986.
2. Currency gets a weight of 1, demand deposits 0.166, savings deposits 0.124, and time deposits 0.081. These weights are proportional to the reserve requirements on these deposits.
3. Or, more correctly, the *Report on Economic and Monetary Union in the European Community*.
4. No firm dates have been agreed for the beginning of stage 3.
5. Of course, the ability of individual governments to monetize their national debt would be rendered impossible under the full stage 3 regime of a single currency.
6. It should be noted that the capital market's pricing debt in this fashion does *not* imply market inefficiency. On the contrary, the market is taking into account both on-balance-sheet and off-balance-sheet sovereign risk and default guarantees.
7. Partly because of a higher "tax" base, such as larger reserve requirements on banks.
8. It might be noted that the seigniorage from a single European currency could be distributed asymmetrically to weaker countries.
9. Note that the presence of Japanese and American banks "as potential competitors" is not reflected in this table.

10. For example, Deutsche Bank owns 10 percent or more of the equity in eighty-six German corporations.

11. A cap of 10 percent of a bank's capital in any one firm and a 50 percent total cap.

12. The host country, however, will bear the responsibility for supervision related to monetary policy, such as liquidity and reserve requirements.

13. To the extent that the EC countries reach harmonized growth rates, however, such gains may be quite small in the longer term.

14. Assuming that entry is immediately granted. For example, it was many years before Citibank gained a full membership to the British Clearing House Association.

Chapter 8: Fiscal Harmonization in the EC, G. K. Shaw

1. It is also the case that countries with high personal income taxes tend also to be countries with high personal benefits, a factor that militates against tax-induced movements of labor services.

2. In the context of an integrated Europe, cross-border shopping need not be restricted to border regions. With the advent of mail-order shopping and the remarkable potential created by fax facilities, cross-border shopping (especially in the case of high-value, low-volume items) becomes community-wide.

3. The evolution of thinking on these issues has, of course, been a continuous and gradual process, as is characteristic of all major research programs. Nonetheless, if one were to indicate the most influential developments, they would certainly include the celebrated Neumark report (1963), the two-volume study of fiscal harmonization edited by Shoup (1967), which was responsible for developing many key theoretical insights, and the more recent and post–Cockfield report study on fiscal coordination edited by Cnossen (1987).

4. Perhaps it should be noted that a theoretical argument exists to deny these distorting effects and to argue that the two modes of taxation are indeed equivalent. This argument, however, relies on extreme assumptions of price flexibility and exchange rate flexibility, which are such as to render the thesis redundant as a guide to real world issues. On this point see especially Shoup 1953 and Biehl 1988.

5. Indeed, this has become so much a part of the conventional wisdom that it has been adopted in a number of public finance textbooks—see the references in Cnossen and Shoup 1987.

6. A zero-rated product differs from a product that is not subject to VAT taxation in that, although the rate of tax levied on the final sale is zero, it is still possible to reclaim the tax paid on intermediate inputs.

7. This proposal now appears to be a dead letter, at least in its original form. Britain strongly objected to the termination of zero rating, and other countries, particularly Denmark, have questioned the need for imposing a maximum limit to the rate of VAT. That position reflects the view of the influential London-based Institute of Fiscal Studies, which has argued per-

suasively that the costs of higher rates are borne solely by the country adopting them.

8. Indeed, the Fredersdorf report (1978) specifically concluded that it was not essential to harmonize the personal income tax.

9. The major concessions included the alternative of a minimum 15 percent rate for VAT, with no upper limit established, acceptance of the principle of zero rating for a very limited range of products, and the substitution of "reference values" for excise duties in place of absolute harmonization.

10. In practice incentives exist from lack of rigorous enforcement of the compensatory procedures—rather akin to the incentive provided by the existence of green exits at custom duty checking points in international airports.

11. As previously noted, this concession appears now to have been granted with the option of a 15 percent minimum rate of VAT with no upper limit in place of the 14 percent to 20 percent band.

12. Although it may be noted that two important papers by Keen (1987, 1989) strongly suggest that such rate harmonization will be potentially Pareto improving on purely efficiency grounds.

13. In the same manner, ad valorem taxation discriminates against those brands of cigarettes offering coupons that could be redeemed for various gifts, since the provision of coupons was reflected in the retail price and thus subject to taxation. After Britain's entry into the EC, this form of promotion was quickly discontinued. For this and related argument see especially Kay and Keen 1987.

14. With unleaded petrol being taxed at a lesser rate.

15. There are, of course, many sophisticated models that attempt to determine the answers to these problems. See, for example, Deaton and Muellbauer 1980, which forms the basis of the attempt of Lee and Pashardes (1988) to estimate the revenue effects of the commission's proposals for the United Kingdom.

16. Although the method differs. In Italy and West Germany the tax paid by the company is fully credited against the taxation of shareholder dividends, whereas in Greece dividends are deducted from the taxable profits of the company. The difference can be substantial if there are significant differences between corporate and individual income tax rates.

17. The credit is based on the dividend plus the tax burden at the normal rate. Thus, for example, assuming for expositional purposes that both the rate of corporate tax and the tax credit were fixed at 50 percent and assuming that a company declared £100 profit, it would pay £50 in corporate tax. If it then paid dividends equal to £25, the shareholders would receive £25 plus a tax credit equal to 50 percent of £37.50, or £18.75.

Board of Trustees

Paul F. Oreffice, *Chairman*
Chairman
Dow Chemical Co.

Edwin L. Artzt
Chairman and CEO
The Procter & Gamble
  Company

Griffin B. Bell
King & Spalding

Winton M. Blount, *Treasurer*
Chairman and CEO
Blount, Inc.

Willard C. Butcher
Former Chairman
Chase Manhattan Bank

Edwin L. Cox
Chairman
Cox Oil & Gas, Inc.

Christopher C. DeMuth
President
American Enterprise Institute

Malcolm S. Forbes, Jr.
President and CEO
Forbes Inc.

Tully M. Friedman
Hellman & Friedman

Christopher B. Galvin
Senior Executive Vice President
  and Assistant Chief Operating
  Officer
Motorola, Inc.

Robert F. Greenhill
President
Morgan Stanley & Co., Inc.

Larry D. Horner
Managing Director
Arnhold and S. Bleichroeder, Inc.

Bruce Kovner
Chairman
Caxton Corporation

Richard B. Madden
Chairman and CEO
Potlatch Corp.

The American Enterprise Institute for Public Policy Research

Founded in 1943, AEI is a nonpartisan, nonprofit, research and educational organization based in Washington, D.C. The Institute sponsors research, conducts seminars and conferences, and publishes books and periodicals.

AEI's research is carried out under three major programs: Economic Policy Studies; Foreign Policy and Defense Studies; and Social and Political Studies. The resident scholars and fellows listed in these pages are part of a network that also includes ninety adjunct scholars at leading universities throughout the United States and in several foreign countries.

The views expressed in AEI publications are those of the authors and do not necessarily reflect the views of the staff, advisory panels, officers, or trustees.

Robert H. Malott
Chairman and CEO
FMC Corp.

Paul W. McCracken
Edmund Ezra Day University
  Professor Emeritus
University of Michigan

Richard M. Morrow
Former Chairman
Amoco Corp.

David Packard
Chairman
Hewlett-Packard Co.

George R. Roberts
Kohlberg Kravis Roberts & Co.

Wilson H. Taylor
Chairman and CEO
CIGNA Corporation

Henry Wendt
Chairman
SmithKline Beecham

James Q. Wilson
James A. Collins Professor
  of Management
University of California
  at Los Angeles

Charles Wohlstetter
Vice Chairman
GTE Corporation

Richard D. Wood
Chairman
Eli Lilly and Co.

Walter B. Wriston
Former Chairman
Citicorp

Officers

Christopher C. DeMuth
President

David B. Gerson
Executive Vice President

Council of Academic Advisers

James Q. Wilson, *Chairman*
James A. Collins Professor
  of Management
University of California
  at Los Angeles

Donald C. Hellmann
Professor of Political Science and
  International Studies
University of Washington

Gertrude Himmelfarb
Distinguished Professor of History
  Emeritus
City University of New York

Samuel P. Huntington
Eaton Professor of the
  Science of Government
Harvard University

D. Gale Johnson
Eliakim Hastings Moore
  Distinguished Service Professor
  of Economics Emeritus
University of Chicago

William M. Landes
Clifton R. Musser Professor of
  Economics
University of Chicago Law School

Sam Peltzman
Sears Roebuck Professor of Economics
  and Financial Services
University of Chicago
  Graduate School of Business

Nelson W. Polsby
Professor of Political Science
University of California at Berkeley

Murray L. Weidenbaum
Mallinckrodt Distinguished
  University Professor
Washington University

Research Staff

Claude E. Barfield
Resident Scholar

Walter Berns
Adjunct Scholar

Douglas J. Besharov
Resident Scholar

Robert H. Bork
John M. Olin Scholar in Legal Studies

Anthony R. Dolan
Visiting Fellow

Dinesh D'Souza
Research Fellow

Nicholas N. Eberstadt
Visiting Scholar

Mark Falcoff
Resident Scholar

Gerald R. Ford
Distinguished Fellow

Murray F. Foss
Visiting Scholar

Suzanne Garment
DeWitt Wallace Fellow in
  Communications in a Free Society

Patrick Glynn
Resident Scholar

Robert A. Goldwin
Resident Scholar

Gottfried Haberler
Resident Scholar

Robert W. Hahn
Resident Scholar

Robert B. Helms
Visiting Scholar

Charles R. Hulten
Visiting Scholar

Karlyn H. Keene
Resident Fellow; Editor,
  The American Enterprise

Jeane J. Kirkpatrick
Senior Fellow

Marvin H. Kosters
Resident Scholar; Director,
  Economic Policy Studies

Irving Kristol
John M. Olin Distinguished Fellow

Michael A. Ledeen
Resident Scholar

Robert A. Licht
Resident Scholar

Chong-Pin Lin
Associate Director, China Studies
  Program

John H. Makin
Resident Scholar

Allan H. Meltzer
Visiting Scholar

Joshua Muravchik
Resident Scholar

Charles Murray
Bradley Fellow

Michael Novak
George F. Jewett Scholar;
  Director, Social and
  Political Studies

Norman J. Ornstein
Resident Scholar

Richard N. Perle
Resident Fellow

Thomas W. Robinson
Director, China Studies Program

William Schneider
Resident Fellow

Bernard Schriever
Visiting Fellow

Herbert Stein
Senior Fellow

Irwin M. Stelzer
Resident Fellow

Edward Styles
Director, Publications

W. Allen Wallis
Resident Scholar

Ben J. Wattenberg
Senior Fellow

Carolyn L. Weaver
Resident Scholar

A NOTE ON THE BOOK

*This book was edited by Trudy Kaplan and
Dana Lane of the publications staff
of the American Enterprise Institute.
The figures were drawn by Hördur Karlsson.
The text was set in Palatino, a typeface designed by
the twentieth-century Swiss designer Hermann Zapf.
Coghill Composition Company, of Richmond, Virginia,
set the type, and Edwards Brothers Incorporated,
of Ann Arbor, Michigan, printed and bound the book,
using permanent, acid-free paper.*

The AEI PRESS is the publisher for the American Enterprise Institute for Public Policy Research, 1150 17th Street, N.W., Washington, D.C. 20036: *Christopher C. DeMuth*, publisher; *Edward Styles*, director; *Dana Lane*, assistant director; *Ann Petty*, editor; *Cheryl Weissman*, editor; *Susan Moran*, editorial assistant (rights and permissions). Books published by the AEI PRESS are distributed by arrangement with the University Press of America, 4720 Boston Way, Lanham, Md. 20706.